OUR SOUTHERN HOME

OUR SOUTHERN HOME

SCOTTSBORO TO MONTGOMERY TO BIRMINGHAM

THE TRANSFORMATION OF THE SOUTH
IN THE TWENTIETH CENTURY

Waights Taylor Jr.

McCAA BOOKS • SANTA ROSA

McCaa Books
1535 Farmers Lane #211
Santa Rosa, CA 95405-7535

First published in 2011 by McCaa Books, an imprint of McCaa Publications.

Permissions acknowledgments for previously published material and
the cover photographs can be found beginning on page 405.

LIBRARY OF CONGRESS CONTROL NUMBER: 2011914422
ISBN 978-0-9838892-0-5

Library of Congress Cataloging-in-Publication Data has been applied for.

Printed in the United States of America
Set in Minion Pro
Cover design and map design by Suzan Reed
Author's photograph by Star Dewar

www.mccaabooks.com

*In memory of
my loving mother and father,
Rose "Rosie" Dawson Taylor and
Waights "Dukie" McCaa Taylor,
and
a dear, beloved friend,
Mattie Ruth Rucker*

CONTENTS

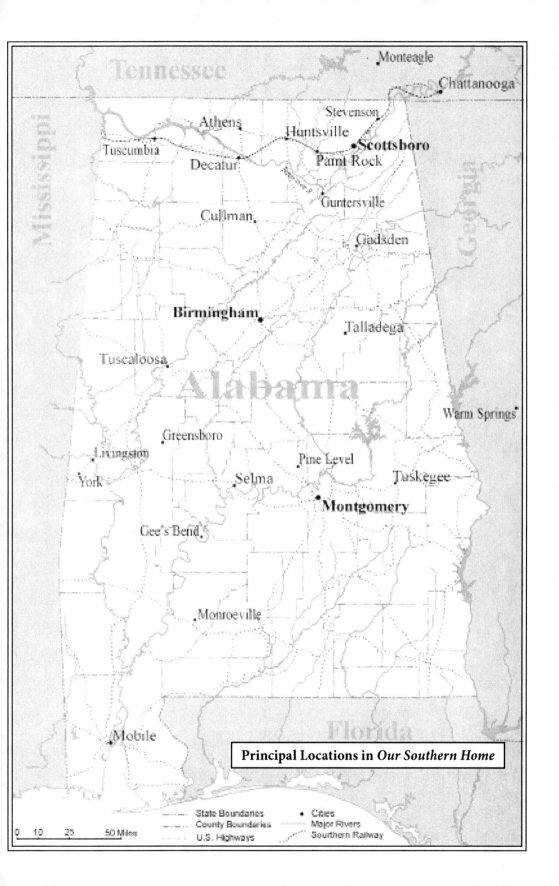

Principal Locations in *Our Southern Home*

INTRODUCTION
UNEXPECTED CONNECTIONS

2004

J UST WHEN YOU THINK you have finished a long journey, something happens that alters the planned itinerary, setting you on an entirely new course into new and uncharted territory. On October 5, 2004, soon after I thought this book was complete, I received the following e-mail out of the blue.

> I did a Google search of "Waights Taylor" while researching our collections here in the Archives at the Birmingham Civil Rights Institute, where I've come across the (rather unusual) name. I wonder (1) if you are related to the person I came across in our collections—Waights Taylor, interviewed in B'ham by a Talladega College professor in 1947—and (2) if you'd email back. (I found a Santa Rosa mailing address for you, but am of the email age and, therefore, too anxious to wait for my message to reach you via post.) By the way, what I'm after is more information on the person/family whose name is in our collection. I will happily tell you more about the particular collection in which Waights Taylor is named if/when you respond with interest. I hope you're willing and able to help me a bit, and I thank you sincerely for your time.
>
> Laura Anderson
> Assistant Archivist
> Birmingham Civil Rights Institute

I immediately responded to Ms. Anderson's e-mail. I told her I was Waights Taylor Jr., the son of the person she was interested in.

The exchanges that followed between Ms. Anderson and me opened a fascinating and unknown door into my father's past. Through her, I learned that Lore and Donald Rasmussen, white professors who taught at the all-black Talladega College in Talladega, Alabama, had interviewed my father in 1947 as part of a research project on race relations in the South. The Rasmussens interviewed fifty-five white Southerners in Birmingham said to be "liberal on the race question." The interviewees were assured that their names and the detailed interview notes would be kept under lock and key, as the times were not tolerant of those who spoke out against the South's racial inequities. Not only were the interviewees' jobs in potential jeopardy, but they could have been subject to state and federal government scrutiny and labeled "Communist" or "un-American" by local politicians and the media. The Rasmussens kept their pledge to the interviewees until 2003 when they donated Don's thesis and all their notes to the Birmingham Civil Rights Institute, since so much time had passed.

Ms. Anderson mailed me a copy of the Rasmussens' notes from their interview with my father. The notes, several pages in length, offer an interesting perspective of the times and the views of a white southern male thought to be "liberal on the race question." Reading the notes, I became aware, for the first time, of my father's involvement in the Scottsboro Boys' tragedy in the 1930s. I then knew I had to go back to the drawing board with my book; the interview notes and the associated events were too rich in new material to be ignored.

The Rasmussens now live in Berkeley, California, near my home in Santa Rosa. I called and arranged to meet with them, thinking we would discuss only their interview with my father. I was in for a big surprise. Lore and Don Rasmussen were truly unknown pioneers and heroes in the years leading up to the civil rights movement in the 1950s.

Lore came to New York City in 1938 at the age of seventeen, fleeing the terrible Jewish persecution by the Nazi regime in Germany. She was able to gain admittance to Teachers College, the noted school of education associated with Columbia University. In 1939, Lore quit Teachers College in protest over the firing of several professors who were accused of being either Communists or too socialist in their views. She then enrolled at the University of Illinois, where she took a course in the Sociology Department taught by a young American professor named Don Rasmussen.

Don was born in Wisconsin to Protestant working-class parents of Scandinavian heritage. Don attended the University of Illinois, receiving his master's degree in sociology in 1937 at age twenty-one. He later received a PhD in sociology from Illinois, using the Birmingham interviews as the basis for his doctoral thesis. Lore and Don were married in 1940 in Illinois after Lore's graduation.

In the fall of 1942, they moved, with their infant son, to Talladega, Alabama, to teach at Talladega College—Lore as a professor of education and Don as a professor of sociology. They quickly found that their experiences with racial prejudice in Illinois paled in comparison to what they experienced in Alabama. One of their early experiences in Alabama is so rich in historical significance and irony that I must retell it here.

Two months after the Rasmussens settled in Talladega, they made a trip to Birmingham at Thanksgiving to shop for some clothing and furniture. While in Birmingham they contacted Louis Burnham, Executive Director of the Southern Negro Youth Congress, whom Lore had met at an NAACP conference in Atlanta a few weeks earlier. The three went to an African American restaurant for a late lunch. Just as they were completing their meal, two policemen entered the restaurant, came right to their table, and asked if they were white or colored. Don responded, as he looked at the back of his hand, "It looks kind of white to me."

The three were immediately taken to a nearby police station where they were booked on charges of violating the Birmingham sanitary code—a code prohibiting the operation of a restaurant that did not separate the races with a ten-foot wall—and for inciting to riot. They were then taken to the city jail where the three were put into separate cells and interrogated for several hours. A friend of Louis Burnham's learned the three were in jail and arranged for a local black dentist to post their bail. All three were released at about three o'clock the next morning.

At their trial several days later, Lore and Don, while not apologetic about what they had done, pleaded guilty with no intent to break the law. The Rasmussens and their colleagues at Talladega College had decided that this was the best course of action. The tensions between some Talladega townspeople and the college were high at the time, and fighting the charges would only exacerbate the situation. The judge lectured Lore and Don on Southern law, telling them "whites have their restaurants and blacks have theirs, and they don't mix." He told them that if he thought they had deliberately flouted the law, he would send them right back to jail. The judge reluctantly accepted their statement that they had no intention of breaking the law and imposed a fine for each of them of twenty-five dollars plus three dollars court costs.

Don told me, both with tongue in cheek and with some regret, that he wished he had written a letter from the Birmingham jail as Martin Luther King Jr. most famously and eloquently did twenty-one years later. Don added wistfully, "I could have at least sent a postcard to someone."

After my meeting with the Rasmussens, I sat quietly at home thinking about this incredible couple and their ties to my father when, over the electronic transom, another Laura Anderson e-mail appeared on November 18, 2004.

I am back to processing the Rasmussen collection this morning after a few weeks away from it and discovered that another interviewee lives in California—Nancy Huddleston Packer. I wonder if she is in communication with the Rasmussens. I would think she would be. She's retired from Stanford, where she was a creative writing instructor in the Stegner program. Her father was the Congressman from Alabama, George Huddleston Sr., as was, later, her brother, Jr. She married Herbert Packer in Birmingham and they moved out to Palo Alto in the fifties. Their daughter, Ann, and son, George, are both writers.

I e-mailed Laura and said I would be very interested in talking to Nancy Packer about her experiences in Birmingham and with the Rasmussens. Laura didn't have a phone number for Nancy, so I called information and got a number in Palo Alto. I dialed the number, and the conversation started something like this.

"Hello, could I speak to Nancy Packer?"

"This is Nancy Packer."

I said, "I want to be sure I have the right person. Is this the Nancy Packer who is a professor of creative writing at Stanford University?"

"Well, I used to be. I'm retired now."

"My name's Waights Taylor and I—"

Before I could finish my sentence, Nancy exclaimed, "Waights Taylor—I know that name!" And from there, another unexpected connection was made, introducing me to the Huddleston-Packer family.

I explained to Nancy how I had come to call her and asked if she remembered being interviewed by Don Rasmussen in 1947 in Birmingham. Initially, she was vague about it, as anyone would be after almost sixty years; but the more we talked, the more she remembered. Nancy and I made a date to meet in her Palo Alto home to discuss our Birmingham backgrounds and the Rasmussen interviews.

Nancy Huddleston Packer is an author, Professor Emerita of English at Stanford University, and the former director of the Stanford creative writing program co-founded by Wallace Stegner. She has published four books, including *In My Father's House: Tales of an Unconformable Man*, a memoir about her father, George Huddleston, the U.S. Congressman for the Birmingham Ninth District from 1915 to 1937.

In 1956, Nancy Huddleston attended a dinner party at the home of a prominent Birmingham attorney, where she met one of the out-of-town guests, a good-looking young Jewish lawyer from the North, Herbert Packer. He was making a brief visit before heading to his new teaching position at Stanford. Nancy was intrigued with this intellectual Yale Law School graduate and the lure of a place far beyond the Alabama border. For two years, Nancy and Herbert had a long-distance romance that culminated in marriage in 1958 in Birmingham. Nancy immediately moved to Palo Alto to join her new husband. I too would move out West a year later, when I moved to Seattle upon my graduation from the University of Alabama.

I met with Nancy Packer in Palo Alto, and we hit it off immediately as we discussed our families, our Birmingham roots, and the Rasmussen interviews. Nancy is a fascinating woman—small in stature with a strong outspoken voice that still carries an unmistakable southern accent. She not only remembered meeting my father at some point in the 1940s or 1950s, but she also knew two of my father's brothers, Macey Taylor and Frank Taylor.

I showed Nancy the Rasmussen notes from my father's interview, and I gave her Laura Anderson's phone number and e-mail address. Nancy said she would definitely like to have a copy of her interview notes, but she had some trepidation when she thought about reading them. I understood this completely, as what I thought and said about issues many years ago was affected by my youthful certainties and panache.

I left Nancy's home realizing I had, in the span of a couple of serendipitous months, found incredible new friends with fascinating connections to my family and my past. As I reflected on all that had transpired, I found myself torn between two points of understanding. My rational self kept telling me these were just coincidental events, while my creative and imaginative self insisted on believing there were more significant meanings to it all. Unable to resolve my conflict, I chose to go with my creative side.

2009

HAVING LEARNED from my unexpected connections about my father's involvement in the Scottsboro events of the 1930s, I spent the next four years on a broader inquiry into Alabama's history in the twentieth century. Besides researching the Scottsboro Boys trials, I accumulated and read a large amount of material on many of the significant racial- and segregation-related events of the period.

More personal and more embarrassing, I also had to face my own cowardice during two of the critical historical moments I had witnessed. I was the quintessential white southern "liberal" who deplored racial intolerance and segregation but said little and did nothing about it. In addition, I had to search for an explanation for something I never clearly understood: my father's transition from a young New Deal liberal to an aging neoconservative.

With these vast amounts of material from numerous sources in front of me, it was apparent I would have to make some tough choices and distill the information into a manageable and coherent story. After I struggled with a number of drafts, my focus slowly sharpened on three broad themes.

The first of these themes is the importance that the accident of birth places on most individuals. The nine Scottsboro Boys, and my father and his four brothers, the Taylor Boys, were all about the same age—all were born between 1908 and 1918—but because of their birth circumstances and skin color, they experienced very different life opportunities and outcomes.

Second, the Scottsboro period in the 1930s represents the nadir in Alabama's segregated history. However, although the state and the South would experience many terrible incidents over the next thirty to forty years, this was also the beginning of a slow ascent—a jagged, but inexorable, climb to the start of the civil rights movement.

Third, many Southerners have yet to fully understand and accept two profound connections that bond blacks and whites together. Over the last three to four centuries, a *historic bond* of interdependence developed between blacks and whites as the region's agricultural base and social order grew under the yoke of slavery and the apartheid of segregation. And in many ways, even more profound is the *human bond* that developed over these many years. Sexual encounters between blacks and whites, most of which were forced by white men on black women (although there were some consensual relations and marriages), led to a genetic bond between the two groups that requires us all to recognize our common human heritage.

Finally, I chose to frame the book around three families, three cities, three individuals, and one obvious but immutable fact. *Change* is that immutable fact. Change is the one constant, illogical as it sounds, for all the individuals and political systems involved in this period, or any other period. Change has many moods: change for the better or worse; change handled as frivolously as coins in one's pocket; change driven by rabid ideological views; and, most importantly, moral and social change pushed by a few on unwilling and unyielding political and social systems. The moral courage and dedication of these few finally led to the legal changes that resurrected the South from its entangled roots with slavery and segregation.

The three families are the nine Scottsboro Boys and their families, representing one big, common family; The Taylor Boys and me, and our families; and Rosa Parks and her family. The stories of these three families are interwoven throughout the book with occasional intentional changes in the voice and tone of the writing as we move from historical events to family events and back. There are even a few whimsical changes of pace to hopefully give the reader a brief respite from the usual complexities of historical events necessarily laden with numerous dates, facts, and characters.

The three cities are Scottsboro, Montgomery, and Birmingham. The events in Scottsboro in 1931 were the symbolic low point in Alabama's sad racial history and segregated past. Rosa Parks was the critical link from the Scottsboro events to the start of the modern civil rights movement in Montgomery. Her growth as a civil rights activist grew out of the Scottsboro Boys trials to her date with destiny in 1955 with the white Montgomery bus driver. Birmingham provided the tragic, penultimate event of the period in 1963—the murder of four young black girls at the Sixteenth Street Baptist Church—which finally persuaded President John Kennedy to draft legislation that became the historic Civil Rights Act of 1964.

The three individuals are Clarence Norris, Waights Taylor, and Rosa Parks. Clarence is one of the Scottsboro Boys, Waights is my father, and Rosa needs no introduction. All three were eighteen years old on the day the Scottsboro events began, and all three had very different life stories in the twentieth century.

This is their story, my story, and the South's story.

1.

A SHAMEFUL DAY
1967

Let us all hope that the dark clouds of racial prejudice will soon pass away and the deep fog of misunderstanding will be lifted from our fear-drenched communities, and in some not too distant tomorrow the radiant stars of love and brotherhood will shine over our great nation with all their scintillating beauty.
Martin Luther King Jr.
Letter from Birmingham Jail, April 16, 1963

MY SINGLE ENCOUNTER with Martin Luther King Jr. came in 1967 and is not a proud moment in my life.

In 1966, my family and I moved from Seattle to the Atlanta area for a new job I had just accepted. My wife Darlene, while supportive of the career move, was quite apprehensive about moving to the Deep South. She was from Montana and had never been to the South, much less lived there. It was a time of turmoil and terror: civil rights marches, murders in Mississippi, and politicians such as Lester Maddox of Georgia and George Wallace of Alabama inflaming public opinion with their bigoted statements and perverse leadership.

After we settled in Atlanta with our two young sons, ages two and three, Darlene had a terrible nightmare that plagued her for twenty months until we moved from the South back to the West Coast in 1968. In this dream, she is always walking alone in a large city (presumably Atlanta or Birmingham) looking for the boys and me. As she rounds a corner, she sees me leaning against a building. I have been attacked by a group of redneck racists, castrated, and left bleeding with our two young sons crying in fear as they cling to my legs. It was a recurring image of the South that haunted her for many years. She still remembers it with a sense of foreboding.

One evening in 1967, my wife and I went out for a quiet dinner alone at the Hyatt Regency Hotel, located on one of the ubiquitous Peachtree streets in Atlanta. We parked our car in the hotel's underground parking garage and had a pleasant dinner in a restaurant in the hotel.

After dinner, we returned to the garage and waited for our car. Waiting with us were two separate groups of people: Martin Luther King Jr. and three or four well-dressed black people were on the other side of the car return area, and a group of four well-dressed white people, two men and two women, stood near us.

I turned to Darlene and said, "Look over there. That's Martin Luther King."

"Are you sure?" she asked.

"Oh yes, that's him," I said.

At that moment, one of the two white men yelled something like, "Well, lookie there Billy, if it ain't the savior of the colored folks. I'll betcha he ate coon livers for supper."

I looked at the men in disbelief, as the other white man yelled out an even more racist epithet. King and his party said nothing and stoically waited for their car as a barrage of racial slurs was hurled at them. King's car arrived first, and he and his party left without saying a thing or acknowledging the presence of the two white men.

My wife and I said nothing during this dreadful encounter. We stood silently, observing a scene that I'm sure King experienced daily. Our car came after King's, and we left the garage in silence. We said nothing to King, we said nothing to the white men, and we said nothing to each other as we drove home. We were shocked and ashamed.

I AM STILL ASHAMED.

Part One

Bound for Scottsboro

1897–March 25, 1931

2.

MARCH 25, 1931

Clarence Norris

CLARENCE WAITED QUIETLY in the shadow of an abandoned warehouse building on the western edge of the Southern Railway yard in Chattanooga for the overdue departure of the freight train. He had chosen this spot carefully to avoid any railroad employees, as he planned to jump the train when it pulled out and hobo his way to Memphis in hopes of finding some work.

Unlike the house in Charles Dickens's *Bleak House*, the railroad yard was a bleak, unsafe place. Only railroad employees or a person trying to jump a train to catch a free, but illegal, ride would choose to be here. Sets of parallel tracks coursed through the yard, interconnected by manual and automatic switches. The yard was littered with material, some useful and some discarded, including railroad ties, rail, switches, frogs, and other track, locomotive, and freight car parts. Loose rock and gravel—the primary building ingredients of a railbed—were everywhere. Numerous buildings, scattered about the yard, were designed in a concrete bunker or shack-like motif and ranged from new structures to old, dilapidated structures long past their useful life.

The forty-three-car freight train finally pulled out of the yard on an unseasonably cool morning at 10:20 a.m. on March 25, 1931. Although its final destination was Memphis, most of the route would be through northern Alabama, roughly paralleling the Tennessee River through the bucolic Tennessee Valley. As the train moved slowly toward the main line, Clarence ran from behind the warehouse, grabbed the side rail of a boxcar, and pulled himself up onto the train. He saw a number of others boarding the train, black and white alike, and more would continue to do so until the train departed the Chattanooga area. He thought little of jumping the train; riding the rails as a hobo had become a standard form of transportation for many of the unemployed in this second year of the Great Depression.

Clarence Norris was eighteen years old, the second of eleven children of poor, black sharecroppers in Georgia. He had finished only the second grade and had started working the cotton fields at age seven. His hardscrabble life consisted of a string of ever-changing menial jobs for little pay and frequent run-ins with white southern cops; he was arrested and jailed for vagrancy more than once, and he had been taunted, beaten, and told to run for his life by the railroad cops in a Birmingham railroad yard. He had just recently arrived in Chattanooga, having taken up the life of a hobo after quitting his job in a Goodyear plant in Gadsden, Alabama, when his girlfriend left him.

Clarence was about to experience a number of unexpected connections that would alter and dictate the course of his entire life. This train wasn't bound for glory. No, this train was bound for infamy in the town of Scottsboro in northeastern Alabama.

Waights Taylor

AS THE TRAIN pulled out of the yard, another young man was on the move, walking across the Quadrangle at the University of Alabama in Tuscaloosa for one of his beloved Shakespeare classes. Although Waights would be early for the eleven o'clock class, he hoped to have a private chat with the professor about a recent lecture.

The beautiful tree-lined campus, only two hundred miles to the southwest of the Chattanooga railroad yard, was anything but bleak and might as well have been in another universe. The Quadrangle, over twenty-two acres in size, was its centerpiece. Bounded on the south side by Denny Chimes, a bell tower named after the university's president, and on the north side by the university library, the Quadrangle consisted mainly of open green space interspersed with majestic water oak and elm trees.

Waights recited to himself the Shakespearean passage he had recently memorized, Henry V's famous St. Crispin's Day speech before the Battle of Agincourt. He knew the entire passage, but one part kept eluding him as he repeated to himself:

> *This story shall the good man teach his son,*
> *And Crispin Crispian shall ne'er go by*
> *From this day to the ending of the world*
> *But we in it shall be remembered,*
> *We few, we happy few, we band of brothers.*

He continually committed to memory famous Shakespearean passages and exhibited an extraordinary ability to match a Shakespearean quote to the conversation or the events of the day for the next sixty-six years.

Waights Taylor was eighteen years old, white, and one of five sons of upper middle class parents from Birmingham. He grew up in a family that enjoyed the pleasures and advantages of education and travel. He received an excellent elementary and secondary education, and was now finishing his freshman year at the university, following in the footsteps of his two older brothers, continuing a tradition his two younger brothers would also follow.

Waights walked slowly across the campus absorbed in his intellectual reverie. Little did Waights know on that cool March morning, as he was bound for class and Clarence was bound for Scottsboro, that in five years he too would become a bit player in the soon-to-unfold tragic drama in the northern part of the state.

Rosa McCauley

WHILE WAIGHTS WALKED to class and Clarence boarded the train, a young woman was also on the move in Alabama. Rosa walked along the beautiful oak-tree-lined sidewalks in the white neighborhood of Pine Level, a small town about seventeen miles north of Montgomery, the state capital of Alabama. She walked to her job as a "domestic" in the home of a white family. She worked two days a week in the home and three days a week in a local shirt factory. Although all work available for young black women was menial, she preferred her days as a domestic, as the working conditions were better and less demanding than in the shirt shop.

In September 1929, Rosa had been a student in the high school associated with Alabama State Teachers College for Negroes in Montgomery. Soon after she started her junior year, she had to drop out of school and return to Pine Level to find work to assist her mother and grandmother, both of whom were in poor health and needed her support.

Rosa McCauley was eighteen years old, the oldest child of James McCauley, a carpenter, and Leona Edwards McCauley, a teacher. She was born in Tuskegee, Alabama, the home of Tuskegee Normal and Industrial Institute (later called Tuskegee University), the black college founded by Booker T. Washington in 1881. When she was a toddler, her parents separated, and her mother, Leona, took baby Rosa and moved to her parents' small farm near Pine Level. Rosa's brother, Sylvester, was born soon after they arrived in Pine Level.

Rosa walked slowly toward the house thinking of the mistreatment she and her family consistently received from whites. As a young child, she and her brother were taunted and threatened by young white children. One time her grandfather had to bolt the family door and stand ready with a loaded shotgun as the Ku Klux Klan terrorized the neighborhood. There was also the constant insult of segregated facilities and bus service. Every time she went to Montgomery and used the local bus service, she was reminded of her second-class status in the community.

Rosa approached the front door of the white family's home, trying to let go of the anger, helplessness, and sadness she felt. She wanted to enter the house feeling positive about her day and the work to come. Of course, just like Clarence and Waights, she had no idea that she too would soon become involved in the Scottsboro drama.

THREE YOUNG PEOPLE, all eighteen years of age, each calling the South home—a young black man, a young white man, and a young black woman— with three very different life stories and outcomes. One would seek and receive redemption and offer forgiveness to his tormentors; one would start his political life as a Franklin Delano Roosevelt liberal and end his life a staunch neoconservative; and one would become an iconic figure of the twentieth century. But, on this day, March 25, 1931, all three were bound *for* Scottsboro.

3.

WARM SPRINGS, GEORGIA

THE GEOLOGY OF WARM SPRINGS, GEORGIA, provided the natural hot springs that attracted Native Americans and the early white settlers to the area. The later arrival of a single individual from Hyde Park, New York, left the area a legacy that today attracts over one-half million visitors a year.

Indians of the Creek Confederacy were the first known users of the warm mineral springs that flow from what is now called Pine Mountain. Legend has it that the Creeks would allow the injured warriors of the Cherokee Nation access to the area to benefit from the springs' healing properties. The U.S. government moved the Creeks out of the area in 1827. The Cherokees followed them in 1838, as they were forced out on the infamous march called the "Trail of Tears." The first resort was developed in the Warm Springs area in 1832, and in 1893, Charles Davis built the 120-room Meriwether Inn that was quite successful until the early part of the twentieth century.

It was Franklin Delano Roosevelt, however, who put Warm Springs on the map. FDR first visited the small town on the southern edge of the Piedmont Plateau, about sixty miles southwest of Atlanta near the Alabama state line, on October 3, 1924, to try the waters that were touted as a balm, and some said cure, for the ravages of polio. While FDR did not experience a cure, he was taken with the soothing effects of the spring waters. His trips there over the next few years certainly restored his body and soul for the tasks that befell him as he led the country out of the Great Depression and through World War II.

In 1926, Roosevelt purchased twelve hundred acres including the old Meriwether Inn, calling it the Georgia Warm Springs Foundation. Over the next several years, he rebuilt the inn, refurbished the pools, built a golf course and tennis courts, and created the first treatment center for polio victims. Roosevelt and a local physician, Dr. James Johnson, also developed the first hydrotherapy treatments used for this debilitating disease.

In 1931 and 1932, FDR built a modest six-room cottage about five miles from his institute to use as a residence on his frequent trips to Warm Springs. The cottage became known as the Little White House when FDR was inaugurated President in 1933. He was sitting for a portrait in the Little White House when he suffered a massive cerebral hemorrhage on April 12, 1945, and died a few hours later. April 12, 1945, is a date as memorable to my father's generation as November 22, 1963, is to my generation, and September 11, 2001, is to the current generation. Where we were and what we were doing at the moment we heard the awful news of those events is etched in our memories as indelibly as if it were an engraver's etching on a memorial plaque.

Clarence Norris

CLARENCE NORRIS was born on July 12, 1912, on a farm near Warm Springs. Clarence was the second of eleven children. He had two surviving brothers and six sisters; a brother and sister died in infancy.

His parents worked as sharecroppers. Sharecroppers worked a portion of the property of a landowner and were required to share the crops resulting from this shared agreement. Most often, but not always, the white landowners would demand a larger share of the crop than agreed on, thus exploiting the labor of the black sharecroppers and their families.

As with many black families in the South, there was little family history available to Clarence. He did know that his father was born a slave, was said to be part Indian, and was much older than Clarence's mother. His father was a tall, handsome man, who worked hard as a sharecropper his entire life to provide for his family, but he was a stern taskmaster. Clarence never developed a close and loving relationship with his father, especially after the day a white man falsely accused Clarence and one of his brothers of setting a fire that destroyed the white man's beehives. Clarence later said, "Daddy stripped us buck naked in front of this man and beat us like we was mules."

Clarence adored his mother, Ida, a loving woman who struggled against the insurmountable odds of racism and poverty to provide for her family. Fishing was one of her real passions, and, from a young age, Clarence would frequently accompany her on her all-day fishing trips, which usually rewarded the family with a large catch of catfish and perch. Clarence said of those days, "Those were good times."

The family always had a large garden of vegetables—potatoes, collards, okra, turnips, tomatoes, beans, cabbages, and yams—since a poor family at that time had to be as self sufficient as possible. They also had several cows for milk, and they raised hogs, some of which were slaughtered each year for their meats.

Beyond their garden and animals, the family subsisted on the cash crops—cotton, wheat, and corn—Clarence's father raised for the white farmer he sharecropped for. All his children and his wife worked in the fields. The children were put to work in the fields when they were six to seven years old. Clarence went to school only a couple of days a week and stopped going altogether after the second grade.

The family moved twice in Clarence's younger years because of the following incidents related to the low status of black sharecroppers in the South.

While living in Warm Springs, Clarence's father bought a red horse and a brand new buggy with rubber tires, quite an elegant rig for the times. It was the family's only mode of transportation and their pride and joy. One day Clarence's father found the horse in a nearby stream shot to death. Again he beat Clarence and his brother unmercifully, thinking the boys had killed the horse. The next day his father found a note on the porch that said, "Your children didn't kill your horse, I did and I've got my shotgun loaded to kill you on sight."

Clarence's father immediately moved to Neal, Georgia, entered into a sharecropping agreement with another white farmer, and sent for his family four months later. Clarence never knew what caused the white man to react so violently; perhaps, he was either jealous or thought that Clarence's father was an uppity black man for owning a horse and fancy buggy.

Sharecropping in Neal came to an abrupt end after the white landowner tried to rape Ida while Clarence's father was away. Clarence described the scene saying, "He had momma on the floor, tearing her clothes and forcing hisself on top of her." The white man left when the children started "screaming and hollering." The family moved to Molena, Georgia, the day his father returned, and they entered into yet another sharecropping agreement with another white man, Mr. Watts. In Molena, Clarence and his brother became good friends and playmates with Watts's sons, George and Zach. Their friendships came to an end in the boys' teens, when George said to Clarence, "Bubba, Momma wants you to call me Mr. George now. Call me that in front of her, but otherwise you don't have to do it."

Clarence didn't care for the farm life and sharecropping, and he constantly sought permission to work elsewhere, much to his father's consternation. In an attempt to punish and control Clarence, his father started beating him as almost a daily ritual. He would be tied to a tree and whipped with tree branches. Both his mother and Mr. Watts beseeched Clarence's father to stop the abusive treatment. Naturally, Clarence's hatred of his father was solidified at this time, and he never let go of the feeling or forgave his father.

In 1928, Clarence's father died in Molena. The family started to drift apart soon after his death: several of his siblings were either married or were soon to marry; his mother started working for a white family as a live-in maid; and Clarence returned to Warm Springs, where he would find work at FDR's institute.

4.

BIRMINGHAM, ALABAMA

B IRMINGHAM'S EARLY HISTORY is defined by two disparate sets of cir-cumstances—one that is well beyond our control in time and out-come, and the other, well within the human will and endeavor to shape. The geology of the area shaped its physical appearance and economic *raison d'être*, while the legacy of slavery, Reconstruction, and the resulting imposition of harsh legal and social racial barriers warped its heart and soul.

The Appalachian Mountains, as unimposing as they are now compared to the Rocky Mountains or California's Sierra Nevada, were a defining presence in the formative years of this country. The thirteen original colonies were bounded to the East Coast by the Appalachians, and the mountains proved to be an economic boon for many areas in their shadows. However, many other areas became home for the poor, white Scotch-Irish, English, and German settlers who would be known as "hillbillies" or, more derogatorily, "poor white trash." In fact, the southern parts of the Appalachian Mountains were called Appalachia, which became synony-mous with the poverty in the area. Many people still think of Appalachia as consisting only of illegal moonshine stills, stock car racing, and "backwards" people like those portrayed in the 1972 film based on James Dickey's novel *Deliverance*.

While geological evolution took millions of years to shape the Appalachians and the northern Alabama landscape with the coal, lime-stone, and iron ore mineral deposits necessary for Birmingham's creation, the white settlers to this land took only three hundred years to evolve a social order that would bring this country to civil war in 1862. The war led to the emancipation of the slaves in 1863, the Thirteenth Amendment to the Constitution abolishing slavery in 1865, and then a period of so-called "Reconstruction" that sought to right the wrongs of the slavery period.

Finally, in the late nineteenth and early twentieth centuries, southern states imposed segregation laws that warped and compressed the society as completely as the geological forces had shaped the Appalachians.

The first recorded instance of the sale of an indentured servant into the New World was in 1619, when a Dutch ship sold twenty blacks as indentured servants to the English colony of Jamestown, in what is now the state of Virginia. Although indentured service continued for some time, it soon evolved into slavery, and in 1661, the first reference to slavery appears in Virginia law. As the southern colonies and territories expanded more and more into a plantation-style agricultural economy, the need for a large number of cheap field hands moved the South to formalize slavery as a way of economic and social life.

In 1705, the Virginia General Assembly passed the Slave Codes, which stated, "All servants imported and brought into this Country...who were not Christians in their native Country...shall be accounted and be slaves. All Negro, mulatto and Indian slaves within this dominion...shall be held to be real estate. If any slave resist his master...correcting such slave, and shall happen to be killed in such correction...the master shall be free of all punishment...as if such accident never happened." The other colonies used the Virginia law as a model for the slave codes they developed in subsequent years.

New York and New Jersey were the last northern states to pass legislation abolishing slavery in 1799 and 1804, respectively; however, all vestiges of slavery did not end until 1827 in New York, and in 1865 in New Jersey with the passage of the Thirteenth Amendment. The southern states, with their reliance on slavery to support their plantation-style economy, continued the practice until forced to change by the Civil War and the Thirteenth Amendment.

Reconstruction, as envisioned by President Lincoln, could possibly have been a successful and noble endeavor. In 1863, Lincoln issued the Proclamation of Amnesty and Reconstruction, a plan based on forgiveness and the hope for a speedy reunification of the states. He intended to let the southern states take the lead in self-reconstruction if they accepted emancipation of the blacks and rejected the reinstitution of slavery. He also planned to grant full pardons to most Southerners and to respect property rights. However, with Lincoln's assassination, the Reconstruction period proved to be a failure from almost all perspectives, and it was formally ended in 1876 after the election of Rutherford Hayes as President. Southern whites slowly regained control of their state legislatures and soon passed laws that formalized the segregation of the races.

Birmingham was still a young city in the early part of the twentieth century, having been established in 1871 in the Jones Valley at the southern reach of the Appalachian mountain chain. Birmingham, named after the industrial English city famous for its production of iron, was surrounded by hills possessing what, at the time, seemed to be endless quantities of coal, iron, and limestone deposits—the necessary ingredients to produce pig iron and steel. This fortunate confluence of natural resources and cheap labor soon transformed Birmingham into the "Pittsburgh of the South." In 1910, the city also earned the sobriquet "The Magic City" because of its rapid industrial expansion and a population that had grown to about 132,000. Birmingham was a town with multiple personalities: it was a free-wheeling example of American capitalism and entrepreneurship; a frontier town where saloons, whorehouses, and murder were a daily norm in districts with names like Pigeon's Roost and Scratch Ankle; a company town where the large mines, factories, and mills controlled workers through company housing and stores; and a segregated town that exploited blacks using perverse forms of neo-slavery—the convict lease program and the fee system.

The convict lease program was used by Alabama, and many other southern states, to produce revenue for state coffers by charging mines, mills, and plantations for the use of state convicts. In some years, Alabama received revenues from convict leases that covered 30 percent of the state's annual budget. The fee system encouraged and allowed local sheriffs and court officials to supplement their incomes by arresting mostly black men, and even boys, for petty crimes or on trumped-up charges. When the men were invariably unable to pay the imposed fines and court fees, the men were sold to the mines for a fee equivalent to the imposed costs. Most sheriffs, who were paid either a small salary or nothing, approached the arrests as if dealing with objects, not people. Estimates vary, but somewhere between one hundred and two hundred thousand convicts were leased to the mines and mills. The men were worked unmercifully and treated brutally. One in ten died of accidents, diseases, or brutal beatings and torture in the mines. In 1928, Alabama was the last state to abolish the convict lease program.*

In addition, a State Constitution was passed in 1901. The keynote speaker, John B. Knox, Esq., made the express purpose of the constitutional convention in Montgomery absolutely clear by saying, "What is it that we want to do? Why, it is, within the limits imposed by the Federal Constitution,

---

* The most comprehensive book on the horrible convict lease program and the fee system, overt forms of de facto slavery used in Alabama and throughout the South, is Douglas A. Blackmon's *Slavery by Another Name: The Re-Enslavement of Black Americans from the Civil War to World War II*. For this book, Blackmon was awarded the 2009 Pulitzer Prize for General Nonfiction.

to establish white supremacy in this State." The State Constitution was a byzantine document that studiously avoided mentioning either whites or blacks in any direct context, yet it would institutionalize laws and practices that would disenfranchise blacks and haunt the entire state for years to come. For example, the new constitution established the Poll Tax, an insidious form of voter registration control that, five years after its implementation, had reduced black adult male voters to only 2 percent of the state's black adult males. A quarter of the white male voters also lost their voting right, since they couldn't pay the annual Poll Tax of $1.50.

The Taylors Arrive in Birmingham

In 1897, twenty-three-year-old Angus Macey Taylor moved to Birmingham from Waynesboro, Mississippi, to start a new business in this booming new city of the South. In 1899, Angus's twenty-seven-year-old brother, James Durward Taylor, joined him in Birmingham. James and Angus were in the business of buying and selling hides, furs, and tallow. They called their new business Birmingham Hide & Tallow Company. In 1909, James moved to New Orleans and opened a similar business, the Taylor Company, leaving the Birmingham business to Angus. Over the next twenty years, Angus's business grew as the demand for leather goods expanded, particularly with the shoe and leather goods manufacturers in the New York City and Boston areas. He became quite prosperous.

Angus and James were descended from English immigrants, and their grandfather, Charles Knight, was a man with a colorful past. Charles Knight's forefathers came from England and were early settlers in the Jamestown settlement in what became the Commonwealth of Virginia. The Taylor family always loved to tell the story, likely embellished in the telling, of Charles Knight's "unfortunate love affair and duel between rivals for the lady's hand." Charles apparently shot the man and immediately left Virginia for the backwoods of Mississippi.

In 1905, Angus married twenty-four-year-old Margaret Boykin McCaa. Margie, as she was always called, was born in Aliceville, Alabama, and was an elementary school teacher for several years. Although Margie did not continue to work after her marriage, she was always involved in civic affairs. She was the Birmingham chairman of the Fourth Liberty Loan Drive supporting World War I. She had a broad interest in art, literature, and music, and instilled this interest in her family. She was instrumental in bringing the first opera series to Birmingham—Massenet's *Thaïs*, and Verdi's *Aida* and *La traviata*. Margie was also quite active in the Women's Suffrage Movement, serving as the first president of the Birmingham Equal Suffrage group in 1915. She made speeches in various parts of town, standing in the back of the family car with the top down with Angus at the wheel, always ready to drive away quickly if the crowd became unruly, as there was widespread hostility to the thought of granting women the right to vote. At this time, Margie, along with the rest of the Alabama suffragettes, was unable to convince the Alabama legislature to approve the Nineteenth Amendment. However, in 1920, two-thirds of the states approved the amendment that stated, "The rights of citizens of the United States to vote shall not be denied or abridged…on account of sex." Margie received a certificate of commendation from Carrie Chapman Catt, of which she was justly proud.

Margie has an interesting and very southern family history. On her father's side, she was descended from John McCaa, a Scottish immigrant who settled in Camden, South Carolina, in 1794. Margie's mother, Sallie Gibbs, was the daughter of Waights Elias Gibbs and Margaret Henry. Colonel Waights Elias was a slaveholding landowner in Mississippi and served in the Confederate Army. Margaret was related to the American Revolution patriot Patrick Henry.

After their marriage, while the city of Birmingham was busy producing pig iron and steel, Margie and Angus were equally busy producing babies from 1906 to 1917. Their first child, born on April 8, 1906, was a daughter named Margaret Henry Taylor. Margaret, a beautiful young girl, unfortunately died on November 12, 1918, at age twelve during the terrible 1918 flu pandemic that killed millions of people worldwide.

After Margaret's birth, the Taylor Boys started to arrive: Angus Macey Taylor Jr. was born on April 20, 1908; George William "Bill" Taylor was born on August 9, 1910; Waights McCaa Taylor was born on September 3, 1912; Frank Marion Taylor was born on February 6, 1914; and Robert Macey Taylor was born on January 9, 1917. These five boys, whose birth recitation sounds like an Old Testament biblical passage, enjoyed their entire young years through college in the same house in Birmingham at 2121 Sixteenth Avenue South on the side of Red Mountain. The mountain, a hill by anyone else's description, overlooks downtown Birmingham and the Jones Valley five hundred feet below.

The family home was large but not grandiose, its most imposing feature being the two tall Ionic columns framing the front. The house was built of dusty yellow brick, trimmed in white, with Victorian stained glass windows in several rooms. The main floor of the house had a large entry hall, a living room, a library, a dining room, a large breakfast room, a kitchen, and a butler's pantry large enough to be an extra room in most homes. The upstairs had four bedrooms and a sleeping porch, which all five boys used for many years. The large backyard had a washhouse where the laundry was done by hand using washtubs and corrugated metal washboards. Behind the washhouse was a stone garage with two rooms for servants above the garage.

No well-to-do upper middle class white family in the South went without black domestic help at that time. The Taylors employed five black domestics: two "mammies," a cook, an upstairs maid, and a butler to perform all the daily chores most of us take for granted today. The mammy in white southern homes dates back to the times of slavery; these black women became an integral part of households and were surrogate mothers to many of the children they raised from infancy. Most white children raised by these women lovingly sang their praises for the rest of their lives; the Taylor Boys joined that chorus in full voice.

Mammy Sophie was a tall, stern woman with a regal air, who dominated the other servants, and, in many ways, the entire Taylor family. Her principal underling was Mammy Jane, a younger lady who continued with the family after Mammy Sophie died in 1920. Clarence E. D. Rucker later became the family chef, chauffeur, and major-domo. E. D. was considered the family philosopher because of his colorful phrases. Two of his most memorable proclamations were "Ef you right, stay right; ef you ain' right, git right!" and the immortal admonition, "Tell a hawg sump'n when a shoat don't know!"

A few years after the family moved into the house, Angus purchased the empty lot alongside the house, and the family christened it the "new lot." Margie planted a vegetable garden in the "new lot," but it was soon abandoned as neither Margie, nor any of the boys, showed much interest or aptitude in gardening. Fortunately for the Taylor family, the garden products were not essential to their needs, and the "new lot" assumed a more productive use as the neighborhood playground.

And use it the boys did. Sixteenth Avenue South included a large number of young boys who comprised a neighborhood gang, and they called the Taylor house a second home and the "new lot" their playground. The gang included Hunter and Miles Copeland Jr., George and Bill Warwick, Burghard Steiner, "Ox" Pruitt, Billy Caldwell, Max Franke, Howard Friedel, Neil Smith Jr., Roy Cohen, and Erle Pettus Jr. and his sister Rosalie. How Rosalie was able to be included in the gang has never been clarified in Taylor family lore, except that she was Erle's little sister.

Although the Sixteenth Avenue South neighborhood was not the wealthiest enclave in Birmingham, it may well have been the most interesting. Several of the "new lot" gang members and their families have fascinating stories to tell.

Gang member Roy Cohen's father, Octavus Roy Cohen, a well-known writer of the time, who started his writing career in Birmingham in the 1920s, published over fifty books and numerous short stories in *The*

Saturday Evening Post, Colliers, and other magazines over the years. His genre was detective mysteries, sometimes featuring a dapper black man named Florian Slappey, whom he described as "a sepia gentlemen." He surrounded Slappey with a number of black characters presented in stereotypical roles popular at the time, complete with clownish attitudes, misjudgments of every situation, and exaggerated black dialect. In a book he published in 1921, titled *Highly Colored,* he had a black character, Mr. Anopheles Ricketts, a tailor, telling a colleague seeking a loan, "Yeh—an' I di'n't git it by lendin' it out at ten puh cent intrus' 'thout no s'curity to no-'count cullud folks liken to what you is." It was pure minstrel show and *Amos 'n Andy* type humor, popular in its day; however, today it would be judged profoundly politically incorrect and insulting to blacks.

Erle Pettus, gang member Erle Pettus Jr.'s father, was a prominent Birmingham lawyer who was appointed U.S. Attorney for Northern Alabama in 1928. He was also a delegate to the Constitutional Convention in Montgomery in 1901, where the state's constitution was written and approved. The Pettus family was also related to Edmund W. Pettus, a brigadier general in the Confederate Army and an Alabama U.S. senator from 1897 until his death in 1907. Edmund's brother, John, was the governor of the State of Mississippi from 1859 to 1863. In 1928, a new bridge over the Alabama River in Selma was named the Edmund Pettus Bridge in honor of Senator Pettus. Little did the family know then that a horrible event would take place on the bridge on March 7, 1965—"Bloody Sunday," when local police and Alabama State Troopers attacked civil rights marchers as they crossed the bridge to march in protest to Montgomery.

Erle Jr. attended Princeton University and Duke University Law School, where he graduated at the top of his class. He was an intelligence officer in World War II, earning numerous medals including five Bronze Stars. After the war he practiced law first in Washington, D.C., and then concluded his legal career with his father's law firm in Birmingham.

Another of the gang members, Miles Axe Copeland Jr. was one of Waights's best boyhood friends; he led a fascinating life, probably the most fascinating of the "new lot" gang. After a short stay at the University of Alabama, he left, telling his parents, "I already know all they can teach me." (Since he had an IQ of 162, genius level, it seems his judgment was not unreasonable.) Miles was an accomplished trumpet player, and in the 1930s, played with many of the country's leading bandleaders of the time, including Erskine Hawkins, Charlie Barnet, Ray Noble, and Glenn Miller. In 1940, as the Second World War raged in Europe and Asia, he used Alabama House of Representatives member John Sparkman (later to be a senator from Alabama for thirty-three years) to get a position with Army Intelligence, and in 1942, he joined the fledgling intelligence service, the

OSS (Office of Strategic Services), led by "Wild" Bill Donovan. This was one of the precursors to the Central Intelligence Agency, and Miles was intimately involved in the creation of the CIA under Allan Dulles after the war. Miles spent most of his CIA years in the Middle East with lengthy assignments in Syria, Lebanon, and Egypt. He retired in London and wrote five books on his CIA and espionage experiences, most notably *The Game of Nations: The Amorality of Power Politics*, and an autobiography, *The Game Player: The Confessions of the CIA's Original Political Operative*. In his autobiography, when he describes his interview for "special assignment" in the CIA, he is asked who were the persons who had influence on his character in his younger years, and he responds, "Then there were Waights Taylor, the neighbourhood intellectual, who taught me *what* to read, and..."

The Taylor Boys and their buddies spent their formative years in the Roaring Twenties, a robust period in American history when it seemed nothing was impossible. It was an exciting time of Prohibition and speakeasies, flappers, jazz, Art Deco, the Model T, radio, and the Harlem Renaissance. However, the boys were more interested in Lindbergh's solo flight across the Atlantic and the era's sports heroes: Babe Ruth, Jack Dempsey, and Bobby Jones. Another sports entity was about to roar onto the national scene: the undefeated University of Alabama football team was invited to participate in the 1926 Rose Bowl against the University of Washington. Southern teams were considered inferior to their eastern and western counterparts, and Alabama was invited only after several eastern teams declined invitations. The boys likely sat around the radio in their living room listening to the game as Alabama fell behind 12–0 in the first half, confirming what many had predicted: a rout of these nice, but inexperienced, football players from the South.

Alabama coach Wallace Wade said only one thing to his players at halftime. "They told me boys from the South would fight." Alabama roared back in the second half on the heroics of quarterback Pooley Hubert and running back Johnny Mack Brown to win the game 20–19. The outcome is called "the football game that changed the South," as Southerners treated the victory as reclamation of lost honor and southern pride for the loss of the Civil War and the nation's view of the South. The boys would have been around the radio once again on January 1, 1927, as Alabama and Stanford played to a 7–7 tie in the Rose Bowl. Alabama football was now definitely a national entity, and the team would play in the Rose Bowl four more times over the next twenty years.

The "new lot" major-domos, the five Taylor boys, enjoyed an enlightened youth well beyond Alabama football heroics. Angus's business was doing quite well, and he and Margie were determined to see that the boys had a good education, as well as life experiences well beyond their southern heritage. Margie, with her five young sons in tow, traveled to Chautauqua, New York, the famous precursor to summer fine arts festivals, in the summers of 1920, 1922, and 1924. Angus would sometimes take one of the boys along on his business trips to New York City and Boston. In their teenage years, the boys spent their summers traveling throughout the United States, as well as South America, Germany, the Far East, and Scandinavia.

When one considers all the chance opportunities for change leading up to a specific birth—chance meetings of individuals, marriages gone awry, immigration patterns of different cultures, and the improbability of a successful conception resulting from a single act of sex—one is certainly tempted to ask, "Am I an accident of birth?"

Whatever the answer to this rhetorical question, the Taylor Boys were the fortunate recipients of that genetic "accident," and were born into an affluent, white, southern family.

5.

TUSKEGEE, ALABAMA

G EOLOGY AND A SINGLE ACT of the Alabama legislature in 1880 molded the history of Tuskegee, Alabama. Geology blessed the area with a soil ideal for agricultural pursuits, and the Alabama legislature provided the impetus for what would become one of the more prestigious black universities in the United States, Tuskegee University.

About ninety miles south of Birmingham, the last remnants of the Appalachian Mountains fade away, and fifty miles south of Warm Springs, the Piedmont Plateau slopes to the flatter sections of central Georgia. The rocky, red clay soil in both states gives way to an area rich in fertile, dark soil atop the chalky, limestone substrata, so much so that it is known as the Black Belt. The geological Black Belt is a swath of land about twenty-five miles wide stretching in a crescent shape for some three hundred miles from southwest Tennessee down through northeast Mississippi and across south-central Alabama, terminating as it crosses into Georgia.

However, the name Black Belt has come to have a broader and more generally accepted geographic definition. The Alabama Black Belt embraces a twenty-two county area in the south-central part of the state from the Mississippi border on the west, through Livingston, Selma, and Montgomery to the Georgia border on the east. An even broader geographic Black Belt definition encompasses agricultural areas in eleven southern states— Alabama, Arkansas, Florida, Georgia, Louisiana, Mississippi, North Carolina, South Carolina, Texas, Tennessee, and Virginia. This broader geographic Black Belt includes as many as 623 counties, and the majority of the population in most of the counties is African American, leading many to assume the name Black Belt refers to the racial composition of the area. Many of the 623 counties continue to be among the poorest in the United States on a per capita income basis.

The first inhabitants in the Alabama Black Belt were, of course, Native American Indians—Choctaws and Creeks. Both were forced to negotiate treaties in 1831 and 1832 ceding all their Alabama lands to the state, and both tribes were part of the infamous "Trail of Tears" march to the Oklahoma Territory. After the 1832 treaty was signed, Macon County was created by the Alabama legislature in December 1832, and Tuskegee, named after a Creek word meaning "warrior," was designated the county seat.

The expropriation of the Indians' lands and their expulsion led to a rush of white settlers, mostly from Georgia and the Carolinas, into Alabama's Black Belt. The migration was so intense that it was called "Alabama fever," Alabama's land and agricultural version of the California Gold Rush to come in 1848. One likely beneficiary of the expulsion of the Choctaws and Creeks and the "Alabama fever" period was Waights's great-grandfather, Sanford Taylor, who moved to the Black Belt region in the 1820s or 1830s. Sanford and his wife, Frances Harbin, acquired from the U.S. General Land Office forty acres in the Black Belt's Monroe County in 1837, and an additional forty acres in adjacent Wilcox County in 1838. Both counties are in the heart of the ancient tribal lands of the Choctaw people.

The geographic Black Belt of Alabama became the agricultural heart of the state's plantation economy, which thrived on cotton production and slavery. The other states in the geographic Black Belt also became agriculturally dependent on slavery with crops of cotton, rice, sugar, and tobacco. The social order and business interests that grew out of the Black Belt were the principal forces responsible for the huge growth in slavery in Alabama and throughout the South from the 1830s forward. The dependence on agriculture and slavery reinforced the strong political resistance to change that led to the Civil War. During the plantation years, the population of Macon County was about 95 percent African American, and even today it's about 85 percent.

In 1880, the State of Alabama was critically short of qualified black educators and teachers. Although the state did not offer blacks equal education choices until forced to by the U.S. Supreme Court ruling in 1954 and the modern civil rights movement, the state legislators even then realized they had a problem too large to ignore, and they passed legislation authorizing creation of Tuskegee Normal School for Colored Teachers. The school opened on July 4, 1881, under the leadership of Dr. Booker T. Washington, the noted educator and leader in the black community. The school was renamed Tuskegee Institute in 1937 and became Tuskegee University in 1985. Dr. Washington best described the dual meaning of Black Belt in his autobiography, *Up from Slavery*.

I have often been asked to define the term "Black Belt." So far as I can learn, the term was first used to designate a part of the country which was distinguished by the colour of the soil. The part of the country possessing this thick, dark, and naturally rich soil was, of course, the part of the South where the slaves were most profitable, and consequently they were taken there in the largest numbers. Later, and especially since the war, the term seems to be used wholly in a political sense—that is, to designate the counties where the black people outnumber the white.

In 1896, Dr. Washington recruited George Washington Carver to join the school as the head of its Department of Agriculture. Carver, a botanical researcher and agronomy educator, remained at Tuskegee for forty-seven years until his death in 1943. Carver became one of the most noted agricultural researchers in the United States and the world. His achievements and awards were numerous. His two most notable scientific accomplishments involved crop rotation and peanuts. Years of cotton-only farming in the Black Belt had depleted the rich soil of its nutrients, and crop yield had declined substantially aided by the growing boll weevil infestations. Carver did not invent crop rotation, but he developed a training program using a mobile wagon, which he and others used to educate Alabama farmers on the need for crop rotation using alternative crops like cowpeas, soybeans, sweet potatoes, and peanuts. However, Carver is probably best known for the work he did with peanuts as a viable crop in lieu of cotton. He reportedly developed over three hundred uses for peanuts from food products to industrial products to cosmetics. This achievement was likely exaggerated, as his admirers and newspapers elevated Carver's life and accomplishments to a mythic status.

One of the more famous programs the school was associated with was the Tuskegee Airmen, the first African American flight squadrons in United States armed forces history. Their training program started in June 1941 at Tuskegee Institute, and flight training was done at nearby Moton Field and Tuskegee Army Air Field. Although the War Department objected to the group's formation, the Tuskegee Airmen were very competent pilots, winning numerous awards in World War II.

One program the school wishes it hadn't become involved in was the U.S. Public Health Service's Tuskegee Syphilis Experiment. The Public Health Service conducted an experiment on 399 black men in the late stages of syphilis from 1932 to 1972. The men, mostly illiterate, were from poor Alabama counties and families. The men were never told what disease they suffered from and were given no medications, as the program had no intention of trying to cure them. The program's intent was to observe these men as the disease progressed and they deteriorated. When a participant died, data was collected by autopsy. Tuskegee Institute let the Public Health Service use its affiliated hospital's medical facilities for the study. Other black institutions were involved, as were local black doctors and a black nurse. The experiment ended only when the story broke in the press in 1972, leading to Congressional hearings. Some U.S. government, Alabama, and Tuskegee Institute officials were unrepentant, claiming the men were "voluntary participants." One study participant said, "I thought they [the doctors] was doing me good." The moral, racist, ethical, sociological, and legal issues raised by this experiment were, and should continue to be, both profound and disturbing to both whites and blacks alike.

In the early 1900s, the town of Tuskegee and the school were doing well. Dr. Washington—a tireless orator, fundraiser, and advocate for education and self-reliance for blacks—had developed a network of wealthy American businessmen, including Andrew Carnegie, John D. Rockefeller, and Julius Rosenwald, the head of Sears, Roebuck and Company. These three men and many others came to be generous contributors to the school's development. Dr. Washington used their donated funds to not only add to his school's needs, but to help establish over five thousand small community schools for blacks throughout the South.

Rosa McCauley

IN 1912, A YOUNG MARRIED COUPLE moved to Tuskegee from Pine Level, Alabama. James McCauley and his wife, Leona Edwards McCauley, were both twenty-four years old and had been living in Leona's parents' home in Pine Level. James, a carpenter and skilled stonemason, saw the Tuskegee building activity created by Dr. Washington's fundraising successes as a good job opportunity. James and Leona found a home near the campus, and James was correct about the job opportunities, although his building assignments frequently took him away from his home to locations throughout the county. Leona, a trained teacher, initially got a job teaching in a local school, but she soon had to resign the position, as she was pregnant with their first child. On February 4, 1913, Leona gave birth to a daughter, Rosa Louise McCauley. Leona kept encouraging James to get a job with Tuskegee Normal School as a carpenter, since the school provided employees with housing and education opportunities unavailable to blacks in most of the South. James, who demonstrated a desire for wanderlust throughout his life, preferred to seek contracting jobs, which made more money but required travel. He also decided to return to his family and hometown in Abbeville, Alabama. So, when Rosa was about two, Leona reluctantly went to Abbeville with James to live with his large family.

Rosa later learned what little she would ever find out about her father's family history from her Uncle George, James's younger brother. George told her that her father's grandmother was a slave and probably part Indian. He told her that little was known about her father's grandfather, although it was rumored he was a Yankee soldier in the area during the Civil War.

James left Abbeville after his family got settled in his parents' home to go north to seek contracting work. Leona was uncomfortable staying in Abbeville with his parents with James not present. She was also pregnant with her second child, so she moved back to Pine Level to live with her parents, Rose and Sylvester Edwards. James returned to his family in Pine Level for a short period but soon left again to find work. After he left, Rosa's baby brother, Sylvester, was born in September 1915. Rosa saw her father when she was five years old, but she did not see him again until she was an adult and married. James and Leona, unable to reconcile their differences— his need for travel and her need for some permanency in their lives—never got back together.

While living with her grandparents in Pine Level, Rosa learned quite a bit about her mother's family history. Rosa's grandmother, Rose, was the daughter of James Percival and Mary Jane Nobles. James Percival was white: a Scotch-Irishman who immigrated to this country as an indentured servant. He came into the United States through the port of Charleston, South Carolina, a major entry point for indentured servants and Africans slated for the slave auction block; he was sent to Pine Level to work for a white plantation owner named Wright. In Pine Level, James met and married Mary Jane, a slave and a midwife. They had nine children, three born before the end of the Civil War and six afterwards. Rosa's grandfather, Sylvester, was the son of John Edwards, a white plantation owner. Sylvester's mother was a slave housekeeper and seamstress in the Edwards's household. She died soon after Sylvester was born, as did John Edwards. Since Rosa's grandfather, Sylvester, was so white, she always thought her great-grandmother, Sylvester's mother, was probably a child of a black woman and a white man.

Rosa's childhood in Pine Level was typical for a black child in the South at the time. Although she and her brother generally played only with other black children, they did have occasional run-ins with white kids over racial slurs. Since Rosa's grandparents owned the house and land they lived on, they weren't considered sharecroppers as so many blacks were. However, she and her brother had to work as field hands and help pick the crops each year. Rosa's grandfather instilled in all his family members the understanding that they didn't have to put up with bad treatment from anyone, especially whites. Rosa lived her life as though that thought was genetically imprinted in her mind.

6.

THREE ODYSSEYS
1928

Waights Taylor—An Intellectual Wandering

WAIGHTS STOOD on the promenade deck of the ship facing the strong wind, blowing a cold sea spray in his face. He wrote in the journal he kept on the trip, "The wind is whipping around the promenade so fast that you can lean against it!! It's a Sou'Wester. Having a big time on this cold, clammy August day in the great north Atlantic."

He and Andy Allison, his good friend from Birmingham, along with other boys from throughout America, were going to Norway, Denmark, and Sweden, where local families would host them as part of a Rotary Club exchange program. It was August 1928 and Waights was fifteen years old, although he would surely have said, "I'll be sixteen next month."

Andy was from a wealthy family in Birmingham that owned a large timber operation in Sumter County, Alabama, and in twenty-one years, Andy and one of his sons to be would play an important role in a life-and-death struggle involving Waights's oldest son, Waights Jr.

Waights's father, Angus, accompanied him by train from Birmingham to New York City to see him off on this grand tour of Scandinavia. Waights departed New York City on July 28 for the ten-day crossing of the North Atlantic. His thirty-seven day trip abroad began on a high note of anticipation and excitement. A few days out to sea, he described in his journal a rare sight for a southern teenager: "Saw an iceberg about 3 miles away. A lone sheep in a field of blue. The moon is full tonight. It is the prettiest thing I ever saw. The waves with gold tinting!"

Their ship arrived in Oslo, Norway, on August 7, and the boys went sightseeing for a few hours. They departed later that day on the same ship for Copenhagen and arrived the next day. Andy remained in Copenhagen with a local family, and Waights departed on a small steamer for Aalborg, Denmark.

"Today is good old Bill's birthday. I guess he is on the Pacific now. I wrote a letter to Kobe [Japan], I hope he gets it," Waights wrote in his journal on August 9 as he steamed toward Aalborg. Waights's brother, William "Bill" Taylor, turned eighteen working as a crewman on his youthful journey to various ports in the Far East. The Taylor Boys were anything but bound to Birmingham and the South; their parents constantly encouraged and aided them to reach well beyond the social confines and racial mores of Alabama and the times.

Waights stayed in Aalborg for ten days with a Danish family, whom he described as, "very nice, quaint people." Andy arrived from Copenhagen on August 11. Waights was delighted, exclaiming in his journal, "I was worried about him, but he is all right, and we are together so everything is 'jake.'" (Jake was a popular slang word used at the time to mean everything is satisfactory.) Their time in Aalborg with new young Danish friends was quixotic: they visited cabarets; played tennis, football, and baseball; went bicycling and swimming; enjoyed fine dinners; and were treated to sightseeing trips all over the west coast of the Jutland peninsula.

On August 19, they departed Aalborg by train and continued on to Göteborg, Sweden, by boat. Their stay was brief, only one night. They left by train for Oslo early the next morning.

Andy and Waights arrived in Oslo the next day, and, much to their joy, found themselves housed in a Norwegian estate. Waights wrote, "Andy and I sure hit it off lucky. We are together in a luxurious home on a Norwegian estate of about one hundred acres. It is the most beautiful home and grounds I have ever seen." They attended local dances, visited the National Art Gallery and the Oslo Ski Museum, and took a boat trip around the fjord near Oslo.

On August 28, Waights and Andy departed Oslo by ship and returned to Copenhagen, arriving the next day. They had lunch in Copenhagen and visited the National Museum Art Gallery and the House of Parliament. Then they took a train to the small town of Jyderup, about forty miles west of Copenhagen, where they would spend the next six days. Initially the boys complained about the slow country life; Waights even described Jyderup as "a rather crude place." However, they came to enjoy the place and their hosts, the Hooge family, immensely. On September 3, Waights celebrated his sixteenth birthday in Jyderup. The "crude place" was now written about quite differently, "The Hooges were certainly fine to me. Mr. Hooge gave me a present, some pictures of the town. It has been a fine day."

The boys traveled by train on September 4 back to Copenhagen, where they would spend the last eight days of this marvelous trip. Over the next several days, Waights saw his first opera, Leoncavallo's *I Pagliacci*, at the Det Kongelige Teater (Royal Danish Theatre) with the King and Queen of Denmark in attendance; he visited Kronberg Castle, Hamlet's castle in Elsinore, about thirty miles north of Copenhagen, as he had already started a love affair with Shakespeare that would continue his entire life; he toured Fredericksberg Castle near Copenhagen and visited the local museums; and, on the last night of their stay, he attended a farewell banquet held at a famous Copenhagen restaurant. Waights wrote of his last days in Scandinavia, "We are really having a wonderful time these last few days in Copenhagen. It all seems like a dream almost."

On September 12, Waights, Andy, and the other boys left Copenhagen at noon on the S.S. United States bound for New York City. The return crossing took twelve days, with brief stops in Oslo and Halifax, and the ship arrived in New York City on September 24. The next day, Waights and Andy left New York City on the Southern Railway Special for Birmingham. As they approached Birmingham, a homesick Waights, eager to tell his loving family about all his adventures and give them the gifts he had bought for each of them while abroad, excitedly wrote, "We'll be in tomorrow, boy it's going to be good. Oh you engineer, open up that throttle!!"

They arrived in Birmingham on September 26, concluding a sixty-six-day odyssey that would serve as a stepping stone in their transition from teenagers to young adults. Waights's last entry in his journal was, "Home at last! Boy it's great!!"

Waights spent the school year of 1928–1929 as a junior at Phillips High School in Birmingham. He spent the summer of 1929 in the White Mountains of New Hampshire; however, he did not keep a daily journal, so a peek back at those experiences is not possible.

In January 1930, Waights graduated from Phillips High School, and, in September, he entered the University of Alabama, where he would prove to be an eager and excellent student, earning a Phi Beta Kappa key for his efforts, and where he would find himself walking across the Quadrangle on March 25, 1931.

Waights and his brothers enjoyed an upbringing best described by Waights in an unpublished memoir he wrote years later. Borrowing from one of Birmingham's nicknames, he wrote, "Could any other world ever have been filled with half the magic of those twelve years from 1918 to 1930?"

Clarence Norris—A Wandering Filled with Challenges

CLARENCE STOOD BESIDE the third tee at the golf course FDR had built in Warm Springs. He wasn't waiting his turn to tee it up; he was working as a caddy for three dollars a round.

He returned to Warm Springs in the summer of 1928 after his father's death, and he, like Waights, was fifteen, going on sixteen. Clarence stayed with relatives, and his cousin Johnny was able to get him a job at FDR's Georgia Warm Springs Foundation. The foundation offered the major employment opportunities for blacks in the area, but, of course, the jobs were all service related—cooks, porters, waiters, gardeners, maids, chauffeurs, caddies, and grounds personnel.

Clarence was hired as a caddy in the daytime; at night, he and another caddy, nicknamed "Red" because of his light skin, would work as greenkeepers, mowing the greens and lawns. Once a week they were allowed to swim in the pool, but only just before they drained it, cleaned it, and refilled it for the white patrons. For this additional work, Clarence and Red were each paid thirty dollars every two weeks.

One night after the two had finished mowing the greens, Red asked Clarence, "Do you want some ice cream?"

Clarence said, "Yeah, but where you gonna get it?"

Red answered, "Follow me."

They slipped into the clubhouse through a back window that was easily opened. When they got inside, Red said, "Eat, take all you want, they never miss nothing." They helped themselves to all the ice cream they could eat and left with golf balls, candy, and a box of cigars each.

Well, Red was wrong; the items were missed. Several weeks later on payday, the boss approached the boys, and noticing a few cigars in Red's shirt pocket asked him, "Boy where did you get those cigars?"

At first, Red tried to bluff by saying, "I bought them." The boss persisted, and Red finally confessed that he and Clarence had stolen them. The boss threatened to call the police but instead fired them on the spot and refused to pay them their back wages.

Clarence returned to Johnny's house and related to him what had happened. Johnny also worked in the clubhouse, and he was tired of both his job and his home life. Johnny said, "Let's go to Birmingham. I've got some money saved and I'll get paid today." That evening Johnny, Clarence, and two other boys jumped a freight train headed for Birmingham.

Clarence was about to start an odyssey over the next three years similar to the journeys Odysseus took in Homer's *Odyssey* and Inman took in Charles Frazier's book, *Cold Mountain*. All three men faced life-threatening events and challenges along the way leading to their destinies.

Clarence departed Warm Springs with a head cold that got progressively worse over the next few days. He left Johnny and the other two boys at one of the stops along the way and struggled to find help until he happened upon a black family's home in the country. He collapsed on their porch, was taken in, was nursed back to health, and then worked for them in their fields for fifty cents a day. After several weeks, they told Clarence he should go home, gave him money for the train ride, so he wouldn't have to illegally ride the rails, and drove him to the depot to return to Molena.

Clarence stayed with his sisters in Molena for a short time and heard there were jobs to be had at a lumber company in West Point, Georgia. He went to West Point, only about twenty miles from Molena, got a job, and moved into a boardinghouse for black men. After about a week, all the men went out for a Saturday night on the town. Clarence decided not to go, since he knew few people in town, and he went to bed early. He awoke later in the night to find the old black man who owned the boardinghouse on the side of his bed, fondling his penis. As Clarence rushed to dress and get out of the house, the old man begged him to stay and promised Clarence anything he had, if only Clarence would cooperate with him.

Clarence moved to another boardinghouse in West Point, owned by a black lady. The old man from the other house found out where Clarence was staying and came over to complain that Clarence was a thief and had stolen his clothes. His new landlady looked through all of Clarence's clothes and saw that none of them were nearly large enough to fit the old man. She told the old man to get out of her house and to leave Clarence alone. The old guy persisted in going around town accusing Clarence of being a thief, but no one believed him.

Clarence soon met his landlady's niece, Annie Pearl. She was a beautiful, tall, brown-skinned woman about two years older than Clarence. He was immediately smitten with her. After a brief courtship, she persuaded Clarence to move with her to Gadsden, Alabama, where good jobs were available in a new Goodyear plant under construction.

Annie Pearl had some education, and she taught Clarence how to recognize numbers and do simple addition. Clarence got a job with Goodyear and worked lots of overtime, using his money to furnish the house they rented. For almost a year, he enjoyed happiness and contentment he had seldom experienced until Annie Pearl fell in love with another man, left Clarence, and moved in with the new man. One night, he talked Annie Pearl into going for a walk with him. As they walked across a bridge in the moonlight, Clarence fully intended to kill her. Annie Pearl, sensing his mood, looked at him and said, "Are you going to kill me, Bubba?" Her question broke the moment, and Clarence soon left Gadsden, his good job, his house, and all its belongings. He went back to the life of a hobo, riding the rails for transportation while seeking that elusive nirvana.

A later stop along the way found Clarence in Birmingham, where he sought overnight shelter in an empty boxcar in the railroad yard. Unknown to Clarence, the railroad cops had seen him in the yard, and they searched the freight cars until they found him. The cops yelled at him, "Get outta there, n-----."* They taunted him, beat him, and finally said to him, "We are going to give you a chance to run for your life." Knowing they were about to shoot him, Clarence jumped into some high weeds just behind a big billboard and ran low in the weeds for some distance as shots rang out behind him until he felt safe. He slept overnight at that spot and awoke the next morning behind a house in a white, well-to-do neighborhood. He knew if he were spotted, he would be in big trouble; he waited until it seemed safe, and then he ran between houses to the street and escaped with no further trouble.

Continuing his life as a hobo, Clarence scratched for an existence throughout Alabama and Georgia, existing alongside the many whites and blacks caught in the same web. Prostitution was rampant among the women as a source of money for survival, and in the hobo jungles there was little racial bias for their services; a black man with a white woman was as common as white on white. Survival and the need for money for the next meal were the common denominators. The threat of arrest for vagrancy was constant, especially for blacks. At one of his stops along the way, Clarence was arrested for vagrancy and received a ten-day sentence at hard labor busting rock in a local quarry.

And then, on March 25, 1931, Clarence found himself in Chattanooga waiting to hop a freight train for Memphis.

Unlike Waights, Clarence never personally wrote about his life from 1918 to 1930. Clarence was illiterate.

Rosa McCauley—A Journey for an Education

ROSA FINISHED PACKING HER SUITCASE, already feeling nostalgic about leaving home again on this hot August day in 1928. She was preparing to make the short trip to Montgomery for the start of the school year. She had spent the summer in Pine Level with her family, but now it was time to return to her Aunt Fannie's house in Montgomery.

Rosa was fifteen years old, and she was about to start the tenth grade in the laboratory high school at Alabama State Teachers College for Negroes. Since there were no public high schools for blacks in the Montgomery area, the college had a laboratory school where young black students studying to be teachers could be trained. This was Rosa's only choice unless she traveled ninety miles to Birmingham.

---

* The N-word is used and quoted in full form throughout the references used for the events in this book. Historical purists, grammarians, and educators may fault me, but I refuse to use its full form in my book. I heard the word used so frequently in the South as a racial epithet and insult that I will not use the word today.

Rosa's mother, Leona, knew and understood the importance of education and was determined to do everything she could to see that Rosa was well educated. Leona had attended Payne University in Selma, Alabama, where she received a teaching certificate. She taught grade school in Tuskegee before Rosa was born and in a school near Pine Level as Rosa was growing up. She started teaching Rosa to read at age three. Rosa could read when she entered first grade in Pine Level, a one-room, one-teacher school with about sixty children in grades one to six.

Rosa was eight years old in the summer of 1921. She'd just finished the second grade, when Leona took her to Montgomery for the first time. Leona had to attend Alabama State Normal School, a black teachers' college (later called Alabama State Teachers College for Negroes) each summer to take courses to keep her teacher's license current. Leona enrolled Rosa in the school's laboratory grade school classes, where the student teachers worked with the children. When Leona and Rosa returned to Pine Level, they learned the Pine Level School had closed, and Rosa and Sylvester had to go to school in Spring Hill, eight miles from Pine Hill. Spring Hill was the church school where her mother had been the only teacher for several years. The children went with Leona in a horse drawn wagon each week to Spring Hill, where they stayed in a friend's home and walked to school each day. They returned to Pine Hill in the wagon for the weekends.

After Rosa finished fifth grade at Spring Hill School, Leona sent her to Montgomery to attend school and to live with Leona's sister, Fannie. Leona had enrolled Rosa in the Montgomery Industrial School for Girls, more commonly called Miss White's School, exclusively for African American girls, run by two white women, Alice White and Margaret Beard from Massachusetts. The teaching staff was all white, and, as one would imagine, the school and the teachers were not well received in the segregated South—the school was burned down at least twice. Leona initially paid Rosa's tuition, although Rosa later had to accept a scholarship and perform menial tasks in the school. The school did receive some support from local white churches in Montgomery, and from Julius Rosenwald, the Tuskegee Normal School supporter.

Rosa had suffered from tonsillitis since she was about two years old, causing her to frequently miss school. Leona decided to have Rosa's tonsils removed by a Montgomery doctor before she started school at Miss White's, but the recovery period caused her to enroll late. Miss White elected to start her in the fifth grade because of her late start, but she did so well, she was moved up to the sixth grade at midterm. Rosa was an excellent student and obeyed the school's strict Christian-based rules without question. Her schoolmate Johnnie Mae Carr later said that Rosa was "very quiet" and always "staying out of trouble." Even though school policy prohibited dancing, most of the girls ignored the prohibition. Carr made it clear that Rosa was not one of those girls; "She was a straight Christian arrow."

After Rosa completed the eighth grade, Miss White, now quite elderly, closed the school. Rosa's experience at the school was probably life altering; she was taught that she had as much self-worth and dignity as any other person—white or black—and that she should aspire to do whatever she wanted with her life.

With Miss White's school closed, Rosa attended Booker T. Washington Junior High School in Montgomery, which had opened specifically for blacks, for the ninth grade. Rosa successfully completed the ninth grade and went back to Pine Level for the summer of 1928 wondering where she would next go to school. Rosa shouldn't have worried; Leona had registered her in the only available high school for blacks in Montgomery, a laboratory class at the Alabama State Teachers College for Negroes.

Leona hugged Rosa goodbye as her suitcase was loaded into the car trunk. She got into the car and waved goodbye, and a family friend drove her to Aunt Fannie's house in Montgomery. Rosa completed the tenth grade at Alabama State and started the eleventh grade at Alabama State in 1929. Unfortunately, she had to drop out after only a month when her grand-mother became ill. Rosa returned home to Pine Level to help care for her grandmother, who died a month after her return.

After Rosa's grandmother's death, Rosa returned to Montgomery and found a job in a factory that made men's work shirts. She went back to Alabama State for a short period, but then her mother became quite ill. Rosa had to go back to Pine Level and care for Leona, who suffered from migraine headaches and swelling of her legs and feet. Sylvester had to drop out of school as well to work to support the family. Leona did get somewhat better, but the stress on family finances and dynamics forced Rosa to remain in Pine Level, doing domestic work and taking care of the farm. Rosa, displaying the stoic and self-effacing attitude that would mark her life, did not want to drop out of school; however, she knew it was her responsibility to take care of her grandmother and mother. She later said, "I did not complain; it was just something that had to be done."

In the early spring of 1931, Rosa, now eighteen, sat on the porch of the Pine Level home with her mother waiting for the arrival of a gentleman caller. She had met the man recently when a mutual friend introduced them. He was a barber in Montgomery and was ten years older than Rosa.

The man stopped the car, walked to the porch, and probably said some-thing like, "Hello Rosa. Hello Mrs. McCauley. I'm Raymond Parks. Just call me Parks."

7.

CHATTANOOGA, TENNESSEE

Double, double, toil and trouble,
Fire burn, and cauldron bubble.

IN SHAKESPEARE'S PLAY *MACBETH*, the weird sisters—the witches—add fillet of fenny snake, eye of newt, toe of frog, tongue of dog, adder's fork, lizard's leg, an owlet's wing, and prophetically, the liver of a blaspheming Jew, to make a brew most potent, as they continue their chant:

For a charm of powerful trouble,
Like a hell-broth boil and bubble.

Had the witches been in Chattanooga the night before the freight train departed for Memphis, their brew would have included a mix of racial prejudice, abject segregation, stereotypical views of black men's sexual prowess, the hallowed sanctity and sexual purity of white southern women, a southern pathological fear of miscegenation, illiteracy, prejudicial lawyers and judges, the U.S. Communist Party, a New York Jewish lawyer, profound anti-Semitism, a biased southern press, outside pressure from places as far flung as Poland and Germany, the Great Depression with its high unemployment, the Alabama Supreme Court, and the U.S. Supreme Court. All of these ingredients led to events that would *"like a hell-broth boil and bubble"* for years to come.

As Clarence waited in the railroad yard for the train's departure, others were gathered in the yard and along the railway through and out of the city, also waiting to jump the train to ride to various points on its route to Memphis. The others included a number of white and black male youths, and two young white women who would serve as the catalyst to ignite the witches' brew.

The sequence and number of people who boarded the train is not absolutely clear, but before the train left the Chattanooga area, all the major participants were on board. Reports vary, but it seems that from six to eight white male youths and from ten to thirteen black male youths boarded the train. There is no doubt that only two young white women were on the train, and thereby hangs a tale. Because of their presence and the events to follow, Clarence and eight of the other young blacks on the train would soon be labeled "the Scottsboro Boys" for the rest of their lives.

Four black youths jumped on the train together as it passed the 23rd Street area in Chattanooga—Haywood Patterson, Eugene Williams, and the brothers, Andrew "Andy" Wright and Leroy "Roy" Wright. They were friends and all lived in Chattanooga at the time. They had decided to ride the freight train to Memphis, where they heard government jobs were to be had hauling logs on boats on the Mississippi River.

Haywood Patterson

HAYWOOD PATTERSON, who would become one of the more tragic figures in this unfolding drama, was eighteen years old. Like Clarence, he was the son of poor sharecropper parents, Claude and Janie Patterson. He was born in 1912, the fourth of nine children, on a farm near Elberton, Georgia, a town about one hundred miles east of Atlanta. His father and mother worked long and hard to provide for the family, and Haywood later said the family never wanted for the basics of food and shelter.

In 1921, when Haywood was nine years old, his father purchased a car, an almost new Model T Ford. The white landowner, the boss, came to Claude and told him to put the car away and get back to work in the fields. Claude was so upset by this incident that he left the farm and looked for work elsewhere. However, at the time, a black man could not easily leave a sharecropper agreement without risking arrest for violation of the contract and likely leaving behind debts incurred to the white landowner. Claude and Janie agreed on a plan, knowing "You had to fox your way out of such a spot."

The day after Claude's departure, Haywood later wrote, "The day after my dad slipped off, my mother, she went crying to the boss. She told him that the old man had left her with the kids and she didn't know where he had gone." The landowner believed her and let the family go, although he insisted they leave behind livestock that was rightfully theirs. They stayed with Haywood's grandfather for a month and then moved to Chattanooga, where Claude had settled and found employment.

Considering how similar this event was to the circumstances of Clarence's father's experience with his red horse and new buggy, it becomes clear that a black sharecropper had little opportunity to climb out of his impoverished situation in spite of his best intentions. Any attempt to better one's lot was seen as a threat by the white social order and was thwarted at every turn.

Haywood was able to make a number of friends his own age in Chattanooga, unlike at the farm, where his only playmates were his brother and sisters. He and his friends frequented the poor black neighborhoods, Blue Goose Hollow and Tandry Flat, and occasionally visited the more upscale black areas of Bush Town and Hog View (the names certainly don't evoke an upscale image). His father had a good job with the American Brakeshoe Company, making forty or forty-five dollars a week until after 1929 and the start of the Great Depression, when his wages dropped to fifteen dollars a week.

Haywood quit going to school at age thirteen, was functionally illiterate, and in 1926 at age fourteen, made his first ride on the rails to Dayton, Ohio. He did so to free his parents of the responsibility of caring for him so they could better provide for his younger siblings. He continued to ride the rails over the next several years, going as far north as Ohio, south to Florida, west to Arkansas, and ending up back in Chattanooga in March 1931.

Unfortunately, there is a lack of detail available on the early lives of the other boys that boarded the train that day. There are even discrepancies about their ages in the various accounts. This is likely attributable to the attention given Clarence Norris and Haywood Patterson in the court proceedings about to unfold, and the subsequent attention they received from their autobiographies.

Eugene Williams

EUGENE WILLIAMS WAS THIRTEEN years old when he boarded the train. Eugene was born and raised in Chattanooga, and he worked as a dishwasher. He was described by the press as a mulatto—a person with one white parent and one black parent, generally of light or chocolate brown color.

Racial labels, such as mulatto, are not only derogatory, but also illogical. The word mulatto comes from the Spanish *mulato*, originally meaning young mule, an offspring of a male donkey and a female horse. Taking it back another step, it's derived from the Latin word *mulus*, meaning the offspring of any two creatures of different species. Why is a person born to a white and black parent always considered black? It's statistically a fifty-fifty proposition, and, yet, the black side always trumps the white side in racial categorization. The influential and eminent evolutionary biologist and natural historian, Stephen Jay Gould, was outspoken on cultural oppression in all forms, particularly racism and sexism. Gould used an interesting barroom-type question to illustrate how cultural perceptions color our view of the facts. He asked, "Which Italian American player for the Brooklyn Dodgers once hit forty home runs in a season?" Few, if any, would get it right, as the correct answer is Roy Campanella. Roy's father was an Italian American and his mother was an African American, yet he initially had to play baseball in the Negro League because society labeled him black.

White European and American heritage has assumed a cultural superiority of the white race, and this paradigm still haunts us today. Imagine our modern culture today without the likes of Halle Berry, Lani Guinier, Eartha Kitt, Barack Obama, Colin Powell, and August Wilson. All have had extraordinary lives and careers. Of course, while one should value and honor their racial roots, Morgan Freeman, the great American actor, was asked by Mike Wallace on *60 Minutes*, "How can we get rid of racism?" Freeman responded, "Stop talking about it. I'm going to stop calling you a white man. And I'm going to ask you to stop calling me a black." However, when you consider the evolutionary tract of the human species, the white paradigm needs to be reversed, as we are all "out of Africa."

Andy Wright

ANDY WRIGHT WAS NINETEEN years old in 1931, and he and his brother, Roy, and his three sisters were born and raised in Chattanooga. He did well in school but had to quit after the sixth grade to help his mother, Ada Wright, support the family when his father died. At age twelve, he took a job driving a truck with a local produce distributor and continued to work there for seven years, until the distributor's insurance company found out about Andy's age, forcing the boss to let him go. He then worked in a furniture store until he heard about the jobs in Memphis and boarded the train.

Roy Wright

ROY WRIGHT WAS TWELVE years old, the youngest of the nine boys destined to become one of the Scottsboro Boys. Roy quit school after three or four years to work in a local grocery store. He also started hanging out with Andy and his friends and was eager to join them on the train to Memphis. This would be Roy's first trip away from home, and both he and Andy left without telling their mother.

In addition to Clarence Norris and the four Chattanooga boys, four other black youths boarded the train separately at different points along the way out of Chattanooga to complete the group of nine who would become the Scottsboro Boys.

Charlie Weems

CHARLIE WEEMS WAS NINETEEN years old in 1931, the oldest of the nine boys, and was from Atlanta. Charlie had had a hard childhood, starting with his mother's death when he was four years old. Of his seven brothers and sisters, only one of them survived beyond childhood. He completed the fifth grade in public school but quit when his father became too old to work. He took a job in a pharmacy to support the family. Later, when his father got sick, he was sent to Riverdale, Georgia, to live with an aunt. He returned to school in Riverdale, but he didn't last long. Charlie quit school again, and he blamed it on his distraction and infatuation with girls. In the winter, he worked on a road gang, and the remainder of the year he worked on a local farm near Riverdale. He left Riverdale for Chattanooga just a few weeks before he was to board the Memphis-bound freight train.

Olen Montgomery

SEVENTEEN-YEAR-OLD OLEN MONTGOMERY was born in Monroe, Georgia, in 1913. He went to school through the fifth grade and had to repeat the third grade. He quit going to school when he was about fourteen (a familiar story with most of these young boys) to help his mother, Viola Montgomery. Olen's first job was delivering groceries, before working in construction, and finally at a fertilizer plant, where he quit when the boss cursed at him. Olen was badly nearsighted and was nearly blind in one eye from a cataract (possibly his sight problems contributed to his problems in school). In March 1931, he went to Chattanooga to seek a better job in hopes of earning enough money to buy a new pair of glasses.

Ozie Powell

FIFTEEN-YEAR-OLD OZIE POWELL was born in rural Georgia. His father, who mistreated his mother, left them when Ozie was a small boy. His mother, Josephine Powell, remarried, moved to Atlanta, and worked for white people, probably in their homes. Ozie went to school for only one year and was essentially illiterate, unable to write much more than his name. He worked at odd jobs when he was very young, and, at age thirteen, started working at sawmills and lumber camps. At age fourteen, he ran away from home for the first time and worked at a highway camp for $2.50 a day. He continued to travel often, and, at age fifteen, he hoboed to Chattanooga and jumped the train bound for Memphis.

Willie Roberson

WILLIE ROBERSON WAS SEVENTEEN years old in 1931. Shortly after he was born in Columbus, Georgia, his parents separated. His mother died when he was two. After that, his maternal grandmother and two of her sisters in Atlanta raised him. He went to school, reaching only the seventh grade. He quit, saying, "I just got lazy and did not care any more for school." He worked as a hotel bus boy but left in 1931, hoping to find better work in Chattanooga. Unable to find work in Chattanooga, he jumped the freight train bound for Memphis, where he planned to look for work and a free hospital to treat his severe cases of syphilis and gonorrhea.

The common denominators binding these nine boys together were many beyond the color of their skin: they all came from poor families struggling to make a living; several of the boys' fathers had died or left the mothers as the sole source of support for the families; two of the boys lost both parents at an early age and were raised by relatives; none of the boys finished elementary school; they all started work at an early age in menial jobs, as their color and lack of education dictated; and they all hoped to find a better job somewhere down the line, as they boarded the train to Memphis.

Victoria Price and Ruby Bates

THE TWO YOUNG WHITE GIRLS that jumped onto the train that cool morning in Chattanooga were bound for their hometown of Huntsville, Alabama. Victoria Price, twenty-one years old, and Ruby Bates, seventeen, said they were returning to Huntsville to get their personal belongings and bring them back to Chattanooga, where they would continue with their new jobs in a cotton mill. In fact, they were returning to Huntsville after an overnight tryst with two young white men in the hobo jungle near the Chattanooga railroad yard.

Huntsville in the 1930s was yet to become the thriving city it is today, a center for technology and for the space and defense industries. In the 1930s, Huntsville was a city of about thirty-two thousand, which included those in the surrounding mill villages, and was in the declining years of its cotton mill and market-driven economy. The town had seven cotton mills that had prospered for years, but the Great Depression took a huge toll on their production and employment requirements.

Victoria and Ruby's early life stories sound startlingly similar to those of the nine black boys they would soon encounter. They were all born into poor backgrounds with little opportunity for a good education or meaningful employment. Most ironic, the nine black boys and two white girls occupied almost identical status in the southern social order, a structure that can be loosely compared to the Indian caste system. At the bottom of the social order is the Dalit, or "untouchables," which would include poor whites and all blacks. However, the South, either by intention or by accident, had developed a subtle split between the two halves of the lowest group. Southern custom treated poor whites and all blacks somewhat equally on matters of economics to maintain a cheap labor pool available to farmers, businesses, and industrial operations. The poor whites were given latitude over the blacks only on social issues concerning the color of one's skin. The implications of this social structure became harshly apparent as the events that occurred on the train unfolded.

Victoria Price

Victoria Price lived with her widowed mother, Ella Price, in a ramshackle, unpainted shack in a racially mixed part of town. She quit school when she was ten years old and started to work at age thirteen. In the 1920s, she was working full time in the Margaret Spinning Mill, making twenty cents per hour for a twelve-hour day. The Margaret Mill, one of seven cotton mills in Huntsville, was an employment choice of last resort, as it was an antiquated facility paying the lowest wages of all the mills. In 1931, the mill cut her wages to $1.20 a day for three twelve-hour days every other week. Victoria was a hard-talking, hard-drinking young woman who would prove to be the principal antagonist of the nine boys throughout the entire ordeal. If any one individual was responsible for the injustices that were about to occur, it was Victoria Price.

Ruby Bates

Ruby Bates had a harsh childhood. Her father was a drunk, and he constantly beat Ruby, her mother Emma, and her two brothers. After Ruby's father was arrested for horsewhipping one of Ruby's brothers, the family left him and moved from town to town in northern Alabama until they settled in Huntsville. They moved into an unpainted shack in a poor part of town, where they were the only white family on the block. Their black neighbors said Emma "took men for money whenever she got the chance." Ruby, who was fifteen years old at the time, took a job in the Margaret Mill. She and Victoria became friends while working in the mill, and they decided to go to Chattanooga to seek better employment.

Victoria and Ruby supplemented their meager mill incomes by working as prostitutes, not an uncommon practice for poor white and black women during the Great Depression. Life was hard and opportunities were very limited. An official of the National Association for the Advancement of Colored People (NAACP) described the girls as "notorious prostitutes." In defense affidavits presented at a later trial, one witness, a Negro boardinghouse owner, swore Victoria and Ruby had rented a room to use for prostitution; they entertained black men on what they called "negro night." Another witness said he heard Victoria "ask colored men the size of his privates." He also added he once heard Ruby boasting that she could "take five negroes in one night and not hurt her."

———

AND SO, THE TRAIN LEFT THE CHATTANOOGA AREA, the die was cast, and the witches had indeed loaded it with a combustible brew that would soon *"boil and bubble."*

PART TWO

THE TRIAL PERIOD

MARCH 25, 1931–JULY 24, 1937

8.

SIXTEEN DAYS IN SCOTTSBORO
MARCH 25–APRIL 9, 1931

The Train Departs Chattanooga—March 25, 1931

THE FREIGHT TRAIN SLOWLY WOUND ITS WAY along the Tennessee River out of Chattanooga and the State of Tennessee, through the southern reaches of the eastern side of the Cumberland Plateau and into the northeast corner of Jackson County, Alabama. Just before the train entered Alabama, the Tennessee River made a sharp turn to the southwest, following a geological marvel, the Sequatchie Valley, which runs for over one hundred and fifty miles between the two principal ridges of the Cumberland Plateau on an almost straight line through Tennessee and into Alabama. Spring was coming to the valley, with a bucolic landscape scattered along the river's banks awaiting the full bloom of what many called the most beautiful valley in the world.

The train tracks parallel the river for some distance; over one hundred and seventy years ago, the Tennessee River had served as a conduit and an observer in another sad day in this country's history—the river was one of the "Trail of Tears," the routes used in the forcible expulsion of the Cherokee Nation from the southeastern states to the Oklahoma Territory.

American history is littered with stories like the "Trail of Tears," and there is no easy way to clear away the debris left behind by the actions of those who preceded us. The Cherokees had inhabited the Southeast, parts of which are now Alabama, Georgia, Kentucky, South and North Carolina, and Tennessee, for nearly one thousand years before the first whites arrived in the area in large numbers in the eighteenth and nineteenth centuries.

The "Trail of Tears," from the Cherokee phrase "nunna dual isunyi"—
"the trail where we cried"—was a direct result of states' rights pressures
President Andrew Jackson was receiving from South Carolina on tariff
issues, and even more so from Georgia on forced Cherokee removal. To
diffuse the pressure he was getting from these two states, Jackson chose to
appease Georgia by forcing the Cherokees to sign a removal treaty. Officials
of the U.S. government and a breakaway group of pro-removal Cherokees
signed the treaty, the Treaty of New Echota, on December 29, 1835. Although
the main Cherokee council, representing the majority of the Cherokee
people, did not sign the treaty document and repudiated it, Congress
approved the treaty by one vote, and on May 23, 1836, President Jackson
proclaimed it ratified. All Cherokee ancestral lands east of the Mississippi
River were ceded in the treaty.

About three thousand Cherokees, mostly members of the pro-removal
group, left for the Oklahoma Territory after the treaty was signed, leaving
behind about thirteen thousand other tribal members who had two years to
leave under the terms of the treaty. As the two-year deadline approached
and the remaining Cherokees showed no signs of leaving the southeastern
states voluntarily, President Martin Van Buren sent General Winfield Scott,
the most decorated and admired American general since George
Washington, to enforce the treaty removal provisions. Scott arrived in
Georgia in May 1838 with about seven thousand soldiers. He and his troops
proceeded to round up the Cherokees at gunpoint in Georgia, Tennessee,
North Carolina, and Alabama, placing them in squalid camps prior to their
forced departure to the West.

One sad irony of the experience is that, in addition to the sixteen thousand Cherokees displaced, wealthy Cherokee slaveholders took about two
thousand black slaves with them. The Cherokees and slaves were forced to
travel twelve hundred miles by one of three routes, including the Tennessee
River. Estimates of the number who died along on the way vary from four
thousand to eight thousand.

The Train Continues to Paint Rock

Now again, in 1931, the Tennessee River would be called upon to serve as
an observer to another tragic event on its banks. This time, it might well be
called the "Trail of Trials and Tears."

Soon after the train left Chattanooga and exited the tunnel under
Lookout Mountain, a single incident started the chain of events to follow.
All who had jumped on the train illegally, black and white alike, tried to
find a car that provided the best protection from the unseasonably cool and
windy day.

Haywood Patterson and his three friends held on to the side of a tank car, as they prepared to look for a more comfortable spot, when a group of white boys walked across the top of the car. One of the white boys stepped on Haywood's hand, and Haywood yelled at him, telling him he had almost lost his grip and fallen off the train. He also said to the white boy, "The next time you want by, just tell me you want by and I let you by." The white boy replied, "N-----, I don't ask you when I want by. What you doing on this train anyway?" Haywood said, "You white sonsofbitches, we got as much right here as you!" The boys traded additional insults and threats, and the white boys started throwing rocks at Haywood and his friends. Rocks and cuss words were hurled back and forth for a short time before things quieted down for a bit.

Clarence, who boarded the train alone, had settled in a boxcar near the rear of the train and was not aware of the initial outburst. He remained alone as the train entered the northeast corner of Alabama and made a stop at Stevenson, a small town about ten miles from the state line, to add another boxcar. Clarence, and most of the others on the train, got off for a few minutes, but the rock throwing continued intermittently between the two groups of boys. Haywood approached Clarence and some of the other black boys he now saw were on the train, and he asked for their help if the fight continued.

Shortly after the train left Stevenson, the whites continued to harass the blacks with rocks and racial slurs. Fed up with the situation, Haywood, his three Chattanooga friends, and the other black boys he had enlisted to their side in Stevenson, jumped into the car with the white boys; a heated, but brief, fight broke out between the two groups. The blacks quickly prevailed in the fight and proceeded to force the whites from the train, which was moving fairly slowly. They were about to throw the last white boy, Orville Gilley, off the train when it sped up, so they pulled him back in, fearing he would be seriously injured.

Clarence, Haywood, and most of the other black boys settled down in a gondola car, hopeful that their trouble with the white boys was over, so they could continue to Memphis with no more incidents. However, this was the South in the 1930s, and the white boys were not going to sit idly around and let themselves be bested by a group of blacks. The white boys walked along the railroad track right-of-way back to Stevenson, found the local deputy sheriff, and complained they had been assaulted by a group of black boys and forcibly thrown from the train. The local deputy sheriff immediately called the Jackson County Sheriff in Scottsboro, Alabama, and told him of the charges and the situation. The sheriff called a posse together and told the men to meet in Paint Rock, Alabama, a small water stop about twenty miles west of Scottsboro.

The posse gathered in Paint Rock and, at about one thirty in the afternoon on March 25, ordered the train to stop. The posse immediately searched the train and found the nine black boys, who were immediately charged with assault and attempt to murder. They also found Orville Gilley and, much to their surprise, two young white girls dressed in overalls.

Clarence, Haywood, and the other boys were stunned and confused, not knowing what the turmoil was about, yet they were not truly surprised, as they had experienced run-ins of one sort or another with white Southern police. While all of this occurred, Victoria Price and Ruby Bates had quietly moved off to the side, almost as if they hoped to go unnoticed, for indeed they knew they could be arrested for having illegally boarded the train.

The absolute sequence of events at Paint Rock is not clear, but after the posse spent a short period of time interrogating the nine boys and the two girls separately, one of the girls told the posse they had been gang raped by the group of black boys. Knowing the personalities of the two girls, it most likely was Victoria Price, the more outspoken and indignant of the two. Victoria may well have said something like, "Those boys had their way with us, all of 'em."

The Four Scottsboro Trials

PRICE'S ACCUSATION propelled a sequence of events over the next sixteen days, and then for forty-five more years, that was almost unparalleled in U.S. legal history and difficult to comprehend even today. The sixteen days in Scottsboro were Kafkaesque in nature and must be considered as they must have seemed to the nine boys—a blur because of the speed with which things were about to occur, and a haze because of the boys' confusion and lack of knowledge of the legal process and of their rights.

Day 1—Wednesday, March 25, 1931

After Victoria's accusation, the mood of the posse turned particularly ugly, and, if not for the deputy sheriff's pleas to the group to let law and order take its course, the boys might well have been lynched on the spot in Paint Rock. At about 4:00 p.m., the posse arrived in Scottsboro with the nine black boys, the two white girls, and Orville Gilley. The nine boys were taken to the two-story Scottsboro jailhouse, the girls were taken for medical examinations by two of the town's doctors, R. R. Bridges and Marvin Lynch, and Gilley was left to his own devices in Scottsboro. Gilley and the girls would normally have been subject to arrest for being on the train illegally, but, of course, the rape accusation now overshadowed any interest in those technicalities.

The boys still did not know how serious their situation was until, late in the afternoon, Victoria and Ruby came into the jail with the sheriff to identify their assailants. The boys were lined up, and the girls were asked to positively identify the boys who had raped them. Only then did the boys come to understand the gravity of the charges, for they knew well a black man accused of raping a white woman in the South was tantamount to getting a one-way ticket to a lynch mob or the electric chair. Victoria did not hesitate as she pointed to six of the boys. When Ruby remained silent, the guards assumed the six must have also raped her. The boys protested, saying not only had they not touched the women, they hadn't even seen them until they got off the train in Paint Rock. Clarence said the women were lying, and as one of the guards lifted his bayonet to strike him, Clarence used his hand to shield his face, receiving a cut to the bone on his hand. The guard yelled at him, "N-----, you know damn well how to talk about white women."

By dusk, a crowd of several hundred people had gathered in front of the jailhouse, as the story of the assault and rape spread like wildfire through the community, becoming more grotesque with each telling. Sheriff Wann pleaded with the crowd for calm, but the situation worsened with time. The crowd, taking on a mob-like lynch mentality, yelled, "Let those n------ out. If you don't, we're coming in after them. Give 'em to us." Around 8:30 p.m., Sheriff Wann had become so concerned he called the governor of Alabama, Benjamin Meek Miller, explained the worsening situation, and asked for state assistance.

Miller, who was adamantly opposed to lynching and the Ku Klux Klan, immediately instructed the state's adjutant general to call Major Joseph Starnes, head of the National Guard Armory in Guntersville, Alabama, twenty-five miles from Scottsboro and the nearest guard unit. Starnes was ordered to mobilize his men and to get to Scottsboro as soon as possible to protect the boys and prevent any lynch mob activity. Major Starnes and twenty-five or thirty of his men arrived in Scottsboro at midnight to find the situation significantly diffused. Only a handful of men remained near the jail, sitting in their cars, quietly waiting to see what would transpire. Starnes encouraged them to go home, and there were no further incidents that night.

While all this turmoil took place around the county jail, the nine boys could see the mob from their cell window and, in fear and horror, only wonder how long they had left to live. Finally, late in the night after the mob had left, the boys drifted off to sleep.

Day 2—Thursday, March 26, 1931

The boys awoke from their restless sleep the next morning to find themselves still alive but probably wondering if they would survive many more nights.

Late that afternoon, the Jackson County Solicitor, H. G. Bailey, met with Judge Alfred E. Hawkins, a judge in the Jackson County Court who would hear the case, to discuss the charges against the boys and the most expedient course of action for the prosecution of the case. The Jackson County Grand Jury had completed its regularly scheduled deliberations only a week earlier, but Judge Hawkins agreed to reconvene the group on Monday, March 30, to consider the charges against the boys. Bailey made it clear to the judge and the press that he planned to seek the death penalty for all nine boys.

The press was allowed to interview Victoria and Ruby, and the nine boys. Victoria told a horrifying story to the press, which was, of course, printed in newspapers everywhere. It was reported that Victoria said, "A whole bunch of Negroes suddenly jumped into the gondola, two of them shooting pistols and the others showing knives. I started to jump, but a negro grabbed my leg and threw me down into the car...I guess you heard the rest. Mister, I never had a 'break' in my life...The only thing I ask is that they give them all the law allows." Ruby, the quieter of the two, would not talk to the press, but she didn't contradict Victoria's story, as she often nodded in agreement. Roy Wright, the twelve-year-old, overheard Orville Gilley telling the press that Roy and the others had raped the girls. Roy denied he had raped anyone, and he told the press he and his three Chattanooga friends were innocent, but he went on to say the other five boys had assaulted the girls. None of the other boys talked with the press except to deny any involvement in the alleged rapes. The press, however, reported that several of the boys had admitted attacking the girls.

The mood in Scottsboro was for quick justice, and there was no doubt in the minds of locals what justice would entail. A Scottsboro newspaper, the *Jackson County Sentinel*, tried to be circumspect when it wrote "that the ends of justice could best be served by a legal process," but the paper more accurately reflected and enflamed local sentiment by adding, "the evidence against the negroes was so conclusive as to be almost perfect."

Judge Hawkins knew he was required by law to find legal counsel for the nine boys, as this was surely to be a capital punishment case. He instructed the seven lawyers in Scottsboro to take the case and represent the nine defendants. However, over the next few days, three of the lawyers were retained by local white residents of Scottsboro to assist Solicitor Bailey, and three others were excused for various reasons, leaving only Milo G. Moody with any interest in the case. Moody was nearly seventy years old, and it was said he was getting a bit forgetful. One associate of his said he was a "doddering, extremely unreliable, senile individual who is losing whatever ability he once had." Moody's interest in the case was the small retainer fee he would receive, as he had few calls for his services these days.

At the same time, one of Chattanooga's leading black citizens and its outstanding black physician, Dr. P. A. Stephens, became aware of the seriousness of the charges against the boys. Knowing four of them were from Chattanooga, he convened a meeting of other prominent blacks in Chattanooga who were associated with a church conference of which he was president. When the meeting participants realized Mrs. Ada Wright, the mother of Andy and Roy Wright, was a member of one of their churches, they proceeded to raise $50 and started to seek a lawyer to assist in the defense of the boys.

Dr. Stephens knew of one white lawyer, Stephen P. Roddy, who might take the case in spite of the small retainer. Roddy dealt mostly in real estate title and police court work. He also dealt in drinking and was frequently observed drunk in public. The police usually ignored his drinking, possibly because of his work in the police court; however, he was arrested and jailed for public drunkenness on at least one occasion. Roddy agreed to take the case for a fee of $120.

Although tensions in Scottsboro had somewhat subsided, late in the day the National Guard transferred the nine boys to a jail in Gadsden, a town about sixty miles south of Scottsboro, where passions about the pending case weren't as extreme.

Days 3, 4, and 5—Friday, Saturday, Sunday, March 27–29, 1931

The boys spent the long weekend in the Gadsden jail, probably not aware a grand jury would hear the charges against them on Monday. Although the published accounts of the Scottsboro trials do not discuss these three days except to recognize where the boys were jailed, it is likely the boys experienced a mix of feelings during these days—periods of boredom at being locked up with little else to do except talk to one another; constant anxiety at wondering what would happen next; moments of terror as they were likely taunted and threatened by their jailers; and fear of the appearance of a lynch mob. A Southern jail was the last place on earth a black person would elect to be in the South.

Day 6—Monday, March 30, 1931

On Monday morning, Stephen Roddy drove from Chattanooga to Scottsboro to attend the Grand Jury hearing. He had told the Chattanooga blacks who hired him, "It is my intention to see that the Negroes get a fair trial." He arrived at the courthouse shortly after nine to find a packed courtroom guarded by Major Starnes and his men.

The Grand Jury had convened at 9:00 a.m., and within a few hours, heard the nine boys plead not guilty, went into a closed session where they heard testimony from Victoria Price and Orville Gilley, and returned to the courtroom prepared to render a decision. However, the Grand Jury was not allowed to announce its decision for twenty-four hours because of confusion over a legal technicality.

Roddy did not identify himself in the courtroom, took no part in the Grand Jury proceedings, did not attempt to see any of the boys, and returned to Chattanooga at the end of the day.

Day 7—Tuesday, March 31, 1931

The Grand Jury returned to the courtroom on Tuesday morning and issued formal indictments against all nine boys. Judge Hawkins immediately announced the trial would start the following Monday, April 6.

The boys were returned to the jail in Gadsden.

Days 8 through 12—Wednesday through Sunday, April 1–5, 1931

Now the boys would have to endure an additional six nights and five days in the Gadsden jail before their trial would begin, subjecting them to a longer period of boredom, anxiety, terror, and fear.

Scottsboro city leaders used this time to prepare for the trial, realizing a large crowd was likely as the interest in the case was widespread. Scottsboro was the marketing center of Jackson County, supporting what was principally an agriculture-based economy. A visitor under normal circumstances would have found a small, attractive town with a population of about four thousand serving a county population of thirty-seven thousand. The county courthouse and its square, a ubiquitous feature in most rural Alabama county seats, was the hub of the business and social activities in the county. Over 90 percent of the county residents were white, a sharp contrast to Alabama counties in the Black Belt region where African Americans comprised 70 to 80 percent of the residents.

The farmers in the area used Scottsboro for all their shopping, trading, legal, and medical needs. In addition, the first day of the trial would fall on the first Monday of the month, the traditional gathering day of local Jackson County farmers and their families in Scottsboro to buy and trade goods and to socialize. The day was called "First Monday," or "Fair Day," or just plain "horse-swapping day."

Day 13—"First Monday," April 6, 1931

Early Monday morning, the boys were sleeping quietly when the guards woke them, took them from the cell, and bound them together in chains and ropes. They knew, from what they had heard at their Grand Jury hearing and from the constant banter and insults from the guards, that their trial would start this day. They were loaded into the back of a truck and transported the sixty miles to Scottsboro like animals bound for the slaughterhouse.

When they arrived in Scottsboro and approached the courthouse, the boys could not believe what they saw. They were terrified to see thousands of white people surrounding the building, rekindling their fears of lynch mobs. "First Monday" and the lure of the start of the trial had indeed attracted a huge crowd. They came by automobile, wagon, horse, and on foot. Estimates of the crowd size varied from five to ten thousand people, some coming from Tennessee and many from distant locations in Alabama. They saw machine guns on the courthouse lawn and probably wondered if they would be executed on the spot. The National Guard had placed two guns at each of the four entrances to the courthouse to maintain crowd control if things got out of hand. It appeared the building was under siege as the crowd was kept fifty yards from the building, and only those associated with the trial were allowed into the building. Later, a limited number of spectators were allowed in to fill the remaining seats in the courtroom. Attendance was restricted to white males twenty-one years of age or older— no women were allowed into the courtroom.

The boys were rushed into the courtroom, only to encounter another sea of white faces awaiting their arrival; not a black person was to be seen, other than the nine defendants. They sat down at the defense table in a state of utter confusion, fright, and loneliness. Since being taken into custody twelve days ago, they had not yet been assigned legal counsel, had not talked to a single lawyer, and had not talked to any of their family members.

When Stephen Roddy arrived in Scottsboro that morning, he felt a different kind of hostility. As he entered the courthouse, he was openly cursed by a number of angry, jeering whites gathered near the entrance. He began to wonder if he should have accepted this case. Roddy initially sat behind the defendants, not with them at the defense table. Several of the prosecution lawyers in the courtroom later said Roddy had clearly been drinking, even calling him "stewed."

Judge Hawkins called the court to order shortly before nine, and immediately asked the counsel for the defendants to come forth. At first, not one lawyer acknowledged the judge's request until Roddy tentatively came just inside the railing separating the spectator seats from the main courtroom area. When the judge asked if he represented the boys, Roddy replied he wasn't their chief counsel but had been asked to assist the boys where possible by persons interested in their well being. Judge Hawkins said, "If you appear for these defendants, then I will not appoint counsel." After a few more exchanges with the judge, Roddy said, "I think the boys would be better off if I step entirely out of the case according to my way of looking at it and according to my lack of preparation of it and not being familiar with the procedure in Alabama. " Judge Hawkins became increasingly annoyed and concerned he would have to postpone the trial, when Milo Moody stood and said, "I am willing to go ahead and help Mr. Roddy in anything I can do about it, under the circumstances." This satisfied Judge Hawkins, who simply said, "All right." He gave the two lawyers thirty minutes with their clients before ordering the trial to proceed. So the trial of nine young men charged with a capital offense carrying a death penalty began with two defense lawyers who were unprepared for the case, one who was described as showing signs of senility, and the other with a history of public drunkenness.

Roddy opened for the defense with a motion to change the venue for the trial based on the inflammatory articles in local newspapers and the need to call out the National Guard to protect the boys. The prosecution quickly disposed of the first item by arguing Roddy presented no witnesses or other substantiating evidence to support his claim. Sheriff Wann and Major Starnes handled the second point, when both testified there had been no credible threats against the boys and they felt the situation was well under control despite their earlier concerns. Judge Hawkins ruled against Roddy's motion and ordered the trial to proceed in the Scottsboro courtroom.

Roddy then told the court he had no objection to having all nine boys tried at the same time. However, Bailey said he wanted to try the boys in separate trials and moved to try Clarence Norris, Charlie Weems, and Andy Wright in this, the first trial. Roddy objected to Andy Wright being in this group based on his age and juvenile status. Bailey chose not to fight Roddy's objection and agreed to try only Norris and Weems as he thought he had the strongest case against these two. At this point, as it was noon, Judge Hawkins called for the lunch recess.

After lunch, an all-white male jury was quickly selected consisting of eight farmers, three merchants, and one mechanic. Solicitor Bailey then called his first witness to the stand at about 2:30 p.m. When Victoria Price, an attractive woman with a slim figure, stood up and walked to the witness chair, a deadly silence enveloped the courtroom, replacing the steady buzz of quiet chatter present since the trial started. She was well dressed and groomed, a stark contrast from the young woman who came to Scottsboro twelve days before in dirty coveralls and a man's hat.

Victoria would prove to be an effective and compelling, if not truthful, witness in this trial and the trials to follow. While her testimony was at times rambling and inconsistent, she spoke in a clear, strong voice, albeit in a style that would make any young English grammar student grimace, using vigorous gestures to make her points, never wavering or showing modesty even when describing the more lurid details. If Victoria had been raised in more fortunate circumstances with a good education, she could have possibly used the inherent skills she demonstrated on the witness stand to become a famous actress like another Huntsville native, Tallulah Bankhead.

Bailey did not have to lead his prime witness to elicit her testimony. After he asked a few opening questions, Victoria gave her entire testimony with few interruptions. Everyone in the courtroom, Judge Hawkins, the lawyers, the jury, the nine boys, and the spectators, listened intently. She explained that she and Ruby Bates left Huntsville for Chattanooga on March 24 to find work, as the mills in Huntsville offered few opportunities. Early the next morning, the proprietor of the Chattanooga boardinghouse Victoria said they stayed at, Mrs. Callie Brochie, went with them to all the mills in the area looking for jobs with no success. The girls decided to return to Huntsville, and Mrs. Brochie accompanied them to the rail yard to see them off.

Victoria said the first part of the train trip was uneventful. She and Ruby decided to move into a gondola to get out of the cool breezes during the stop at Stevenson. Although seven white boys already occupied the gondola, Victoria made it clear it was just a friendly exchange with no sexual undertones, saying it "wasn't in no loving conversation." It seems she was setting the stage for her testimony to come in hopes of avoiding any suggestions she and Ruby had sex with the white boys. Shortly after they got settled in the car, she said twelve Negroes jumped into the gondola, two with pistols, and all with open knives. She said a terrible fight ensued, and the twelve blacks threw or forced all the whites off the train but Orville Gilley.

Then she said the real trouble started when Clarence said to her, "Are you going to put out?" She replied, "No, sir, I am not." She said six of the blacks then grabbed her, adding, "It took two of them to take my clothes off and took three of them to ravish me." She methodically pointed to the six she said had raped her: Clarence Norris, Charlie Weems, Haywood Patterson, Olen Montgomery, and Roy and Andy Wright. She said she was "beaten up" and "bruised up," as the assaults continued until the train got to Paint Rock. She claimed three of the twelve involved in the assault jumped off the train before it reached Paint Rock, thus accounting for the discrepancy in the number of blacks said to have boarded the train compared to the number arrested at Paint Rock. She put her clothes back on and lost consciousness as she stepped off the train. She said the next thing she remembers is being bound for Scottsboro.

In his brief cross-examination, Roddy tried to show Victoria was of questionable character, but the court quickly prohibited this line of questioning as being irrelevant. When Roddy realized all his questions would be objected to by Bailey and sustained by Judge Hawkins, he said that was all and concluded his cross-examination at shortly after three. Victoria, the state's principal witness, had been on the witness stand for forty-five minutes, yet, in this short period of time, she had succeeded in playing to all the latent fears white Southerners had about black men—their insatiable sexual appetite, their desire to sexually assault and control white women, and their complete lack of understanding or remorse about their perverse nature.

Solicitor Bailey didn't rest his case with Victoria's testimony. He called the two doctors who had examined the girls within an hour and a half of the alleged rapes. He first called Dr. R. R. Bridges, one of Scottsboro's most prominent citizens. Dr. Bridges' family had lived in the area for generations, and he occupied what many considered to be the finest home in the city. Dr. Bridges testified that his examination showed Victoria had sexual intercourse prior to his examination, and Ruby Bates had "a great amount" of semen in her vagina. He did not support Victoria's contention she was "beaten up" or "bruised up." He said she had small bruises on the top of her hips and a few "short scratches," but emphasized they were minor. He found no bruises or tears in or around her genital organs, saying, "She was not lacerated at all. She was not bloody, neither was the other girl." He added the semen he found was "non-motile." He said the girls were quite calm during his examination, showing no signs of hysteria as they chatted nervously. When asked by Bailey if it was possible for the girls to have been continually raped by the six boys without suffering apparent injuries to their genitals, Bridges replied it was "possible."

Dr. Bridges' testimony provided numerous avenues for cross-examination, yet the defense pursued none of these. Roddy again tried to attack the girls' backgrounds by asking Dr. Bridges if the girls had admitted to having frequent indiscriminate intercourse, only to have the question objected to by Bailey and sustained by Judge Hawkins. Roddy asked Dr. Bridges if either of the girls had a venereal disease, and this was also disallowed, ending the cross-examination.

Dr. Marvin Lynch was then called to the witness stand. Dr. Lynch was a young doctor, who had been in practice only three years. His testimony was quite similar to that of Bridges. Concerning the "great amount" of semen found in Ruby Bates's vagina, he said, "there was, I guess, probably two spoonfulls in the vaginal canal." However, he said that with Victoria, "We only got enough semen out of the vagina to make a smear." He agreed neither girl was hysterical and said their conversation was normal and calm. Lynch said he found slight bruises and scratches on the girls' bodies but said the "vagina was in good condition on both of the girls. There was nothing to indicate any violence about the vagina."

After Dr. Lynch concluded his testimony, Judge Hawkins adjourned the court, since it was late in the afternoon. The boys were taken to the Scottsboro jail for the night and were relieved that the crowds they encountered in the morning were largely gone. Most of the crowd, sensing the case would not go to the jury that day, had left several hours earlier.

Later that night, Clarence was sleeping restlessly in his cell with the others when the cell door clanged open, and several deputies ordered Clarence to come with them. They took him to another room in the jailhouse and promptly threatened him if he didn't admit to the rape charges. When Clarence protested, denying he had raped anyone, the deputies severely beat him. As they returned him to the cell, they kept repeating the threats if he didn't confess to the rape charges. Clarence crawled back into his bunk, refusing to talk to his cellmates. He lay there the rest of the night wondering what more could possibly happen and how he would deal with it all at the trial in the morning.

Day 14—Tuesday, April 7, 1931

A smaller crowd, numbering fewer than three thousand, was gathered in the courthouse square the next morning. Apparently, First Tuesday did not attract as many locals into town in spite of the widespread interest in the trial. Judge Hawkins called the court to order at 8:30 a.m., and Solicitor Bailey continued with his case against Clarence and Charlie.

Although Clarence and Charlie were not charged with having raped Ruby Bates, she was called to the witness stand to corroborate Victoria's testimony. Ruby was an attractive young woman, yet very much the opposite in character to Victoria. Ruby was soft spoken and lacked the self-confidence Victoria had displayed on the witness stand. Solicitor Bailey had to ask Ruby direct questions with frequent prompting to elicit her testimony. Ruby's account of the events differed from Victoria's on several points. The fight was more of an argument than a fight, and the white boys immediately jumped off the train after being confronted by the black boys. She did testify that two boys held her at knifepoint and with a gun, while a third boy raped her, although she could not identify any of her alleged assailants.

Roddy did raise an interesting point in his cross-examination of Ruby, but he failed to press the point forward in any useful way in the defense of the boys. He asked Ruby if the reason she initially told the posse only about the fight and not the rapes was because she and Victoria were traveling with some of the boys. Ruby denied his allegation, saying she and Victoria traveled alone to Chattanooga and were alone on the return to Huntsville.

Clarence and Charlie watched in complete confusion as the state paraded five more witnesses to the stand. One witness proved extremely damaging. Luther Morris, a farmer who lived near Stevenson, testified he was in his barn about thirty yards from the tracks when the train passed. He said he saw several of the black boys "put off five white men and take charge of two girls." When Roddy tried to get Morris to admit he might be mistaken, he replied with conviction, "I think I saw a plenty." Three of the witnesses corroborated parts of earlier testimony, and one actually testified about the Paint Rock events in a manner that could be construed in the boys' favor. James Broadway, who happened to be passing through Paint Rock on his way to Huntsville when the train and posse arrived, was asked to join the posse by the deputy sheriff. Broadway testified he never heard Victoria Price make a complaint to either himself or anyone else about any mistreatment by any of the defendants. Broadway was history after his testimony, as the prosecution did not call him to testify in any subsequent trials. Roddy did not use Broadway's testimony to any further advantage in the trial, either in cross-examinations or summations.

Solicitor Bailey rested his case, confident he had presented and developed a compelling case against Clarence and Charlie, hinged primarily on the dynamic and explosive testimony of Victoria Price.

Stephen Roddy was faced with the insurmountable task of presenting a credible defense. He had been given no time to prepare for the case and was left with an option defense attorneys use only as a last resort—put your defendants on the witness stand to plead their own case. Roddy, recognizing the risk involved in his decision, first called Charlie Weems to the stand. Charlie, a lanky six footer, proved to be an effective and consistent witness. He responded to Roddy's questions in a direct manner, never giving the impression he was evading the issue or struggling for time to find an answer. He admitted there had been a brief fight, but added the white boys jumped off the train and were not pushed by the black boys. On cross-examination, Charlie did not yield to the pressure from the prosecution. Bailey was unable to unnerve him or get him to change his testimony. Charlie said there were no girls in the gondola during or after the fight. He did say several black boys also jumped off the train, which would account for the difference between the number of blacks who boarded the train in Chattanooga and the nine boys who were found on the train in Paint Rock. Charlie adamantly denied raping the girls and said, "I never saw these girls at all and never had anything to do with them...There wasn't a soul in that car with me and Patterson except those negroes and one white boy...I had nothing to do with the raping of the girls. I never saw anything done to the girls."

Roddy then called Clarence Norris to the stand, a decision he would come to regret. Clarence said he did not take part in the fight, having observed it from the top of a boxcar next to the gondola, and he described the fight in much the same way Charlie Weems had. Within just a few questions of Bailey's cross-examination, Clarence became completely unnerved and said, "...everyone of them have something to do with those girls after they put the white boys off the train." Clarence said Roy Wright held a knife on one of the girls and the other seven boys took turns raping her. Clarence insisted he did not participate in the rapes.

Roddy sat stunned. What little case he thought he had was now completely demolished by Clarence's testimony. Roddy's objections to Bailey's questions were consistently overruled, and he finally asked for, and got, a brief recess. Roddy tried to get Bailey to agree to a plea bargain —guilty pleas for life imprisonment instead of death sentences for the two boys. Bailey refused, as he sensed a complete victory and saw no need to compromise. After the recess, Roddy tried to rehabilitate Clarence as a defense witness to no avail. Roddy's questions showed Clarence recalled little detail of the rapes. He had told Bailey he saw the girls plainly during the assaults, even though he could not recall if they were naked or what they were wearing. Clarence also said there were eight rapists, while the girls testified twelve boys raped them. Roddy could not get Clarence to recant either of his claims; he said, "I saw that negro just on the stand, Weems, rape one of those girls. I saw that myself," adding the other seven "all raped her, every one of them."

An area newspaper reporting on the trial wrote, "Mr. Roddy then sighed and turned the witness over to the state."

The prosecution then called Arthur Woodall as a rebuttal witness. Woodall testified he found a knife in Clarence's pocket when the boys were searched at Paint Rock. Victoria Price was called to the stand and confirmed the knife was hers. She said Clarence had taken it from her on the train along with $1.50 she had in her pocket. Bailey rested the state's case, confident he had now linked Clarence to the rape.

When Judge Hawkins asked the defense attorneys to make their closing argument, both Roddy and Moody declined. Attorney Snodgrass and Solicitor Bailey presented the state's closing argument, asking for the death penalty for both defendants.

Early in the afternoon, Judge Hawkins gave to the jurors a balanced set of instructions, detailing the law involved in the case and the options the jurors had in reaching a verdict. Hawkins made it clear to the jury that the burden was on the state to prove beyond all reasonable doubt the accused were guilty.

Even as the jury was clearing the room, the jury selection process for the second trial had begun. Within the hour, a jury was impaneled and Haywood Patterson was brought into the courtroom to stand trial alone. Haywood's trial started much as the first trial. Victoria Price was called again as the state's first witness, and she proved equally effective and dramatic in her testimony, even adding details she apparently had forgotten in the first trial. Most damning, she was adamant that Haywood's "private parts penetrated my private parts." Roddy again tried to probe her past and reputation, and, even though the state objected, Victoria insisted on answering some of the questions. When asked if she was a prostitute, Victoria said, "I don't know what you are talking about. I do not know what prostitution means. I have not made it a practice to have intercourse with other men. I have not had intercourse with any white man but my husband; I want you to distinctly understand that."

Solicitor Bailey called Ruby Bates to the stand in hopes of getting her to corroborate the rape charge Victoria had leveled against Haywood. Ruby again was an ineffective witness for the state. She finally conceded she could not positively identify which boys had intercourse with Victoria.

Ruby had just concluded her testimony when the bailiff informed Judge Hawkins that the Norris-Weems jury had reached a verdict. As the Patterson jury was escorted out of the courtroom, they passed the Norris-Weems jury, but no exchanges took place between the two groups. The Norris-Weems jury took their seats as a deadly silence descended over the courtroom. The court clerk read the verdict: "We find the defendants guilty of rape and fix their sentence at death in…" Before the clerk could finish reading the verdict, the courtroom broke into a loud roar of applause and cheering. Some in the courtroom even ran outside to tell the large crowd in front of the courthouse the verdict, and the crowd added to the raucous shouts and cheers. Judge Hawkins tried to restore order in the courtroom the old fashioned way; he banged his gavel and called for order but could not be heard or was ignored by the cheering courtroom crowd. Hawkins finally had to order the National Guard to clear the courtroom of the more boisterous spectators before any semblance of calm could be regained in the courtroom. Norris and Weems looked straight ahead and appeared emotionless during the verdict announcement and demonstrations; their true states of mind probably bordered between fear and resignation.

Roddy realized he finally had an issue favoring the defense, and he called Major Starnes to testify. Starnes had been in the jury room with the Patterson jury during the reading of the verdict and the ensuing outburst by the crowd, and he admitted that the sequestered jury had heard the crowd reaction. Roddy moved that the Patterson trial be declared a mistrial, citing a 1923 U.S. Supreme Court ruling; the high court had overturned the convictions in an Arkansas trial, finding that crowd noise and mob mentality influenced the outcome. Hawkins denied Roddy's motion and ordered Patterson's trial to proceed.

Bailey called Dr. Bridges to the stand, and he testified much the same as he had in the first trial. Dr. Lynch was not called, presumably because his testimony in the first trial was not as favorable as Bridges' for the state's case. The state called a new witness, Ory Dobbins, who was in his barn near the tracks when the train came past. Dobbins was adamant when he said, "I saw two girls and these colored people, and as it got by, one of the colored men grabbed a woman and threw her down." Roddy declined to cross-examine Dobbins.

Again, the only witnesses Roddy had to offer were the defendants. He called Haywood Patterson, a brash, outspoken young man who displayed what Jewish people called *chutzpah*. While he wouldn't have understood the term at the time, he would later have the opportunity to learn the meaning first hand. Unfortunately, all the whites at the trial saw Haywood as an uppity n-----, one of the worst attributes a black person could be labeled in the segregated South. Haywood's testimony proved to be erratic, inconsistent, and generally contradictory. He denied having been involved in the fight in spite of all the previous testimony to the contrary. He first said, "I saw all but three of these negroes ravish that girl [Victoria]. I do not know none of their names that ravished the girl; Weems was one; I saw him ravish her," but later denied he had seen the girls until the train got to Paint Rock. However, he consistently denied that he or his three Chattanooga friends raped the girls.

Even putting aside Haywood's attitude in this all-white southern courtroom, Roddy knew Haywood's testimony was so ambivalent and contradictory the jury could only think he was lying. In hopes of rehabilitating Haywood's inconsistent testimony, Roddy decided to call Haywood's three Chattanooga friends. First up was Roy Wright, the twelve-year-old, who described the fight similarly to the testimony of others, although he added that fourteen black boys were involved in the fight. Roy also said he later saw "nine negroes down there with the girls and all had intercourse with them…I saw that with my own eyes," while denying that he and his three Chattanooga buddies were involved. After Roy concluded his testimony, Judge Hawkins adjourned the court. The boys were escorted back to their cells by the National Guard, as the trial spectators and other onlookers gathered outside the courthouse to listen and cheer to a local Scottsboro band playing military marches and the national anthem.

There is no record of the mood and demeanor of the nine boys that night; however, it is not hard to imagine what might have transpired. Of course, the guards would have continued their taunts and threats against the boys, and the guards likely boasted about the guilty verdicts and death sentences handed down in the first trial. It's also likely the boys argued and made accusatory comments to one another about the proceedings and some of the testimony. Clarence, Haywood, and Roy were probably harshly criticized or threatened by their co-defendants for implicating the others while denying involvement in the alleged rapes.

Day 15—Wednesday, April 8, 1931

On Wednesday morning, the courthouse square was less crowded than the day before, and the National Guard had removed their machine guns from the courthouse entrances, although the crowd still numbered about two thousand. There was no band that morning, but a Scottsboro Ford dealer did parade twenty-eight new Ford trucks around the square blaring music to the crowd.

Haywood's trial resumed Wednesday with brief testimony from Andy Wright, Roy's older brother, and Eugene Williams. They both admitted there was a fight but denied seeing anyone with a gun or seeing any girls being raped. Andy added he didn't see the girls until the train arrived at Paint Rock.

Roddy then called Ozie Powell in hopes that his testimony would help Haywood. Ozie said he did follow some black fellows who planned to throw the white boys off the train, but the fight was over by the time he got to the gondola. He testified he saw no knives or guns, heard no gunshots, and saw no girls on the train.

Olen Montgomery was the last witness called in the Patterson trial. He said he spent his entire time on the train in a rear car, and he was not aware of any fight or the presence of any girls. He said, "I was by my lonesome."

After both the state and defense rested their cases, Roddy and Moody again declined to make a closing statement, and the state made a brief summation. Judge Hawkins then charged the Patterson jury much the same as he had the first one, and the jury started deliberations at 11:00 a.m.

The third trial was called to order at 11:15 a.m., only fifteen minutes after the Patterson jury exited the courtroom. Olen Montgomery, Ozie Powell, Willie Roberson, Eugene Williams, and Andy Wright were to be tried as a group. Solicitor Bailey had purposely held the trials of Norris, Weems, and Patterson first, since Victoria had positively identified them as her assailants. Bailey was concerned he would have to depend on Ruby Bates as his principal witness against these five boys.

Bailey's concern was short-lived. Victoria continued to be a compelling and dramatic witness. This testimony, her third and final performance at Scottsboro, proved to be even more explicit and colorful, providing the details necessary to implicate all the boys. She said, "...the one sitting there with the sleepy eyes, Olen Montgomery; he ravished me; he had intercourse with me." She added that Olen was the first of the boys to rape her, while Eugene Williams held her at knifepoint, Willie Roberson held her legs, and the other boys shouted, "Pour it to her, pour it to her." She said Olen, Eugene, and Andy raped her, and Ozie and Willie raped Ruby. Bailey now had the testimony he was missing—positive identification of these five defendants as participants in the rapes. Roddy made a futile attempt to undermine Victoria's testimony, but she held fast to her story, and she added additional details as she responded to Roddy's cross-examination. Victoria said it took three boys to remove her coveralls, and Weems was the leader. She added there were seven gunshots during the turmoil.

Just before Judge Hawkins was planning to adjourn the court for lunch, the Patterson jury advised him they had reached a verdict, less than twenty-five minutes after starting their deliberations. After Patterson's jury was settled in the jury box and the jury for the third trial was clearly sequestered and out of earshot, Judge Hawkins sternly warned everyone in the courtroom he would tolerate no outbursts when the verdict was announced. He said he would have the twenty-five National Guardsmen he had posted around the courtroom bring anyone who violated his warning to the bench, and he would have them jailed. As the court clerk read the verdict, one could hear a pin drop in the courtroom. Patterson was found guilty and sentenced to death. Quiet reigned supreme in the courtroom, although no one was surprised at the verdict.

The trial resumed after lunch, and Ruby Bates was called to the stand. Bailey's concern about Ruby proved to be correct; she was a weak witness for the state. Although she testified she had been raped six times, and all the boys had raped either her or Victoria, she was unable to positively identify any of the six she claimed raped her.

Dr. Bridges was called and testified again much as he had in the first two trials; however, he did add some new information. Willie Roberson was suffering from serious cases of syphilis and gonorrhea. Bridges said, in his opinion, Willie could have assaulted the girls, even though it would have been extremely painful for him to do so.

Roddy again had no choice but to call the five defendants to testify on their own behalf, as he had no other witnesses or evidence to present. There were no witnesses available to testify on the character or backgrounds of the boys, and of course, not one white person in the Scottsboro area had offered to do so.

Ozie Powell was called to the stand first. Ozie said he and Willie Roberson jumped on the train together in Chattanooga but separated soon after boarding. He said he had nothing to do with the fight and did not see any girls on the train. Ozie held fast to his story through a tough cross-examination by Bailey.

Willie Roberson came next and was a sad sight to see and listen to. Willie had a head of very bushy hair and a difficult time speaking clearly. He was later measured to have an IQ of less than sixty-five. Courtroom observers spoke of him in very derogatory terms, calling him "that ape n-----." Willie had decided to hobo to Memphis in hopes of finding work, so he could afford treatment for his venereal diseases. He corroborated Ozie's testimony, saying they got on the train together but separated soon thereafter. He said he spent most of the time on the train in one car, a boxcar in the rear three cars forward of the caboose, where he tried to lie still because of the pain in his private parts.

Andy Wright followed Willie to the stand. Andy insisted he did not take part in the fight except to help pull Orville Gilley back on the train. He added that several blacks who took part in the fight were not on the train when it got to Paint Rock. Andy withstood a ferocious cross-examination by Bailey and stuck to his story.

Olen Montgomery took the stand next and told a story similar to Willie Roberson's. Olen said he stayed in one car, an oil tanker, near the end of the train for the entire trip to Paint Rock. He said he did not see anything, no fight and no girls. Olen was blind in his left eye, and he had only 10 percent vision in his right eye. He said he was going to Memphis in hopes of finding work to help pay for a pair of glasses. Olen held firm to his story under cross-examination.

Eugene Williams was the last of the five to testify. His testimony was the same as he gave in the Patterson trial, and he continued to insist there were no girls in the gondola when the fight took place. On cross-examination, Bailey showed Eugene the knife Victoria claimed was used to threaten her and hold her down. Eugene said the knife was his and was in his pocket the entire trip until it was removed from his pocket by one of the posse members at Paint Rock.

After the defense rested, Bailey called Victoria back to the stand. She testified she had seen the knife in the hands of Williams and Weems, and they held it to her throat while she was raped. Bailey recalled several witnesses to reinforce their earlier testimony and closed the state's case by calling Orville Gilley for the first time. Gilley testified he saw the five defendants in the gondola along with the two girls. The state rested. As before, the defense made no summation statement, and the jury in the third trial was given the case at 4:20 p.m.

The trials were not over yet. Even though the state was required by Alabama law to try Roy Wright, the last of the nine boys awaiting trial, in a juvenile court because of his age—unless the state obtained a waiver in a separate proceeding—Solicitor Bailey was determined to bring all the boys to trial at this time. Bailey approached Stephen Roddy and offered him a deal: Roy Wright would agree to plead guilty, and the state would agree to a sentence of life imprisonment, not death. Roddy refused, knowing that under Alabama law a defendant's rights to an appeal were forfeited by a guilty plea. Roddy told Bailey he would make the defense brief and proceeded to do so. In Bailey's summation, he did ask the jury to consider life imprisonment for Roy because of his age. Within an hour, Roy Wright's trial was over and went to the fourth jury to start deliberations in two days in trials seeking the death penalty for eight boys.

Neither of the two juries now out for deliberation reached a verdict by late Wednesday night, and Judge Hawkins dismissed the court and the juries, sending everyone home for the night. The boys were returned to their cells, six of them still unsure of what their fate was to be; after all that had transpired over the last three days in the courtroom, their hopes cannot have been too high.

Day 16—Thursday, April 9, 1931

The court came to order the next morning with everyone in high anticipation of the two verdicts yet to come. The third jury was ready with a verdict soon after the court was convened and found all five—Ozie Powell, Willie Roberson, Andy Wright, Olen Montgomery, and Eugene Williams— guilty and sentenced them all to death. The fourth jury had still not reached a verdict at noon, and the jury advised Judge Hawkins they were deadlocked. Judge Hawkins called the jury into the open courtroom and had them polled. In spite of Bailey's request for life imprisonment for Roy Wright, seven jurors were insisting on the death penalty. After the jury foreman told Judge Hawkins he saw no opportunity for compromise and a verdict, Hawkins reluctantly declared a mistrial.

Late in the afternoon, Judge Hawkins called the eight boys found guilty to the bench and asked if they had any statements. Only Haywood Patterson spoke up, "Yes, I have something to say. I'm not guilty of this charge." They then stood stoically in front of Judge Hawkins as he sentenced each of them to death on July 10, 1931, in the electric chair at Kilby Prison, an Alabama state prison near Montgomery. Although there were tears in his eyes, as this was the first time Hawkins had been called on to issue a death sentence in his five years on the bench, the tears did not reflect any consideration of leniency on his part.

The nine boys were taken back to the jail in Gadsden, never to return to Scottsboro, yet they would forever be known as the Scottsboro Boys.

Sixteen Days in Scottsboro

VIEWED FROM AFAR, with little knowledge of the racial situation in the South, the prosecution's case appears overwhelming. The testimony of Victoria Price was compelling and devastating for the boys, and the preponderance of the testimony of other witnesses seems to corroborate the charges. Possibly most damaging, the testimony of three of the boys —Clarence Norris, Haywood Patterson, and Roy Wright—was incriminating, as all three said they saw the others boys have intercourse with the girls.

However, come nearer to the courtroom, slowly circle and enter, and an entirely different picture emerges. Today, individual capital punishment cases can take years to get to a courtroom. Yet in the short span of sixteen days, nine young black boys were arrested for raping two young white girls, indicted by a grand jury, tried in four separate trials, found guilty, and were all, except one, sentenced to death.

A first-year law student, or even a law layman, can identify the many legal mistakes made in preventing these nine young men from getting a fair trial. First, and foremost, is the speed with which events were allowed to unfold. A period of thoughtful reflection and consideration is required in any complicated legal proceeding, especially one where capital punishment is a possible outcome. The boys were given no chance to secure adequate lawyers; the court did not go out of its way to find and assign defense lawyers; the court gave the defense lawyers finally assigned to the case no time to review and prepare a case; the juries were all white, as blacks were systematically excluded from juries; the crowd's reaction to the first verdict was heard by the second jury; and the four trials were held in a revolving-door fashion with no opportunity for the defendants or their lawyers to regroup and prepare a better defense.

———

THERE WERE, HOWEVER, two spectators in the courtroom, Lowell Wakefield and Douglas McKenzie, who observed all this. Their report on the Scottsboro trials would initiate actions far beyond anything the Alabama legal and political systems could have ever imagined.

9.

DIFFERING STRUGGLES
THE REMAINDER OF 1931

The Scottsboro Boys

AFTER THE SENTENCING on April 9, the boys were returned to the Gadsden jail and placed in one large cell already occupied by about ten other black men. That night, the pressure of the past sixteen days and the death sentences finally came to a head for the boys. They decided to attempt a breakout instead of waiting for the executioner: the boys started cursing the guards, banging on the cell bars, and demanding food; a guard brought them cold biscuits; the boys threw the biscuits down and cursed the guard; the guard walked over to the cell to curse the boys; he was grabbed by Clarence and Haywood, and they tried to get his gun and keys; the guard screamed for help, and in short order the cell area was full of guards; the guards entered the cell with their guns drawn and told the blacks not involved in the rape case to get out; the guards beat the boys until they were a bloody mess; and, the guards handcuffed the boys together and left them in the cell in their bloody condition. The next day, they were chained together and moved to the Jefferson County Jail in Birmingham. This was a more secure location with larger facilities. They were still subjected to daily verbal, and sometimes physical, abuse at the hands of their jailers, which would continue throughout their imprisonment. They all sat in the Birmingham jail not sure or aware of what was to happen next, except that, all but one, had a date with the electric chair on July 10. The boys were about to become embroiled in another struggle, as a tug of war was about to ensue over who should represent them in any appeals or subsequent trials.

The two courtroom observers in Scottsboro were Lowell Wakefield, a member of the Communist Party of the United States of America (CPUSA) and the International Labor Defense (ILD) who lived in Birmingham, and Douglas McKenzie, an organizer for the League of Struggle for Negro Rights. Charles Dirba, a member of the CPUSA's Central Committee and the assistant secretary of the ILD in New York City, read about the case in *The New York Times*. He immediately called Wakefield and asked him and McKenzie to attend the trial and report their observations back to him. After the first day of court proceedings in Scottsboro on April 6, 1931, Wakefield informed Dirba they had another Sacco-Vanzetti case on their hands, and it looked like the trial would lead to a legal lynching.

The CPUSA would reach its zenith in the United States in the late 1930s through a combination of events: the Great Depression, the attraction of American socialists to communism following the Russian Revolution, and the issues of racial and social oppression in the United States. The ILD was the legal defense arm of the CPUSA. The alarm Wakefield sent to Dirba, and the actions to follow, would lead to an explosion of protest from people all over the world to the events at Scottsboro. The ILD formally decided to defend the boys on April 10, 1931, the day after the death sentences were pronounced, starting a struggle for the hearts, minds, and defense of the Scottsboro Boys. Besides being interested in the boys' defense, the CPUSA and ILD saw this case as a major opportunity to push their agenda and expand their membership, especially among African Americans, a group that had largely ignored the Communists.

The ILD wasted no time in securing its beachhead in the case. Formal protests were sent to court officials and the Governor of Alabama during and after the Scottsboro trials. Immediately after voting on April 10 to defend the boys, ILD headquarters in New York City sent Allan Taub, a top ILD lawyer, to Chattanooga to work with Lowell Wakefield in seeking complete control of the case. The two initially worked through Stephen Roddy, but to no avail. Undaunted, they approached Dr. P. A. Stephens, the Chattanooga minister, and asked to meet with the Chattanooga Negro Ministers' Alliance on April 18. Joseph Brodsky, the ILD chief legal counsel, joined Taub and Wakefield for the meeting, and it went well. They told the Alliance the ILD would accept full responsibility for all costs associated with the case. While no formal agreement was reached with the Alliance, Taub informed the ILD in New York City that the situation was approaching a satisfactory conclusion. At the same time, the ILD knew a good southern lawyer was needed to work with their defense team, so Taub and Wakefield secured the services of George W. Chamlee Sr., a Chattanooga lawyer. Chamlee, who once served as the attorney general of Chattanooga's county, came from a prominent Tennessee family, and his grandfather was a decorated Confederate veteran. Although Chamlee had once written a magazine article defending lynching in certain circumstances, he was one of the few lawyers in Chattanooga willing to work with the ILD, as he had defended Communists and other left-leaning activists.

Meanwhile, the NAACP was considering whether to involve itself in the case. The NAACP, initially called the National Negro Committee, was founded in 1909 on Abraham Lincoln's birthday, February 12, in New York City by a multiracial group of individuals interested in the struggle for civil and political rights and justice for all people. In its early years, the NAACP led legal and public protests against a number of racial injustices: protested Woodrow Wilson's introduction of segregation into the Federal Government; succeeded in having African Americans commissioned as officers in World War I; decried D. W. Griffith's racially charged film, *Birth of a Nation*; and constantly protested and publicized lynching. At this time in its development, the NAACP was a more conservative organization than it would become in later years. The organization's primary focus was on legal and political issues, and they were generally content to work with the white power base and courts to effect change, even if it came slowly and incrementally.

Walter White, born in Atlanta, Georgia, in 1893, was the NAACP Executive Secretary when the Scottsboro events unfolded. He moved forward in a much more tentative fashion than the ILD. He sent no observers to the trials, depending instead on gleaning his information on the proceedings from newspapers, many of which were biased Southern papers. As he read about the trials, he seemed satisfied that the boys were receiving adequate defense counsel. White, not wanting to alienate his supporters and the organization's reputation, did not want the NAACP involved in a rape case concerning nine young blacks unless it was clear they were innocent or were denied their rights to a fair trial. Mr. White's hesitancy on the matter would prove fatal on this occasion and several to follow in securing a meaningful position for the NAACP in the case.

On April 10, White received a phone call from the ILD asking him to meet with ILD representatives and Clarence Darrow the next day to discuss the case. Darrow, the famous lawyer and civil libertarian, was a member of the NAACP's Board of Directors and had been asked by the ILD's Joseph Brodsky to serve as chief counsel in any appeal to the Supreme Court. White immediately sent a special delivery letter to Darrow's hotel in New York City saying, "I have no objection to the I.L.D. because it is a Communist organization. On the other hand, it has been our experience that it is impossible to cooperate with them in any legal case. In all instances they have been more interested in making Communist propaganda than they have in any immediate results." The meeting did not take place, as White assured Darrow the NAACP was in control, and White was confident the NAACP's Legal Committee would approve taking the appeal forward once the court transcripts were available for review. White then contacted Dr. Stephens, the black minister in Chattanooga who had recommended Stephen Roddy, and asked him to get a copy of the Scottsboro court transcripts. After a series of delays, White had to send Stephens a check on April 24 for twenty-four dollars to pay for the transcript, and the copies did not arrive until sometime later, another miscalculation and delay.

Meanwhile, the ILD's Taub and Wakefield remained in Chattanooga to meet with other black churches to elicit their support for the ILD position. Brodsky traveled to Birmingham on April 20 to have what would prove to be the first of many meetings with the boys. Brodsky explained to the boys that the ILD would pursue their defense with a strong team of lawyers that had the broad support of thousands of black and white workers across the country and the world. Clarence Norris said of Brodsky that he was "over six feet tall and weighed two hundred pounds. He spoke with the roar of a lion." The boys, struggling to understand this white man with a northern accent, nonetheless liked what they heard and agreed to sign or mark an affidavit assigning responsibility for their defense to the ILD.

Walter White continued trying to sort out the NAACP's position on the Scottsboro case. However, on April 20, White finally realized the NAACP was being outflanked by the ILD, when he read in an article in *The New York Times* that Taub and Wakefield were in Chattanooga making speeches and gaining support for the ILD position. He immediately contacted Dr. Stephens in Chattanooga, told him of the ILD's Communist connections, and advised him to have someone tell the boys not to sign any agreement until the NAACP had reviewed the trial transcripts, decided on its course of action, and met with the boys. Stephens asked Roddy to drive to Birmingham.

On April 23, Roddy met with nine very confused boys. He told them the ILD was a radical group; he emphasized that the group was interested only in furthering its communistic agenda; and he urged them to sign a statement he had prepared asking the ILD to cease its defense of the boys. The boys signed and marked the statement. After the statement was released to the press, Walter White relaxed and reassured his constituency that everything was under control.

White had again underestimated the ILD. The ILD pressed forward on two fronts. First, the ILD, realizing all the boys were minors and legally required their parents' approval of any legal representation, sought out and contacted all the boys' parents they could find. It was a masterstroke and invites one to wonder why the NAACP never contemplated or did the same. Although it's an unattractive answer, it may be that the NAACP suffered from class consciousness as all racial and social groups do; the NAACP was run by upper middle class, well-educated blacks and whites, and they may have been unwilling to deal with blacks at the lower end of the socioeconomic structure, even if they were not consciously aware of it. Whatever the reason, the result of the NAACP's inaction with the parents would prove fatal in the organization's attempts to represent the boys.

The ILD's Brodsky and Taub located several of the boys' parents in Chattanooga: Ada Wright, Andy and Roy Wright's mother; Claude and Janie Patterson, Haywood Patterson's parents; and Mamie Williams, Eugene Williams's mother. It was the first time anyone had bothered to talk to the parents about the case, and the parents were surprised and delighted with the experience; unlike the usual white-black conversation in the South, Brodsky and Taub did not talk down to the parents or tell them what to do, but rather, they explained the situation and asked for the parents' support. Neither the Chattanooga Negro Ministers' Alliance, Stephen Roddy, nor the NAACP had taken time to talk to the parents about the case; thus, the parents quickly agreed to sign a statement supporting the efforts of the ILD. The parents then wrote their sons and told them to ignore the preachers and Roddy, and to let the ILD coordinate their defense.

To ensure that the boys heeded their parents' advice, Brodsky decided to have a few of the parents taken to Birmingham to meet with their sons. On April 24, Wakefield and Chamlee accompanied Ada Wright, Mamie Williams, and Claude Patterson to the Birmingham Jail, and they saw their sons for the first time since the boys left Chattanooga on March 25. The meeting was quite emotional for both parents and sons, and the parents urged their sons to re-sign with the ILD just twenty-four hours after they had signed Roddy's statement on behalf of the NAACP. The boys agreed, signing an affidavit prepared by Wakefield; the new affidavit said Roddy's document was signed without their parents' advice or consent, and they now understood Roddy and the NAACP did not serve their best interests.

On April 25, all the boys except Roy Wright were taken from their cells in Birmingham and transferred to Kilby Prison near Montgomery. Kilby is the Alabama state death house, and the eight boys were moved in preparation for their executions on July 10.

Walter White, now under pressure from many NAACP chapters and other liberals in the United States to defend the boys, realized he needed a new approach. White's new strategy was to find a prominent white Alabama lawyer to lead the defense, as he felt this strategy had the best chance of gaining not only the support of the boys and their parents, but more importantly, sympathetic white Southerners and the courts. Although White would again prove to be wrong, he moved ahead with this strategy. The NAACP's first choice was George Huddleston, the U.S. Congressman for the Birmingham district. Huddleston was known as a fiery liberal in the state, but the NAACP would find, to their chagrin, that his racial views were certainly not liberal in this case.

The head of Birmingham's NAACP chapter then suggested they approach one of Birmingham's most prominent and successful criminal lawyers, Roderick Beddow. Walter White met with Beddow in Birmingham on May 13. Beddow expressed interest in the case but had some serious concerns about it, especially the testimony of Clarence Norris and Roy Wright, where they said they saw the other boys rape the girls.

Two days later, May 15, White went to Kilby Prison and met with the boys for the first time. He told the boys the only reason the ILD was interested in their defense was to exploit them to further the ILD's agenda. White said the NAACP would get the best attorney in Alabama to represent them and would take the case to the U.S. Supreme Court, if necessary. Willie Roberson, Ozie Powell, Clarence Norris, and Charlie Weems signed the affidavit White had prepared. Andy Wright and Haywood Patterson said they wanted to write their parents before making a decision. Olen Montgomery and Eugene Williams decided to stay with the ILD.

On May 16, White issued a statement to the press saying the NAACP had retained a prominent Alabama attorney for the case and had the support of most of the boys. He also made some condescending statements about the boys' parents, saying they were undereducated and didn't understand the forces at play in the continuing struggle for the boys' support. He would come to regret these comments.

The ILD responded immediately, took the parents back to Kilby Prison the next day, May 17, and again got the boys to repudiate the NAACP and support the ILD.

White then sent Williams Pickens, the NAACP's field secretary in Kansas City, to Chattanooga and Birmingham with three objectives: get the parents out of the ILD's control, formalize an arrangement with Roderick Beddow, and gain the support of the boys—a large order when considering all that had transpired.

On May 31, Pickens and Beddow went to Kilby Prison to talk to the boys. They covered much the same ground as previous visits had, and Beddow decided the boys were innocent after he talked to Norris and Wright about his concerns. Beddow told them all he wouldn't have them sign anything, as it would prove futile after the many reversals that had occurred, but he would defend them if they wanted him to.

Judge Hawkins planned to hold the hearing for arguments for a new trial on May 7, but when two court officials had deaths in their families, it was postponed to June 5. So, on June 5, ILD and NAACP lawyers finally met in a courtroom in Ft. Payne, Alabama, thirty miles southeast of Scottsboro. Roddy represented the Chattanooga Negro Ministers' Alliance and the NAACP, and Brodsky and Chamlee represented the ILD. Both groups asked Judge Hawkins to rule on which group should represent the boys. Hawkins said the decision of representation was up to the defendants, as he didn't care how many lawyers the defense had. He let both groups continue in the hearing. Both groups petitioned the court for a new trial, but after presenting their arguments and examining a number of witnesses, Judge Hawkins denied the petition for a new trial, meaning the death sentences were still intact.

Even though the issue of final representation of the boys was still unresolved, on June 22, the ILD was able to get a stay of execution after filing an appeal to the Alabama Supreme Court.

Clarence sat in his bunk in Kilby's death row, staring at the wall. Boredom was his constant companion interrupted by periods of harassment and terror. Twice a week the boys were taken from their cells buck naked and marched to the showers. There they were treated to streams of water, racial epithets, and sexual invectives about their taste for white women coupled with a reminder of the hot seat, the electric chair, awaiting them down the hallway. Clarence shared a cell with Olen Montgomery, which was a godsend since Olen could read and write, and he was happy to share his meager talents with Clarence. Clarence, as all the boys, was thoroughly confused by the constant pressure from the ILD and NAACP concerning representation, although he was favoring the NAACP at this moment. On August 14, 1931, Clarence had Olen write a letter to Walter White expressing this view and his frustrations: "My dear friend Just a few lines to let yo her from me this leaves me well at present and i trully hope when these few lines rech your kine hands they will fine all well and doing fine Mr Walter me and the other boys was talking about yo to day i think all them is made it up in they mine that yo was write...i am to glad for some body to help me out of this truble becase i do not know eny thing about what I am charge with So i am looking for yo to do what yo can for me...i shure would be glad if yo would send me some camel smokes"*

On August 16, Walter White visited the boys again to make his final appeal for their support. He was unable to convince all the boys that they

---

* The letter is shown as it was written to show the struggle blacks had at this time in the South to get even a rudimentary education. Clarence's letter reads, "My dear friend: Just a few lines to let you hear from me. This letter leaves me well at present, and I truly hope when these few lines reach your kind hands, they will find all well and doing fine. Mr. Walter, the other boys and I were talking about you today. I think all of them have made their minds up that you were right...I am too glad for somebody to help me out of this trouble because I do not know anything about what I am charged with. So, I am looking for you to do what you can for me...I sure would be glad if you would send me some Camel smokes."

would be best served by the NAACP, and Andy Wright summarized the feelings and thoughts of most of the boys when he said to White, "Mr. White, if you can't trust you mother, who can you trust?" Roderick Beddow withdrew from the case telling White that he and his firm could not go forward without full support of all the boys. On August 31, White turned in desperation again to Clarence Darrow, now seventy-four years old and in failing health. Darrow said he couldn't prepare an appeal or be lead attorney because of his health, but he agreed to make one of the oral arguments to the Alabama Supreme Court if it was necessary. When Beddow learned that Darrow would be involved, he agreed to stay with the case.

Three boys still remained aligned with the NAACP: Ozie Powell, Clarence Norris, and Charlie Weems. Josephine Powell, Ozie's mother, originally supported the NAACP, but the ILD convinced her to switch alliances, and in September Ozie wrote the NAACP and advised them his mother told him to go with the ILD. Soon after, Ida Norris got Clarence to switch to the ILD, and Charlie Weems, the final holdout, came over to the ILD in early December. It was unanimous; the ILD now had the full support of all the boys and their parents. The NAACP was checkmated.

The ILD used the support of the parents to the fullest advantage of both the boys and the ILD. In the fall and early winter of 1931, the ILD arranged a speaking tour for five of the mothers: Janie Patterson, Viola Montgomery, Ida Norris, Mamie Williams, and Ada Wright. Accompanied by ILD personnel, the mothers split up and visited numerous cities in all areas of the country: the South, the Northeast, the Midwest, the Southwest, and the West Coast. The pace was intensive, but the mothers, reticent and unsure at first, became quite adept at exhorting crowds to the injustices being done to their sons. Each stop included a speech, a plea for contributions to the defense fund, and a request that protests be sent to Alabama officials. The court, the governor's office, and the Alabama Supreme Court received thousands of letters and telegrams from all across the country and the world. Most of the protest came from ordinary U.S. citizens, but a large number of prominent liberal persons, including Theodore Dreiser, Albert Einstein, Langston Hughes, Fiorello La Guardia, Thomas Mann, John Dos Passos, and H. G. Wells also sent letters of protest. Rallies were held and protests were received from England, France, Germany, Poland, Holland, and Russia. Alabama officials reacted quite negatively to this input from outside their state and their country, considering the bulk of it Communist-inspired; and it certainly harmed the boys' position with state officials.

The NAACP tried one more move, not accepting the finality of the situation. Clarence Darrow and Arthur Garfield Hays, another NAACP lawyer, went to Birmingham on December 27 to work on the pending appeal to the Alabama Supreme Court. The ILD obviously knew about Darrow and

Hays's trip to Birmingham; that evening, the ILD had a telegram, signed by the Scottsboro Boys, sent to Darrow and Hays decrying their involvement in the case unless they worked with the ILD. Darrow immediately contacted Lowell Wakefield in the Birmingham ILD office and requested a meeting to discuss the situation. Darrow hoped to arrange a compromise allowing both groups to work together to represent the boys. The next evening, December 28, Darrow, Beddow, and Hays, representing the NAACP, met with Brodsky, Chamlee, and Irving Schwab, representing the ILD. The two groups discussed and argued the situation for hours to no avail. The ILD was insistent that the NAACP lawyers work under the ILD banner, and the NAACP would not agree to work directly with the Communists. Darrow, frustrated with the lack of progress, suggested that all the lawyers agree to work for the boys independent of either the ILD or the NAACP. The ILD representatives said they would have to get the New York office's approval for such an arrangement. The meeting adjourned after midnight, and the next day the ILD New York office replied that they would accept Darrow and Hays as ILD lawyers (ignoring Beddow) only if they repudiated the NAACP before joining the ILD team. Hays advised Walter White he saw no room for compromise, and withdrawal from the case was the only course of action open to the NAACP.

On January 5, 1932, the NAACP formally announced their withdrawal from the case saying, "By formal resolution of the Board of Directors following the Association's Annual Business Meeting yesterday afternoon, the National Association for the Advancement of Colored People has withdrawn from the defense of the 8 boys sentenced to death in Scottsboro, Alabama, placing the entire responsibility for the fate of the boys upon the Communists operating through the International Labor Defense."

In spite of all the actions by the ILD and the NAACP, the more important issue was the state of mind of the nine boys after this struggle for their allegiance. Did they truly believe that they were best served by the ILD? Did they understand the political and social forces at play in trying to win their approval? Probably not; however, they seemed to have had an intuitive understanding of how they might best be served. They were bombarded by philosophical and political ideas and arguments that made little sense to them, yet their internal barometers likely sensed the correct decision based on their life experiences and their parents' guidance in the white-controlled world they lived in.

In Clarence Norris's autobiography, he relates the boys' reaction to some of the NAACP's public statements: "The NAACP put out in the papers that we were too dumb and ignorant to realize we were being used by the Communists. Not too long afterwards we all signed with the ILD and decided to stick with them."

Hollace Ransdell

AFTER THE FOUR TRIALS concluded in Judge Hawkins's courtroom, another individual became involved in the Scottsboro case, and she would provide one of the more accurate and insightful reports on the trials that had just transpired. The American Civil Liberties Union (ACLU) was interested in the case because they saw it as a classic example of poor, illiterate youths being denied their constitutional and civil rights to a fair and proper trial. Although the ACLU never offered counsel to the boys as the ILD and NAACP did, they communicated with both organizations about the situation, and, when the ILD became the sole defense counsel for the appeals to the Supreme Court, the ACLU publicly supported the ILD.

On April 29, 1931, Forrest Bailey, an ACLU director, sent a letter to Hollace Ransdell asking her to travel to Alabama and investigate the recently concluded Scottsboro trials. Ransdell was an activist, journalist, and economist, and had performed other assignments for the ACLU. Ransdell, born in Colorado on March 23, 1894, did her undergraduate work at the University of Chicago, and received a Master's degree in Economics from Columbia University. Ransdell was in Louisville, Kentucky, when she received Bailey's letter, having just concluded a teaching assignment at a school for young women in the textile, garment, and tobacco industries.

The ACLU was founded in 1920 by Roger Baldwin, who also became its executive director for the ACLU's first thirty years. It was founded to combat what was an almost complete disregard for the constitutional and civil rights of many citizens at that time. Ironically, one of the other founders and early board members of the ACLU was Helen Keller, the woman who overcame her deafness and blindness to become one of the most famous and admired women in America at the time. Helen was born in the northern Alabama town of Tuscumbia in 1880. Her father, Arthur Keller, was an officer in the Confederate Army, and her mother, Kate Adams Keller, was a cousin of Robert E. Lee. Tuscumbia is about one hundred miles directly west of Scottsboro. Draw a straight line on a map of Alabama from Scottsboro west to Tuscumbia, and it will also pass near Huntsville and Decatur, cities that had a significant role in the Scottsboro case history.

Of course, the ACLU's activities are well known today, and both the right and the left criticize them, since they defend cases for clients as disparate as the Ku Klux Klan and anti-war groups. In 1920, the ACLU defended immigrants against the right to free speech and deportation in what was called the Palmer Raids. The then Attorney General of the United States, A. Mitchell Palmer, responded to social and political turmoil in the country by rounding up individuals thought to be anarchists, and many, who were immigrants, were deported without due process. In 1925, the ACLU and Clarence Darrow defended John Scopes, a Tennessee high school teacher charged with breaking the state law that prohibited teaching "any theory that denies the story of the Divine Creation of man as taught in the Bible." The trial is best known for the famous exchanges that took place between Clarence Darrow and William Jennings Bryan, the counsel for the prosecution. Darrow was an avowed agnostic, while Bryan believed the Bible was the word of God and the fundamental truths of the history of man and the earth.

Forrest Bailey's April 29 letter to Ransdell said, "There is something you can do. Can you go down to Scottsboro and saturate yourself with the whole situation as regards those eight Negro boys? The Civil Liberties Union is not officially in on the case, but it looks as if we may be in on it before long…It is quite clear that things are in a frightful mess…It is important that you should keep your mind open and not allow yourself to be swayed either way by anything else than an impartial survey of the facts… My blessings and hopeful prayers go with you."

After receipt of the letter, Ransdell immediately left for Birmingham, and, over a ten-day period from May 6 to May 15, visited Birmingham, Tuscaloosa, Montgomery, Huntsville, Scottsboro, and Chattanooga. She interviewed numerous people including Walter White, Judge Hawkins, Jackson County Medical Examiner Dr. Bridges, Scottsboro's Sheriff Wann, the mayor of Scottsboro, black clergymen in Birmingham and Chattanooga, Huntsville's Sheriff Giles, strangers and private citizens in Scottsboro and Huntsville, and, most importantly, Victoria Price and Ruby Bates, and the eight boys in Kilby Prison awaiting their execution. Ransdell's approach was to ask direct and provocative questions about the entire situation: the trials, racial attitudes, social backgrounds, and economic conditions. Having never been to the Deep South, Ransdell was shocked by the racial hatred and fear she heard expressed about African Americans.

After Ransdell arrived in Birmingham on May 6, she met with Walter White that evening, and he explained the situation to her from his and the NAACP's perspectives. The NAACP had decided to approach George Huddleston, the U.S. Congressman from Birmingham and a lawyer, who was known to be "stubbornly independent and often radical," especially because of his support for federal relief in the Great Depression. Forrest Bailey wrote to Huddleston on behalf of the NAACP, saying, "We are venturing to suggest to you that you would be rendering a high public service in behalf of justice and the reputation of your State if you would interest yourself in the eight Negro boys under death sentence as a result of the recent trial at Scottsboro. We have today requested a representative of this organization to call on you in Birmingham to present the facts that she has been able to gather as a result of close study of the case." Ransdell was the representative Bailey referred to, and White asked her to meet with George Huddleston the next day on behalf of the ACLU and the NAACP.

The next morning, May 7, Ransdell met with George Huddleston. That evening she wrote a report to Bailey on the meeting, explaining, "He met me coldly and spoke hostilely of the American Civil Liberties Union. Said he was not interested in the Scottsboro case and regarded the ACLU interest in it as stupid meddling on the part of Northerners who did not understand the 'peculiar problems of the Southerners'...I then asked him if he would be interested if he were convinced beyond the shadow of a doubt that they were innocent. 'No', he roared. 'I don't care whether they are innocent or guilty. They were found riding on the same freight car with two white women, and that's enough for me!...It doesn't matter to me what the women had done previously, I'm in favor of the boys being executed just as quickly as possible! You can't understand how we Southern gentlemen feel about this question of relationship between negro men and white women'...Well, this is enough to let you know how the liberal 'friend of labor' stands on the negro issue."*

Ransdell left her meeting with Huddleston realizing the issue of race was much deeper and more strident than she had ever imagined. Huddleston's point of view would be underscored throughout the remainder of her stay in the Deep South.

In Ransdell's visit to Scottsboro, the officials she interviewed closed their doors and interrogated her instead, convinced she was a Communist spy sent to discredit them. In 1974, when interviewed by Mary Frederickson for the Southern Oral History Program, Ransdell told of her chilling reception by Scottsboro officials. She said, "I interviewed the judge and the sheriff and the mayor of the town. So finally they all got together and in this meeting there was the judge of the trial, the doctor who examined the girl... And they shut the door and two policemen stood on each side of the door and the policemen came and guarded the room all around. I sat in the chair...They said 'We're very surprised. We'd like to know what organization sent you down here. No respectable organization would send a white woman down to ask about a lot of n------'...That was their attitude, you see...I must be straight from Moscow or something like that...Then they

---

* I asked George Huddleston's daughter, Nancy Huddleston Packer, about her father's reported outburst, and she doubted it was true. She said it was completely out of character for the father she knew and loved. She went on to say that, while he may have declined to be involved in the case, his temperament and views were absolutely inconsistent with such a strident outburst. However, Ransdell's meeting with Huddleston illustrates the depth of racial feelings about blacks in the South at the time of the Scottsboro Boys' case. On occasion, people who normally appear liberal or at least tolerant on race relations in the South let their deep-seated fears instilled over generations come to the surface.

said 'Well, you are a very foolish woman. We advise you to get out of town. We won't be responsible for your safety if you're not out of town within the next hour.' They offered to take me down to the train and put me on the train. I said no, I can take care of myself, thank you." Ransdell left Scottsboro later in the day with no further incidents with the town officials or the residents.

Ransdell concluded her trip to Chattanooga on May 15. She left the South that evening and returned to her home in New York City. She surely struggled with how to structure her final report to Forrest Bailey. On the one hand, she had uncovered a number of factual matters about the case and the participants that had never come out in the courtroom, but, more importantly, she now had a much broader sense of the social and economic conditions that spawned the racial divide and hatred in the South. Ransdell resolved the issue by producing a report that was both enlightening and damning concerning the Scottsboro events and the social structure of the South on race relations.

On May 27, 1931, Hollace Ransdell sent her twenty-two-page report on her entire trip to Forrest Bailey. It was titled "Report on the Scottsboro, Ala. Case," and it was complete, explosive, revealing, and provocative. Since it was researched and written shortly after the trials, when memories were still fresh and raw, it is the most complete account of the situation in addition to the trial transcripts. The report tells a chilling tale of the trials and the chief participants. Ransdell uncovered the true story about the lives and backgrounds of Victoria Price and Ruby Bates, which was not brought up in the trials, since, if Stephen Roddy made an attempt to press the girls on their backgrounds, Judge Hawkins would not allow that line of questioning. Ransdell's report was never published, although copies were sent to a number of individuals and news organizations.

The two most important findings in Ransdell's report are the backgrounds of the two girls, Victoria Price and Ruby Bates, and the general attitude of many Alabama whites to the situation. One section of Ransdell's report is subtitled, "Why the Two Girls Made the Charge?" and deals with the first issue. She submits that you can't understand the answer to this question without understanding the conditions these two young women grew up in. Price and Bates worked in the worst mill in Huntsville and lived at the bottom of the white social structure in the South; they were called "the lowest of the low" by respectable whites. One social worker said of them, "These mill workers are as bad as the N------. They haven't any sense of morality at all. Why, just lots of these women are nothing but prostitutes. They just about have to be, I reckon, for nobody could live on the wages they make, and that's the only other way of making any money open to them."

On May 12, Ransdell visited Ruby and her mother, Emma Bates, and her two brothers in their clean, but unpainted, shack in a Negro section of Huntsville. She found Ruby to be "a large, fresh, good-looking girl, shy, but a fluent enough talker when encouraged. She spits snuff juice on the floor continually while talking, holding one finger over half her mouth to keep the stream from missing aim." The family lived among and played with Negroes and had no "intense feelings" about sexual relations between whites and blacks. Ruby Bates was considered by the social workers to be "quiet and well behaved until she got into bad company with Victoria Price." But, faced with the Scottsboro situation, Ruby and Emma now agreed with "respectable" white opinion and wanted to see the eight Negro boys put to death by either legal means or a lynching party.

Ransdell met with Victoria Price and her mother, Ella Price, in their unpainted shack in Huntsville. Ransdell described Victoria as "a lively, talkative young woman, cocky in manner and not bad to look at...Like Ruby, Victoria spits snuff with wonderful aim." Victoria had a reputation as a prostitute in Huntsville, but she told Ransdell "that in spite of her low wages she never made a cent outside the walls of the mill." Walter Sanders, chief deputy sheriff in Huntsville, knew of Victoria's prostitution, but he didn't bother her, saying she was a "quiet prostitute, and didn't go rarin' around cuttin' up in public and walkin' the streets solicitin', but just took men quiet-like."

The second important finding in Ransdell's report is subtitled "Why the Boys Were Hated." In her visit to Scottsboro, she describes the town as "a charming southern village." She says, "The people on the street have easy, kind faces, and greet strangers as well as each other cordially...It came as a shock, therefore, to see these pleasant faces stiffen, these laughing mouths grow narrow and sinister, these soft eyes become cold and hard because the question was mentioned of a fair trial for nine young Negroes terrified and quite alone. Suddenly those kindly-looking mouths were saying the most frightful things." In her meeting with Judge Hawkins, who was sure he had done everything he could to give the boys a fair trial, she came away convinced, "They all wanted the Negroes killed as quickly as possible in a way that would not bring disrepute upon the town." One Scottsboro resident said to Ransdell, "We white people just couldn't afford to let these N------ get off because of the effect it would have on other N------." The strong sentiment in the town was best summed up by "The N----- must be kept in his place."

Ransdell concludes her report writing, "With the contrasting picture in mind can any person not poisoned with race prejudice still maintain that the Scottsboro trial as 'fair and just' and that the eight Negro boys deserve execution?"

Ransdell's qualifier that "any person not poisoned with race prejudice" was well chosen, since most Alabamians who read or heard of the report refuted Ransdell's basic findings and contentions as another example of northern meddling and lack of understanding of southern race relations. Whites and blacks got along fine in the South, so the myth went, assuming, of course, that whites were in complete control over the blacks.

Another agency, working independently of Ransdell, conducted a series of investigations on the Scottsboro case in May and June of 1931. The Commission on Interracial Cooperation (CIC) had its Interstate Secretary for Alabama and Tennessee, James D. Burton, conduct investigations with a particular emphasis on the backgrounds of Victoria Price and Ruby Bates. The CIC was an interracial group of people, founded in Atlanta, Georgia, in 1919, whose objective was to improve southern race relations. The CIC was a conservative organization compared to the ILD, and much like the NAACP, preferred to foster improvements in race relations in the South within the existing framework of the southern political and social situation. The CIC's early years were mostly spent trying to prevent lynching, as it had become a serious problem after World War I. The results of the CIC investigations confirmed much of what Ransdell had reported, and the CIC's findings did get some attention in the South. However, the CIC leadership did not publish any reports, fearing it would cause more harm than good; thus, the net effect of the CIC investigations on the case was minimal.

George Chamlee and the ILD were doing investigations of their own and found much the same information on the backgrounds of Victoria Price and Ruby Bates. In addition, the ILD discovered that the two girls practiced prostitution while in Chattanooga with both white and black men. Chamlee also tried to find the lady and the house where Victoria stated on the witness stand in Scottsboro that she and Ruby had spent the night in Chattanooga. Chamlee could find neither a Mrs. Callie Brochie nor her house, and assumed Brochie must have been a figment of Victoria's vivid imagination.

All these findings, whether by Hollace Ransdell, the CIC, or the ILD, had little impact on court officials, politicians, or public opinion in the South, particularly in Alabama. The prevailing point of view was that the boys deserved to die, and many white people would just as soon see them lynched as die in the electric chair. One "kind-faced, elderly woman" Ransdell interviewed on the streets in Scottsboro summed up local sentiment best. The woman told Ransdell that "if they re-tried the Negroes in Scottsboro, she hoped they would leave the soldiers home next time. When I [Ransdell] asked why, she replied that next time they would finish off those 'black fiends' and save the bother of a second trial." The *Jackson*

County Sentinel, a Scottsboro newspaper, published an editorial on April 23, 1931, stating in part, "...we are told that we must have negro jurors on any jury trying the blacks if they are to get their 'rights.' A negro in Jackson County would be a curiosity—and some curiosities are embalmed, you know."

Rosa McCauley

LEONA MCCAULEY invited Raymond Parks to join her and Rosa on the porch of their home in Pine Level. Raymond sat down, and all three had a pleasant chat, although most of the conversation was between Raymond and Leona, as Rosa was quite shy. In fact, the next time Raymond came to visit, Rosa hid under the blankets in her bed, and no amount of entreaties by her mother could get her to come out and see Raymond. Initially, Rosa was not particularly attracted to Raymond as he was very light skinned, and Rosa had an aversion to white men, even white-looking black men other than her grandfather. Raymond was persistent; he continued to drive to Pine Level in his red Nash Rambler hoping to woo this young lady. Rosa finally relaxed a bit and agreed to go with Raymond on rides in his car. She knew very few black men who owned a car; her experiences had been that a black man with a car was either a driver for a white person or a family. She was about to learn that Parks, as he preferred to be addressed, and as Rosa would address him her entire life, was quite different than the black men she had come to know in her life. He loved to talk, and he would spend hours telling Rosa about his upbringing and his activities. More significantly, Parks was the first black activist Rosa had met. Parks started Rosa in her own personal struggle to overcome her shyness and begin her life's journey toward activism.

On their car rides, Parks told Rosa about his early years and his life before meeting her. He was born on February 12, 1903, in Wedowee, Alabama, about eighty miles northeast of Montgomery near the Georgia border. His father left home soon after Parks was born and died in a fall from a house roof on a construction job. Parks lived with his mother in a house in the middle of an all-white neighborhood, and, when he was school age, he couldn't go to school in Wedowee because there were no schools for blacks in the area. His mother taught him to read and write, and later he attended school in Roanoke, a town near Wedowee, for a short period, but he had little formal education. After his mother died when he was sixteen, he got his first job as a sexton in a white Baptist church in Roanoke. He left Roanoke in his early twenties, moved around a lot working odd jobs, learned how to barber in Tuskegee, and now lived in Montgomery where he worked as a barber.

Parks told Rosa about the problems he had with his light complexion, which may partially explain the attitude he developed to life in the Deep South. Rosa was most impressed by his lack of fear of white people, with whom he displayed no "Uncle Tom" attitudes. Parks told her he tried to get along with everyone, but if pushed or threatened by a white person, he would speak up forcefully, defending himself as necessary. He told Rosa he had been a member of the NAACP for some time, and he told her about the Scottsboro Boys. He explained that he and a few friends were quietly and secretly raising money for their defense in hopes of keeping the boys out of the electric chair. This was the first time Rosa had heard about the case, and she listened in fascination and disgust as he described the trials and verdicts just recently concluded.

As Rosa got to know Parks better throughout 1931, she became much more comfortable with him and admired his courage and activism. However, she had grave concerns for his safety, knowing what a rabid racist would do to a man like Parks if he became aware of his activities on behalf of the Scottsboro Boys. Parks told Rosa that he and his friends were very careful; in fact, he never revealed the names of the others working with him; he called them all Larry.

The Taylor Boys

WAIGHTS COMPLETED his freshman year at the University of Alabama as the intense struggle between the ILD and NAACP was building up. The Taylor family had its own struggle at this time, albeit much less significant than the life-threatening situation faced by the Scottsboro Boys, as Angus Sr.'s booming business of the 1920s was now suffering from the effects of the Great Depression. All the Taylor family members were struggling to live within their reduced means, although the family was absolutely intent on seeing that all the Taylor Boys got a college education.

The Taylor Boys, while all out of the same genetic mold, were, of course, very different in personality and interests. Angus, the oldest, was a natural leader, a trailblazer, an entrepreneur, and an excellent athlete. Bill was the scientist and engineer, a prodigious reader, and, according to Waights, was the best student of the lot. Waights was considered the family intellectual, loved music and theater, and was also an excellent student. Both Bill and Waights earned the highest academic honors available in their chosen majors; Bill earned a Tau Beta Pi key in Engineering, and Waights was awarded a Phi Beta Kappa key in his dual English and Journalism majors. Frank was very laid back, a big kidder who loved to make fun of all around him. He was not the best student, and, yet, he would develop an advertising and public relations business that was the envy of his brothers and all his competitors in Alabama. Macey, the youngest, was shy and retiring in his elementary school years, but he blossomed in high school and college, and was the only Taylor brother to earn dual degrees at the university: a BA as an undergraduate, and a LLB in Law.

Throughout the 1930s, at least one of the Taylor Boys was always attending the University of Alabama: Angus graduated in 1930 with a degree in Business; Bill graduated in 1932 with a degree in Aeronautical Engineering; Waights graduated in 1934 with degrees in Journalism and English Literature, and continued at the university in 1935 to work toward his graduate degree in English Literature, a degree he never completed; Frank graduated in 1936 with a degree in Business; and Macey, the kid of the family, was a freshman in high school in 1931 and started at the university in 1935, graduating with degrees in Business and Law in 1940. All the boys enrolled in Reserve Officer Training Corp (ROTC) classes and graduated as 2nd Lieutenants in the U.S. Army, not likely appreciating how soon they would be called to serve their country.

However, it was not all classes and military training, as Angus, leading the way as usual, joined a fraternity, Delta Kappa Epsilon; the Dekes were the oldest social fraternity at the university, and the fraternity house occupied such a choice spot on the campus that it was known as "The Mansion on the Hill." All the brothers followed in Angus's footsteps and became Dekes, so a Taylor Boy was a member of that house for all fourteen years from 1926 through 1940.

When Waights returned to the campus in September 1931 for the start of his sophomore year, his friend and traveling companion on the trip to Scandinavia in 1928, Andy Allison, enrolled at the university as a freshman and also joined the Dekes. Waights and Andy would continue their friendship throughout their college years. After college and World War II, Waights and Andy would come together again in circumstances that neither would ever have imagined.

As the Taylor Boys looked for ways to either make some additional money or reduce their college expenses, Angus, ever the entrepreneur, made the first move. He and a fellow Deke, Walter Brownell, put together a plan to create a flying enterprise called "Alabama Airway, Inc." Walter had learned to fly while he was in England, and as wild as it sounds, they were successful in selling the idea to a few university students and some Tuscaloosa businessmen. They got together enough money from the stock they sold in the company to buy a WACO 10 biplane with an OX-5 engine.* Bill Taylor, the soon to be Aeronautical Engineer, took all his savings and

---

* A new Waco 10 with an OX-5 engine sold then for $2,450, but a used one could be had for about $500.

bought stock in the company; Walter taught Bill to fly, and Bill soloed after six hours of dual instruction. Walter gave flying lessons to company members as part of their investment and to others who paid for them. On weekends, the fledging operation sold ten-minute flights to the public to raise money. However, the Depression and an ill-conceived business plan soon broke the company, and the airplane was sold.

Even putting Angus's failed flying venture aside, from 1931 on, the Taylor Boys had to really start tightening their budgets and expenditures. As the Depression started taking its toll on their father's business, all the boys sought financial assistance and looked for jobs. Bill and Waights got part-time jobs as teaching assistants in their respective departments and ate their meals in a dormitory, which was cheaper than the dining room in the Deke house.

THE SUPREME COURTS
1932

The Supreme Courts

A S 1931 CAME TO A CLOSE, the Scottsboro Boys waited anxiously for some resolution to their pending appeals. They knew a tug of war was going on for their defense, as the ILD and NAACP vied with them individually, with their parents, and with the public to garner their approval. Clarence Norris sent a letter to Walter White on November 10, 1931, reading, in part, "My delay in writing was due that I cannot write myself and I were waiting on the other boys to answer your letter, but I don't think any of them did. So another disinterested party wrote for me...I don't know where my mother is in favor of your Association or not. I don't think she is. Mr. Beddow were here twice talking to us. but since I've heard that he won't take the case unless the ILD lay off and Mr. Chamlee says he is going through with the case. but at that I believe you know best...Answer soon."

Alabama Supreme Court

After the answer came in the formal withdrawal of the NAACP from the case on January 5, 1932, the ILD rushed to prepare its arguments for the Alabama Supreme Court appeal. In the meantime, the court was inundated with mail and telegrams demanding justice for the Scottsboro Boys, much of it instigated by the ILD, and often in language that was meant to intimidate and even threaten the court.

The Alabama Supreme Court convened the appeal on January 21, 1932. Before the lawyers were allowed to argue the case, Chief Justice John C.

Anderson angrily admonished the lawyers for the threatening mail the court had received. George Chamlee told the court the ILD did not instigate the mail, but it was obvious the justices were not convinced. Joseph Brodsky presented most of the arguments for the defense, focusing on four principal issues: One, the trials were not fair, and Brodsky offered numerous examples supporting that argument. Two, the trials were conducted under a state of siege and mob mentality, and Brodsky cited the presence of the National Guard and the crowd reaction when the first guilty verdict was announced. Three, the boys were not provided adequate defense counsel. Four, the juries were all white, depriving the boys of their rights under the Equal Protection Clause of the Fourteenth Amendment to the Constitution.

The next day, January 22, Alabama Attorney General Thomas G. Knight Jr., the son of court Associate Justice Thomas G. Knight, presented the state's rebuttal to the defense claims, dismissing all the defense arguments as irrelevant or lacking an understanding of southern traditions and the importance placed on protecting southern womanhood.

On March 24, 1932, the Alabama Supreme Court issued its decision. To no one's surprise, by a vote of six to one, the court upheld the guilty verdicts and death sentences of seven of the boys. The eighth, Eugene Williams, was granted a new trial since he was a supposedly a juvenile at the time of the crime and his conviction. The court's decision, written by Justice Knight, the Attorney General's father, held that the trials were fair, that there was no mob mentality in evidence during the trials, that the National Guard was present to ensure the accused a fair and safe trial, and that the State of Alabama had the right to define qualifications for jurors (presumably as the state interpreted the Fourteenth Amendment). Chief Justice Anderson was the dissenting vote, arguing that the state did not convince the court that the defendants got a fair and impartial trial.

It seems inconceivable that Attorney General Knight Jr. presented the state's case to the court while his father, Associate Justice Knight, served on the court, or that Justice Knight would have heard the case, much less write the majority opinion. One or the other of them, and maybe both, should have withdrawn and allowed others to present the case and rule on it.

Most Alabamians and Alabama newspapers heralded the court's majority decision. However, there were a few dissenters, who, while not proclaiming the boys innocent, argued that new trials were certainly appropriate: the Birmingham *Age-Herald*, the Birmingham *Post*, and the Selma *Times-Journal*, along with a few individual Alabama white citizens. Meanwhile, the ILD, under the guise of the Communist *Daily Worker*, attacked the decision in vociferous terms, calling the verdicts a result of class and race prejudice, even attacking Chief Justice Anderson's dissent as meaningless.

U.S. Supreme Court

Despite all the bombastic rhetoric on both sides, the ILD immediately appealed the Alabama court's decision to the U.S. Supreme Court. The Supreme Court held a preliminary hearing on May 27, 1932, and agreed to hear the case. On October 10, 1932, the court heard the arguments in the case. The ILD hired an eminent constitutional lawyer, Walter Pollack, to present the boys' case, and Attorney General Knight represented the State of Alabama. Many of the same arguments were presented as had been used with the Alabama Supreme Court, with the exception that Pollack put more emphasis on the exclusion of Negroes from Jackson County juries.

The U.S. Supreme Court rendered its decision on November 7, 1932, finding by a vote of seven to two that the boys had been denied "The right of the accused, at least in a capital case, to have the aid of counsel for his defense, which includes the right to have sufficient time to advise with counsel and to prepare a defense, is one of the fundamental rights guaranteed by the due process clause of the Fourteenth Amendment...In a capital case, where the defendant is unable to employ counsel and is incapable adequately of making his own defense because of ignorance, feeble-mindedness, illiteracy, or the like, it is the duty of the court, whether requested or not, to assign counsel for him as a necessary requisite of due process of law, and that duty is not discharged by an assignment at such a time or under such circumstances as to preclude the giving of effective aid in the preparation and trial of the case."

Justice George Sutherland, who delivered the court's majority opinion, further stated, "In the light of the facts outlined in the forepart of this opinion—the ignorance and illiteracy of the defendants, their youth, the circumstances of public hostility, the imprisonment and the close surveillance of the defendants by the military forces, the fact that their friends and families were all in other states and communication with them necessarily difficult, and, above all, that they stood in deadly peril of their lives—we think the failure of the trial court to give them reasonable time and opportunity to secure counsel was a clear denial of due process."

The U.S. Supreme Court chose, as the central issue in their finding, the failure of the Scottsboro court to provide the boys adequate legal counsel, ignoring the other issues brought to it by the ILD lawyers, especially the issue of exclusion of blacks from juries in Jackson County. The effect of the ruling meant the case would go back to the Scottsboro court and Judge Hawkins for retrial. The citizens of Scottsboro and Jackson County were in no mood for a new trial, having decided the boys had been fairly treated, were guilty, and deserved to die; they blamed the ILD and their Communist supporters for the trouble and bad name their community was receiving from Northerners and the northern press.

The Communists, mostly through the *Daily Worker* and from radical left-wing writers and authors, were publishing some vitriolic and harsh indictments of the U.S. legal, social, and political systems that went well beyond their stated objective to represent the Scottsboro Boys. Nonetheless, the ILD and their persistence and efforts got the case to the U.S. Supreme Court, resulting in this landmark decision.

Felix Frankfurter, whom Franklin Delano Roosevelt would appoint in 1939 to the U.S. Supreme Court, was then a faculty member at Harvard University's law school. He wrote an article in *The New York Times* on November 13, 1932, titled *A NOTABLE DECISION—The Supreme Court Writes a Chapter on Man's Rights*. Frankfurter explained how the court based its landmark decision on the Fourteenth Amendment, which requires that no State can deprive a U.S. citizen of life, liberty, or property without due process of law. Frankfurter concluded his article by saying, "But the court, though it will continue to act with hesitation, will not suffer, in its own scathing phrase, 'judicial murder.' Here lies perhaps the deepest significance of the case."

The boys were told of the court's decision, but realizing it meant another trial in the state of Alabama, the news did nothing to lift their spirits. The boys knew better than their ILD attorneys the poor chances a black man had in a southern court, especially on the charge of having raped a white woman, and that the death penalty was still a very real threat. During the period of time that at least one Scottsboro Boy remained in an Alabama prison, the state executed 108 men in the electric chair: 16 whites and 92 blacks. Clarence Norris's autobiography best expresses the constant fear the boys felt about execution, as he describes the night five men were executed in Kilby Prison: "There was nothing to do but stare at the walls and think about dying…That was the night they killed Bennie Foster, John Thompson, Harry White, Ernest Waller and Solomon Roper. Mass murder was all it was…They killed them one behind the other. I had nightmares for many nights after they went…I thought I was a goner and it was only a matter of time."

The ILD also came to a realization. In spite of the Communists' continuing rhetoric through the press and leaflets criticizing the U.S. social, economic, political, and legal systems, they now realized, having won the appeal to the U.S. Supreme Court, they had to mount a credible and effective defense or face the mounting criticism that the boys' well-being was not their primary interest. Although Joseph Brodsky and George Chamlee were highly competent lawyers, they recognized the need for a prominent criminal lawyer to lead their defense team. Clarence Darrow and Arthur Garfield Hays were obviously not available. As the ILD considered possibilities, one name kept rising to the top of their list: Samuel S. Leibowitz.

Rosa McCauley Parks

ALTHOUGH PARKS ASKED ROSA to marry him on their second date, the subject remained unresolved throughout 1931 and most of 1932 as they continued their courting relationship. Parks did continue his quiet fund-raising activities on behalf of the Scottsboro Boys.

Rosa learned more about his activities and commitment to the Scottsboro injustice, including that Parks was a founding member of the NAACP chapter in Montgomery. In addition to the NAACP membership, he kept informed on activities in the Negro world by reading respected magazines and newspapers published by blacks: *The Crisis, The Pittsburgh Courier, New York Amsterdam News*, and *The Chicago Defender*. Parks also kept current copies of these magazines and newspapers in his barbershop, so his customers could read them. Parks was also an avid admirer of the poetry of Langston Hughes. In January 1932, Hughes visited the Scottsboro Boys in Kilby Prison and read some of his poetry to them.

When the Scottsboro Boys were arrested and charged with rape, Parks was so enraged by the events that he secretly started a legal defense fund and pursued it with a passion from the case's inception in 1931. He attended bimonthly meetings of the National Committee to Defend the Scottsboro Boys, and he and other black men discussed ways to raise money for the defense fund. Parks wouldn't let Rosa attend any of the meetings with him, telling her she couldn't run fast enough if there was trouble. He was concerned for her safety, as Parks and his committee met quite secretly, recognizing the dangers inherent in their activities.

Parks didn't let Rosa forget about his desire to marry her, and, finally, in August 1932, she agreed. Parks asked Leona McCauley for permission to marry her daughter, and she also agreed. On December 18, 1932, Rosa McCauley and Raymond Parks were married in her mother's home in Pine Level.

Rosa Parks was proud of her husband. Although she struggled with her emotions and concerns about his safety, she knew he was doing the right thing. More importantly, and unknown to Rosa at the time, Parks, with his membership in the NAACP and his work on behalf of the Scottsboro Boys, was like the White Rabbit in *Alice's Adventures in Wonderland*. Parks had led Rosa to a door; once she opened and stepped through the door, she would enter a new world and never look back.

Aldous Huxley and Ariel

IN THE FALL OF 1932, Waights was into his junior year at the University of Alabama. He may have read about the U.S. Supreme Court's decision in the Scottsboro Boys' appeal, but he certainly didn't read or hear about Rosa and

Raymond's marriage. Even with the financial pressures he and his family were experiencing, he continued his pursuit of higher education in a world completely separate and different from Clarence and Rosa's.

Waights's education at the University of Alabama was strongly influenced by two of the most prominent professors in the liberal arts program: Hudson Strode, a Professor of English, and Clarence Cason, the founder and head of the newly created Department of Journalism. Strode fed Waights's passion for Shakespeare, and Cason sculpted his journalism skills for his future professional career.

Hudson Strode was an eminent Shakespeare scholar, and the author of a number of books on Europe, Central and South America, and, most notably, a three-volume biography on Jefferson Davis, the President of the Confederate States of America. Strode also started the second university-level creative writing program in the United States, following the example set by the University of Iowa in 1922.

In 1932, Waights was a student in Strode's Shakespeare class studying *The Tempest*, when he read Aldous Huxley's newly published novel, *Brave New World*. Huxley's book had created quite a stir with its oppressive view of the world as it developed into a highly controlled society. The book opens in London in the year A.F. 632. The calendar in "the brave new world" is set from the date of Henry Ford's death, as he is the utopian society's symbol of capitalism, mass production, and consumer consumption. Huxley's satirical utopia has achieved universal happiness through use of an automated reproductive process replacing the womb. The process produces a broad spectrum of individuals from the highly intelligent to the semi-moronic. The masses are controlled using sleep conditioning and a number of pleasurable activities enhanced with a pleasure drug. Uninhibited sex is allowed, but marriage and parenthood are forbidden. Education, books, and anything else that might broaden knowledge are also forbidden. People who break the rules are sent to uncontrolled savage reservations. John the Savage, the book's protagonist, is the product of an illicit love affair and lives on a savage reservation in New Mexico. John has access to books, including an anthology of Shakespeare's works. John is brought to London as a curiosity, but ultimately commits suicide, as he can't cope with "the brave new world."

Waights noted that on or about page 158 in Huxley's novel, the following exchange takes place between the Station Master and John the Savage concerning the speed of the Bombay Green Rocket, which had flown John back to London.

"Twelve hundred and fifty kilometres an hour," said the Station Master impressively. "What do you think of that, Mr. Savage?"

John thought it very nice. "Still," he said, "Ariel could put a girdle round the earth in forty minutes."

Waights knew immediately that Huxley had, in effect, misquoted Shakespeare. It was not Ariel, Prospero's magical spirit in *The Tempest*, but rather, the impish fairy-clown Puck from *A Midsummer Night's Dream* who, in response to Oberon's entreaty to "Fetch me this herb, and be thou here again, Ere the leviathan can swim a league," responded, "I'll put a girdle round the earth in forty minutes." Perhaps Huxley's pre-publication editors and readers were not well schooled in Shakespeare or had merely forgotten their Shakespeare.

In defense of Huxley, he was born into an intellectual family in England, was educated at Eton and Oxford, and was surely well versed in Shakespeare. In fact, the title of his book was taken from *The Tempest*, when Prospero's daughter Miranda marvels at the beauty of the men shipwrecked on her island.

> O wonder!
> How many goodly creatures are there here!
> How beauteous mankind is! O brave new world
> That has such people in't!

Possibly Huxley had a simple lapse in memory when he wrote the passage attributed to Ariel, or, more likely, his mind was focused on *The Tempest* because of the title of his book. Waights, being a bright and precise young man, took it upon himself to set the record straight. He wrote a polite letter to Huxley, addressed to his publisher in New York City, complimenting him on his new book and explaining the mistake in his attribution to Ariel.

Several weeks passed, and Waights had forgotten about the letter, when a postcard arrived in his mailbox. It was postmarked New York City and was from the Algonquin Hotel, the in spot for the intelligentsia and literati crowd of the day. The card was handwritten and said.

> You are quite right about Ariel.
> One has holes in the memory,
> Patches of blindness,
> Moments of temporary insanity.
>
> Yours,
> Aldous Huxley

At first, Waights was rather taken with himself for having corrected a famous author, especially one supposedly well versed in Shakespeare. However, he soon realized his vain reaction was a shallow response. He later wrote, "What was rather amazing to me, other than the fact that he bothered to answer my letter at all, was the graceful way he went about it. Instead of just saying, 'Yes, I made a mistake,' he strung together three metaphors describing his error, all on a penny postcard! Even in a casual act, the power of his great writing shone through."*

Just as Waights knew little or nothing about Clarence or Rosa at this time, it is almost certain neither of them knew about the literary issue Waights raised with Huxley. Although Rosa loved to read, it is unlikely she read *Brave New World*. If she had, she probably wouldn't have caught Huxley's error. Even if he wanted to read the book, Clarence would have been unable to do so.

---

* Purchase a recently published copy of *Brave New World*, and you will find on page 158, John the Savage even now saying, "Still, Ariel could put a girdle round the earth in forty minutes."

11.

THE PERFECT LAWYER
AND THE PRINCIPLED JUDGE
1933

The Perfect Criminal Lawyer—Samuel S. Leibowitz

O N St. Patrick's Day, March 17, 1897, the same year twenty-five-year-old James Durward Taylor and his brother, twenty-three-year-old Angus Macey Taylor, moved to Birmingham to start a new business, a ship from Europe, the Kensington, docked at a New York City pier. Among those arriving that day were three immigrants from Romania: Isaac Lebeau, his wife Bina, and their four-year-old son, Samuel. They were Jewish and had left Romania because of the anti-Semitic policies and practices of the Romanian government and people. While Jews were allowed and required to pay taxes in Romania, they couldn't vote or own land, and they were denied all other civil rights afforded other Romanian citizens. Although Isaac operated a prosperous dry goods business, he left his homeland with its anti-Semitic policies that preceded Nazi Germany's atrocious efforts by about forty years and took his chances in the New World.

Isaac settled his family in the East Side of Manhattan, and, as James and Angus in Birmingham, in a few short years he had established a prosperous business in Brooklyn. His friends told him he should change his name, saying Lebeau was too foreign and strange to Americans. Isaac resisted at first but finally agreed to Americanize Lebeau (Lee-Beau) to Lee-beau-itz or, more simply, Leibowitz. Young Samuel, never a stellar student in elementary or high school, did excel in elocution, as he enjoyed memorizing famous speeches and speaking, two traits that would serve him well in his future profession. Samuel's other two passions were baseball and the Yiddish theatre. His favorites were the team that would soon become the Brooklyn Dodgers and the Thomashefsky's People's Theatre, a Yiddish theater led by Boris and Bessie Thomashefsky, the grandparents of the current Music Director and Conductor of the San Francisco Symphony, Michael Tilson Thomas.

After high school, Isaac insisted Samuel pursue an education in law. Although Samuel was not excited about the idea, he followed his father's wishes, as most sons of a first-generation immigrant would do. He started at Cornell University in 1911, made the Dramatic Club his freshman year, and developed an interest in law as he pursued his passions for debate, baseball, and track. Upon graduation with BA and LLB degrees, he decided to pursue criminal law, realizing his Jewish and immigrant background, and lack of connections in the legal world would prevent him from finding employment in a major New York law firm.

Over the next fifteen years, Samuel developed into one of the more successful, if not most successful, criminal defense lawyers in New York City. Over that period of time, he established a near-perfect acquittal record; he handled seventy-eight first-degree murder cases and won acquittal for seventy-seven of the individuals, while the other trial ended in a hung jury. Samuel used his early skills of memorization and elocution, coupled with thorough and exhausting preparation, to find the seams and niches in the prosecution's case and the witness's testimony. He became especially adept at unnerving prosecution witnesses, frequently turning their testimony completely around or, at least, bringing it into serious doubt. He was also able to use his acting skills and a good voice to connect with jurors, especially on an issue like police corruption, which many New Yorkers considered widespread among their men in blue. Samuel would play to all the preconceived notions: accusing the police of fabricating or withholding evidence, coercing witnesses, and even torturing suspects.

Samuel was a Democrat with no interest in radical causes, he was not a crusader except for his defendants in the courtroom, he had little interest in social and economic inequities, and he was not opposed to the death penalty—Samuel and the ILD were at opposite ends of the political spectrum.

William Patterson, the new ILD National Secretary, and Joseph Brodsky and other ILD officials were worried about their supporters' reactions to someone with Leibowitz's views. However, Patterson knew it was important for the ILD to show a real commitment to the boys' defense to diffuse on-going criticism that the ILD and the Communists were interested only in fostering their own agenda. In January 1933, Patterson sent

Leibowitz a letter formally asking him to become the lead defense lawyer in the boys' defense. The letter read in part, "We are anxious to engage the most competent and able trial lawyer in this country for the purpose of insuring the best legal defense possible...We have no money to offer you as a fee...We do not ask you as a condition of your acceptance as trial counsel to give up any of your social, economic or political views."

Although Leibowitz was familiar with the ILD, he knew few details of the Scottsboro cases. After Leibowitz read the trial transcripts and realized how poorly the defense was handled, he had no doubt he could get the boys free. The ILD's politics were of no concern to him, but he was most interested in their success in funding and successfully appealing the case to the U.S. Supreme Court. Three days after receiving the ILD letter, he wrote back to Patterson, saying in part, "While, as you are quite aware, your organization and I are not in agreement in our political and economic views, your letter arouses my sympathetic interest...we Americans have a common tradition of justice. And if it is justice that these black men be adjudged innocent—if it is justice, I repeat—I cannot believe that the people of Alabama will be false to their great heritage of honor, and to those brave and chivalrous generations of the past, in whose blood the history of their State is written. If the views I have expressed match yours, then I will accept the task of conducting the defense."

Patterson wrote Leibowitz a week later accepting his conditions: "The views you have expressed do not match ours, and yet despite the wide gulf that lies between us ideologically we stand ready to accept your services as trial attorney in the cases of the nine innocent Negro boys in Scottsboro." Patterson went on in his letter to tell Leibowitz, in a polite but direct fashion, that his views of the South were naïve and grossly misconceived. On these latter points, Patterson could not have been more correct.

Leibowitz had no experience in southern courts, knew little of the South's true racial situation, other than the "brave and chivalrous" views he expressed in his letter, and had never experienced the virulent anti-Semitism he would come to know in the South. His friends and his wife advised him against taking the case, but he was convinced he could handle the court and jury in Alabama as he did in New York.

Leibowitz was to be sorely tested and disappointed.

The Principled Judge—James E. Horton Jr.

ON MARCH 6, 1933, Judge Alfred Hawkins convened a hearing in his Scottsboro courtroom to consider a defense petition for a change of venue for the new trials. Leibowitz was unable to attend because of a prior court commitment in New York, and George Chamlee was the sole representative for the defense. Chamlee argued that the boys could not get a fair trial in Jackson County or any of the nearby counties, much to the chagrin of the court and the residents of Scottsboro. Chamlee pressed the court to assign the case to Birmingham. The next day, March 7, Judge Hawkins announced his decision; he would grant a change of venue, not to Birmingham, but rather to Morgan County's Decatur, Alabama, located on the banks of the Tennessee River about fifty miles west of Scottsboro. Judge Hawkins also declared the new trial would convene in Decatur on March 27 with Judge James Horton Jr. presiding.

Decatur was incorporated in 1821 and was named, at the insistence of President James Monroe, after Stephen Decatur, a naval hero in the War of 1812. The city was initially located on Cherokee Indian lands, but in the 1830s, President Andrew Jackson had the Indians forcibly removed; thus, the boys' ordeal would continue on the "Trail of Tears." In 1864, during the Civil War, the city was burned to the ground, except for three buildings, by northern troops in the Battle of Decatur. The city rebuilt slowly after the war and really prospered starting in the late 1880s when the Louisville & Nashville Railroad opened a huge repair shop in the city, attracting other industries and merchants to support the railroad operation. The Great Depression would prove brutal for Decatur when the railroad closed its shops in 1933, and other businesses and banks were forced into bankruptcy as a result.

More important to the upcoming trial of the Scottsboro Boys, Decatur whites were convinced of the boys' guilt, were no more tolerant or understanding of the poor publicity the state had received over the case, were incensed by the U.S. Supreme Court decision infringing on their state's rights, and unhappy with the northern lawyers who were coming to town to defend the boys. Alabama Attorney General Thomas Knight had not opposed the change of venue because he knew, as the ILD did, that the situation would be no better for the defense and the boys in Decatur than it had been in Scottsboro.

The new judge, James Edwin Horton Jr., was definitely a member of the old southern white gentry. His southern pedigree was impeccable—pioneers, planters, politicians, and Confederates—and would serve him well through his entire life. Horton's grandfather was an early Alabama pioneer from Virginia; he settled in northern Alabama in Madison County near Huntsville in the early part of the nineteenth century, developed a large plantation, and served several terms in the Alabama state legislature. In 1857, Horton's twenty-four-year-old father moved to the adjacent county to the west, Limestone County, developed extensive farming interests, and owned several slaves. When the Civil War started in 1861, Horton's father served as an aide-de-camp to General Daniel Donelson, a nephew of

Andrew Jackson. Horton's father did reap one benefit from the war; he met the general's daughter, Emily, and married her. In 1878, their son, James Edwin Horton Jr. was born. Young Horton attended Vanderbilt University for a year where he studied medicine, but then he transferred to Cumberland University in Lebanon, Tennessee, where he received a BA degree in 1897 and a law degree in 1899. In addition to overseeing his family's farming interest, Horton worked as a clerk in the Probate Court in Athens, the county seat of Limestone County just fifteen miles north of Decatur; opened a private practice in Athens for a few years; served in the Alabama state legislature for five years; and in 1922 was elected as one of two circuit judges in the newly created Eighth Circuit Court in northern Alabama serving Cullman, Lawrence, Limestone, Madison, and Morgan counties. Horton was very popular in his home district, where friends and close acquaintances called him Jim Ed; he was easily reelected in 1928 and was now in the fifth year of his second six-year term.

Horton's background and record gave the prosecution no reasons for concern; he was a solid son of the South, and he would certainly uphold the virtues of southern white women and help find these scurrilous Negroes guilty of a most heinous crime. The defense lawyers had no reason to doubt otherwise, although Leibowitz still held to his convictions that he could show a jury how disreputable these two white girls were and get an acquittal for the boys. Both the prosecution and defense lawyers were in for big surprises.

The boys were moved from Kilby Prison to a jail in Decatur: a decaying, unsanitary, and insecure building. The jail's condition was so bad, the county had not used it for white prisoners for over two years. The Morgan County sheriff told Judge Horton he needed at least thirty National Guardsmen to help his men ensure the prisoners didn't escape, as escape from the facility had become so common that the local newspaper ignored it unless the escapee was a serious felon. Leibowitz was denied access to the boys in Kilby Prison, and his first opportunity to meet and interview them was in the Decatur jail. Clarence Norris best described the facility in his autobiography: "The Decatur jail was a hellhole...the State thought it was all right for 'n------.' It was filthy, dust everywhere, big holes were in the floors and walls, plaster fell down around our heads...But the bedbugs! There were millions of them, large as grains of rice. They crawled all over us at night and sleep was hard to come by. The bloodsuckers almost drained us dry. We raised hell about these bugs and they gave us some powder to kill them. But they just ate that stuff and came back for more."

The First Decatur Trial

THE STATE DECIDED TO RETRY Haywood Patterson first, and then proceed with the other boys one by one. However, before Patterson's trial started, a pretrial hearing was necessary to consider several motions and challenges the defense wished to make.

Pretrial Hearing—Monday, March 27, 1933

Judge Horton called the pretrial hearing to order on Monday, March 27. The contrast between the judge and the two principal lawyers was striking. Judge Horton was fifty-five years old, over six feet tall, lean, with a full head of hair. He carried himself with an almost regal bearing that was not intentional or pretentious, but simply represented his character and upbringing; many said he looked like Abraham Lincoln without a beard. If one compares the beardless portrait of Abraham Lincoln painted by George Peter Alexander Healy* in 1860, the year Lincoln was elected President at age fifty-one, to a photograph of Horton, the resemblance is unmistakable. Horton's demeanor in the courtroom was direct, but quiet and in control.

Samuel Leibowitz was thirty-seven years old, about six feet tall, but any physical comparison with Horton ended there. Leibowitz had a plump frame, oval face, balding head, and although he dressed well, he did not make an immediate imposing impression. However, in the courtroom, he was a showman, using his skills from his Cornell days in drama and debate to the fullest advantage.

Attorney General Knight was thirty-four years old, short in stature and lean, and quick to blush when embarrassed or threatened. Out of court, he was a charming southern gentleman, frequently holding forth, as if in his own court, with reporters and admirers in the local hotel over bourbon and branch water. Knight saw the Scottsboro case as an opportunity to further his ambitions for higher political office. To this end, in the courtroom, his persona turned from a Dr. Jekyll to a Mr. Hyde; he became edgy, hotheaded, and bellicose as he resorted to any tactic to win a case.

Knight was born and raised in Greensboro in the heart of Alabama's Black Belt. Knight's father was a delegate to the Constitutional Convention in Montgomery in 1901, when the state's byzantine constitution, a document that legally disenfranchised blacks in Alabama, was passed. Rodgers and Hammerstein understood that racism and bigotry were not inherited traits in an individual when they wrote the song "You've Got To Be Carefully Taught" for their seminal musical *South Pacific*. Thomas Knight Jr. had been "carefully taught"; he firmly believed in the superiority of whites, and "knew" blacks were inferior and had to be managed and controlled.

Leibowitz and the ILD lawyers had decided, before the new trials started, to challenge the validity of the Scottsboro trials based on the systematic exclusion of Negroes from Jackson County juries. Samuel Leibowitz opened the pretrial hearing in Decatur by making a motion

---

* Healy's portrait of Lincoln is in the Corcoran Gallery of Art in Washington, DC.

asking Judge Horton to quash the indictment issued by the Jackson County Grand Jury, arguing that the grand jury had been selected from county jury rolls that excluded Negroes in violation of the Fourteenth Amendment. Leibowitz first called three white witnesses: a Scottsboro newspaper editor, the head of the Jackson County jury commission, and a clerk to the jury commission. Leibowitz was able to get each of the men, all considered outstanding members of the community, to readily testify that, to their knowledge, a Negro had never served on a Jackson County jury. Each man testified that a process of selection, not exclusion, chose the juries. They offered with little prompting, as it was a well-known and established fact, that Negroes weren't qualified for jury duty because they were illiterate, exhibited poor judgment, and were of questionable character. When Leibowitz pointed out that many Negroes in Jackson County were well educated and quite literate, in fact more so than many illiterate whites who were allowed to serve on juries, the newspaper editor admitted it was so. He agreed that some Negroes "has got education enough"; however, he added, "they will nearly all steal." The jury commissioner could not recall the general state requirements for jury duty, saying the state's qualifications were irrelevant since Negroes weren't excluded for cause; they just weren't discussed.

The testimonies of these three gentlemen were Leibowitz's first encounters with the depth of white racial prejudice in the segregated South. These men were surprised and shocked at the implications in Leibowitz's questions and inferences. They generally answered honestly, if not always easily, because the situation described was not evil or contrived in their minds, but simply, the southern way of life they had known since birth. They knew no other way of life, and accepted and conducted the South's segregated customs and laws as unconsciously as one breathes.

Leibowitz then called to the witness stand, one by one, nine black men from Jackson County. All were literate men with good jobs including a Pullman porter, the owner of a dry cleaning business, the former trustee of a Negro school, and a plasterer. Leibowitz established their educational backgrounds, their literacy, their family and religious backgrounds, and showed they were honest, intelligent men of good character and sound judgment. When asked if they had ever been called for a jury, of if they knew any black person who had, they all replied no.

Pretrial Hearing—Tuesday, March 28, 1933

On March 28, the second day of the pretrial hearing, Attorney General Knight started his cross-examinations of the black witnesses. He was, at best, patronizing toward the black men, but generally was quite abusive, as he badgered them, shouted at them, and threatened them. He walked up to

John Sanford, the plasterer, a soft spoken and humble man, as he asked him a question and threatened him by nearly pointing in his eyes. Leibowitz objected strenuously, and Knight, his face turning a deep red, was visibly upset and angry. Judge Horton immediately intervened and calmed the two attorneys down. Knight continued his questioning, calling the witness by his first name, John, a common practice among southern white men when addressing a black man. Leibowitz leapt to his feet and objected, insisting that Knight "Call him Mr. Sanford please." The courtroom gasped, and Knight was livid, but he replied in an even voice that he was "not in the habit of doing that." Again Horton had to intervene strongly to calm the two men down. Knight tried to attack the intellectual integrity of each of the black witnesses by asking them to precisely define terms like "moral turpitude"; however, Knight was unable to show that the broader points Leibowitz had made were invalid. Knight finally argued that no proof had been offered the court that there were no black names on the jury rolls in Jackson County. Leibowitz countered that he wanted the entire jury rolls from Jackson County brought to the Decatur courtroom, and he would have every name on the rolls read aloud to the court to prove they were all white. After the lunch recess, Judge Horton suddenly announced the defense's motion was denied. Expecting that ruling, the defense asked for a one-day recess, which Horton granted.

Leibowitz was not surprised by the judge's decision, but he was pleased to have his evidence in the trial transcript if an appeal was necessary. Leibowitz also knew now that Knight, in spite of his gentlemanly attitude outside the courtroom, had racist views as prejudicial and deeply seated as the earlier white witnesses. Although Leibowitz was unsure how to characterize Judge Horton, he realized he was in for a tough battle in this courtroom.

Pretrial Hearing—Thursday, March 30, 1933

During the one-day recess, rumors ran amok in Decatur that Leibowitz and the defense would next attack the jury rolls and system in Decatur and Morgan County. Decatur and Morgan County had a larger black population than Scottsboro and Jackson County—the 1930 U.S. Census shows Morgan County with a total population of 46,176 of which 8,311, or 18 percent, were black, compared to Jackson County's total population of 36,331 of which 2,688, or 7 percent, were black. When court convened on Thursday morning, March 30, the rumors proved true as Leibowitz opened by making a motion that the case be dismissed because the jury rolls and juries of Morgan County were as biased against blacks as those in Jackson County. Leibowitz now had the attention of the entire Decatur community, many of whom made up the courtroom spectators, and the many more who gathered on the courthouse square.

Leibowitz proceeded to show, as he had in the Jackson County motion, that the jury commissioners in Morgan County had no blacks on the jury rolls and had no intention of putting any blacks on the rolls for much the same reasons as expressed by the Jackson County officials.

Leibowitz called Arthur Tidwell, a Morgan County jury commissioner, to the stand. Agreeing to Leibowitz's request, Judge Horton had the sheriff bring the jury rolls, a huge, red leather bound book, into the courtroom. After introducing the book as evidence, Leibowitz asked Tidwell if all the names in the rolls were white citizens.

Tidwell said, "I don't know." Leibowitz, becoming quite aggressive, asked Tidwell if he was being honest.

Tidwell, clearly angry and threatened, rose in his seat and responded, "Do you mean to say that I would swear falsely?" Leibowitz snapped back that he meant nothing and was only asking a question.

After Knight objected to the intimidating nature of Leibowitz's line of questions, Judge Horton intervened to prevent the exchange from getting completely out of hand. Leibowitz had Tidwell study the rolls page-by-page to see if he could identify Negroes in the book. By the end of the day's court session, he had been unable to identify a single Negro name on the rolls.

Leibowitz's black witnesses were quite an impressive group of educated, successful black men. Among the group that testified were doctors, ministers, businessmen, and civic leaders: most had college degrees and several had more than one. The black men were resolute and direct in their testimony. Each testified that, to their knowledge, a black person had never been called to serve on a Morgan County jury.

Knight attacked the integrity of the Morgan County black witnesses even more harshly than he had the Jackson County black men; he challenged their credentials, their education, and their standing in the community, but he could not move them from their principal contention that they were qualified to be jurors but had been denied an opportunity to do so. One black witness was particularly honest and direct; Knight asked Dr. N. E. Cashin, a physician who was educated at Phillips-Exeter Academy, one of the oldest preparatory schools in the United States, and the University of Illinois, if he knew this county had a jury commission. Cashin replied, as he looked at Knight with a look of disgust and disdain, "I know it is supposed to have one." Leibowitz announced to the court that he was ready to call hundreds of Negroes to prove they all had been excluded from the rolls.

Leibowitz did a masterful job of making his case, but his approach infuriated the Morgan County officials and the courtroom spectators. Their agitation at this challenge to their presumptive rights was one of shock and intrusion.

Pretrial Hearing—Friday, March 31, 1933

Judge Horton called the pretrial proceedings to an end at noon on Friday, March 31 and denied the motion to dismiss the case because the jury rolls and juries of Morgan County were biased against blacks, but said the defense had made a *prima facie* case on its motion. This was satisfactory with Leibowitz, because it meant the judge, in legal terms, had ruled that the evidence, on its face, supported the motion and was sufficient to prove the point on appeal unless rebutted by the state. Judge Horton recessed the court for the lunch break, instructing the lawyers to be prepared to start jury selection for the trial of Haywood Patterson after lunch. Leibowitz, Knight, and Horton likely didn't recognize it at the time, but they had set the stage for what would become one of the more significant U.S. Supreme Court decisions of the twentieth century.

The white citizens of Decatur and Morgan County did not take kindly to the attack Leibowitz had made on their jury commissioners and their southern traditions. Although the mood of the crowd in and around the court house had been non-threatening, and even festive, when the pretrial hearing started on Monday, by the end of the week the talk on the street became quite acrimonious toward Leibowitz with comments as extreme as "He ought to be hung, the Jew bastard." Captain Joseph Burleson, the National Guard commander of the unit assigned to Decatur for the duration of the trials, overheard some of the talk on the street and reported it to Judge Horton. When the court convened after lunch, Judge Horton announced he had a few words for the prospective jurors and the courtroom spectators before the jury selection process began. In a very serious tone and demeanor, Judge Horton said in part: "Now gentlemen under our law when it comes to the courts we know neither native or alien, we know neither Jew nor Gentile, we know neither black nor white, native or foreign born, but to each it is our duty to mete out even handed justice...and we must be true to ourselves, and if we are true to ourselves we can not be false to any one, nor to any people."

Judge Horton then allowed the jury selection process to begin; he, Leibowitz, and Knight questioned prospective jurors for the remainder of the day until twelve men had been selected. The jury included a draftsman, three farmers, a mill worker, two bookkeepers, a merchant, a barber, a bank cashier, an automobile salesman, and one unemployed man. Horton recessed the court Friday evening and sent the jury to a hotel where they would be sequestered throughout the trial with instructions not to discuss the case or to read newspaper articles concerning the case. Leibowitz returned to the apartment building where he and his wife, Belle, were staying to find that Captain Burleson had assigned five of his thirty guardsmen to protect Leibowitz and his wife. Knight, who was staying in the same apartment building, advised Belle to return to New York, as he was unsure the situation could be contained. Belle declined and stayed with Samuel.

First Decatur Trial—Monday, April 3, 1933

Haywood Patterson's trial opened Monday morning, April 3, nearly two years to the day after his first trial at Scottsboro had begun. Haywood was escorted into the courtroom dressed in a pair of poor fitting coveralls and sat at the defense table with Leibowitz on his right, and Chamlee and Brodsky on his left. The prosecution team included Knight, Assistant Attorney General Thomas Lawson, Morgan County Solicitor Wade Wright, and Jackson County Solicitor H. G. Bailey.

Before any witnesses were called to the stand, Attorney General Knight told the court he wanted any witnesses for the defendant that were present in the courtroom to be called. Leibowitz assured the court and Knight that no defense witnesses were present in the courtroom. Knight's concern was not unfounded; the prosecution had been unable to locate Ruby Bates since she had left her home in Huntsville on February 27 to points unknown. Knight knew Ruby's absence would hamper the prosecution, and he also knew she could be a problem for the prosecution. On January 5, 1932, Bates wrote a letter to Earl Streetman, a man she was dating. In the letter, she refuted claims made by another Streetman girlfriend, "I want to make a statement too you Mary Sanders is a goddam lie about those Negroes jazzing me those police man made me tell a lie." She concluded the letter with a P.S.: "This is one time that I might tell a lie But it is the truth so God help me." Bates gave the letter to an ex-prize fighter, Marion Pearlman, to deliver to Streetman. Pearlman was later arrested after an informant told the Huntsville police Pearlman had a letter written by Bates concerning the Scottsboro case. The police found the letter on Pearlman. The Huntsville police arrested Bates, and under the threat of one hundred days on a chain gang, she signed a notarized affidavit saying she was too drunk to know what she wrote in the letter, and her "evidence against the negroes at Scottsboro was absolutely the truth."

Knight opened the prosecution's case by calling Victoria Price to the stand, and, in less than twenty minutes, took her through testimony similar to what she had given in the four Scottsboro trials. Samuel Leibowitz rose slowly from his chair as he prepared to cross-examine Price; he was sure she was lying, and he was equally sure he could find a hole in her story that would convince the jury of her deception and more damning, her willingness to lie and send eight innocent boys to the electric chair. He approached

Price, and with a smile on his face, said pleasantly, "Miss Price, shall I call you Miss Price or Mrs. Price?" Victoria replied coldly, with a look of distrust and hate, "Mrs. Price."

Leibowitz then proceeded with a three-hour cross-examination and found himself with a prosecution witness who would not yield to his highly touted courtroom skills. Victoria was at turns recalcitrant and forgetful (or at least said she couldn't remember), especially with difficult and challenging questions, complained she couldn't understand the words Leibowitz used, and refused to be drawn into making obvious conclusions about apparent factual discrepancies and contradictions. Some of the exchanges between Leibowitz and Price in the transcript of the trial read like a B-movie script for a southern courtroom scene. More importantly, in the following exchanges between Leibowitz and Price, he was able to elicit from her responses that proved to be either false, or aided in proving her responses were likely false based on the testimony of later witnesses.

Leibowitz: Little pieces of rock gray in color?

Price: This chert is what I heard it called.

Leibowitz: Kinda gray rock?

Price: Yes sir.

Leibowitz: Broken rock with jagged ends?

Price: It is sharp.

Leibowitz: It is very sharp?

Price: Pretty sharp.

_____

Leibowitz: Of course when the negroes got off of you, you were wet all over were you not?

Price: No I wasn't wet?

Leibowitz: On your private parts?

Price: I wasn't wet.

Leibowitz: On your private parts?

Price: Why sure.

Leibowitz: And each negro wetted you more and more?

Price: Sure did.

_____

Leibowitz: You said six negroes raped you?

Price: Six negroes raped me.

Leibowitz: And you say six negroes raped Ruby Bates?

Price: To the best of my knowledge.

———

Leibowitz: Some of these negroes were pretty heavy were they not when they were lying [laying] on top of you?

Price: Yes sir.

Leibowitz: With you on your back on this rock?

Price: Yes sir.

Leibowitz: They didn't spare you in any way, didn't try to make it comfortable for you in any way?

Price: No sir.

Leibowitz: Just like brutes?

Price: Yes sir.

Leibowitz: You lay on your back there for close to an hour on that jagged rock screaming?

Price: Yes sir.

Leibowitz: Was your back bleeding when you got to the doctor?

Price: I couldn't say.

———

Leibowitz: To the best of your recollection did you find a single drop of blood on your back when you were at the doctor's office?

Price: I won't answer, I don't remember.

Leibowitz: After you had been on your back on this jagged rock for an hour with six burly negroes on top of you?

Price: I won't answer, I don't remember.

———

Leibowitz: The last negro had just finished raping you you say when you reached Paint Rock?

Price:	Just about five minutes before the train stopped. [The train arrived at Paint Rock just before two p.m.]

—————

Leibowitz:	Do you know a man by the name of Lester Carter?
Price:	He was on the train.
Leibowitz:	Do you know him?
Price:	No, I don't know him.
Leibowitz:	Never saw him before in your life?
Price:	No sir.

Knight next called Dr. R. R. Bridges, one of the two Scottsboro physicians who had examined Price and Bates about two hours after the train arrived in Paint Rock. Knight had Dr. Bridges give an account of his examination of the girls that was essentially the same testimony he had given in the Scottsboro trials. Leibowitz's cross-examination of Dr. Bridges was much more successful than his efforts with Price. Dr. Bridges was not an antagonistic witness, and Leibowitz was able to get him to testify that the girls' vital signs, pulse, and respiration were normal, and that they were calm and not distressed or hysterical, contrary to what might be expected in women who had suffered a multiple rape trauma a few hours before. Far more damning to the prosecution's case was the following exchange when Leibowitz got Bridges to testify the spermatozoa in Price's vagina were non-motile.

Leibowitz:	As you looked through the microscope you saw these little tadpoles there?
Bridges:	Yes sir.
Leibowitz:	They were not moving?
Bridges:	No sir.
Leibowitz:	They didn't move, they were dead?
Bridges:	I couldn't say they were dead but non-motile.
Leibowitz:	Non motile means to the best of your judgment that they were dead?
Bridges:	Yes sir.
Leibowitz:	In other words you were not able to discover any single spermatozoa from this woman who

> claimed she had been raped by six men, you were
> not able to discover any spermatozoa you could
> say definitely was alive?

Bridges: Yes sir, that is right.

Leibowitz then got the doctor to testify that recently discharged spermatozoa into a woman's vagina could live for a week to ten days. Judge Horton also asked a number of questions on this issue to make sure he understood it correctly, as the implication was clear; if two women had suffered multiple rapes two to three hours before Dr. Bridges and Dr. Lynch examined the spermatozoa deposited in their vaginas, some significant portion of any remaining spermatozoa would have been quite active, not non-motile. Leibowitz also got Dr. Bridges to testify that his attention was not called to the bloody head wound Price claimed she suffered; he saw no blood on her head or scalp, there were no signs of hysteria in the two young women, he found no blood on Price's back or in her vagina although there were some minor bruises in both locations, and there was no evidence of any choking around Price's throat.

The jury sat passively, sometimes even glassy-eyed, through Dr. Bridges' testimony; however, Judge Horton frequently leaned over the bench to ask questions directly to Dr. Bridges and to listen to his testimony. Leibowitz's cross-examination of Dr. Bridges concluded the first day of Patterson's trial.

Although Leibowitz was unable to get Price to concede on any significant point, he was able to show in many areas that her story was implausible and likely untrue, especially in the areas Dr. Bridges testified on. However, the press and the courtroom observers judged his cross-examination of Victoria Price based on which side of the Mason-Dixon Line they resided. The northern press reported the cross-examination factually and pointed out some of the possible inconsistencies in Price's testimony, including those revealed by Dr. Bridges' testimony. However, most southern newspapers excoriated Leibowitz for his cross-examination tactics, praised Price for her fortitude under his relentless pressure, and ignored Dr. Bridges' testimony, saying it was unfit for print. The mood among courtroom attendees became even more prejudiced and hostile against this New York City Jewish lawyer, as they perceived him as badgering and questioning the veracity of a young southern white woman against the word of nine young black boys.

First Decatur Trial—Tuesday, April 4, 1933

Court resumed Tuesday morning, April 4, with Dr. Bridges concluding his testimony. Knight then asked for a brief recess so he and Dr. Lynch, the

Scottsboro physician who assisted Bridges in the examination of the two girls, could confer with Judge Horton. Knight asked Horton to excuse Lynch as a witness since his testimony would be quite similar to that of Dr. Bridges. Horton agreed, and as the others returned to the courtroom, Lynch asked Horton if he could speak to him privately. Horton and Lynch went into a men's restroom in the courthouse, guarded by a bailiff to keep others out. Lynch told Horton that Knight was incorrect; his testimony would not be a repeat of Dr. Bridges', and based on his examination of the two girls, he did not believe they had been raped—he was convinced they were lying. Horton was appalled, and said, "My God, Doctor, is this whole thing a horrible mistake[?]" Horton pleaded with Lynch to testify, but the young doctor said his career and life in Jackson County would be ruined if he did. Horton did not insist that Lynch testify, as he knew Lynch was correct.

As Horton and Lynch returned to the courtroom, Horton struggled to maintain his usual calm outward demeanor while his mind raced with the serious alternatives before him. He could force Lynch to testify; he could call the trial to an end, but his decision would be based on one man's opinion; or he could depend on the jury to see the obvious contradictions and lies in Price's testimony. Horton decided on the latter course, and he instructed Attorney General Knight to call his next witness.

Knight called five Jackson County men in succession who had testified in the Scottsboro trials. Four of the witnesses' testimony actually favored the defense more than the prosecution, although none of their accounts touched on the central issue of whether or not the girls were raped. The fifth witness, Arthur H. Woodall, was more effective for the prosecution. Woodall testified during cross-examination by Leibowitz that he found a pocketknife on one of the Negroes when he searched him at Paint Rock, and the Negro told him he got the knife "off the white girl Victoria Price." After Woodall's testimony, the state rested its case.

Horton called for a brief recess, after which it was Leibowitz's turn. He realized he faced an incredible hurdle; his past cases had required him only to convince the court or jury of reasonable doubt of his client's guilt to win an acquittal. In this courtroom, Leibowitz now knew he had to prove Haywood's case well beyond a reasonable doubt.

The first witness for the defense was Dallas Ramsey, a middle-aged black man from Chattanooga. In Leibowitz's cross-examination of Victoria Price on Monday, the following exchange took place:

> Leibowitz: [Didn't you go] To a place called in Chattanooga, Hoboes Jungle?

Price:	No sir, I stayed with a woman by the name of Callie Brochie.
Leibowitz:	Isn't it a fact you all went over in the jungle there and built a fire?
Price:	I didn't go to any jungles.
Leibowitz:	You and Ruby Bates and these two men?
Price:	I didn't go to any jungles.

Ramsey testified he lived in a small shack about three hundred yards from the Chattanooga rail yard next to the hobo jungle. The hobo jungle was where people who rode the rails camped, slept, and cooked their meals as they waited for trains to come and go. Ramsey testified that he and a friend, E. L. Lewis, saw both Victoria Price and Ruby Bates sitting in the jungle at about six o'clock on the morning of March 25, 1931, the day of the alleged rapes. He talked to Price briefly; she asked Ramsey what time the Huntsville train left, and he told her about nine o'clock. He said Price also told him "my old man has gone uptown to look for some food." Later in the morning, Ramsey saw Price, Bates, and a "white man" get on the train bound for Huntsville. Knight was unable to get Ramsey to change his testimony during a fierce cross-examination.

Leibowitz next called George Chamlee, the defense team lawyer from Chattanooga, to the witness stand. As with his preparation for Ramsey's testimony, Leibowitz had questioned Price the day before about Mrs. Callie Brochie and her boarding house on Seventh Street in Chattanooga. Price testified at the four Scottsboro trials and at this trial that she and Ruby Bates stayed in Brochie's boarding house. Leibowitz was trying to show she was lying.

Leibowitz:	Did you ever meet a man by the name of Florian Slappy?
Price:	No sir.
Leibowitz:	Do you know a lawyer by the name of Evans Chew?
Price:	No sir.
Leibowitz:	Do you know a man by the name of Epic Peters?
Price:	No sir.
Knight:	I don't think that is relevant cross examination.

Horton:	Is there anything further you want to ask in regard to these parties?
Leibowitz:	Nothing further.
Leibowitz:	By the way Mrs. Price, as a matter of fact the name of Mrs. Callie you apply to this boarding house lady, is the name of a boarding house lady used by Octavius [Octavus] Roy Cohn in the Saturday Evening Post stories – Sis Callie, isn't that where you got the name?
Knight:	We object.
Horton:	Sustain the objection.

Although Leibowitz's line of questioning was disallowed, he had set the table for Chamlee, who had lived or had his office on Seventh Street for twenty-five of the last forty years. He testified he never knew or heard of a boarding house or a Mrs. Callie Brochie on Seventh Street. He said further that his research of Chattanooga city directories for the years 1930, 1931, and 1932 showed no one named Callie Brochie, and his inquiries of the homes and business along the eight blocks of this well-to-do neighborhood yielded the same result—no one knew of a woman named Callie Brochie ever living on the street. Knight did not challenge Chamlee's testimony with a cross-examination, thus ending the second day of the trial.

And, yes, Leibowitz was referring to the same Octavus Roy Cohn who lived near the Taylor family on Sixteenth Avenue South in Birmingham in the early 1920s, and, whose son, Roy, was a member of the Taylor Boys' "new lot" gang.

The mood of local courtroom attendees became more and more hostile towards Leibowitz over the first two days of Patterson's trial, and this hostile mood was rampantly spreading throughout Morgan County. Most of the hostility was directed at Leibowitz's cross-examination style and technique with Victoria Price. Rumors abounded about meetings being held to discuss the appropriate actions to deal with Leibowitz and the boys.

First Decatur Trial—Wednesday, April 5, 1933

On Wednesday morning, April 5, Judge Horton called the court to order and directed Leibowitz to continue with his defense case. Leibowitz told the court he intended to call six of the Scottsboro Boys to testify, as who could better describe their actions the day these horrible accusations were made. He started by calling Willie Roberson. Leibowitz could not have made a worse first choice; besides having an unattractive appearance—short, stocky, with hair pointing in all directions—Roberson always seemed to be disconnected from events around him as he stared vacantly into space. He was later diagnosed to have an IQ of sixty-four and the mental aptitude of a nine-year-old. Roberson also was suffering from syphilis, which he contracted in 1930. At this time, he was probably suffering mostly from the sores on his private parts; however, left untended over years, the disease can spread to the brain and lead to death. He testified he rode in the back of the train the entire trip from Chattanooga to Paint Rock.

The next witness was Olen Montgomery, who was completely blind in his left eye and had limited sight in his right eye. He testified he was traveling alone and spent the whole trip in an oil tanker car near the end of the train. Knight did not cross-examine either Roberson or Montgomery, as their testimony was essentially the same as they gave in the Scottsboro courtroom.

Ozie Powell was called to the witness stand next, and Leibowitz may have later regretted doing so. Powell testified he saw some black boys jumping over a gondola and then saw some white boys jumping from the train, but he denied he was involved in the fight. Knight didn't pass on cross-examining Powell; he immediately confused Powell, who answered yes to a question and then reversed himself by saying no to the same question. Judge Horton tried to help Powell by asking him if he understood the questions, but Powell continued to answer in a muddled fashion. Leibowitz tried to rehabilitate his witness by asking him one simple question: "Ozie tell us about how much schooling you have had in your life?"

Ozie answered, "I ain't had over about three months."

Judge Horton called for the noon court recess as Powell stepped down from the witness stand.

When the court convened after the noon recess, Judge Horton ordered the jury taken from the courtroom. He then slowly looked, with a stern expression, around the entire courtroom at the lawyers, court officials, reporters, observers, and attendees and said, "The court wishes to make an announcement." *The New York Times* reporter, Raymond Daniell, best described Judge Horton's announcement when he wrote, "He then delivered his warning in phrases that fell from his lips like the bullets he promised to lynchers." Judge Horton had learned from Captain Burleson that his undercover men had attended a meeting of about two hundred young men in a hall near the courthouse where "There was talk there...of riding the New York lawyer out of town and lynching the Negroes." Horton had immediately ordered Burleson to double his guards at both the jail and Leibowitz's apartment and also instructed him to be prepared for any mob action that might occur including, as a last resort, shooting to kill. Horton, with a voice rising in anger on occasion, said, in part, to the courtroom:

Now gentlemen this is for the audience, and I want it to be known that these prisoners are under the protection of this court. The Sheriff and his deputies, and members of the National Guards are under the direction and authority of this court. This court intends to protect these prisoners, and any other persons engaged in this trial. Any man or any group of men that attempts to take charge outside of the law, are not only disobedient to the law, but are citizens unworthy of the protection of the State of Alabama, and unworthy of the citizenship which they enjoy...I absolutely have no patience with mob spirit, and that spirit that would charge the guilt or innocence of any being without knowing of their guilt or innocence. Your very civilization depends upon the carrying out of your laws in an orderly manner...Now gentleman I have spoken straight words; I have spoken harsh words, but every word I say is true, and I hope we will have no more of any such conduct. Let the jury return.

The courtroom attendees sat stunned and in silence as the jury members retook their seats in the jury box. Although Samuel Leibowitz must have been concerned about the events leading to Judge Horton's announcement, he proceeded with the presentation of the defense's case as if nothing had happened.

Leibowitz continued his case by calling Andy Wright and Eugene Williams to the witness stand. Each of the boys testified much as they had in Scottsboro; they admitted there was a fight with the white boys but denied ever seeing the two white girls until the train arrived at Paint Rock, and they absolutely denied raping them. The two boys stuck to their testimony quite well under a tough cross-examination by Knight.

Haywood Patterson then took the witness stand in his own defense. Leibowitz had Patterson tell the court about the events on the train in his own words with little interruption from Leibowitz except to deal with Knight's persistent objections. Patterson's testimony was quite similar to that of the other five boys, but where he really showed his mettle and determination was in his responses and demeanor under Knight's cross-examination. Patterson refused to be intimidated by Knight, frequently answering him in ways that both confused and infuriated Knight. In one exchange with Knight, Patterson made such a subtle point that Knight didn't at first understand the response, and, when he did, he reverted to a southern white man's racist response to a black man.

> Knight: I will ask you if you haven't stood in Kilby Prison and mocked those girls crying while you were raping them?

Patterson:	No sir, I haven't mocked no girl crying, how could I mock them – how could a man rape a girl with a man hanging on the side when we taken him and put him back and saved his life.
Knight:	I will ask you if you didn't mock those girls out at Kilby?
Patterson:	Mock this girl.[?]
Knight:	How she cried?
Patterson:	What girl?
Knight:	The one you are being tried for raping?
Patterson:	I haven't raped any girl, I haven't seen any girl.
Knight:	You didn't do that?
Patterson:	No sir, I didn't do such a thing as that; I pulled this white boy back up on the train and saved his life.
Knight:	Stop talking except when you are being talked to.

Knight's questioning was based on the assertions of a prisoner on death row next to Patterson's cell in Kilby Prison, who claimed he'd overhead Patterson say the girls were crying while Patterson raped them. The governor of Alabama had commuted this prisoner's sentence to life imprisonment. Knight later called him as a witness, but Horton would not allow him to testify. Ignoring the possibility that this witness might not be acceptable to the court, Knight persisted in his line of questioning. Patterson answered Knight by pointing out the obvious to anyone in the South; if a black man had just saved a white man's life—Patterson had pulled the white boy, Gilley, back onto the train after he was forced over the edge during the fight—and put him back in the gondola they all occupied, it was inconceivable he would proceed to rape the white girls in front of the saved white man. Even an uneducated black man knew this would be a one-way ticket to the electric chair or a lynch mob. When Knight finally understood the implications of Patterson's testimony, he responded as many southern white men would: "Stop talking except when you are talked to." A later exchange between the two further infuriated Knight.

Knight:	I will ask you if when you were in Scottsboro – you were tried at Scottsboro?
Patterson:	Yes sir, I was framed at Scottsboro.

Knight:	Framed at Scottsboro?
Patterson:	Yes sir.
Knight:	Who told you to say you were framed?
Patterson:	I told myself to say it.

Patterson concluded his testimony while under Knight's cross-examination with determination and defiance, as he answered Knight, "I told you I don't know, I told you at the beginning I don't know about [train] speed, I told you I guess maybe twenty five."

There was much churning in Decatur and elsewhere that evening after Judge Horton recessed the court. The talk on the streets of Decatur was about Judge Horton's strong statement from the bench. While it didn't stop the general anger and hate boiling up against Leibowitz and the boys, it did quell the lynching threat for the moment. Leibowitz returned to his heavily guarded apartment, where he and his wife likely discussed their safety and the madness they were experiencing in the South. Clarence Norris and Charlie Weems waited anxiously in the old Decatur jail for the return of Patterson and the five boys who testified. Norris and Weems had waited all week in the jail, as they were not called to testify. Boredom and trepidation were their constant companions, and they were eager for courtroom news from the other boys. It is not surprising Leibowitz chose not to call Norris; his testimony at the Scottsboro trials, where he said he saw all the boys rape the girls, but denied he took part in the attacks, made him ripe fodder for any prosecution cross-examination. Weems, who was a good witness at Scottsboro, may have been withheld from testifying since he and Norris were tried together at Scottsboro, and Weems's Decatur trial was scheduled to start right after Patterson's.

The ILD and the U.S. Communist Party had to this point in the trial kept reasonably quiet, as both groups told Leibowitz they would. However, after Judge Horton's stern announcement and what it revealed, the *Daily Worker* wrote scathing articles about the trial and called Judge Horton the "lyncher in sheep's clothing." The party urged their members and others to send telegrams to the court objecting to the proceedings and pleading for the boys' release. Over the next two days, the court was inundated with telegrams demanding the release of the boys and decrying the extreme racial and social injustices in the South. Horton tried unsuccessfully to keep the contents of the telegrams from the jurors.

First Decatur Trial—Thursday, April 6, 1933

On Thursday morning, April 6, Leibowitz first called Percy Ricks to the witness stand. Ricks was the fireman on the train on March 25, 1931. As fireman, his responsibilities were to support the train engineer by keeping the boiler adequately supplied with coal and water. The coal and water were stored in large quantities in the tender, a car located directly behind the locomotive, and it was the fireman's further responsibility to resupply the tender with coal and water at interim stops along the route of the train.

Ricks testified that when the train stopped at Paint Rock, he immediately climbed on top of the tender and prepared to add water to the tender water tank. From this location above the top of most of the cars on the train, he could see the armed white men spread along the entire length of the train, and he observed them arresting a number of Negroes at various cars on the train. He said he also saw two white women get off the train, and added, "They ran toward the engine, one behind the other, then they turned, they seen this crowd of men when they run down toward the engine and they saw they were meeting them and then they started back the other way, and the posse was coming that way and they stopped then and there."

The inference of Ricks's testimony was clear; the girls ran from the train to avoid being apprehended by the posse. Morgan County Solicitor Wade Wright, in a tough cross-examination of Ricks, was unable to get him to change any significant detail of his testimony. Unfortunately for the defense and the boys, this was a moot point, as Ricks was black, and an all-white jury in a southern courtroom would likely ignore his testimony, since many white Southerners believed blacks were habitual liars.

Leibowitz then called Dr. Edward Reisman as an expert witness for the defense. Dr. Reisman was forty-eight years old and had been a practicing gynecologist for the past twenty-three years in Chattanooga. Reisman corroborated the critical points Leibowitz had gotten from his cross-examination of Dr. Bridges: a large amount of semen with motile spermatozoa would be present in the vaginas of women who had intercourse with six men only a few hours earlier; spermatozoa will remain motile for at least twenty-four hours after intercourse; the vital signs and calm demeanor of the women during the examination by Dr. Bridges was not consistent with what Dr. Reisman would expect in two women just raped by six men. The prosecution's cross-examination of Dr. Reisman was brief and did not change Dr. Reisman's conclusions. As Dr. Reisman stepped down from the witness stand, Leibowitz felt he had established a strong position for reasonable doubt with the testimony of the two doctors.

Leibowitz was now prepared, in his mind, to discredit the testimony of the prosecution's prime witness, Victoria Price, with his next two witnesses: his star witnesses, Lester Carter and Ruby Bates. He envisioned their testimony would compel the jury to return a verdict of not guilty.

At about ten o'clock, he called Lester Carter to the witness stand. Twenty-one-year-old Carter came into the courtroom wearing a new, well-tailored men's suit highlighted with a brightly colored tie. Lester Carter was the person Victoria Price said she didn't know until she met him in the Scottsboro jail. Carter proceeded to give testimony that contradicted most of what Victoria Price had testified happened prior to the alleged rapes.

Carter said he was in the Huntsville jail in January 1931 for vagrancy when he met Victoria Price and Jack Tiller, a married man she had been jailed with for adultery. Soon after they were released, Price introduced Carter to Bates. On the night of March 23, the four of them went to the Huntsville hobo jungle for the night, where, Carter testified, "I had intercourse with Ruby Bates and Jack Tiller had intercourse with Victoria Price." During the night it started to rain, so they moved into a boxcar, continued their sexual liaisons, and during interludes in their sexual tryst, discussed hoboing to Chattanooga. Tiller, concerned about his marital status, said he would meet them in Chattanooga later. On March 24 at about three o'clock in the afternoon, Price, Bates, and Carter jumped a train in Huntsville bound for Chattanooga. Carter said they arrived in Chattanooga at about seven o'clock that evening. They met Orville Gilley in the rail yard, and the four of them spent the night in the Chattanooga hobo jungle. Carter said he and Bates had sex that night, but he wasn't sure if Price and Gilley did. He said he never heard of Mrs. Callie Brochie, and that the girls could not have stayed with her, as the girls were in the hobo jungle the entire time they were in Chattanooga. After they got moving the next morning at about four o'clock, Gilley and Carter left to look for some food, and when they returned, the girls were sitting with a group of Negro men in the hobo jungle. Shortly after that, they walked back to the rail yard, waited for the Huntsville bound train, and boarded it between ten and eleven on the morning of March 25.

Carter described the events leading up to the fight, and the fight itself, much as the others had testified. However, he said the girls were in the gondola just ahead of the gondola in which the fight took place, and therefore the girls did not see the fight. Carter said he jumped off the train soon after the fight started because he quickly realized the black boys hopelessly outnumbered the white boys. Carter's testimony also matched up well with the earlier testimonies of Dallas Ramsey and Percy Ricks.

Solicitor Wright cross-examined Carter, and the difference in his approach and deference to this white defense witness—one with a story that repudiated much of what Price had claimed—compared to the black defense witnesses was striking and appalling. Wright generally treated Carter with respect, and he seldom challenged him as he told his story about the events leading up to the claimed rapes, whereas Wright and Knight ruthlessly attacked and challenged each black witness. Wright did get Carter to testify that Joseph Brodsky, the New York ILD lawyer, paid for his room and meals while Carter was in New York City discussing the case with Brodsky. Carter also said he paid eleven dollars for the suit he was wearing in the courtroom out of money Brodsky had given him. Wright ended his cross-examination with Carter's entire testimony pretty much intact.

George Chamlee then called E. L. Lewis to the witness stand. Lewis was the man with Dallas Ramsey the morning of March 25, when Ramsey, testifying earlier, stated he and Lewis saw the girls and had a brief conversation with them. Lewis confirmed Ramsey's story. He also testified he had seen Victoria Price in the Chattanooga hobo jungle several separate times in the company of both black and white men well before March 25. Knight's cross-examination of Lewis was for naught; Lewis held to his story.

It appeared Leibowitz was about to rest the defense's case, although he said he would only rest with the proviso that he be able to put more witnesses on after the prosecution's rebuttal testimony. After some arguments between the defense and prosecution over the admittance of earlier evidence and testimony, Leibowitz received a note and announced to the court that he did have another witness—Ruby Bates. Leibowitz set up a dramatic scene as Ruby Bates entered the courtroom escorted by May Jones, a social worker in Birmingham, who was hired to bring Bates from Birmingham to Decatur. All eyes were on Bates as she walked from the rear to the front of the courtroom; even Judge Horton rose from the bench and moved to the railed enclosure to get a better look. Bates wore very stylish clothes and looked out of place in this southern courtroom. The courtroom broke into a buzz of talk and murmurs, and the prosecution lawyers were clearly disturbed and concerned. After Bates got to the front of the courtroom, Horton gaveled the court back to order.

Leibowitz's direct examination of Bates was over in about fifteen minutes. To verify that Bates knew Price, Victoria was brought into the courtroom from an anteroom, where, as the two girls glared at one another, Bates confirmed it was Victoria Price. Victoria was so angry and agitated that Knight had to intervene and tell his star witness to "keep your temper." Price left the courtroom and Leibowitz continued his questioning. Bates verified the story Lester Carter had just told, and said she testified falsely in the Scottsboro trials because Victoria Price said if they didn't, they might go to jail. She said Price told her everything to say. She explained that after she left Huntsville on February 27, 1933, she first went to Montgomery, where she met with no one special. About twelve days later she arrived in New York City where she later met with the famous Reverend Harry Emerson Fosdick, the pastor of Riverside Church. Fosdick was a liberal theologian and outspoken in his opposition to racism and injustice. After Bates told him her story, he encouraged her to return to the South and tell the truth. Fosdick sent her to Dr. Charles Clingman, the rector of the

Episcopal Church of the Advent in Birmingham, and Dr. Clingman arranged for May Jones to escort Bates to Decatur. Leibowitz closed his direct examination with the question central to the case, "Did any of those negroes rape you?"

Bates replied, "No sir."

Knight walked slowly towards Bates to begin his cross-examination. He knew he had to discredit her in the eyes of the jury or his case was in real jeopardy. Under the pressure of a tough cross-examination, Bates proved to be as poor a witness as she had been in the Scottsboro trials. She played easily into Knight's hands with her quiet demeanor and lack of self-confidence, as he relentlessly pressed her on points from her testimony in the Scottsboro trials. Knight would read a damning passage from the Scottsboro trial transcript, and Bates would either say she didn't remember or "Victoria Price told it that way and I told it just like she said." During one of these many exchanges, a spectator in the courtroom broke into laughter over Bates's confusion. Leibowitz objected strenuously, and Horton told the man and the entire courtroom to refrain from laughing, as this was a very serious matter before the court. After a few more exchanges like this, Judge Horton told Knight to move on, as Bates had made it clear that her Scottsboro testimony was untrue. Knight was not happy with Horton's ruling, since Knight's position was that her Scottsboro testimony was true, and her testimony today was untrue. Knight also asked Bates where she got money for her travels and the fancy clothes she was wearing. Bates said she had saved some money, and a man she met in Montgomery gave her more money for her trip to New York. Once in New York, she worked for a lady named Margaret, and although Bates couldn't remember the lady's last name, she borrowed fifty dollars from her. When she met with Dr. Fosdick, he gave her money for the new clothes she was wearing. She rode a bus, which cost twenty-nine dollars, from New York back to Birmingham. Knight's intent was to show that Bates's new testimony was bought by New York money. He even suspected, but was never able to prove, that Bates went to New York at the behest of the ILD.

Knight then moved to three items in his cross-examination that he was sure would cast doubts in the jurors' minds as to the credibility of Ruby Bates. First, he produced the affidavit Bates had signed under duress from the Huntsville police in 1932, refuting the letter she had written saying she was not raped by any Negroes on the train. When Knight asked if the statement in the affidavit was true, Bates replied, "No, I didn't tell the truth then."

Second, Knight asked Bates if she remembered coming to Birmingham in early February 1933 to discuss the *habeas corpus* hearing concerning Roy Wright, the youngest of the Scottsboro Boys, since she might be used as a witness in those proceedings. Bates said, "Yes sir." Knight then pressed Bates about the discussion at this meeting, where Victoria Price, Solicitor Bailey, and two other men were present. He asked Bates, "Did I not tell you the only thing I wanted was the truth?"

Bates replied, "Yes."

Knight finally reminded Bates about what she told him in Birmingham; you said that "what you swore to at Scottsboro" was "what happened on that train." Bates responded it was not she, but Price, who told him that. She denied remembering any direct questions from Knight about the events on the train.

Third, Knight asked Bates if Dr. Carey Walker in Huntsville treated her for syphilis soon after the Scottsboro trials, and if she told the doctor she contacted syphilis from one of the Negroes who raped her. Bates agreed the doctor had treated her for syphilis, but she denied telling him she got it from one of the defendants because she didn't know where she got it. Dr. Walker later told the court, "She said she got it on this train from these negroes." Knight concluded his cross-examination, having clearly discredited Bates with the locals in the courtroom and probably the jury as well. Judge Horton recessed the court late Thursday afternoon with clear instructions to Leibowitz to have Ruby Bates back in the courtroom the next morning at 8:30 a.m.

The mood in Decatur and surrounding communities turned angry and hostile again Thursday night in spite of Horton's stern announcement from the bench on Tuesday. Morgan County locals, their white neighbors in adjacent counties, and much of the South were adamant in their belief that Bates had sold out to Yankee money, and that she was a hopeless liar. Raymond Daniell wrote in *The New York Times*, "The defection of Ruby Bates caused an immediate and bitter resentment among residents of this and neighboring counties." Mary Heaton Vorse, a reporter for the *New York World-Telegram*, wrote that she overheard a man behind her at the trial whisper, "It'll be a wonder if ever he [Leibowitz] leaves town alive."

Groups of men gathered in Morgan County and Huntsville, and again discussed lynching the defense attorneys and the defendants. When Captain Burleson heard the talk, he added guards for Leibowitz and Bates, and had 150 men ready to move to Huntsville if the situation demanded it. Fortunately, nothing but a lot of racist rhetoric and burnt crosses took place.

Bates's testimony was viewed from other perspectives both during and after the trial. Haywood Patterson later wrote in his autobiography, "Attorney General Knight, he tried to break her [Bates's] story but he couldn't." Clarence Norris wrote in his autobiography, "He [Knight] accused Ruby Bates of having been paid off. But he didn't shake her story." Quentin Reynolds wrote in his Leibowitz biography, *Courtroom*, "Knight wasn't able to do much with her." Mary Heaton Vorse wrote in the *New York World-Telegram*, "Samuel Leibowitz is showing himself to be more than a great trial lawyer; he is the supreme artist."

First Decatur Trial—Friday, April 7, 1933

Judge Horton called the court to order at 8:30 a.m. on April 7. The prosecution called two doctors as expert witnesses, including Dr. Carey Walker, who confirmed that Bates told him she got syphilis from one of the defendants. Knight then recalled Ruby Bates and Haywood Patterson, and briefly questioned them about areas covered in earlier testimony. Both Leibowitz and Knight rested their respective cases after the witnesses were questioned. Judge Horton then instructed the lawyers to present their closing arguments to the jury.

Jackson County Solicitor Bailey opened for the prosecution and gave a reasonably low-key argument calling for a guilty verdict. Morgan County Solicitor Wade Wright followed Bailey with a rambling speech in a fundamentalist evangelical style, as he stirred up all the racial and anti-Semitic undertones present in the trial. Wright was a preeminent member of an all-day singing group: it was a southern tradition among evangelical and Pentecostal groups to gather for a day of worship, singing, and eating. He had a booming voice, and he used it well to stir up the passions and prejudices of the locals in the courtroom and the jury. Once he got rolling, a few people in the courtroom shouted out "Ahhh-men," as if they were in a revival service. Leibowitz sat stunned and in disbelief, and Knight was even embarrassed, as Wright proclaimed that Ruby Bates "couldn't tell you all the things that happened in New York because part of it was in the Jew language." Of Lester Carter, he said, "That man Carter is a new kind of man to me. Did you watch his hands? If he had been with Brodsky another two weeks, he would have been down here with a pack on his back a-trying to sell you goods." Wright closed his anti-Semitic tirade saying, "Show them that Alabama justice cannot be bought and sold with Jew money from New York."

Leibowitz leapt to his feet with a motion for a mistrial after Wright's comment about "Jew money." Horton denied the motion but instructed the jury to disregard Wright's comments about "Jew money"; however, the damage had been done.

Samuel Leibowitz, the perfect criminal lawyer from New York, now had to follow this bigoted tirade with a summation for the defense that would both calm the courtroom and bring it back to reason. Leibowitz proceeded to talk without notes for several hours over the remainder of the court session on Friday. He was eloquent, articulate, and precise, as he tried to show the jury the obvious examples of reasonable doubt inherent in several witnesses' testimony. He tried to diffuse Wright's bigoted tirade saying, "What is the argument of the learned solicitor?...What he is saying is, 'Come on, boys; we can lick this Jew from New York. Stick it into him. We're among home folks.'" Concerning the "Jew money" comment, Leibowitz explained to the jury that he was not getting paid for his legal services or expenses. He added that he was not a crusader for social equality but was here "to see that the law guaranteeing equal protection to all races in our courts is observed."

When it was apparent that Leibowitz could not conclude his summary until very late Friday, Judge Horton decided to recess the court for the day and finish the summary statements the next day.

First Decatur Trial—Saturday, April 8, 1933

The court reconvened at 8:30 a.m. on April 8, and Judge Horton instructed Leibowitz to conclude his summation. As Leibowitz continued on, the toll of the past two weeks in the courtroom and the constant threats to his life were etched in his face; he appeared near exhaustion. He ended his summation at ten o'clock Saturday morning asking the jurors to either acquit or condemn Patterson to death, and then he recited the Lord's Prayer. The passion and interest the jury exhibited during Wright's final argument was absent; the jury sat stone-faced throughout Leibowitz's three-hour summary.

Attorney General Knight followed Leibowitz with the final argument for the prosecution. Although Knight's comments were generally more constrained than Wright's, he could not contain his own racial prejudice completely when he referred to Patterson as "that thing" before he said to the jury, "If you acquit this Negro, put a garland of roses around his neck, give him a supper and send him to New York City."

Judge Horton then delivered his instructions to the jury in his quiet, somber voice. While his demeanor was determined, his face was weary, showing the strain of the past two weeks of pretrial hearings and the trial itself. He knew that several of his rulings during the proceedings had not been well received locally or throughout much of the South. Horton's instructions were balanced as he directed the jury.

> Take the evidence, sift it out and find the truths and untruths and render your verdict. It will not be easy to keep your minds solely on the evidence. Much prejudice has crept into it. It has come not only from far away, but from here at home as well.

Throughout the morning, as the lawyers were giving their summations, messenger boys continued to hurry in and out of the courtroom with telegrams for Horton. Most of the telegrams were from ILD and Communists, or their supporters, demanding release of the Scottsboro Boys and decrying the racial and political injustices in the South. Horton tried to diffuse the impact of the telegrams on the proceedings by saying to the jurors:

> Things may vex you. I might say that the court may have been vexed about a great many things. It may have been evident to you that a great many telegrams came in here to me since I have been here. But, gentlemen, they do not affect me whatever or the great principle which the court desires to see done, and that is to see justice done in this case.

Horton closed his remarks to the jury with a statement that could have come only from his heart.

> We are a white race and a Negro race here together—we are here to live together—our interests are together. The world at this time and in many lands is showing intolerance and showing hate. It seems sometimes that love has almost deserted the human bosom. It seems that only hate has taken its place. It is only for a time, gentlemen, because it is the great things in life, God's great principles, matters of eternal right, that alone live. Wrong dies and truth forever lasts, and we should have faith in that.

At 12:45 p.m., Judge Horton gave the case to the jury, and they began their deliberations in the same small anteroom used by defense witnesses during the trial. Since the trial of Charlie Weems was scheduled to immediately follow Patterson's trial, Leibowitz asked Judge Horton to postpone Weems's trial until Monday, April 17, to give the defense time to better prepare for his case and to prepare a motion for a change of venue to Birmingham. After Horton agreed to the postponement, the courtroom quickly emptied except for the lawyers who collected their papers and discussed Judge Horton's jury instructions, and the reporters who were busy working on their stories for tomorrow's newspapers.

Haywood Patterson was taken back to the Decatur jail, and he explained to the other boys the day's proceedings. Haywood had already told the boys they had the finest, smartest attorney he had ever seen in Samuel Leibowitz, and now he explained to them how fair Judge Horton had been in what he told the jury to consider in reaching a verdict. While the boys waited anxiously for Haywood's verdict, they began to sing spirituals as they did most evenings. In particular, Olen Montgomery and Ozie Powell had good voices and loved to sing, and the National Guard troops assigned to the jail would request songs for a cigarette or some whiskey. The boys sang old favorites throughout the afternoon and into the early evening, songs like "Let's Go Down to Jordan" and "I'm on the Battlefield for My Lord." Later that evening, all the boys awaiting trial were taken back to the higher security Birmingham jail for safekeeping. Haywood was left alone with the guards to think about the verdict to come. At 11:35 p.m., the jury advised Horton that they had not reached a verdict, and Horton ordered the jury locked up in their hotel rooms for the night.

First Decatur Trial—Sunday, April 9, 1933

At ten o'clock Sunday morning, Palm Sunday, April 9, Judge Horton received a phone call in his Athens home with the news that the jury had reached a verdict. He hurried to complete dressing and was in the Decatur courtroom before eleven o'clock. Patterson, the lawyers, and the reporters were already in the courtroom when Horton arrived; however, the spectator seats were only half occupied, as the Sunday church hour was approaching in Decatur. Horton had the jury brought in. The entire courtroom was quiet and tense, and, while a few of the jurors were smiling as they entered the courtroom, they immediately tensed up when they saw the demeanor of the courtroom. Horton had the court clerk bring the jury's decision to him, and he read to the courtroom that the jury had found the defendant guilty and set the punishment as death in the electric chair. The courtroom was silent, Leibowitz slumped back in his chair as if he had been run through with a rapier, and Patterson sat stoically smoking a cigarette, not showing any emotion. Patterson understood more than anyone else in the courtroom the depths of racial prejudice that led to this verdict.

After the verdict was rendered, Judge Horton stated he would sentence Patterson the next day, Monday, April 10. The defense lawyers explained they would not be available during the following week, and Judge Horton postponed the sentencing to April 17 with Attorney General Knight's concurrence.

Judge Horton thanked the jurors for their efforts and called the proceedings to a close. Leibowitz told Judge Horton he was "one of the finest jurists I have ever met." He added, "I believe wholeheartedly that if the verdict in this case had been left to your Honor, this Negro would have been acquitted."

After the court was adjourned, jury members told the press they voted unanimously for a guilty verdict a few minutes after they started their deliberations. They said they did not even consider the testimony of Ruby Bates, yet chose instead to believe Victoria Price. The only holdup to a final verdict was the question of the punishment; one juror held out for life imprisonment, but finally yielded to the other eleven and agreed to the death penalty on the third ballot.

Haywood Patterson was taken back to the Decatur jail, transferred to a police vehicle, and taken to the Birmingham jail to join the other boys.

Leibowitz and his wife, Belle, started their return trip to New York City. Courtroom spectators returned to their Palm Sunday activities, satisfied that justice had been done.

Monday through Sunday, April 10–April 16, 1933

A crowd of over three thousand people greeted Samuel Leibowitz at New York City's Pennsylvania Station. Even though he didn't win an acquittal in the case, he was treated as a returning conquering hero and carried out of the station on the shoulders of the crowd as they chanted his name. When asked by a *New York Herald Tribune* reporter what he thought of the jury in this case, Samuel Leibowitz lost his composure for the first time in his legal career and exploded in an emotional outburst, "If you ever saw those creatures—those bigots whose mouths are slits in their faces, whose eyes pop out like a frog's, whose chins drip tobacco juice, bewhiskered and filthy, you would not ask how they could do it." Leibowitz knew he had made a huge mistake soon after he made his remarks.

There were meetings throughout New York City the remainder of the week, including a rally in a Harlem church with four thousand in attendance, and a mass meeting in Brooklyn with about the same number. Of course, southern newspapers reported on all these activities, but most damning to Leibowitz and the defense were the articles and reactions to his ill-chosen words to the *Herald Tribune* reporter.

Monday, April 17, 1933

Monday morning, April 17, Judge Horton called the courtroom to order. Joseph Brodsky and George Chamlee were present for the defense, and Attorney General Knight represented the state. Samuel Leibowitz was preparing to board a train in New York City for his trip to Decatur and the start of the trial of Charlie Weems.

The first order of business was the sentencing of Haywood Patterson. Horton asked him if he had a statement. Patterson replied, "I ain't had a fair trial. Ain't seen no girls on that train." Horton told Patterson the jury disagreed and had found him guilty, and he did what Alabama law required a judge to do with a jury verdict that also fixed the punishment; Horton sentenced Patterson to die in the electric chair in Kilby Prison on June 16, 1933. Brodsky immediately filed a notice of appeal along with an incomplete motion for a new trial. Horton dismissed Brodsky's appeal, saying he would not accept an incomplete motion.

Horton called for the Weems's trial jury-selection process, but before anything was put into motion, he said he was quite bothered by Leibowitz's rash comments to a New York reporter the week before. Horton said he didn't know if Leibowitz had made the comments, but their very existence made a fair and just trial impossible. Horton then ordered a continuance of the case until such time as he was convinced a fair and impartial trail could be had.

Judge Horton had stopped Charlie Weems's trial and the trials of any of the other boys. He also put Patterson's June 16 execution on hold until a hearing was held on the pending defense motion for a new trial. Horton then called Knight to task for an inflammatory statement attributed to Knight in a Decatur newspaper, saying Knight's statement only added to the tense atmosphere in the community and the court. Knight leapt to his feet when Judge Horton concluded and said he had no apologies for his statement to the newspaper, as Leibowitz's statement was the "wail of a contemptible loser" to the people of Morgan County and the Patterson jury.

After Horton ended the court session, Haywood Patterson and Charlie Weems were removed from the courtroom under heavy guard and returned to the Birmingham jail that evening. Leibowitz heard about Judge Horton's decision to postpone Weems's trial before his train left the New York City area, and he was able to get off at a transfer station and return home to consider his next move.

12.

A REMARKABLE DAY
1933

Birmingham Jail

CLARENCE WAS ABOUT TO GO NUTS sitting in the Decatur jail day after day while Haywood's trial unfolded. Clarence did receive money from both the ILD and in letters from all over the world, and he used the money to buy cigarettes and shots of whiskey from the Decatur guards. But he missed that nice brown-skinned girl in the Birmingham jail, so he was delighted when he realized all the boys were being returned to Birmingham. All, that is, except Haywood, and then Clarence felt bad about Haywood being left alone in the Decatur "hellhole" of a jail to face the "crackers." It's difficult to characterize a jail as a place you'd rather be, but compared to the jails in Scottsboro, Gadsden, and Decatur, and Kilby Prison, the boys came to consider the Birmingham jail a "convict's paradise." They learned if you had money, "You could buy women, clothes, food, liquor, whatever" with the help of the guards.

One night after Clarence got back to the Birmingham jail, he gave his guard three dollars to go to the women's section of the jail and bring Ernestine to his cell for a few hours of female companionship and sex. Ernestine was Clarence's beautiful brown-skinned girl who was serving twenty years for murder. Clarence bought her an iron, and she not only served his sexual appetite, she also ironed his clothes. Although Clarence was happy for her when she got her parole a few months later, he missed his sexual trysts until he established an arrangement with another young lady named Lillian.

After Haywood Patterson and Charlie Weems were returned to the Birmingham jail on April 17, 1933, everything changed. The guards, upset at yet another delay in the trials for the boys, cut off most of their privileges—visitors, special food, liquor, and women—and started harassing the boys again. The next day, the boys refused to push their breakfast trays out through the small slot in the bottom of their cell doors. When the guards tried to come into the cells to get the trays, Haywood set his bed on fire, and the boys were herded into a dayroom. Unknowingly, the guards had played into the boys' hands. The boys had fashioned weapons out of the plumbing in their cells, and they had knives they had purchased from the jail trustees. The boys were now in a group, armed, and prepared to fight the guards if necessary. The Jefferson County sheriff finally joined the outbreak and ordered the jail guards to keep the boys locked up in the dayroom, to ignore them, and not to feed them. After two days of this impasse, the boys and the sheriff reached an agreement to end the stalemate: the boys surrendered their weapons, and the sheriff guaranteed good treatment. The sheriff lived up to his word, and that night the boys were served the best meal they ever had in the Birmingham jail. Clarence later wrote about life in the Birmingham jail, saying, "Life is funny, we would laugh about it. We had the death sentence over our heads, but we were eating and dressing better than a lot of men on the outside, including our guards...But I would much rather have been on the outside looking in."

Pawns in Ideological and Political Disputes

AFTER JUDGE HORTON'S RULING ON APRIL 17, he announced that on June 22, 1933, he would hear defense motions for a new trial for Patterson and a change of venue for Weems's trial. Although all the parties involved in the case should have welcomed a brief respite from the extremely combative and grueling Patterson trial, over the next nine weeks, the exchanges and actions between the parties intensified. The ideological positions and interests of the parties and some individuals were more paramount than the innocence, guilt, or lives of the Scottsboro Boys, now mere pawns in a larger game.

Leibowitz wrote a letter to Horton saying the postponement was welcomed by both sides and said he planned to bring the case before the United States Supreme Court on the issue of race discrimination. However, he took strong issue with Horton's use of his New York City statement as the reason for the postponement, saying, "The sentiment expressed by many of the unthinking in your State that a Negro is a chattel and that he can be referred to as 'my n-----' just as the master refers to 'my dog' is symbolical of that attitude which excludes worthy citizens from service upon juries solely because their skins are black."

The ILD and NAACP did not sit idly by through this latest contretemps. The ILD issued a statement charging the reason for the postponements "was solely the tremendous world protest against the lynch verdict handed down against Haywood Patterson." The ILD organized a huge protest march in Washington, DC, on May 7 with Ruby Bates and Lester Carter in attendance; however, the protest became more about Communist Party issues and positions than about the plight of the Scottsboro Boys. The NAACP, while still not directly involved in the boys' defense, issued its own statement, saying it was necessary to "remove from the already overwhelming prejudices which militate against them the additional burden of communism." The ILD responded that the NAACP had made every "effort to do what the white lynch gangs have tried to do and failed—eliminate the one organization, the International Labor Defense, which has thus far prevented the murder of these innocent victims…" Even while the rhetoric was flying between the ILD and NAACP, negotiations between the two parties and Leibowitz were being conducted, resulting in an agreement whereby the NAACP agreed to help pay for the future legal costs of defending the boys.

The opinion of the press continued divided along the Mason-Dixon Line, although a number of southern newspapers outside of Alabama started to agree that the boys were innocent. The only newspaper of note in Alabama to change its view after the Patterson trial was the *Birmingham Post*, which stated that Patterson should not have been found guilty since the defense raised a number of reasonable doubt issues. The *Post* added, "We love justice enough to want it done regardless of the fact it may seem to play into the hands of unfair radicals."

Prior to the trial in Decatur, three white, prominent Alabamians formed a small group in support of the Scottsboro Boys and their defense: Kenneth Barnhart, a professor of sociology at Birmingham-Southern College; Rabbi Benjamin Goldstein of Temple Beth Or in Montgomery; and Dr. Henry Edmonds, founder and pastor of the Independent Presbyterian Church in Birmingham and chairman of the Alabama Interracial Committee. The three men met often to discuss how best to organize support for the boys, given the racist and political attitudes of most Alabamians concerning the case. On March 26, all three spoke at a Birmingham rally for the boys in a Negro church. Barnhart wanted to see the boys get a "square deal," and the state to abide by the Fourteenth and Fifteenth Amendments to the U.S. Constitution instead of ignoring them. Goldstein and Edmonds supported the ILD in its defense of the boys and called upon all in attendance to contribute to the ILD defense fund.

The reactions of the bodies these three gentlemen served were swift and conclusive. Barnhart was denied employment by Birmingham-Southern College for the academic year 1933–34, and Goldstein was forced to move to New York City by his Montgomery congregation and local politicians.

Edmonds yielded to angry criticisms from Alabama Interracial Committee members for his ILD supportive statements by conceding he had gone "too far." Edmonds was also protected by his high standing in Birmingham religious circles and the community for the social outreach programs he had created in the area.

Two other prominent white Alabamians were ostracized and forced to leave the state over the Scottsboro case: Mary Craik Speed, a descendant of a distinguished Black Belt family, and her daughter, June. Mrs. Speed was a disciple of Norman Thomas, the socialist, pacifist, and six-time presidential candidate of the Socialist Party of America. Mrs. Speed and June became interested in the case in 1931 and by 1933, were supporting the ILD. Twenty-three-year-old June was addressing a May Day rally in Birmingham in 1933, when she was arrested for disorderly conduct and speaking without a permit. She refused to pay the fine of fifty dollars, choosing instead to serve fifty-three days of a one-hundred-day sentence. Upon release from jail, she and her mother immediately moved from the state.

Attorney General Thomas Knight kept a careful eye on his political future and ambitions. He planned to run for lieutenant governor in the 1934 elections, and it was reported he would run for governor in 1938. He closely monitored the developments in the Scottsboro case, as he believed his future political aspirations were closely tied to a successful prosecution of the boys.

In 1932, the ILD lawyers had planned to file a writ of *habeas corpus* in an attempt to get Roy Wright and Eugene Williams released from jail under a bond. The appeal never came to pass because of a disagreement over payment between the ILD lawyers and the Birmingham attorney they hired to handle the appeal. The two boys' statuses had been in limbo since that time; however, Judge Horton was granted authority to hold a hearing on June 2, 1933, where he assigned Roy and Eugene over to juvenile court, formally breaking their cases away from the other seven boys.

Otherwise, while the turmoil continued among the various parties and factions involved in and surrounding the Scottsboro Boys, Judge Horton spent most of his time in his Athens home and office, as if in the quiet eye of a storm, thinking about Patterson's trial. He was preparing for the June 22 hearing, and it was no secret he had reservations about the guilty verdict. As he pondered his position, he even approached Knight and asked the Attorney General to agree to *nol pros* in any future proceedings (an agreement whereby the prosecution agrees to proceed no further in a case) along with a pardon for Patterson. Knight initially said he would consider it but finally rejected the suggestion, indicating that the state fully intended to proceed with the prosecutions. Knight's response did not surprise Horton.

A Remarkable Day in an Alabama Courtroom

ON JUNE 22, 1933, Judge Horton called the Athens courtroom to order to hear the defense motion for a new trial. The Athens courtroom was full with spectators and reporters, and was used for the hearing because the Decatur courtroom was in a previously scheduled session. George Chamlee and Osmund Fraenkel, a noted constitutional lawyer, represented the defense and Attorney General Thomas Knight represented the prosecution. Samuel Leibowitz did not bother to attend the hearing since the defense fully expected Horton to deny their motion, necessitating an appeal to the next higher court.

As soon as Judge Horton took his seat, he said he would hear no preliminary arguments and immediately began reading a prepared statement. It would take Horton over an hour to read his eighteen-page statement as he opened with:

> The case is now submitted for hearing on a motion for a new trial. As human life is at stake, not only of this defendant, but of eight others, the Court does and should approach a consideration of this motion with a feeling of deep responsibility, and shall endeavor to give it that thought and study it deserves.

> Social order is based on law, and its perpetuity on its fair and impartial administration. Deliberate injustice is more fatal to the one who imposes than to the one on whom it is imposed… The law wisely recognizes the passions, prejudices and sympathies that such cases as these naturally arouse, but sternly requires of its Ministers freedom from such actuating impulses.

Horton then proceeded to read what was obviously not a statement, but a decision, and, as he read, smiles broke out on the faces of Chamlee and Fraenkel; Knight was clearly agitated, as his face turned a bright red.

The courtroom was absolutely quiet as Horton read a carefully thought out and crafted decision. He made it clear he would not rule on the specific details of the defense motion, but rather, "The vital ground of this motion, as the Court sees it, is whether or not the verdict of the jury is contrary to the evidence. Is there sufficient credible evidence upon which to base a verdict?" Before dealing with that question, he put forth a number of prior court rulings of both the Alabama and U.S. Supreme Courts, supporting setting aside verdicts of juries when the verdict is contrary to the evidence. One decision by the Alabama Supreme Court even noted that juries, while not consciously violating their duty, could be moved by passion, bias, or prejudice to render an incorrect verdict.

Horton presented his examination of the testimony and the evidence in such a well-organized and well-presented manner that the outcome of his analysis was never in doubt. He summarized the background of the case, the earlier trial at Scottsboro, and the recently concluded trial at Decatur. He then explained that the key prosecution witness to the alleged rapes was the alleged victim, Victoria Price, and he stated that if Price's accusations and testimony were true, it should have been possible to corroborate important elements of her claims. Horton expanded on this rationale, saying:

> With seven boys present at the beginning of this trouble, with one seeing the entire affair, with some fifty or sixty persons meeting them at Paint Rock and taking the women, the white boy, Gilley, and the nine Negroes in charge, with two physicians examining the women within one to one and one half hours, according to the tendency of all the evidence, after the occurrence of the alleged rape, and with the acts charged committed in broad day light, we should expect from all this cloud of witnesses or from the mute but telling physical condition of the women or their clothes some one fact in corroboration of this story.

Horton listed nine issues in "the rich field from which such corroboration may be gleaned," and he proceeded to summarize how he searched for testimony that either corroborated or contradicted Price's testimony.

First, he looked for testimony from the "seven white boys on the gondola at the beginning of the fight, and Orville Gilley, the white boy, who remained on the train, and who saw the whole performance." Horton noted that the prosecution called none of the seven white boys, including Orville Gilley who supposedly witnessed the rapes, to the witness chair. The defense did call Lester Carter, the white boy who jumped off the train when the fight started, and his testimony contradicted Price's.

Second, Horton asked, "Next was Victoria Price hit in the head with a pistol?" Dr. Bridges said Price did not call his attention to a head wound during his examination, and he found no wound on Price's head.

Third, Horton asked, "Next, was she thrown and abused, as she states she was, upon the chert—the sharp, jagged rock?" Again, Dr. Bridges testified he found no laceration or bleeding on Price's back, only a few small bruises that appeared to be a few days old. Horton accepted Lester Carter's testimony to conclude these bruises were likely the result of Price's sexual activity with Jack Tiller the night before she left Huntsville for Chattanooga, and the night she spent in the Chattanooga hobo jungle likely having sex with Orville Gilley.

Fourth, Horton explored the "semen in the vagina and its drying and starchy appearance in the pubic hair and surrounding parts." Dr. Bridges testified he found patches of semen, which were more or less dry, encrusted in heavy dirt and dust on Price's inner thighs. In examining her vagina for semen, he found none or little in the walls of her vagina, but rather had to reach with a swab back to her cervix to extract even a microscopic amount of semen. Price had testified she was repeatedly raped, and her private parts became "wetter and wetter." Horton concluded this part of Dr. Bridge's testimony did not corroborate Price's; in fact, it contradicted it.

Fifth, Horton asked, "What of the coat of the woman spattered with semen, and the blood and semen on the clothes and the bleeding vagina?" These were all things Price claimed she suffered as a result of the rapes. Horton noted that Dr. Bridges said he did not see any blood coming from Price's vagina. She mentioned nothing to Dr. Bridges about semen or blood on her coat or dress, and Dr. Bridges observed none during his examination. Again, there was no corroboration of Price's testimony.

Sixth, Horton asked "What of the physical appearance of these two women when the doctors saw them?" Dr. Bridges testified that the women were neither hysterical nor nervous when they came to his office, and their respiration and pulse were normal. Horton noted one would not expect such normal physical attributes after the horrible experience the women claimed to have endured.

Seventh, Horton asked, "Was there any evidence of semen on the clothes of any of the Negroes?" Assuming the six boys repeatedly raped Price, as she claimed, it is entirely logical to assume there would have been some spots of semen on at least some of their clothes. The arresting officers at the train examined the boys' clothes and pants, and not one witness testified at the trial "as to seeing any semen or even any wet or damp spots on their clothes."

Eighth, Horton explored the likelihood that live, or motile, spermatozoa, would have been found in the vagina of a woman from so many recent semen discharges. Again, Horton turned to Dr. Bridges' testimony. The doctor testified the spermatozoa he examined from the small sample of semen he was able to extract from around Price's cervix was non-motile, or dead. He said spermatozoa survive the longest in areas around the cervix and can survive for days, certainly for several hours. Horton, again referring to the fact that Price had sex the two nights before she boarded the train, said, it "becomes clearer and clearer that this woman was not forced into intercourse with all these Negroes upon that train, but that her condition was clearly due to the intercourse that she had had on the nights previous to this time."

And ninth, Horton said the claims of Price that her clothes were stained with semen and blood could not be corroborated. None of the witnesses, including Dr. Bridges, testified to seeing any such stains on her clothing, and Price washed her clothing before the Scottsboro trials started, so the purported evidence had effectively been destroyed.

Horton then explored the testimony of the state's witness and, finding no corroboration for Price's testimony, concluded "her evidence is so contradictory to the evidence of the doctors who examined her that it has been impossible for the Court to reconcile their evidence with hers." Horton didn't stop here; he then asked, "Next was the evidence of Victoria Price reasonable or probable? Were the facts stated reasonable?" After a further discussion of her testimony, he concluded, "Her manner of testifying and demeanor on the stand militate against her. Her testimony was contradictory, often evasive, and time and again she refused to answer pertinent questions…the proof tends strongly to show that she knowingly testified falsely in many material aspects of the case."

Only once in his decision did Horton refer to the testimony of Ruby Bates when he wrote, "…a statement by Ruby Bates that she had been raped which experience the said Ruby Bates now repudiates." Horton purposely avoided using Bates's testimony as a justification for his decision, as he probably considered her an unreliable witness because of her poor performance on the witness stand, and he likely felt his decision would be considered stronger and received better if he ignored her completely.

Judge Horton concluded with some strong language directed at his view of the character and motives of the two women as he set forth his decision:

> History, sacred and profane, and the common experience of mankind teach us that women of the character shown in this case are prone for selfish reasons to make false accusations both of rape and of insult upon the slightest provocation, or even without provocation for ulterior purposes. These women are shown, by the great weight of evidence, on this very day before leaving Chattanooga to have falsely accused two Negroes of insulting them, and of almost precipitating a fight between one of the white boys they were in company with and these two Negroes. This tendency on the part of the women show that they are pre-disposed to make false accusations upon any occasion whereby their selfish ends may be gained…

> The testimony of the prosecutrix in this case is not only uncorroborated, but is also bears on its face indications of improbability and is contradicted by other evidence, and in addition thereto the evidence greatly preponderates in favor of the defendant. It, therefore, becomes the duty of the Court under the law to grant the motion made in this case…

It is, therefore, ordered, and adjudged by the Court that the motion be granted; that the verdict of the jury in this cause [case], and the judgment of the Court sentencing this defendant is hereby vacated and set aside and a new trial is ordered.

The courtroom sat silent and stunned. Chamlee and Fraenkel couldn't contain their joy at the decision as they smiled broadly at one another, but Knight continued to seethe and burn red. After the court was adjourned, Knight declared in a trembling voice that the state would proceed with a new trial of Patterson, possibly as early as September 1.

———————

WELL BEFORE JUDGE HORTON held his court hearing on June 22, Knight sent a person from his office to talk to Horton about the upcoming hearing. This representative explained to Horton that Knight and the state intended to pursue the case because a *nol pros* withdrawal, as Horton had suggested, would be tantamount to surrender to the Communists and their socialist agenda. He then threatened Horton that if he overturned the jury's verdict, he would not likely be reelected to the bench in 1934.

Jim Ed smiled wryly at Knight's representative and replied, "What does that have to do with the case?"

13.

BACK TO BUSINESS AS USUAL
1933

The Fallout from Judge Horton's Decision

JUDGE HORTON'S DECISION created a wide range of reactions all over the map and the political spectrum; he was alternately praised and pilloried from many quarters. The northern press was effusive in their support of his decision with the exception of the *Daily Worker*, which continued to call Horton the "chief lyncher." A number of southern newspapers agreed with Horton's decision, although with less abandon. Alabama newspapers were adamantly opposed to the decision; the one exception was the *Birmingham Post*, which agreed with his decision that the boys were innocent and praised Horton by saying, "...political considerations mean nothing to him whatever." Several prominent Alabamians supported Horton's decision, including the incoming president of the Alabama Bar Association, Leo Oberdorfer. However, this seeming groundswell of support for Horton's decision wilted against state officials who made it abundantly clear they intended to pursue the prosecutions of the Scottsboro Boys. The fact is the boys were effectively not much better off than they were before Horton's decision. They were still in jail, future trials awaited them, and the threat of the death penalty was as real as ever.

One valid criticism was leveled at Judge Horton concerning his decision. Many asked why he didn't just throw the case out altogether if he felt so strongly about the facts, as he detailed in his decision. Horton certainly seemed to think this would be appropriate given his request to Knight to *nol pros* the case and pardon Patterson. Horton also hoped Knight would decide not to continue the prosecution once his decision was made public. Possibly, Horton thought a future jury couldn't possibly find the boys guilty faced with the facts in his decision. If Judge Horton had thrown the case out, a remarkable day in an Alabama courtroom would have been extraordinary. As it was, all of Horton's assumptions about the future of the case proved to be wrong.

The day after Horton rendered his decision, Attorney General Knight announced that Orville Gilley would testify at the next trial. He said Gilley had returned from California, volunteered to testify, and had signed an affidavit supporting all the details in Victoria Price's testimony. Knight was also determined to see that Judge Horton not be the judge at the next Patterson trial. To engineer this change, Knight got the support of Alabama Supreme Court Chief Justice John Anderson. Anderson wrote Horton, asking him to step aside voluntarily. At first Horton resisted, but in October 1933, he reluctantly acquiesced to the Chief Justice and withdrew from the case. Judge William Callahan, the other judge in Horton's Eighth Circuit Court, was immediately assigned to handle the case.

The Prejudicial Judge—William W. Callahan

WILLIAM CALLAHAN, a seventy-year-old Decatur resident, was the antithesis of James Horton Jr. in his background, education, legal training, and personal and courtroom personas. On the eve of the Battle of Gettysburg, during the Civil War, June 30, 1863, William Washington Callahan was born on a small farm in Lawrence County, the county just west of Morgan County. His childhood was spent on the farm, and his formal education ended with high school. He found work in a local law office, and, as one could still do at that time, he read law as he worked and was admitted to the bar in 1886. He first worked as a lawyer and was then a member of the Alabama legislature as a state representative until he was elected a judge in the Eighth Circuit Court in 1928, the same year James Horton was reelected unopposed. The characteristics Morgan County residents associated with Callahan leave the impression that he was a "good old boy" in all the senses of the phrase. He was known in the community as a good storyteller and was thought to have good "common sense." His courtroom persona matched the widely held views of those outside the South of the southern judge: prejudicial, demanding, and unyielding. Attorney General Knight had gotten exactly what he wanted in a trial judge.

The Second and Third Decatur Trials

WITH THE ASCENSION of Judge Callahan to the throne of the Decatur courtroom, the trials could now proceed without abandon in the racially charged, anti-Semitic, anti-Communistic atmosphere of the 1930's South. Leibowitz and the defense team soon realized they were now facing two chief prosecutors: Attorney General Knight and Judge Callahan. They would find themselves hopelessly thwarted at every turn in Callahan's courtroom with a future appeal their only alternative to the inevitable outcome.

The witnesses in the new trials were the same as in Patterson's previous trial with a few exceptions: Ruby Bates wouldn't respond to Knight's subpoena to testify, fearing for her life if she returned to Decatur, so the court agreed to let her testify by deposition; Orville Gilley was a new witness for the prosecution; the defense had to call Dr. Bridges to get his medical testimony in front of the jury because the prosecution chose not to call him to avoid a lengthy cross-examination. Judge Callahan set out to make his courtroom a much different atmosphere than Judge Horton's. Callahan banned all cameras and typewriters from the courtroom and around the courthouse, and required the press to sit behind the rail, denying them the prime seating they enjoyed in Horton's courtroom. Callahan told the governor he did not want or need the National Guard around or in the courtroom, since he knew the good people of Morgan County would not cause any trouble.

Samuel Leibowitz and Joseph Brodsky arrived in Decatur accompanied by two New York City policemen. The men weighed about 250 pounds each and were assigned to them as bodyguards. They found the situation much more tense and fraught with danger than prior to the first Decatur trial. Since the last trial, there had been an alarming increase in the number of racial lynchings and killings in Alabama and nearby states. In July, three black men from Tuscaloosa were accused of raping and killing a twenty-one-year-old woman. When the ILD sent lawyers to Tuscaloosa to defend the men, an angry local mob formed near the courthouse and denounced the presence of the Communists in their community. A National Guard unit had to be called to escort the three ILD lawyers safely out of town. Tuscaloosa police then took the three black men to a secluded spot in the county and turned them over to a firing squad. Two of the men died; one survived but was later forced to leave the county. None of the police or members of the firing squad were ever prosecuted. In Tuscaloosa in September, a mentally retarded white woman accused an aging black man of rape. The police, after investigating the accusation and finding it lacking, dismissed the charges and released the black man, but seven white men came to his house and shot him to death. Recent lynchings also occurred in Georgia, Louisiana, Maryland, Mississippi, North Carolina, South Carolina, and Texas. During the trial, there were lynchings in Missouri and Tennessee. The situation appeared to be out of hand and dangerous, yet Callahan resisted all requests for additional police and National Guard.

Before the trials started, Leibowitz, Brodsky, and Chamlee became so concerned about the situation they sent a telegram to Clarence Norris's former employer in Warm Springs, Georgia. Besides the other lynchings that had recently occurred in Alabama and other states, their telegram said that "a Negro named Royal was lynched in very city of Decatur in August and a mob visited the Decatur jail to lynch a prisoner named Brown. Only removal to Huntsville jail before mob arrived prevented his assassination." The three defense counselors urged Franklin Delano Roosevelt's intervention with Alabama Governor Miller, requesting adequate protection for themselves and their clients. Roosevelt, who was inaugurated President on March 4, 1933, did not respond to their telegram and took no action with the governor.

Patterson and Norris Pretrial Hearing—November 20–25, 1933

On Monday, November 20, 1933, against this backdrop of fear and denial, Judge Callahan opened the hearing preceding Patterson's trial. The seven boys were brought into the courtroom to face, what must have seemed to them, round six in an endless prizefight. Roy Wright and Eugene Williams were left in the Birmingham jail, as they were now officially under custody of the juvenile court. Callahan had finally yielded to the pressure from the governor for more security by agreeing to the assignment of nineteen armed, civilian-clad deputies to the court. The men had been recruited in the Birmingham area for this purpose, and Callahan immediately assigned two of them as personal guards for Leibowitz, instructing the men to accompany him everywhere, adding, "I mean everywhere, too."

The courtroom was only half full of spectators, as Knight and others had asked the residents of Morgan County not to come to the courtroom in hopes this would help take some of the publicity off the trial. Callahan learned that two photographers had taken pictures in front of the courthouse in violation of his order. He had the two brought into the courtroom and threatened them with a contempt of court citation if they took additional pictures, saying, "There ain't going to be no more picture snappin' around here."

The first day of the hearing then started with Leibowitz making a motion asking the court to grant a change of venue. To support his contention that a change of venue was necessary, Leibowitz presented six affidavits to the court containing the results of over five hundred interviews with residents of Morgan County about their opinions of the Scottsboro Boys trials. Before he left New York, Joseph Brodsky had asked a twenty-seven-year-old New York lawyer named David Schriftman to come to Decatur to conduct the interview survey. When Schriftman agreed to come, Brodsky added, "Be careful, be careful David."

Schriftman drove his high-mileage Chevy roadster to Alabama alone and wisely decided to change his New York license plates to Tennessee plates. After arriving in Decatur, he hired three Southerners to help him with the survey. Schriftman even adopted a southern style of speech, which he later said, "I must admit, I was pretty good at." The four men fanned out over Decatur and the county, posing as salesmen of household products. Schriftman was stunned by the hostility, hatred, and threats of violence in all the interviewees' responses. Ruby Bates and Samuel Leibowitz were the prime targets of most of the vitriolic anger: Bates for recanting her testimony, and Leibowitz for being "the Jew lawyer from New York." Schriftman had also filed an affidavit with the court stating that, in his opinion, an impartial jury could not be found in Morgan County, and that the defense lawyers' lives were in danger. One Decatur resident had said, "If them lawyers, especially that Jew lawyer, Leibowitz, comes here, it will be a one-way trip…He will never go back to New York if he comes here again and we'll take the others, too."

At the hearing, Attorney General Knight demanded that Brodsky and Schriftman take the stand. Knight was particularly vicious in his cross-examination of Schriftman, challenging his methods and the validity of the interviewee-selection process, and the responses in the affidavits. Schriftman later said of Knight, "It was very apparent, to me, that he had put the mark on me as a potential special victim. Little did I realize the extent to which he would go to accomplish that." The prosecution then presented to the court a large number of affidavits from Morgan County residents stating they had no prejudice against either the defendants or their lawyers.

The second day of the hearing, November 21, Callahan denied the defense's motion for change of venue, stating the defense had failed to prove their charge that local prejudice precluded a fair trial. Leibowitz then again entered two separate motions to quash the indictments issued in Morgan County and Jackson County, alleging that the jury commissioners in both counties excluded blacks from the jury rolls in violation of the Fourteenth Amendment. Callahan agreed to accept the evidence the defense had put forth in Horton's court on the Morgan County motion and then adjourned the court until Thursday, saying he wanted to study the motions and the evidence on Wednesday. When court was reconvened on Thursday, November 24, Callahan announced he was denying the motion to quash the Morgan County indictments, saying he was not convinced the evidence supported the defense's contention that the Fourteenth Amendment had been violated. On the Jackson County motion, Leibowitz called for the county's jury rolls and got the court to agree to have all the names read along with their racial classification. After several boring hours of reading the rolls, to everyone's surprise in the courtroom, the clerk read aloud, "Hugh Sanford. He's a Negro."

Over the remainder of the day and part of the next, six names of men who were identified as black were found on the rolls. Leibowitz believed the names were added after the fact and arranged for a handwriting expert to come from New York to examine the rolls. On Saturday, November 25, the handwriting expert arrived in Decatur, spent several hours examining the jury rolls under a powerful microscope, testified the names had been added after the March 1931 Grand Jury names had been chosen from the rolls leading to the indictment, and identified the clerk who wrote the names in the rolls by analyzing handwriting samples. However, the expert lost all credibility with the court and the spectators when he testified he was paid fifty dollars a day by the defense for his services. Judge Callahan denied the defense motion, saying the expert witness's testimony had made a confusing issue even more confusing and adding he could not impugn the Jackson County officials without more substantive evidence. Callahan concluded the hearing and said Patterson's trial would start first thing Monday morning, adding he wanted the attorneys to wrap up the case in three days.

Patterson's Second Decatur Trial—November 27–30, 1933

Monday morning, November 27, Haywood Patterson was brought into the Decatur courtroom to begin his third trial. Callahan did everything he could to move the trial along, generally at the expense of Leibowitz and the defense team. The jury was selected by three o'clock that afternoon, with Callahan prodding Leibowitz to "hurry it along" and "that's enough on that" as he questioned prospective jurors. The ILD was delighted with the proletarian makeup of the jury, but Leibowitz was decidedly unhappy with the jury: nine farmers, a truck driver, a house painter, and a merchant. He knew this jury was much like the jury in the last Patterson trial: an undereducated group of white men who could be easily influenced by their racial and anti-Semitic biases.

Soon after the jury was sworn in, Victoria Price was called to testify for the prosecution for the sixth time, and she repeated the story and accusations she had made in all the preceding trials. A new prosecution mantra did start to appear early in Price's testimony today. When asked what one of the black boys yelled as they jumped into the gondola to fight the white boys, she replied, "All you white sons-of-bitches unload."

As soon as Leibowitz started to cross-examine Price, the tenor of the trial was set; Callahan did not allow Leibowitz to ask any questions pertaining to Price's past, her relationship with Jack Tiller or Orville Gilley, or to probe the time the girls spent in the hobo jungles in Huntsville and Chattanooga. Throughout Patterson's trial, Callahan consistently sustained

Knight's objections and overruled Leibowitz's. Even more controlling, Callahan acted like both a prosecutor and a judge by disallowing Leibowitz's questions to witnesses before Knight had entered an objection on behalf of the state. The proceedings became nothing more than a kangaroo court with Callahan constantly interrupting Leibowitz with admonitions like "treat the lady with more respect," and "The more I shut you off, the better shape you're in." He directed Leibowitz's questioning, saying "Let's don't take up time on that; that is a waste of time," and "go on to something else."

Orville Gilley took the stand for the prosecution and was an engaging young man; when asked if he was a hobo, he described himself as "an entertainer. I recite poetry and take up collections." He upheld all the essential facts in Victoria Price's testimony. When asked early in his direct examination if he heard any exclamations from any of the black boys as they jumped into the gondola to fight the white boys, he responded exactly as Price had, saying he heard one of them say, "All you white sons-of-bitches unload." Leibowitz tried to show that the state coerced Gilley to testify with a carrot and stick approach; the carrot was money he was paid by the state, and the stick was a threat of prosecution. Leibowitz's line of questioning appeared to have little impact on the court or jury.

The other witnesses' testimonies were quite similar to the earlier trials, and, although Dr. Bridges and Lester Carter repeated their favorable testimonies for the defense, Callahan repeatedly prevented Leibowitz from using it to the defense's benefit. During Leibowitz's examination of Carter, he tried to question Carter about the nights Carter was with Victoria and Ruby preceding March 25, 1931. Callahan continually prohibited Leibowitz from pursuing this line of questioning, finally exclaiming to Leibowitz that his questions were no more than "a vicious attempt to get something before the jury that I have ruled is improper."

Closing arguments started on November 29 with comments from the prosecution, first by Morgan County Solicitor Wade Wright and then by Jackson County Solicitor H. G. Bailey. Wright was his usual bombastic self, but he did refrain from issuing an anti-Semitic remark as he had at the first Decatur trial of Patterson. Bailey was more subdued as he asked for a guilty verdict on the evidence. Both men referred to the statement attributed to one of the black boys, "All you white sons-of-bitches unload."

Leibowitz then spoke for the defense. He tried again to lean heavily on the medical testimony of Dr. Bridges. He attacked the character of Victoria Price, calling her, Bates, Gilley, and Carter "'bums,' 'loafers,' 'scum,' upon whose word neither side could rely." He called on the jury to believe Dr. Bridges, a respected local physician, rather than the contradictory testimony of Price, "a white girl tramp." Leibowitz had again misjudged the southern courtroom with his attacks on a white woman's character, even one at the low end of the social order.

On Thanksgiving morning, November 30, as Attorney General Knight made his closing argument, Leibowitz leapt to his feet and said Knight's words were only an emotional appeal to the jury. Knight responded, "It is an appeal to passion."

Leibowitz immediately made a motion for a mistrial, which Callahan denied amidst chuckles and backslapping among the courtroom spectators. Knight then continued his passionate appeal by challenging the jurymen's manhood in front of their friends and neighbors in the courtroom; he called upon the jury to protect Alabama's womanhood by returning a guilty verdict. Knight also brought up the "All you white sons-of-bitches unload" statement. By this time, the jury must have perceived the implications of this statement. Knight wanted the jury to understand that even if they were unsure of the rape charge, this statement was a challenge to the southern social order between whites and blacks, and it could not go unpunished.

At 10:30 a.m., Judge Callahan took a two-hour recess so he and others could go home for their Thanksgiving dinner. At 1:30 p.m., he started his charge to the jury on the law in the case and the evidence; it was a thinly veiled appeal to the jury to bring in a guilty verdict. It is difficult to interpret Callahan's charges any differently, considering statements like, "It is the glory of the law of this State and of the States of this Union that its protecting wings encompass all womanhood." Callahan dismissed one of Judge Horton's key arguments in Horton's decision granting Patterson a new trial: the need to corroborate the testimony of the prosecutrix. Callahan said that the law "would authorize a conviction on the testimony of Victoria Price alone...[the law] does not require corroboration."

When Callahan started his charge, Haywood Patterson sat upright, alert and interested in what the judge had to say. As Callahan proceeded, Patterson slowly sank dejectedly into his chair, fully realizing the implication of Callahan's remarks. A number of times Callahan even changed to a more stern tone of voice and glared at the defense table as he read his charge. Callahan concluded his charge by explaining to the jury the forms for a guilty verdict. He was preparing to give the case to the jury when Leibowitz rushed to the bench and whispered in Callahan's ear that he had failed to give the instructions for an acquittal verdict. Callahan agreed that he had failed to give the complete instruction and explained to the jury they had to be convinced beyond a reasonable doubt of Patterson's guilt as charged or he should be found not guilty. The jury took the case under consideration at three o'clock.

Norris's First Decatur Trial—November 30–December 6, 1933

The moment the Patterson jury was behind closed doors, Clarence Norris was brought into the courtroom for the start of his second trial, the first being on April 6, 1931, in Scottsboro. The jury-selection process started immediately, but was not concluded by the end of the day, much to Callahan's displeasure. He adjourned the court, instructing the sheriff to have twelve more prospective jurors in the courtroom the next day at 8:30 a.m., since the jury pool was so depleted from having pool members excused for one reason or another. Callahan also sent the Patterson jury to their hotel, as they had not yet reached a verdict, telling them to return to their deliberations in the morning.

The next morning, December 1, the Norris jury-selection process dragged on for hours, as it was difficult to find twelve men without preconceived opinions about the case. Leibowitz again moved for a change of venue, but Callahan denied the motion. Finally, a jury was selected, and, at 5:00 p.m., as Judge Callahan prepared to swear the new jury in, Patterson's jury signaled it had reached a verdict by knocking on the jury door with a single, loud knock. In the ten minutes it took deputies to bring Patterson to the courtroom, Callahan returned to business, swearing in the Norris jury and instructing them not to discuss or read about the case.

The deputies arrived with Patterson, manacled at the wrist, and escorted the tall, well-built young man down the aisle to his seat beside Norris. The Norris jury was then escorted from the courtroom, and Callahan signaled the bailiff to open the jury room door. Twelve somber, grim-faced men walked into the courtroom. The jury foreman handed their decision to the court clerk, who read the verdict: guilty as charged, along with a death sentence. Patterson looked like a caged animal ready to lunge forward. He stared at the jury and Callahan with a malevolent leer, his body twitching with anger. Clarence sat in a dreamlike trance during and after the Patterson verdict was read; it was as if he foresaw the results of his trial.

Callahan said he would sentence Patterson in a few days, adding, "I make it a rule never to sentence a man if I can help it on the day the jury brings in a verdict. I don't believe in yanking him around." Callahan then informed Leibowitz he had thirty days to file a motion for a new trial. Leibowitz requested the thirty days run from the date the trial transcript was delivered to the defense, but Callahan denied the request.

In his autobiography, Clarence Norris wrote of Judge Callahan, "This judge was a redneck from the word go. His robes might as well have been those of the Ku Klux Klan. It didn't matter to him if we were innocent or guilty, he was determined to send us to the electric chair. He didn't make no bones about that."

Clarence had now been in jail two years and eight months, as had all the boys. This trial was to be, as that esteemed philosopher, Yogi Berra, would say years later, "déjà vu all over again."

Clarence can be forgiven for being prejudiced about Callahan, since his judgment wasn't far from the mark. Clarence's jury—nine farmers, a carpenter, an oil salesman, and a railroad employee —was essentially a carbon copy of Patterson's jury. Clarence's trial was hopelessly similar to Patterson's: the same witnesses, the same testimony, the same control by Callahan over the defense and the testimony, the same biased charge to the jury, and, of course, the same guilty verdict with the death penalty.

The jury brought the guilty verdict against Clarence into the court-room on December 6 after deliberating for fourteen hours over two days. The length of the deliberation was never a question of guilt for the jury, which they agreed to early in their deliberation, but the form of the punishment—life imprisonment or death in the electric chair. Judge Callahan passed sentence on Patterson and Norris, ordering they be put to death in the electric chair in Kilby Prison on February 2, 1934. Leibowitz immediately filed a notice of appeal, which acted as a stay of execution until the appeal was exhausted.

Then, as if someone yelled, "Get out of Dodge [Decatur]," within an hour, all seven boys were in a heavily guarded patrol wagon on their way back to the Birmingham jail. Patterson and Norris would be transported from Birmingham to death row in Kilby Prison. Within two hours, the two New York bodyguards escorted Leibowitz to the Decatur train station. The court also ordered three Alabama deputies to accompany Leibowitz, his bodyguards, and the New York newspaper men on the train to Chattanooga beyond the Alabama state line. Rumors were adrift that Leibowitz's life was in danger in Decatur, and the train passed through Huntsville, Paint Rock, and Scottsboro, where more trouble might be expected. None came to pass.

14.

SOUTHERN "LIBERALS"
1933–1935

ALTHOUGH THE SCOTTSBORO BOYS were in the Birmingham jail for all of 1933 until the trials started in Decatur in November, the Taylor Boys followed the case in the Birmingham newspapers with only a modicum of interest. The Taylor family knew their close friend and minister, Dr. Henry Edmonds of the Independent Presbyterian Church, was concerned about the plight of the Scottsboro Boys and had called on people to support the ILD defense fund. However, the pressure of other things commanded most of the family's attention: the Taylor Boys focused on college and job opportunities; Angus Sr. struggled to keep his business afloat in the Depression through a series of bank loans; and Margie started work as a travel agent, both to keep busy and to supplement the family income.

University Life Ends

WITH THE EARLY YEARS of the "new lot" gang behind them, the Taylor Boys started the slow process of breaking apart from each other and the family. While Waights, Frank, and Macey continued their college days, Angus and Bill graduated from the university and entered the job market in the depths of the Great Depression.

The Importance of Being Connected

Angus found a job with the help of family connections, an essential necessity at any time but especially during the Depression. He worked as a clerk in the U.S. Federal Court in Birmingham in the office of Judge W. I. Grubb, a family friend. Angus used this opportunity to start studying law, and in 1934, he became a lawyer when he passed the State of Alabama bar exam. In late 1934, Angus's newly earned law degree paid off when he was hired by the Federal Bureau of Investigation. The FBI sent Angus to Virginia, where he completed his training to become a special agent in time to return to Birmingham for the Christmas holidays.

Bill, fresh out of the university in May 1932 with his Aeronautical Engineering degree, wanted to fly. He tried to qualify for the Navy's cadet flying school, but he failed the physical exam twice because of a high pulse rate detected during an exercise test. Bill, sorely disappointed, continued to send out resumes to aircraft manufacturers and airlines, but he received only polite rejections or heard nothing, as no one was hiring. In 1933, he found a job as a draftsman with the Alabama Highway Department for seventy-five dollars a month. It kept him busy, but he was bored, and in March 1934, he found a job as junior engineer with the United Fruit Company in Tela, Honduras. United Fruit had a huge banana operation in Tela, and Bill did survey work for the construction of irrigation canals, drainage ditches, and railroad tracks. Bill's work in Tela was completed in November, and, although the company wanted him to stay on, he returned home from Honduras just in time to be with the family for Christmas.

Waights, Frank, and Macey were home for Christmas from the university, and the family celebrated the holidays together. It was the last time the entire family would be together at Christmas.

After the Christmas holidays, Angus departed for San Francisco to start his first assignment in the FBI office in the beautiful city by the bay. Bill, determined as ever to find work in the aviation field, went job hunting in Washington, DC, and New York City. As always with the Taylor family, Bill had connections in both cities. He pursued an unsuccessful lead in Washington with Walter Brownell, Angus's partner in their ill-fated "Alabama Airways, Inc." operation at the university, and then immediately went to New York City.

Bill had a letter of introduction from Judge Grubb to his good friend, Robert Thach, the chief legal officer for Pan American Airways. Over the next two days, Bill learned three valuable life lessons: the importance of a high-level contact in a big company, timing, and good luck. Pan Am was in the process of hiring about twenty engineers for a challenging and adventurous project, the establishment of bases in Hawaii, Midway, Wake, Guam, and Manila to support the China Clipper flying boat service they planned to introduce across the Pacific Ocean in 1936. Bill met briefly with Thach, who was preparing to leave the office on an extended business trip, and Thach arranged for Bill to meet with the project chief engineer the next day. Bill met with the chief engineer, who liked both Bill's aeronautical degree and recent civil engineering work experience, as this project required both skills, and Bill was hired on the spot. Bill thought he would be returning to

Birmingham whatever happened on this trip, but now he found himself checking into the local YMCA. The next day, January 30, 1935, he would formally join Pan Am to start a career with them that lasted almost eighteen years. When news of Bill's employment reached the Taylors in Alabama, he received a telegram reading, "Happy landings and bon voyage. Good luck and love," signed, "Whole Dam Family."

In August 1935, Angus Sr. suffered a partial stroke, and while Angus and Bill couldn't come home, the other boys were close at hand. Macey postponed his return to the university that fall to help Angus Sr. get to work and back each day, as he was determined to work, even if for only a few hours a day.

Angus was transferred from San Francisco to Honolulu's FBI office in September 1935, and Bill's work in the Pacific was complete in December. Bill was reassigned to Pan Am's maintenance facility in Alameda, California. On his return flight to the United States, the China Clipper stopped at Honolulu, and Angus was there to greet Bill with leis and lavish parties.

University Life Continues

In the fall of 1933, Waights entered his senior year at Alabama, and Frank started his sophomore year. Waights continued some Shakespeare courses with Hudson Strode, but his primary focus was now on his journalism major under the tutelage of Clarence Cason. Frank was working toward his business degree, but his real enjoyment and interest were his extracurricular activities; by the time he graduated in 1936, he was a Brigade Commander in ROTC, the editor of the university yearbook, the *Corolla*, vice-president of the Inter-Fraternity Council, and a member of at least five honorary societies—he was a "Big Man on Campus."

You Gotta Be a Football Hero

After Alabama's victories in the Rose Bowl in 1926 and 1931, the school was now a recognized football powerhouse nationwide, and Alabama football had become a primary passion, almost a religion, for most Alabamians. In 1932, Waights and Frank met a tall, muscular freshman from Arkansas, Paul William Bryant.

Paul arrived at the University of Alabama in the fall of 1931, having been recruited at the end of his high school senior year by Alabama Assistant Coach Hank Crisp. For the past several summers, Coach Crisp had made a recruiting trip looking for talented high school football players in southern Arkansas, an area that turned out an inordinate number of good players considering its population and size. In 1931, he returned to the university with two players who would become legendary in Alabama football lore:

Paul Bryant and Donald Montgomery Hutson. Coach Crisp had one problem to resolve with Paul; although he was a high school senior, he didn't qualify for a diploma because he hadn't completed the mandatory courses. Crisp had a solution to the problem, and Paul was determined to return to Tuscaloosa with him, as it was now the Mecca of southern football with its Rose Bowl successes. To solve his high school degree problem, Paul spent his first year in Tuscaloosa attending the local high school to complete the course work he needed for a degree. As there were no formal scholarship programs at that time, football players like Paul were expected to perform menial tasks for the athletic department and the university. For his room, tuition, meal money, and a few dollars for his personal needs, Paul cleared dining room tables, performed ground maintenance around the campus, including the football stadium, and was assigned the glorious job of cleaning toilets and showers.

Paul was born in 1913 in Moro Bottom, a place a few miles north of Fordyce, Arkansas. A place was about all you could call Moro Bottom; since it was so small, it wasn't even recognized as a dot on a map. Paul was the eleventh of twelve children of William and Ida Bryant. The Bryants were farmers, and their vegetable crops and chickens and hogs fed the family well, with some left to sell to neighbors and local markets. Paul grew up in a simple four-room house with no electricity or running water. Some would call them "po' white trash," but if a Bryant heard you utter that epithet, you had a fight on your hands. Their situation and station in life were similar to that of Victoria Price and Ruby Bates with two significant differences. First, the area around Fordyce was largely self-sufficient. Compared to Huntsville, Alabama and its dependence on cotton mills, the Great Depression had less impact on the Fordyce area, and the Bryant family's farm was a good example of that self-sufficiency. Second, unlike the dysfunctional families Victoria and Ruby grew up in, Paul's was supportive and loving. Paul was never an outstanding student, but football would become his salvation, leading him out of Moro Bottom to become one of the most famous and successful college football coaches of all time.

The other Arkansas kid, Don Hutson, was born in 1913 in Pine Bluff, thirty-five miles northeast of Fordyce. Actually, Don was never referred to as "the other" in reference to Paul. However, even Paul later called himself "the other end," as he played the end position opposite to Don throughout their varsity years. Don's father worked for the railroad in Pine Bluff and his mother was a schoolteacher, so Don's family was a notch up the social ladder from Paul's. Don was also an excellent student; thus, he didn't have to join Paul at Tuscaloosa High School. Don and Paul roomed together at Alabama, and, although Don's family was reasonably well off, he worked at menial tasks at the university as all the football recruits did. Don started his freshman year in 1931 and, after he graduated in 1935, had an eleven-year National Football League (NFL) career with the Green Bay Packers, establishing eighteen NFL records including career touchdown receptions, a record that would go unbroken for over forty years.

Paul started his freshman year at the university in 1932, joined the Sigma Nu social fraternity, and pursued his two interests in life: football and pretty young women. Paul was now called "Bear" by most people, a nickname he earned as a teenager when he wrestled a live bear on the stage of the only theater in Fordyce for one dollar a minute. It was later said he lasted about three minutes with the bear but never collected his three dollars, as the owner and his bear skipped town right after the event.

The friendship Frank and Bear established would serve them both well years later when Bryant returned to the university as the head football coach in 1958. Bear contacted Frank soon after he returned to Alabama, and together they developed *The Bear Bryant Show*. The live television show aired every Sunday afternoon during the football season. Although modest in production early on, the show became the model for all football coaches' programs to follow. The show featured Bear discussing the previous day's game, using film clips from the game to highlight his points, and talking about the prospects for the next week's game, always playing up the opponent no matter how poor their record might be. The show was a huge success, and Frank and Bear shared in its substantial economic rewards.

Waights graduated in May 1934 with a degree in journalism, earning a Phi Beta Kappa key for his academic excellence. He continued his education in the fall, doing graduate work in journalism while working as a teaching assistant for Clarence Cason in the Department of Journalism. Macey joined Waights and Frank at the university that fall for the start of his freshman year in a liberal arts program with an eye on a law degree. Macey may have been son number five, but his achievements would equal, and in many ways surpass, his elder brothers.

The fall of 1934 would also bring a wonderful nonacademic achievement to the campus: a football team that many arguably call the greatest team Alabama ever fielded. The 1934 team had a perfect record, 9–0, scored 287 points to their opponents' 32 points, and was led by three All-Americans and "the other end": quarterback Millard "Dixie" Howell, end Don Hutson, tackle Bill Lee, and Bear Bryant. The Crimson Tide capped their perfect season with a victory in the Rose Bowl on January 1, 1935, when they beat highly favored Stanford 29–13. On January 6, Waights, Frank, and Macey were among the five thousand supporters, faculty, and students to greet the returning heroes to Tuscaloosa.

Southern "Liberals"

WHITE SOUTHERNERS have been and continue to be cautious and conservative people. However, in the 1930s into the 1960s, those who called themselves liberal fell into one of two categories. The first category, a southern liberal, was a rare breed in the South. A true southern liberal believed and followed a broad liberal path on most issues: economic, social, political, and racial. The second category, the southern "liberal," comprised the vast majority of those who called themselves liberals. A southern "liberal" would usually agree with most economic and social liberal issues and was likely a Democrat prior to about 1964. However, southern "liberals," when brought face-to-face with racial and segregation issues, frequently drew the line and fell back to a position supporting segregation. They would shuck-and-jive as they tried to explain some tortured rational for their position, but their meaning was obvious.

In 1947, Donald Rasmussen, a young, white professor at the all-black Talladega College in Talladega, Alabama, interviewed Waights. Rasmussen was interviewing Southerners thought to be liberal on race issues for his PhD thesis. When asked about his liberal racial views and background, Waights answered with an emphasis on two University of Alabama professors who had considerable influence on his early thoughts.

> I cannot trace the origin of my liberalism. It developed gradually, perhaps chiefly out of the great happiness of my family...I believe that segregation must go in all aspects...Professor Cason was a brilliant young man and he had a considerable influence on my thought. He was definitely my ego ideal at that time and he had written a book, which devoted a couple of chapters to race relations in the South. His were not radical ideas but were definitely liberal. At 37 and during the year that I was teaching he shot himself. Some people thought that the reason for his shooting himself was on account of his liberal views. During the year that I was teaching, I also fell under the influence of Professor Gelders. He was a radical and I associated with him. Professor Gelders entertained Negroes in his home and he did many unorthodox things. One day he was severely beaten and he was asked to leave the university.

Waights didn't realize it, but the two college professors he somewhat idolized represented the bookends of southern liberalism.

A Southern Liberal—Joseph Gelders

Waights's memory was faulty on one point in his interview with Rasmussen in 1947. Joseph Gelders did not leave the University of Alabama after being severely beaten; the beating happened in Birmingham almost two years later. In August 1936, Gelders tried to get a young Communist, Bart Logan, out of jail in Bessemer, a steel town near Birmingham. Logan, a labor organizer in the steel industry, the dominant industry in the area at the time, was jailed for having violated a local ordinance against possessing anti-American material. Late in the evening on September 23, 1936, Gelders was walking to his Birmingham home when he was attacked from behind by four men, clubbed with a sawed-off baseball bat, thrown into their car, driven to a remote location, stripped of most of his clothing, and beaten senseless. Gelders did recover, and, because he was from a well-known Birmingham family, the incident created much local press demanding the assailants be apprehended. With the help of an eyewitness, the leader of the assailant group was identified as Walter Hanna, a U.S. Steel security employee at the heart of the company's anti-union activities. Even though this witness identified Hanna as the man he saw throw the bat into a field, and Gelders identified him as the man who first struck him, the Birmingham police made no arrest, and two grand juries would not issue indictments against any of the assailants.

Joseph Gelders was born in Birmingham in 1898 into a prominent Birmingham Jewish family. His family had emigrated from Germany, settled comfortably into the South and its culture, and prospered in Birmingham, where they owned and operated a fine downtown restaurant. Gelders received his physics degree from the Massachusetts Institute of Technology, returned to Birmingham, and then accepted a physics profes-sorship at the University of Alabama. Gelders was a lanky, soft-spoken, bespectacled young man, the quintessential college physics professor, his appearance belying the radical liberal he was to become. Initially he seemed content with his teaching position at the university, although his liberal views were certainly at odds with most at the university. As the Depression started, he was appalled at the startling worsening levels of poverty that developed in the South among both blacks and whites, and he was equally bothered by the lack of state and federal government intervention to assist those most impacted by the chronic economic conditions.

However, in 1934, when mostly black mine workers went on strike against U.S. Steel Corporation in Birmingham, Gelders had a radical epiph-any. The violence that erupted during the strike led to murders of strikers and strikebreakers, and bombings of black scabs' homes. Gelders, in seek-ing answers to this awful event, turned to the writings of socialist writers, and, after he read Marx and Engels, he decided to join the Communist Party. After being accepted by the Party, Gelders went to New York, where he was trained to be the secretary of the National Committee for the Defense of Political Prisoners (NCDPP), a group outside the formal leadership of the U.S. Communist Party. In the summer of 1936, he was sent back to Birmingham as a NCDPP representative, but his real assignment was to be the Party's secret operative in the South. He went on to become an advisor to Allan Chalmers and the Scottsboro Defense Committee on Alabama political, religious and social issues, and key Alabama individuals involved in the trials.

Gelders left the state of Alabama after this terrible episode and settled in Washington, DC, where he became involved in New Deal politics. From 1936 to 1941, Wisconsin Republican Senator Robert La Follette Jr. conducted a series of Senate hearings called the Subcommittee Investigating Violations of Free Speech and Rights of Labor. The subcommittee investigated the surveillance, physical intimidation, strikebreaking services, and private police systems used by large corporations to prevent workers from organizing. In January 1937, the subcommittee looked into the practices of Birmingham's U.S. Steel, and Gelders was called as a witness. Gelders described for the subcommittee what he had experienced. The subcommittee's reports resulted in no direct legislation correcting the situation, nor did it lead to any prosecutions in the assault on Gelders. However, it created such a spate of bad publicity in the Birmingham and national press against the big corporations, that Birmingham's U.S. Steel directed its security and vigilante forces to stop all forms of physical abuse; the period of payroll vigilantism had come to an end in Birmingham.

After his work in Washington concluded, Gelders moved to California and earned his PhD in Physics at the University of California in Berkeley. He died in California in 1950 at age fifty-two.

Of course, Joseph Gelders wasn't the only southern liberal active at this time. Gelders's daughter, Marge Gelders Frantz, was an activist in Birmingham at age fifteen. Others included Virginia and Clifford Durr, Myles Horton, Charles Morgan Jr., and Aubrey Williams—all will make an appearance later.

A Southern "Liberal"—Clarence Cason

Waights's mentor in the Journalism Department, Clarence Cason, was not an accidental journalist, but he was a southern "liberal." He was born in 1896 in Ragland, Alabama, a small town forty miles northeast of Birmingham. Cason graduated from the University of Alabama in 1917 and earned an English literature master's degree at the University of Wisconsin. He developed his own ideas of journalism while at Wisconsin and the University of Minnesota, and honed his journalism skills at several newspapers. Cason was determined to broaden the base of journalistic education, one that was essentially learned on the job at that time, with a liberal arts-based approach encouraging critical thinking and analysis as an adjunct to one's reporting and writing.

Cason returned to Alabama in 1928 to start the university's new journalism program. Waights was a student in Cason's journalism program in 1931, the first year it was offered as a full major. Cason, along with Hudson Strode, were two of the best-known and well-liked faculty members at Alabama; in fact, the student editors of the 1935 university yearbook, the *Corolla*, dedicated the yearbook to Cason for his teaching excellence and work with campus organizations. Cason not only developed the university's new journalism program, he continued his work as a journalist; his articles and essays appeared in the *Yale Review,* the *New York Times Magazine,* the *Baltimore Sun,* and other newspapers and publications. In 1934 and 1935, Cason was working on what was to be his last book, *90° in the Shade.* It was a compilation of new essays along with older pieces, which set forth his views on the South, its strengths and shortcomings, and his thoughts on a subject anathema to most Southerners, race relations.

As time for publication of the book approached in May 1935, Cason expressed concerns to close friends about the content of the book and how it might be received. Apparently, he became convinced it would be so poorly received he would have to leave Tuscaloosa. His friends tried to tell Cason his concerns were unfounded and the book would be well received; one even suggested he "go fishing and forget the whole thing." Cason was unable or unwilling to take their advice and in the late afternoon or early evening of May 7, 1935, he committed suicide with an automatic pistol in his office in the Journalism Department. Cason's wife, alarmed her husband hadn't returned home, went to his office at midnight and found his body sitting in a chair. When the news spread the next morning, the whole campus went into mourning. Waights was devastated, and, if Cason's wife hadn't found him the evening before, Waights may well have been the first one to stumble upon the gruesome scene, as Waights generally met with Cason daily to discuss his classwork assignments.

Waights struggled to complete the few weeks remaining in the school year. The loss of Cason drained all his enthusiasm for school, and he abandoned his plans to continue in the fall to complete his master's degree. A few weeks after the spring semester ended, he got a job with the *Mobile Register* newspaper as an editorial writer. It was a short-lived experience, and he was back in Birmingham by the end of 1935. Waights always said he resigned from the newspaper because he couldn't abide by their conservative editorial policies, although he may well have been fired because of his liberal views, as was another writer the year before, who wrote an article about mixed racial heritage.

Reading Cason's book today, one is hard pressed to understand his concerns; yet, considering the events swirling around Cason at the time—the Scottsboro case, lynchings in Tuscaloosa, an Alabama College professor harassed by forty members of the Tuscaloosa Ku Klux Klan, and the firing of the writer by the *Mobile Register* over the article about people of mixed racial heritage—it is easier to understand his concerns. The book was generally well received by reviewers in the South and North, and did not cause a firestorm of criticism. The titles of several of the essays in Cason's book give a sense of the material: *Shadows of the Plantation, Pulpit and Pew, Politics as a Major Sport, Fascism: Southern Style,* and *Black Figures in the Sun.* In the latter essay, Cason wrote, "Quite aside from such abstract concepts as human freedom and justice, can the South longer afford to jeopardize its economic future by continuing to harbor various delusions which are calculated to keep so large a part of its population in poverty and ignorance? No idealistic philosophy should be required to make the most practical-minded southern business man realize what he is losing in economic productivity and purchasing power because of the South's persistent failure to accept the Negro as a valuable human resource well worth developing."

Cason concluded *90° in the Shade* with these thoughts: "On the whole, the South would profit from a nice, quiet revolution...What I have in mind is a revision of the region's implanted ideas, a clarification of issues, a realistic and direct recognition of existing social problems, a redirection of the South's courage and audacity, and a determination that the southern conscience shall be accorded the reverence due a sacred thing...the present and future of the South may yet prove worthy of the glamorous reputation of the ante-bellum years."

Although it was not exactly a revolutionary book or proposition, and was certainly nostalgic and even naïve about times gone by, Cason conceded the issues and his hopes for "a nice, quiet revolution" with his suicide. Twenty years later the revolution started, and while absolutely necessary, it would not be "nice" or "quiet."

It never could have been.

A Neophyte Activist Starts to Grow

AFTER THEIR WEDDING in Pine Level in 1932, Rosa Parks and Raymond Parks went back to Montgomery to live in a rooming house near her old school, Alabama State Teachers College for Negroes. Parks knew education was very important to both Leona and Rosa, and he encouraged Rosa to go back to school. Rosa was delighted to do so, and in 1933, she proudly earned her high school diploma. Rosa's determination to earn her high school degree is underscored when it is understood that only about 7 percent of blacks in the South had the opportunity for a complete high school education. Even with her diploma in hand, Rosa could only find work not requiring a high school diploma. She found a job as a nurse's assistant at St. Margaret's Hospital in Montgomery and did sewing on the side for white clients to supplement their income.

Rosa and Raymond Parks read the Birmingham and other Alabama newspapers concerning the Scottsboro Boys with extreme interest; they devoured the information and looked for articles well beyond Alabama in all the magazines and newspapers Raymond subscribed to. Rosa had become as knowledgeable as Raymond about the case, but he still refused to let her attend his meetings of the National Committee to Defend the Scottsboro Boys. While they were living in the rooming house, Raymond attended the committee's late night secret meetings alone. Rosa said, "He didn't want me to go because it was hard enough if he suddenly had to run. He wouldn't be able to leave me, and I couldn't run as fast as he could." Of course, Raymond told her he was concerned for her safety, which was certainly true, but it was also equally true that the black culture was male-dominated, and the men considered it their duty and right to conduct business alone. Rosa and other early black female activists, who set the stage for the civil rights movement, would experience the harsh realities of male dominance because gender bias and discrimination are not unique to any one cultural group.

Regardless of Parks's intent, his activist work was dangerous. In a house they lived in later, the men who met there called it the "shot-gun house" because a single bullet would pass through all the rooms the way the rooms lined up one behind the other. Rosa would sit quietly on the back porch in fear and despair over the events requiring the men to meet in such a clandestine fashion. At one of the meetings, Rosa sat on their back porch crouched over with her head between her knees. After the meeting, Raymond had to lift her up and help her back into the house.

On another occasion, Parks came home late from a meeting and had to sneak in the back door because two motorcycle cops kept cruising up and down the street in front of the house. Rosa was sitting on the front porch as this happened and said, "I was so frightened, I was shaking," until she realized Parks was safely in the house.

Although Rosa's mother and grandfather had instilled in her a strong sense of self-determination, it was in this period from 1932 to 1935 when she really became an activist. Initially, she observed and learned from Parks as he worked on behalf of the Scottsboro Boys. However, her interest in and growth as an activist would soon far surpass Parks's interest. The neophyte southern activist had been unleashed, and the world would later look back in awe.

15.

THE SUPREME COURTS REDUX
1934–1935

Chicanery—Southern Style

AFTER HAYWOOD PATTERSON was found guilty on December 1, 1933, Samuel Leibowitz advised Judge William Callahan the defense would file a motion for a new trial. Callahan told him he had thirty days to do so. Leibowitz asked that the thirty days be counted from the date the trial transcript was available for review, but Callahan denied the request, telling Leibowitz he could apply for a continuance if necessary. On December 29, the defense filed a motion for a new trial and asked for a continuance; Callahan granted the request, continuing the hearing to January 25, 1934. At the January 25 hearing, the defense requested another continuance because the trial transcript had not arrived in a timely fashion, and Callahan continued the hearing again to February 24.

At the February 24 hearing, as the defense prepared to argue their motion, Attorney General Thomas Knight objected. Knight justified his objection, as well as explained some nuances of Alabama law to the defense; an original motion for a new trial had to be filed before the close of the current term of a court, and the term of the Morgan County Circuit Court ended on December 23, 1933. Osmund Fraenkel asked, if this date was correct, why had Judge Callahan granted two continuances, why had Knight not objected at the earlier hearings, and why, given two lives were at stake, could some accommodation not be reached in the interest of fair play and justice. Callahan and Knight ignored the defense's questions and plea, and Callahan ruled his earlier continuances were "null and void," as he had no authority after December 23.

The defense should be faulted for not knowing important and critical details about Alabama law. Callahan and Knight knew they had the defense boxed in when the original motion was filed on December 29, six days late, and yet, the prosecution continued to string the defense along until the February 24 hearing. However, there was an even more sinister prosecution motive at play in the legal cat-and-mouse game with the defense; although the defense had lost its opportunity for a ruling on a motion for a new trial from Callahan—which they knew full well would have been denied—they were still preparing for an appeal to the Alabama Supreme Court.

To properly prepare for an appeal to the Alabama Supreme Court, the defense was required to prepare and submit a bill of exceptions, a document listing all the exceptions Leibowitz entered into the record during the Decatur trials and the other exceptions to the conduct of the trial that the defense wished to bring before the higher court's attention in arguing the appeal. The defense lawyers pored over the Alabama law code to ensure they met the bill of exceptions filing requirements. They learned Alabama law required a filing no later than ninety days from the date a motion for a new trial was denied by the lower court, or no later than ninety days from the date the trial judge entered the judgment in the case. Chamlee argued the ninety days should proceed from the February 24 hearing, but the other ILD lawyers considered this much too risky and decided to assume the due date was ninety days from the judgment date.

The defense then had to decide whether the judgment date was December 1, the date Patterson was found guilty, or December 6, the date he and Norris were sentenced. A careful review of the court records by Chamlee showed that Callahan had written and dated the judgment in his own hand on December 6. The ILD lawyers now felt confident that December 6 was the correct start date for the ninety-day countdown, meaning the end due date was March 6, 1934; however, to be prudent, they decided to have the document to the court in Montgomery by March 1 in case the state argued the judgment date was December 1.

When Joseph Brodsky and Osmund Fraenkel got back to New York City on February 25, the ILD legal team had only a few days to prepare, print, and deliver the document. The team worked around the clock, and on the afternoon of February 28, a courier took the large document to the Newark Airport for the last flight that day to Birmingham. Callahan and Knight had pushed the defense team to the brink of the filing deadline with their strategy of granting two continuances and then basically declaring the whole motion process moot.

Then, as if scripted by the evil hand of a malevolent spirit, a Hollywood screenwriter, or just plain bad luck, the airplane carrying the bill of exceptions crashed just north of Washington, DC. A copy of the document sent by regular mail did arrive in Montgomery on March 5, and the ILD lawyers still thought they had met the filing deadline, since the judgment was dated December 6.

In May 1934, Alabama voters also had an opportunity to weigh in to the Scottsboro case saga in the Democratic Party primary election before the general election in the fall. The Scottsboro case would prove to be a factor in two races, and winning the Democratic primary was tantamount to winning the general election, as the Republican Party was essentially a nonentity in Alabama and the South at that time. Attorney General Knight was handily elected lieutenant governor over his opponent. Many Alabama newspapers endorsed Knight, suggesting his noteworthy role in the Scottsboro trials was reason enough to vote for him. It was thought Knight's opponent would have strong voter support in northern Alabama, yet Knight outpolled him in Morgan and Madison counties, and the race was close in the adjacent counties. Judge William Callahan was reelected unopposed for one of the two seats on the Eighth Circuit Court. Judge James Horton, who had run unopposed in the 1928 election for the Eighth Circuit Court, stood for reelection only after close friends and the local bar association convinced him to do so. He came in second in a field of three in the May primary, requiring a runoff between Horton and the number one vote getter, Aquilla Griffith. In the June runoff election, Griffith won almost 60 percent of the votes and beat Horton handily. Griffith later admitted to exploiting Horton's Scottsboro trial decision to his advantage. While Horton had earlier asked, "What does that have to do with the case?" when told he would likely not be reelected if he overturned Patterson's guilty verdict, it did prove to have everything to do with the election.

Alabama Supreme Court

ON MAY 25, 1934, the Alabama Supreme Court heard the arguments in the appeals for new trials for both Patterson and Norris: Leibowitz, Fraenkel, and Chamlee represented the defense; and Attorney General Knight led the prosecution team. Leibowitz opened for the defense, asking the court to overturn the convictions since Jackson County systematically excluded Negroes "solely because of their race and color" from the jury rolls and jury service. Leibowitz added that the names of Negroes shown on the jury rolls were "brazen, rank and amateurish forgery." Fraenkel then presented the arguments concerning Judge Callahan's conduct of the trials.

Knight followed for the state, and, as the defense had feared, he immediately said Patterson's appeal should not even be before the court since "the judgment was entered on December 1," and the defense had failed to deliver the bill of exceptions within the statutory ninety days of that date.

Fraenkel replied that Knight's "previous declaration about the date of the judgment should in common decency preclude him from claiming otherwise." Unfazed by Fraenkel's entreaty, Knight turned to the Norris appeal. Knight ignored the defense's arguments about Callahan's conduct and focused on Leibowitz's jury exclusion arguments. Knight contended it was not for him or the court to determine whether the names on the jury rolls were forged, adding, "If this court, with no evidence showing that Negroes were excluded, holds that systematic exclusion of Negroes took place, then the court is constituting itself the jury commission of every court in Alabama."

On June 28, 1934, the Alabama Supreme Court announced its unanimous decisions. The court, agreeing with Knight's position on the Patterson trial judgment date, ruled the bill of exceptions was late, struck it from the court record, refused to hear Patterson's appeal, and upheld the decision of the lower court. Norris's appeal was heard since the bill of exceptions had arrived within ninety days of his trial's judgment date, December 6; however, the court upheld all of Callahan's rulings and his conduct of the trial, and denied the appeal. Concerning the defense's claim that Negroes were systematically excluded from Jackson County jury rolls and jury service, Justice Lucien Gardner wrote, in the court's opinion "the jury commission did not 'automatically or systematically exclude anybody,' and that the question of race or color was not mentioned, and no one excluded on account thereof." The court set the date for the executions of Patterson and Norris for August 31, 1934.

The defense lawyers knew they had a problem with the ruling in Patterson's case. The Alabama Supreme Court's decision to strike the bill of exceptions from the record in Patterson's case meant that his case could not be appealed to the U.S. Supreme Court. Federal law prohibited a case being appealed to a federal court without exhausting all appeals at the state level, and, technically, there had been no appeal to a state court.

Hoping the U.S. Supreme Court would ignore this technicality, the ILD sent Chamlee to Montgomery on July 9, where he filed an application for a rehearing with the Alabama Supreme Court. This filing put the executions on hold since the state court was in recess until October. On October 4, after the Alabama Supreme Court opened its fall session, it denied the request for a rehearing and set the executions for December 7, 1934. The ILD then asked the Alabama Supreme Court to grant a sixty-day stay of execution to give the defense adequate time to prepare an appeal to the U.S. Supreme Court. On November 16, the Alabama Supreme Court granted the request, moving the execution date to February 8, 1935.

On January 7, 1935, the U.S. Supreme Court announced it would review the appeals of Haywood Patterson and Clarence Norris on February 15, thus suspending their death sentences until the court conducted its review and made its ruling.

Haywood and Clarence sat in Kilby Prison awaiting execution throughout this period of scheduled executions, attempted appeals, denied appeals, stayed executions, and rescheduled executions. The question, "What constitutes cruel and unusual punishment?" is oft debated in discussions on capital punishment. Clearly, the emotional and psychological stress implicit in the process Haywood and Clarence were subjected to would seem to fit a form of "cruel and unusual punishment." The two young men struggled almost day-to-day with the issue of life and death, and now their struggle was to take another unfortunate but familiar turn.

Chicanery—Northern Style

Samuel Leibowitz returned to New York City on December 6, 1933, after the two Decatur trials were concluded. He was exhausted from the pressures of the courtroom, the constant threats to his life, and lack of sleep. Early in his career Leibowitz had established a pattern when handling a case; at night, instead of trying to sleep soundly, he would lay in bed mulling over his strategy, preparation, and conduct of a case. This approach served him well over the years, and he continued it in the Scottsboro cases. His wife, Belle, was determined to get him away for a while, and, after the May 25 hearing before the Alabama Supreme Court, she finally got him on a French liner bound for Europe in late June for a ten-week tour of the Continent. They returned to the United States in early September, where Leibowitz would find the case in chaos as a result of news reports alleging illegal activities by the ILD.

Just after noon on Monday, October 1, 1934, Leibowitz heard some news that rocked him on his heels and would change the complexion of the defense effort and team. He was told that three men had been arrested in Alabama and Tennessee on charges of attempting to bribe the prosecution's chief witness in the Scottsboro case, Victoria Price. It was said the men were associated with the ILD. Leibowitz immediately called Joseph Brodsky and demanded to know what was going on. Brodsky came over to Leibowitz's office and did not deny the charges, telling Leibowitz that the ILD had been negotiating with Price about a payoff since June through a Birmingham man named Pearson. Brodsky said, seemingly ignoring the legal implications of the situation, the effort was "good propaganda for the cause" had it worked. Leibowitz hit the ceiling, yelling at Brodsky that the ILD had "assassinated the Scottsboro boys with that sort of business." Leibowitz and Brodsky parted with the issue unresolved. Later that day, Leibowitz met with several NAACP officials to discuss the turn of events.

The next day, October 2, *The New York Times* published an article with more details on the alleged attempted bribery. The article reported that on Saturday, September 29, 1934, a Birmingham man, J. W. Pearson, drove to Huntsville, Alabama, where he picked up Victoria Price and continued driving with her toward Nashville, Tennessee. In Nashville, they were to meet with two men who were prepared to give Price $1,000 in cash if she would sign an affidavit refuting her testimony in the seven trials of the Scottsboro Boys. Pearson had driven only a few miles north of Huntsville when his car was pulled over by Huntsville police, and he was arrested and charged with attempted bribery on a warrant sworn to by Price. The next day, September 30, the two men they were to rendezvous with in Nashville were arrested by Tennessee police and also charged with attempted bribery on warrants sworn to by Pearson and Jack Tiller, Price's bodyguard. The two men gave their names as Daniel Swift, a New York attorney, and Sol Kone, also of New York.

This appeared to be anything but an accidental bust; the ILD had considered a bribe possibility for some time, and the Huntsville police reacted accordingly when tipped off by Price. George Chamlee, the Chattanooga lawyer on the ILD defense team, had told the ILD office in New York in May 1933 that Price had indicated she might consider changing her story for the right sum of money. At the time, nothing came of her supposed interest; however, in June 1934, Pearson said he met with Swift in Chattanooga where the two men discussed the bribery attempt. Pearson approached Price in late August and offered her $500 to change her testimony. On September 27, Pearson told Price the offer was being increased to $1,000, at which point Price went to the Huntsville police with the story about the bribery attempt. The Huntsville police told her to string Pearson along, and they would arrest him when he was in her company. The trap had been set, and it snapped shut very effectively.

After Swift and Kone were arrested in their Nashville hotel, having just arrived from Cincinnati in a charted airplane, they were taken to the Nashville jail for booking. As they got out of the car at the jail, the October 2 *Times* article reported that one of the officers making the arrest said, after he found $1,500 in $1 bills still in the car, "You're leaving your money," and one of the men replied, "It's not my money." It was reported that Sol Kone was an attorney in the office of Joseph Brodsky, the chief attorney for the ILD and a member of the defense team. It was further reported that Daniel Swift was an alias for David Schriftman, a young New York attorney. Schriftman was, of course, the young man who had worked for Brodsky during the Decatur trials in November 1933.

On October 3, Leibowitz issued a statement about the alleged bribery attempt and his involvement in the case. Leibowitz said he would withdraw as the Scottsboro Boys' counsel unless the Communists agreed to withdraw from the defense team. He maintained that he knew nothing of the two men who allegedly tried to bribe Victoria Price. To make his position absolutely clear, he said, "Until all secret manoeuvrings [maneuverings], ballyhoo, mass pressure, and Communist methods are removed from the case, I can no longer continue." Leibowitz added that he was not giving up on the Scottsboro Boys and concluded by saying, "I have given of my best and am prepared to do so to the end that the Scottsboro boys shall not die."

Like a ball of yarn rolling down a steep hill, unwinding as it tumbled, the next day, October 4, the ILD announced that Leibowitz was no longer the chief attorney on the case, and the *Daily Worker* trumpeted the clarion call on October 8 when it called Leibowitz a member of the "Alabama lynch rulers," as they spread "lying stories of attempts to bribe Victoria Price and other slanders." Also on October 4, the governor of Tennessee honored a request from the governor of Alabama and granted extradition of Daniel Swift and Sol Kone to Alabama. The two men were rushed to Huntsville by Alabama authorities where they joined J. W. Pearson in the Huntsville jail. After a few weeks, ILD lawyers arranged for the release of Swift and Kone under bonds of $2,000 each. On November 27, all three were indicted in Huntsville on charges of attempted bribery. Their cases were called to trial in the Huntsville Circuit Court on May 29, 1935, but Swift and Kone did not appear, forfeiting their $2,000 bonds. The court took no further action against any of the three men, and Pearson was released.

During this time of deception and turmoil over legal maneuverings and bribery attempts, no one bothered to ask, "What about the boys?" Knight was satisfied with his election outcome and was sure his prosecution tactics in the Scottsboro case were partially responsible. The ILD and the Communists were content with their bribery attempt, as it was seen as an acceptable propaganda ploy, although they now denied the accusations and claimed the charges were slanderous lies by Leibowitz and the southern political establishment. Leibowitz was determined to wrest control of the case away from the ILD, convinced he could achieve what the NAACP had been unable to do in 1931. The NAACP, still unwilling to take a firm public stand on the boys' behalf, was more worried about being caught in the cross hairs in any Leibowitz-ILD fight and what it might do to the association's reputation.

The approach and tactics of the two parties was quite similar to the 1931 struggle between the ILD and NAACP. Leibowitz made the first bid, announcing on October 10 that he, with the help of a newly formed group of Negro clergymen in Harlem, had secured signed affidavits from Patterson, Norris, and some of the boys' parents authorizing Leibowitz to take full control of the appeals. Leibowitz demanded that the ILD's Brodsky turn over all records in the case to him within the next two days.

On October 11, Brodsky's public statement made it sound like the ILD intended to fully comply with Leibowitz's request and cede control of the case to him; however, the ILD quickly trumped Leibowitz's first move, as the group was not about to give up control of the appeals so easily. On October 13, one of the ILD's attorneys, Benjamin Davis, and an associate visited the boys in Kilby Prison. Davis told Haywood and Clarence the charges of bribery were lies perpetrated by "Alabama lynchers" and Leibowitz. The two boys reversed their decision of a few days ago and signed an affidavit assigning responsibility for their appeals exclusively to the ILD.

The game was now on in earnest between the ILD, and Leibowitz and his supporters, now organized as the American Scottsboro Committee. The struggle between the two became heated, and the mudslinging was relentless for the next three months. Over this period of time, Haywood, Clarence, and their parents would change allegiances at least five times, as the seemingly endless process of entreaty and deception went on. The ILD propaganda about Leibowitz and his supporters got particularly ugly; the ILD said Leibowitz had joined Attorney General Knight's camp in his zeal to win the boys' support and claimed Haywood had been brutally tortured to force him to support Leibowitz. For his part Leibowitz tried to appeal to southern concerns about the ILD and the Communists in hopes of eliciting support for his position and that of the American Scottsboro Committee. When he asked Alabama Governor Benjamin Miller to bar ILD personnel and their agents from Kilby Prison and the Birmingham jail, Miller icily refused to do so. Leibowitz then asked Will Alexander, founder and head of the southern-based Commission on Interracial Cooperation, to intercede with the boys on Leibowitz's behalf. Alexander also refused to help.

Leibowitz still failed to realize that he was as disliked and despised in the South as much as the ILD and the Communists. Alabama politicians and newspapers delighted in the struggle between Leibowitz and the ILD; to most Southerners, they were just two sides of the same coin. Even after Leibowitz said he would welcome additional southern lawyers on the defense team, Alexander and other liberal Southerners still refused to support Leibowitz and the American Scottsboro Committee.

Haywood and Clarence sat through this maddening exchange between the ILD and Leibowitz thoroughly confused and disheartened. Clarence later wrote, "So there we were, stuck in the middle again. The people who had our lives in their hands were fighting among themselves. The press had a field day, the Southern press loved it…It was a mess." Clarence finally favored Leibowitz as his defense attorney, while Haywood vacillated between the ILD and Leibowitz.

The fight and ongoing impasse between the ILD and Leibowitz was broken when the U.S. Supreme Court announced, on January 7, 1935, that it would hear the appeals. The two antagonists quickly realized they had to reach some accord to be properly prepared for the upcoming appeals. Leibowitz and the ILD agreed that Leibowitz and Chamlee, who had joined Leibowitz in repudiating the ILD, would handle Clarence Norris's appeal, and Osmund Fraenkel and Walter Pollack would handle Haywood Patterson's.

Chicanery ploys and the control games finally came to an end as the lawyers prepared their briefs and oral arguments for the U.S. Supreme Court.

Coda to Chicanery—Northern Style

WHAT YOU HAVE JUST READ about the bribery attempt of Victoria Price —and the subsequent arrest, extradition, and trial—is based on the events as reported in 1934 by *The New York Times* and other newspapers. The arresting officers and Madison County Sheriff B. F. Giles supplied most of the material in the newspaper articles to reporters. The books published since that time on the Scottsboro Boys write of this bribery episode based on these available news accounts.

On March 25, 2011, I attended a commemorative event for the Scottsboro Boys for the eightieth anniversary of the start of their tragic drama. The event was held in Scottsboro, Alabama, at the recently opened Scottsboro Boys Museum & Cultural Center. Even while many of Scottsboro's current residents would prefer to see the memory of the Scottsboro Boys left in the dust bins of history, the museum's mission is to preserve their memory and integrity, and to advance reconciliation, healing, and cultural diversity. The museum's Board of Directors, led by founder and chairperson Sheila Washington, hosted the commemorative event.

Among the scheduled speakers at the event was a New York City National Labor Relations Board attorney named Aggie Scribner Kapelman. Aggie is the daughter of David Schriftman (aka Daniel Swift). While the story Aggie told about her father will soon unfold on these pages for the first time, one must know that on July 30, 1937, David Schriftman had his name legally changed to David Scribner, largely because of the personal humiliation he felt to his character and honesty from his arrest on bribery charges. Aggie told the some two hundred people at the Scottsboro museum that her father was innocent of the bribery charges, and that Alabama authorities had essentially kidnapped him, when they extradited her father and Sol Kone to a Huntsville jail to face bribery charges in a Huntsville court. Aggie added that she had documents that supported her father's innocence, and she left a copy of the documents for the museum's archives.

I introduced myself to Aggie and explained to her that a book I had written was being prepared for publication later this year. I told her I would like to get copies of the documents she claimed supported her contention that her father was innocent. I told her I couldn't commit to making any changes or additions to my book until I had completed a review of the documents and drawn my own conclusions about their significance. I added that I might also be precluded from making any changes dependent on my publisher's timetable. She said she completely understood my caveats and would send me copies as soon as she got back to New York. After I returned home, I received a number of documents from Aggie via e-mail, FedEx, and fax. The material included the following documents from which I reconstructed the sequence of events described in the documents.

On October 4, 1934, an extradition hearing was held from 2:00 p.m. to about 3:45 p.m. before the Governor of Tennessee, Hill McAlister. The transcript of the hearing shows that the State of Alabama, led by Attorney General Thomas Knight, persuaded the governor to sign their request to extradite Sol Kone and Daniel Swift to Huntsville. Knight had Victoria Price, Jack Tiller, Victoria's paramour and now "bodyguard," and James H. Pride, Morgan County Solicitor, at the hearing in case he needed them to testify. Both Victoria and Tiller had signed affidavits on October 1, 1934, swearing that Swift, Kone, and Pearson had offered Victoria a bribe. Pride signed a petition on October 1, 1934, asking Tennessee to extradite the two men, and he further stipulated that Morgan County Sheriff B. F. Giles would be the agent of the State in the matter. None of the three was required to testify.

On October 4, 1934, at about the same time the extradition hearing was in progress, a hearing seeking a writ of *habeas corpus* for Daniel Swift was held before Nashville Criminal Court Judge Chester K. Hart. Swift's attorneys convinced Judge Hart to issue a writ of *habeas corpus* ordering Nashville's Davidson County Sheriff L. A. Bauman and Huntsville's Madison County Sheriff B. F. Giles to "have the body of Daniel Swift... before me...the 5th day of October 1934, at 9 a.m. to be dealt with according to law." Three men—a Deputy Criminal Court Clerk; Frank Scheiner, Swift's attorney; and Charles Norman Jr., the brother of one of Swift's attorneys—immediately took the writ to the jail to seek Swift's signature on the writ. They asked Sheriff Bauman if they could see Swift to get his signature on the papers. Bauman asked if the papers were a *habeas corpus* proceeding, and he was told they were. The signed writ and the order were filed with the court on October 4, 1934, at 3:38 p.m.

On October 10, 1934, Charles Norman Jr. swore to and signed an affidavit describing the events that unfolded on October 4 after the writ of *habeas corpus* had been filed with the court. Norman said that some time after two o'clock he observed a car with Alabama license plates move from the front to the rear of the jail, where he then observed an Alabama officer escort Kone and Swift into the car and get in himself. Even though Sheriff Bauman knew a writ of *habeas corpus* had been issued, Norman then observed one of Bauman's deputies directing the car out of the jail court-yard to the street. With copies of Judge Hart's writ of *habeas corpus* and order in hand, Norman and Dick Taylor, a court officer in Judge Hart's Criminal Court, ran to the front street. Both men attempted to jump on the moving car's running board, but only Norman was successful in doing so. As Norman held the car door with one hand, he held the documents to the window with his other hand, displayed the documents to the car occupants, and yelled it was a writ of *habeas corpus* for Kone and Swift. The deputy sheriff driving the car said he didn't care what Norman had and told him to get off the car. After holding on to the car for about six blocks, Norman had to jump off for his own safety. Sheriff Bauman certainly knew of the writ, and it is highly likely that the Alabama officers did as well; however, both authorities had either ignored a legally served writ, or as agents of their respective authorities, had ignored attempts to serve the writ. The Alabama car driven by the deputy sheriff, serving as an agent of the court under Sheriff Giles, should have stopped to verify the validity of Norman's claim. Upon reading the writ, he would have been legally obligated to return Kone and Swift to the Nashville for the hearing before Judge Hart on October 5. It is not unfair to conclude that the Alabama authorities "kidnapped" Kone and Swift.

On October 9, 1934, with Daniel Swift now in custody in the Huntsville jail, an arrest warrant was issued for him. The warrant was preferred by Victoria Price and signed by Madison County Inferior Court Judge W. H. Blanton.

On November 2, 1934, a preliminary hearing was held on the charges against Kone and Swift before Judge Blanton. The hearing would determine if the charges against Swift and Kone were sufficient to send the case to the Grand Jury to seek an indictment. Victoria Price was the prosecution's principal witness. Over the course of a long, rambling testimony, frequently prompted by Solicitor Pride, she testified that Pearson, who introduced himself to Victoria as a distant relative named Charley Price, visited her three times before the arrests took place. She said Kone visited her two times, and Swift two times, but she then corrected it to several times. She also testified that Swift visited her four to six weeks after the November 1933 trial in Decatur, when he asked her to write her life story. She said he offered her $10 a copy, but she corrected it to $10 a page when prompted by Solicitor Pride. At one of the purported meetings with Price and Swift she said, when asked if she wanted to read the affidavit they wanted her to sign, "I told him I didn't want to read it." When asked about the affidavit she signed against Kone and Swift, she said, "I didn't swear to no affidavit until they was arrested." She also said that she recognized all three men from the November 1933 trial but added she didn't know their names at the time. As we go forward in this complicated tale, it is important to remember the number of times Victoria claimed Swift visited her in Huntsville after the November 1933 Decatur trial.

On November 2, 1934, at the preliminary hearing in Huntsville, Daniel Swift entered a statement to the charges. Swift denied the bribery charges, challenged the jurisdiction of the Inferior Court, and charged Sheriff B. F. Giles and his men of ignoring, and continuing to ignore, Judge Hart's writ of *habeas corpus*.

On November 5, 1934, Daniel Swift signed a $2,000 bond stipulating forfeiture of the bond unless he appeared "at the next term of the Circuit Court of Madison County, Alabama, there to await action by the Grand Jury and from term to term thereafter until discharged by law, to answer a criminal prosecution for the offense of Bribery." Swift was released from jail on November 5 and immediately returned to New York City.

On November 27, 1934, the Madison County Grand Jury issued an indictment charging Daniel Swift with bribery. The copy of the Grand Jury indictment does not have the actual date the indictment was issued. *The New York Times* reported the indictment's issuance date, which occurred three weeks after Swift and Kone were released on bond.

On December 4, 1934, after Daniel Swift got back to New York City, he had a copy of the statement he had made to the Inferior Court on November 2, 1934, notarized. He filed the notarized copy in a New York City court, presumably to have his position on record in New York if any questions on his part in the events came up.

On May 28, 1935, the Huntsville Circuit Court rendered a *nolle prosequi* decision in the cases of Daniel Swift, Sol Kone, and J. W. Pearson. The entries on the trial dockets read, "May 28, 1935 – Nolle Prossed on motion of Solicitor." The prosecution had conceded the charges couldn't be proved, the evidence indicated a fatal flaw in the case, or the defendants were innocent. The court's statement does not specify which of the three *nolle prosequi* conditions led to the decision.

That is, as best as can be reconstructed from the above court records, the sequence of events that led to the formal end of the charges against Kone, Swift, and Pearson. It is now time to hear from one of the three accused men, David Scribner (aka Daniel Swift), formerly named David Schriftman.

David Scribner always maintained to family members, friends, and business associates that he was innocent of the charge of bribery, and that he was illegally taken from the Nashville jail to the Huntsville jail by the Alabama authorities. For years, his wife urged him to write his account of the events, and he studiously avoided doing so, apparently intent on putting the events behind him and focusing on what became an illustrious career in labor and civil liberties law.

In 1986, when he was eighty years old, Scribner sat down and finally put pen to paper. He was at his summer home in Pembrooke, Maine near the Bay of Fundy. He gave the notes he wrote and the audiotape he made to his daughter, Aggie, one or two years before he died on April 10, 1991. A working mother with two young children, Aggie did little with the material for years. She was finally motivated to take some action when the off-Broadway production of Kander and Ebb's musical *The Scottsboro Boys* was staged in March and April 2010. When she heard about the upcoming eightieth commemorative event in Scottsboro, she immediately contacted the Scottsboro museum and prepared to come to the event with her family. And thus, here we are now on this page.

David's [let's use Scribner's first name to avoid confusion with the change in his last name] notes tell a much different and more chilling version of his arrest and the subsequent events. First and foremost, he denies any guilt, making it clear he never bribed or intended to bribe Victoria Price. His initial encounter with anything that became part of the subsequent events was in September 1934, when Joseph Brodsky first called him to his office. He found Brodsky in an excited state as he explained to David the phone call he had received from Pearson about Victoria's interest in changing her testimony in the next trial of Haywood Patterson. Pearson told Brodsky that Victoria wanted to come to New York to speak to defense counsel, but he added that she did not have the money to make the trip. Pearson suggested that Brodsky send someone to Nashville to meet with him and Victoria to discuss and make arrangements for her to travel to New York. Later that day, Pearson called Brodsky to make final plans for the meeting in Nashville, and Brodsky put David on the call. David talked to Pearson for about two minutes about the upcoming meeting. David said this phone conversation was his only encounter with Pearson; he never met with him in person. He never met with him in Chattanooga as reported in *The New York Times*, or at any of the meetings that Victoria later testified to in the preliminary hearing in Huntsville on November 2, 1934. Further, David added that he had never been in Chattanooga.

David said he left New York with a feeling that they were walking into a dangerous trap; however, his confidence in Brodsky's judgment overruled his intuition. When David arrived in Nashville, he proceeded to the hotel Pearson had arranged for their meeting. As he sat in the lobby waiting for Pearson, a burly man approached him and said he was from the sheriff's office. He asked David if his name was Schriftman. When David did not answer, the man said, "come along" and hustled him out of the lobby into a waiting car. *The New York Times* had reported that, when Kone and David got out of the car, the arresting officer said he found $1,500 in $1 bills still in the car and said to the men, "You're leaving your money," and one of the men replied, "It's not my money." David's notes of this moment are much different. He said he had a few hundred dollars in large bills in his rear pocket. When David got out of the car, he patted his rear pocket and noted his money was missing. He said it had either fallen out of his pocket or was filched by the sheriff's officer. David said nothing to the officer's inquiry about the money, thinking that the less he said the better. He also said the money was intended for his and Kone's expenses, plus any subsequent expenses to get them, Victoria, and Pearson back to New York.

Upon arrival at the Nashville jail and when booked, he drew a name out of the air, Daniel Swift, in a moment of indecision and uncertainty about what was going on. This was the first time and only time David had used this alias. He said that when Victoria and Pearson later referred to him in affidavits and court proceedings, they always called him Daniel Swift, adding, "The significance of that is quite obvious."

On his fifth day in the Nashville jail, David saw a well-dressed man and a young woman standing near his cell. The man was talking rapidly to the young woman as he pointed at David. David recognized Alabama Attorney General, now Lieutenant Governor Elect, Thomas Knight, and Victoria Price. Soon after they left the cellblock, David was hustled out of his cell and out the back door of the jail by Nashville authorities, handed over to another man, and into a waiting car. Kone was already in the back seat. David was seated next to Kone, and next to Kone was Jack Tiller, holding a large revolver in his lap. Victoria was in the front seat next to the driver, an Alabama deputy sheriff. David's account of Charles Norman's valiant attempt to serve the writ of *habeas corpus*, while he hung to the moving car's running board, is much the same story. As the car left Charles Norman in the dust, not a word was spoken until the car was well beyond the Tennessee-Alabama border. The deputy sheriff finally relaxed and said to Kone and David, "Don't worry, we'll get you to the Huntsville jail-house safe and sound. There may be a nasty crowd gathering there now because word gets around fast in these parts." David wrote of the ride saying, "Notwithstanding these assurances the ride was a nightmare, what with the sheer malevolence in Victoria's face as she stared at us, and the nervous handling of the deadly revolver by Jack Tiller."

At the preliminary hearing on November 2, 1934, Victoria testified that Swift had visited her in Huntsville two times, and then corrected it to several times. She also testified that Swift came to see her four to six weeks after the November 1933 trial in Decatur, when she was asked to write a book for $10 a copy and then, with the prosecution's prompting, corrected it to $10 a page. Of Victoria's testimony that day, David wrote, "She didn't just lie—she was a creative liar, never fazed by inconsistencies in her testimony and responded to every effort of the prosecution to change or adjust her blatant improbable answers to keep her on the prosecution's course. Nor was she embarrassed by any obvious errors as to time and place." When David returned to New York after he was released from the Huntsville jail on November 5, 1934, he methodically went through his diaries and other records of his whereabouts at the times Victoria claimed he was in Alabama. He was able to find positive proof that he was not in Alabama during any of the time periods she said their meetings took place. For example, on one of the occasions Victoria said Swift met with her, David was able to prove he was in a courtroom defending a group of workingwomen accused of rioting because they held a demonstration at the headquarters of the Home Relief Bureau. David also talked to the trial judge, who readily agreed to come to Alabama and testify as a witness on David's behalf, if necessary. David wrote, "I concluded my research, covering every day of the period during which Victoria Price testified that I visited her in Alabama. I had absolute proof she lied."

So, how does one measure David's credibility as a witness on his own behalf almost eighty years after the events in question? First, it's important to consider his character as represented by his long, illustrious legal career after his arrest. For years, he worked tirelessly with clients on cases related to labor, civil liberties, and civil rights. He was General Counsel for the United Electrical, Radio and Machine Workers of America union in the 1940s and 1950s. He represented many people called to testify before the House Un-American Activities Committee. He handled cases for the families of the students of the Kent State tragedy and the Attica Prison uprising leaders. He argued four cases before the U. S. Supreme Court, winning all four. He represented either the petitioner or respondent in five cases seeking a *writ of certiorari* from the U. S. Supreme Court and won favorable rulings in three of those cases. On March 4, 1983, at the 46th Anniversary Meeting of the National Lawyers Guild, David, a founding member of the Guild, was honored for his dedicated service to the struggles of working people and for the advancement of civil liberties.

Second, how does one compare the credibility of the two competing witnesses who had a voice in these events: Victoria Price and David Scribner? If Judge Horton were involved in this case, he would ask, "Was the evidence of Victoria Price reasonable or probable? Were the facts stated reasonable?" He would likely conclude as he did in 1932 that "Her manner of testifying and demeanor on the stand militate against her. Her testimony was contradictory, often evasive, and time and again she refused to answer pertinent questions...the proof tends strongly to show that she knowingly testified falsely in many material aspects of the case." How he would have ruled on David's "testimony" is, of course, speculative, but it is probable he would have said, after considering the history of the case and the motivations of Victoria Price and the political aspirations of Thomas Knight, that David Scribner was a credible witness.

After personally reviewing all the material Aggie Scribner Kapelman provided me, I am persuaded that her father, David Scribner, is innocent of the charge of bribery and that he was illegally "kidnapped" by the Alabama authorities when they steadfastly refused to acknowledge or consider a writ of *habeas corpus* in the matter.

However, there are aspects of this sordid event that will never be fully understood. What was Pearson's role in all of this? Was he a publicity seeker? Was he an agent of the prosecution? Was he an honest Southerner looking for a way to aid the Scottsboro Boys?

What about Thomas Knight? Did he engineer the whole episode? Did he persuade Pearson, Victoria, Jack Tiller, and the police authorities to support him in this scheme? Or, did he just take advantage of the moment when Victoria said she went to the sheriff with the story of the bribe attempt? His racist views and political ambitions concerning the Scottsboro Boys certainly provided him with the motivation to take full advantage of this situation.

What about Joseph Brodsky? When Samuel Leibowitz challenged him about the reported bribe, he did not deny it but said the effort was "good propaganda for the cause" had it worked. It seems likely in his discussions with Pearson that Brodsky understood some money was on the table in dealing with Victoria. Did he purposely withhold this aspect of the deal from David and Kone? Did he just send them to Nashville knowing the situation was fraught with danger?

Those are questions we'll never know the answers to. So, the events that appeared to be northern chicanery are either entirely another example of southern chicanery, or more likely, both the North and South dipped into the chicanery pot in attempts to enhance their positions.

Now, let's leave this current discussion of events that occurred almost eighty years ago and return to Samuel Leibowitz when he appeared before the U. S. Supreme Court to present his oral arguments challenging the State of Alabama's systematic exclusion of Negroes from jury duty.

U.S. Supreme Court

ON FEBRUARY 15, 1935, as Samuel Leibowitz walked slowly toward the steps of the U.S. Supreme Court building in Washington, DC, he paused and stared nervously at the imposing structure, the apex of American jurisprudence and home of its ultimate arbiters. Leibowitz was normally quite calm when he entered a courtroom, but today was different; it was his first appearance before the high court, and he felt the pressure of the moment and its significance, both to himself and his client. Lawyers who had appeared before the high court advised Leibowitz to avoid becoming too emotional as he presented his arguments. When Chief Justice Charles Evans Hughes called on him to proceed with his oral arguments, he immediately relaxed and outlined his arguments in a quiet, controlled voice, explaining the State of Alabama's accepted practice of excluding Negroes from jury duty even though the state's laws did not explicitly call for such exclusions. The eight justices listened attentively; the ninth justice, James C. McReynolds, a southerner, had excused himself from hearing the appeal. However, Leibowitz could not contain his usual courtroom persona when he started to talk about the forged Jackson County jury rolls. He exclaimed in an emotional appeal that this forgery was an affront against both the defendants and the court.

Chief Justice Hughes immediately demanded, "Can you prove this forgery?"

Leibowitz replied, "I can your honor, I have the jury rolls here with me."

Hughes said, "Let's see them," and, for the first time in the memory of many court observers, the sitting justices examined a piece of evidence during the oral arguments of an appeal. As Leibowitz explained how the six names were fraudulently added to the document, Hughes examined the jury rolls carefully with a magnifying glass and said, passing the rolls to the next justice, "It's as plain as daylight." The other seven justices studied the document, several nodding their agreement with Hughes's assessment. Leibowitz even thought he saw Justice Brandeis smile ever so slightly at him.

Thomas Knight Jr. rose to present the state's arguments. Knight, now Alabama's lieutenant governor, was assigned by the state as a "special counsel" to specifically argue the Scottsboro case appeal before the high court. Knight, who had appeared before the high court several times, defended the state's procedures for selecting jury members, arguing it was a process of "selection," not exclusion. Concerning the appearance of six Negro names on the jury rolls, he said, somewhat incongruously, "I cannot tell you whether or not those names were forged. I simply take the position that I do not know."

On April 1, 1935, the U.S. Supreme Court issued its opinions in the Norris and Patterson appeals, both written by Chief Justice Hughes. In the Norris appeal, the court was unambiguous and unanimous in its finding that Negroes had been barred from jury duty in both Jackson and Morgan Counties. The high court, in ordering a new trial for Clarence Norris, condemned both the "sweeping characterization of the lack of qualifications" of Negroes by Alabama officials in justifying their jury selection process, and the obvious addition of six forged Negro names to the Jackson County rolls. Underscoring the importance of Judge Horton's earlier ruling that the defense had made a *prima facie* case on its motion concerning the exclusion of Negroes from juries, the opinion said, "That testimony in itself made out a *prima facie* case of the denial of the equal protection which the Constitution guarantees..." and added, "We are of the opinion that the evidence required a different result from that reached in the state court. We think that the evidence...established the discrimination which the Constitution forbids. The motion to quash the indictment upon that ground should have been granted."

Hughes's opinion repeated the court's finding that the defendant's *prima facie* case was also convincing in the Morgan County trials, adding, "And, upon the proof contained in the record now before us, a conclusion that their continuous and total exclusion from juries was because there were none possessing the requisite qualifications cannot be sustained."

In the Patterson appeal, the eight justices had to deal with two competing issues: a valid legal technical issue versus a moral issue. Legally, the high court seldom heard appeals that lower courts had denied on the basis of legal fact, as the Alabama Supreme Court had done in striking Patterson's bill of exceptions from the record since it was filed past the statutory deadline. However, the high court was faced with the moral issue that one of the two men found guilty on the same evidence would be granted a new trial, while the other faced the immediate prospect of execution. The high court issued a King Solomon-reasoned opinion in Patterson's appeal saying, "...we cannot ignore the exceptional features of the present case...We are not satisfied that the [state] court would have dealt with the case in the same way if it had determined the constitutional question as we have determined it." Implicit in the high court's opinion was a strong message to the Alabama court that failure to grant Patterson a new trial would result in another review of the case by the high court as Chief Justice Hughes wrote in the opinion, "At least the state court should have an opportunity to examine its powers in the light of the situation which has now developed…we vacate the judgment and remand the case to the state court for further proceedings."

The reactions to this latest major event in the Scottsboro cases were as varied and predictable as before. As usual, newspapers were generally split along the Mason-Dixon Line. An editorial in *The New York Times* said, "This judgment shows that the highest court in the land is anxious to secure and protect the rights of the humblest citizens." The *Montgomery Advertiser* blasted the opinions in an editorial: "Mr. Hughes's pontifical deliverance [of the opinion] is a lot of baloney. The *Advertiser* may be dumb, as well as 'lost and ruint' but to save itself it cannot see what the political rights and privileges of Negroes in Alabama have to do with the guilt or innocence of the gorillas who are charged with criminal assault upon two women."

The Communist Party hailed the high court's decision as "a smashing confirmation of the correctness of the defense policy," and the ILD added it was "proof of the might of mass pressure and mass protest."

Leibowitz was ecstatic with the high court's decisions, immediately calling them a "triumph for American justice." He thought the State would stop the prosecutions; however, he said if they were to continue, it would be by grand juries and petit juries selected from jury rolls including Negroes. Leibowitz, as usual, underestimated Alabama politicians; Lieutenant Governor Knight announced the day after the opinions were released that the State of Alabama would seek new indictments to retry the Scottsboro cases. Knight added that about ninety jurors in seven trials had found the defendants guilty, and, but for Roy Wright, they were all sentenced to die. Knight made it clear that it was his duty and obligation to prosecute the cases, and he would continue to do so.

The news of the high court's opinions delighted eight of the nine Scottsboro Boys. Patterson alone understood the implications of being retried in Alabama, as he shouted from his cell, "You must think I'm drunk if I believe that," as he added with boisterous laughter, "A new trial—a new trial."

The Legacy of the High Court's Decisions

IN SPITE OF ALL THE VARIED REACTIONS to the high court's opinions and the continued plight of the Scottsboro Boys, there was one historic fact from this moment. For the second time in the Scottsboro Boys' case, the U.S. Supreme Court had issued a landmark ruling concerning the conduct of the trials. The first ruling, in November 1932, had found the Scottsboro Boys were denied the right to secure proper defense counsel saying, "…we think the failure of the trial court to give them reasonable time and opportunity to secure counsel was a clear denial of due process." And now, this ruling, concerning the systematic exclusion of Negroes from juries in Alabama, struck at the very heart of one of the more onerous aspects of segregation: the South's denial to a large group of its citizens, based solely on the color of their skin, of their right to a trial by a jury of one's peers embedded in the Sixth and Fourteenth Amendments to the Constitution.

To this day, the U.S. Supreme Court makes constitutional decisions in a deliberate, sometimes frustratingly slow manner, and while the court tries to maintain a position uninfluenced by popular public and political opinion, it is frequently unable to do so. Michael Klarman shows and argues convincingly in his book *From Jim Crow to Civil Rights: The Supreme Court and the Struggle for Racial Equality* that the court's "constitutional interpretation almost inevitably reflects the broader social and political context of the times." One of the more egregious examples of this is the *Plessey v. Ferguson* decision in 1896 that upheld the constitutionality of racial segregation in railroad accommodations under the doctrine of "separate but equal." The South used this decision to continue and expand the "separate but equal" doctrine to many institutions and facilities, most notably education, resulting in the educational disenfranchisement of generations of black children, thus exacerbating the economic plight of blacks. "Separate but equal" was the law of the land until 1954 when the Warren Court issued its historic decision in *Brown v. Board of Education* overturning the "separate but equal" doctrine. Chief Justice Earl Warren wrote in the unanimous decision, "We conclude that, in the field of public education, the doctrine of 'separate but equal' has no place. Separate educational facilities are inherently unequal." This historic decision set the legal table for the civil rights struggle soon to follow.

Although the two U.S. Supreme Court landmark decisions in the Scottsboro cases were Pyrrhic victories for the Scottsboro Boys, as they were still imprisoned and faced the possibility of death sentences, their ordeal provided two legal stepping stones to the historic events of the 1950s and beyond.

The boys certainly didn't understand, and most of those around them failed to comprehend, the significance of the decisions and events unfolding in the moment and the changes they portended.

16.

PATTERSON'S FOURTH TRIAL
1935–1936

Alabama Implements U.S. Supreme Court Decision

AYWOOD PATTERSON AND THOMAS KNIGHT were the only two people who clearly understood that the trials and ordeals of the Scottsboro Boys were anything but over. When the newly elected governor of Alabama, Bibb Graves, instructed all Alabama state courts to follow the U.S. Supreme Court decision, many took it to mean that the state was prepared to take a different course of action on the Scottsboro case. Graves's instructions to the state courts said, "This decision means that we must put the names of Negroes in jury boxes in every county. Alabama is going to observe the supreme law of America." John Temple Graves, II, a respected Birmingham newsman, wrote in an editorial piece for *The New York Times*: "Prompt action by Governor Bibb Graves to have the names of Negroes placed in Alabama jury boxes in conformity with the decision and his statement that 'Alabama is going to observe the supreme law of America' are being taken as fresh examples of political realism and an executive courage…It is safe to suggest that the South is not half as shocked at the prospect of Negro jurors as it is at the threat of another Scottsboro trial."

On April 30, 1935, Leibowitz, encouraged by these recent activities, wrote Governor Graves and asked him to end this judicial merry-go-round and release the boys. If this was unacceptable, Leibowitz suggested to Graves that he appoint an impartial committee of prominent Alabamians to review the case and make a recommendation on its disposition. Leibowitz added that he would comply with any decisions made by the committee. Yet again, Leibowitz misread and misunderstood the situation and the South when Governor Graves's only response was a "deadening silence."

On May 16, 1935, the Alabama Supreme Court, yielding to the higher court's decisions, overturned the original indictments against the boys; however, the court made it clear that new indictments and retrials were entirely proper. Thomas Knight, in an uncharacteristically slow response to the Alabama Supreme Court decision, announced in September that he would ask for a special session of the Jackson County Grand Jury to seek new indictments. Perhaps Knight had planned a long summer vacation or decided to wait until the fall when more attention would be focused on the activities. In any case, on November 13, 1935, the Jackson County Grand Jury of seventeen white men and one black man, returned indictments against each of the nine boys on two counts: one, the rape of Victoria Price, and two, the rape of Ruby Bates. The lone black member of the grand jury was Creed Conyers, a farmer from Paint Rock and chairman of the Board of Trustees of the Paint Rock Negro Schools. Local residents said it was the first time in their memory that a black had served on a Jackson County jury as the court moved to comply with the recent U.S. Supreme Court ruling. Trying to imagine Conyers's reception and willingness to be a meaningful participant on the grand jury is best summed up by Birmingham's John Temple Graves, II, in another editorial piece for *The New York Times* on November 17: "The letter of the court's injunction is being served, perhaps, but its spirit will not prevail until the white men themselves are convinced that it is safe, comfortable and wise to rub elbows in jury rooms with their colored brothers." For Knight and the state, the more important consideration was Alabama law, which required only a two-thirds vote of a grand jury's members to return an indictment, thus, making Conyers's participation moot even if he voted against returning the indictments. The new trials were to be held in Decatur, and Judge William Callahan announced the first trial would start on January 20, 1936.

Scottsboro Defense Committee

AFTER THE U.S. SUPREME COURT DECISIONS in the Norris and Patterson appeals, the brief peace treaty between the ILD and Leibowitz dissolved as the two parties got back to business as usual, attacking each other privately and publicly over the spring and summer of 1935. Their impasse was broken by the realities of the world situation: the terrifying rise of fascism in Europe embodied in Hitler's Germany. At the Seventh Congress of the Communist Party International meeting in Moscow in July and August 1935, the party announced it would develop popular fronts with all organizations opposed to fascism to counteract the growth of power in Hitler's Germany. This new policy required the U.S. Communist Party and the ILD to do some nimble two-step footwork to abandon their existing "popular front from below" policy; this policy opposed all organizations in power such as Roosevelt and the New Deal, all Socialist parties, and most labor unions, and focused instead on the poor and unemployed. Now the party had to step back from its aggressive support "from below" of the poor and unemployed and its organization efforts with blacks, and accept a policy that embraced those it had shunned in the immediate past. The ILD did this as good soldiers do when following a commander's orders, and quickly realized they needed a new tack in their dealings with Leibowitz and the others involved in the Scottsboro case.

In September 1935, the ILD contacted the NAACP and suggested they form a broad coalition to oversee and conduct the Scottsboro defense. Initially the NAACP was, as ever, wary of the true ILD intentions and refused to meet with them. However, the NAACP finally acquiesced, and an initial meeting was held in October with representatives from the ACLU, the American Scottsboro Committee, the ILD, the League for Industrial Democracy,* and the NAACP. Leibowitz was not at the meeting, and the group knew this was a major problem, as he had the support of eight of the boys, and Haywood Patterson was also leaning his way. The ACLU and the NAACP were particularly opposed to Leibowitz's continued participation on the defense team. However, after several more meetings to discuss the issues, the group agreed to proceed if Leibowitz would agree to a compromise: continue serving as chief counsel for the defense, but let a southern lawyer handle the majority of the courtroom work.

Leibowitz agreed to the compromise, and on December 19, 1935, the Scottsboro Defense Committee (SDC) was formed as a legal entity. The ACLU, the ILD, the League for Industrial Democracy, the Methodist Federation for Social Service,[†] and the NAACP signed the formal joint defense effort agreement. At the last moment, the American Scottsboro Committee refused to sign the agreement; it seems the committee felt it had no place with the new organization after Leibowitz agreed to compromise, and it disbanded and ceased its activities shortly thereafter. The SDC agreement created an executive committee made up of one person from each participating organization. The executive committee's first task was to find a notable person to serve as SDC Chairman.

The SDC executive committee selected the Reverend Dr. Allan Knight Chalmers its chairman. Thirty-eight-year-old Dr. Chalmers was the pastor

---

* The League for Industrial Democracy was founded in 1905 by a group of notable socialists. Its early purpose was to educate Americans about the labor movement, socialism, and industrial democracy.

[†] The Methodist Federation for Social Service was founded in 1907 to seek justice and attention to the human suffering among the working class.

of the Broadway Tabernacle Congregational Church in New York City, a church with a rich history of supporting the abolition movement and other liberal social reforms. Chalmers was born in Cleveland, Ohio in 1897, and attended Johns Hopkins University where he received his degree in 1917. He was determined to serve his country in World War I, but after failing the physical examination for both the Army and Navy, he went to France and served as a second lieutenant in the Second French Army at the Verdun battlefield. He came home from Europe a devoted pacifist, horrified by what he saw and experienced, and remained so for the rest of his life. Chalmers was a soft-spoken, determined man, a good listener, and an excellent conciliator with the ability to charm whomever he was dealing with. Chalmers left Broadway Tabernacle in 1948 to join the faculty at Boston University where he was a mentor to a young divinity student from Atlanta, Martin Luther King Jr. Chalmers continued to support and counsel King until King's assassination in 1968.

Although Chalmers wanted the newly formed SDC to immediately establish a working relationship with a like-minded group in Alabama, he and the other SDC members knew their initial focus had to be the preparation and conduct of the first trial in Decatur on January 20, 1936. The SDC and Leibowitz had agreed in their compromise to add a southern lawyer to the defense team to handle the day-to-day activities in the Decatur courtroom. In fact, some hoped that Leibowitz would stay out of the Decatur courtroom altogether. They hired a Huntsville lawyer, forty-nine-year-old Clarence Watts, after Judge James Horton advised them that Watts was the best lawyer in the area for their needs. Horton also advised the SDC and Leibowitz to focus on the medical testimony, as Horton considered it the most damning evidence against the prosecution's case.

Watts, who reluctantly agreed to become involved in the case, was a member of a prominent Huntsville-area family. For eight years, he worked as secretary to the Huntsville district member of the House of Representatives in Washington, DC. During those years, he attended Georgetown University where he received his law degree in 1913. He was paternalistic—considering himself to be a kindly, father figure to the blacks he associated with—in his racial views, as were many of his fellow well-to-do Alabamians. However, he did believe, and stated publicly, that Victoria Price was not raped, and this position, along with Horton's endorsement, was what mattered to the SDC and to Leibowitz.

Haywood Patterson's Fourth Trial, January 20–24, 1936

THE TWO RULINGS favorable to the defense by the U.S. Supreme Court had minimal impact on the overall conduct of the subsequent trials. The State of Alabama complied with the letter of the law required by the high court's rulings, but certainly not with the broader intent to ensure the Scottsboro Boys* a fair trial. Nothing illustrates this more dramatically than Haywood Patterson's fourth trial. At an arraignment hearing on January 6, 1936, Haywood and the other eight boys pleaded not guilty to the new indictment, and Judge Callahan angrily denied a defense motion for a change of venue to a federal court.

Judge Callahan called Haywood's fourth trial to order on Monday, January 20. With two major exceptions and several minor ones, this trial can be viewed as an instant replay of Haywood's previous trial under Judge Callahan. The first major exception was the jury selection process; twelve black men were called, along with eighty-eight white men, for the prospective juror pool. Although the black men were in the juror pool, all other aspects of segregation and southern racial prejudices were present in the courtroom. The twelve men were not allowed to sit in the jury box with the white men, but were required to sit in separate chairs set up for them adjacent to the jury box. When one confused, and obviously scared, black man was called with a group of twelve for review during the normal selection process, he mistakenly tried to take a seat in the jury box. Callahan immediately admonished the man, "Here, boy, sit over there." None of the twelve black men was selected for the jury panel; seven were excused for cause, and the prosecution used its peremptory challenges to reject the remaining five. Haywood later said of the jury's composition, illustrating a complete understanding of the racial undertones present in the courtroom, "I didn't want no scared Negroes judging me."

Although Samuel Leibowitz was in the courtroom, Clarence Watts conducted most of the defense's case. Watts did a credible job of representing Haywood as he constantly battled with the prosecution and its witnesses, and, most frustratingly, with Callahan. Watts's presence in the courtroom, as a local southern lawyer for the defense, proved to be of no measurable value to the outcome of the trial. If anything, Callahan treated Watts more roughly and rudely than he had Leibowitz at the earlier trial.

Victoria Price testified for the eighth time, and was on the witness stand for less than an hour since Callahan refused to let the defense ask her questions about her movements and actions the few days before the alleged rapes. Orville Gilley, the self-proclaimed hobo poet and star prosecution witness at the last Decatur trials, was not available as a witness at this trial, as he was in jail in Tennessee for assaulting and robbing two women.

---

* I continue to use the word "boys" for the Scottsboro defendants, not as a pejorative description, but as a consistent term of reference throughout the book. After almost five years of jail and legal proceedings, the "boys" were now young men.

As before, Callahan's demeanor throughout Haywood's trial was biased and prejudicial. He constantly prodded the defense to move faster, made and sustained objections of his own against the defense even though the prosecution had made no objections to the testimony, made frequent aside comments to the jury prejudicial to the defense's case, and would not allow the defense to probe the medical testimony of Dr. Bridges. Knight cross-examined Lester Carter, a defense witness who was with the girls on the freight train, about Carter's coast-to-coast wanderings. Leibowitz asked Callahan why, if Knight could probe the movements of Carter, the defense was not permitted to do so with Victoria Price. Callahan was furious and threatened to cite Leibowitz for contempt, as he shouted, "I won't have insinuations that you were denied something that somebody else got." Several times during the trial Watts moved for a mistrial based on Judge Callahan's comments and conduct, and Callahan always angrily dismissed the motions with a statement like he "did not want to hear any further argument." Of Callahan, Haywood said, "He couldn't get us to the chair fast enough."

After closing arguments and Callahan's instructions to the jury, which were quite similar to the ones at Haywood's last trial, the case was given to the jury late in the evening on Wednesday, January 22. However, the jury did not begin its deliberations until the next morning when Callahan started the jury selection process for Clarence Norris's trial. This time the jury pool consisted of five black men and ninety-five white men. Again, none of the five black men was selected for the final jury: one was excused for cause and the other four were dismissed by the prosecution's use of peremptory challenges. A chilling episode that clearly illustrates the depth of the courtroom and community prejudice against the boys took place during the jury selection process. Callahan asked a group of twelve prospective jurors to raise their hands if they had a "fixed opinion" about the case, and none of the men raised as much as a finger. Watts then pointed out to the court that three of these men had served on the juries in the last two Decatur trials where they found Haywood and Clarence guilty and sentenced them to death. Although the court record is not specific, presumably the three men were dropped from the jury pool.

Late Thursday afternoon, January 23, just after the Norris jury was selected and sworn in, the Patterson jury was ready with a verdict after deliberating for about eight hours. The two juries walked past each other as the Patterson jury entered the courtroom, and the Norris jury walked to the witness room; it was a scene reminiscent of the jury crossings that took place in the 1931 trials in Scottsboro. John Burleson, the jury foreman, handed Callahan the slip of paper with the verdict, and Callahan had the court clerk read it aloud, "We, the jury, find the defendant Haywood

Patterson guilty as charged, and"—now the second major exception in this trial occurred.

The clerk concluded with the jury's decision to "fix his punishment at seventy-five years in prison."

The clerk handed the piece of paper back to Callahan, and he seemed perplexed as he studied it. The prosecution team looked shaken by the verdict. Victoria Price wandered around mumbling "Twant fair" after she heard the verdict in the witness room. Samuel Leibowitz was not ecstatic, but he was pleased, as the verdict had at least taken a turn away from a death sentence.

The verdict was due to the actions and convictions of one man, John Burleson, the brother of National Guard Captain Joseph Burleson, who guarded Leibowitz and the Scottsboro Boys at Patterson's trial in Judge Horton's court in 1933. Thirty-five-year-old John Burleson was born and raised in Morgan County, was a devout Methodist, did not smoke or use chewing tobacco, and did not drink liquor. He graduated from Morgan County High School, spent two years at the Gulf Coast Military Academy, a West Point preparatory school in Gulfport, Mississippi, left the academy to pursue a career as a professional baseball player, and returned a few years later to his family's farm to become one of the county's most prosperous farmers. He entered the jury pool with an open mind and later said he wanted to see "justice done no matter whether a man is black, yellow, red or white." He was surprised when the prosecution didn't exempt him from the jury. Throughout the trial he became convinced that Victoria Price was not telling the truth, and he went into the jury room for the deliberations determined to find Patterson innocent. The other eleven jurors were equally determined to find Patterson guilty and sentence him to death. Rather than suffer a hung jury, Burleson decided to try to save Patterson's life, and he was able to get the other jurors to go along with a sentence of seventy-five years. Some will argue that Burleson should have held to his not guilty position, pushing the immediate case to a hung jury. The outcome of such an action would have been another Patterson trial and another jury, which would have surely found him guilty and sentenced him to death. Although there were still many bumps and turns to come for the Scottsboro Boys, Burleson's decision probably represented the turning point in the Scottsboro Boys' case. Lest it appears the Burleson brothers were completely enlightened Southerners, they both considered segregation of the races a necessity, and blacks inferior to whites; however, they were honorable men who did not let their prejudices overcome their sense of justice and duty.

Friday morning, January 24, the trial of Clarence Norris was scheduled to begin, but the preliminaries hit an early snag when Leibowitz and Knight were unable to agree on how to handle the medical testimony of Dr. Bridges, who was near death in Scottsboro. Neither party would take the responsibility of bringing the doctor to the court, nor would Knight agree to Leibowitz's suggestion of using a narrative abstract of the doctor's earlier testimony, although Knight had agreed to such an arrangement in Patterson's just concluded trial. Judge Callahan offered to break the impasse by postponing the Norris trial, but he wanted to proceed with the trials of Andy Wright and Charlie Weems on Monday, January 27. Leibowitz wouldn't agree, saying the doctor's testimony was equally important for all the trials, and Callahan postponed the trials indefinitely with a hope of resuming them in April.

After the Norris jury was dismissed, Callahan had Haywood brought into the court and formally sentenced him to seventy-five years in the state penitentiary. When asked by Callahan if he had anything to say before he was sentenced, Haywood replied, "Yes sir, Your Honor, I am not guilty and I don't think justice has been done me in my case."

Haywood Patterson realized the implication of the sentence. The thought of seventy-five years in an Alabama prison was more than he wanted to endure, saying, "It was no victory for me...I knew I was going to be driven to a slow death...I would have been better off with the death sentence." Haywood would prove to be absolutely right in his assessment of the situation, as his remaining years would prove to be anything but enjoyable.

All Hell Breaks Loose

AFTER HAYWOOD WAS SENTENCED on January 24, the out-of-town participants in the case departed Decatur that afternoon. Samuel Leibowitz boarded a train for Chattanooga for the first leg of his trip to New York. Clarence Watts drove to his home in Huntsville. The state organized a caravan of five cars to take the nine boys back to the Birmingham jail; three of the cars held three boys handcuffed together in the back seat with two police officers in the front seat. Two carloads of state highway patrolmen escorted the caravan. Thomas Knight's car, driven by a black chauffeur, followed the caravan.

In the car carrying Ozie Powell, Clarence Norris, and Roy Wright, an event occurred that would instantly negate any benefit the defense thought it had achieved with the jury's verdict in Haywood's trial. About twenty miles south of Decatur near Cullman, Alabama, Ozie suddenly pulled a four-inch switchblade from his pocket with his free right hand, reached over the back seat, and slashed the fleshy part of the double chin of deputy sheriff Edgar Blalock, who was riding shotgun in the front seat. A scuffle ensued in the car, and, after the car was brought under control and stopped by the driver, Morgan County Sheriff J. Street Sandlin, the sheriff's gun fired. Ozie was seriously wounded when the bullet penetrated the upper part of his skull and remained embedded about an inch deep in his brain.

After the police officers got the situation under control, Knight, who had stopped his car to assist, had his chauffeur drive the wounded Blalock to a nearby hospital in Cullman. The doctor who treated the deputy sheriff said the wound was not critical, and although it took twelve sutures to close the six-inch long cut, Blalock recovered with no problems.

Ozie was driven to a Birmingham hospital, still handcuffed to Clarence and Roy, where a neurosurgeon successfully removed the bullet from his brain; however, the surgeon put Ozie's odds of survival at fifty-fifty. Ozie did recover, but the doctor said he would likely suffer some permanent brain damage. The doctor was right. Clarence later said of Ozie's injuries, "He was never the same as he was...He was really a little off after that. He had brain damage of some kind. It was a goddamn shame." Olen Montgomery, when asked why Ozie did it, said he didn't really know, but he "hasn't real good sense no way I dont believe."

As usual in incidents like these, there were conflicting stories about the event. The one fact not in contention was that Ozie did slash Blalock across the lower chin with a knife. Beyond that point, Sandlin and Blalock maintained that the three boys had planned to escape, and that Ozie's slashing of Blalock's throat was the start of their escape attempt. The two officers said the boys then attempted to take possession of the car by trying to grab Sandlin's pistol. Sandlin said the pistol was inadvertently fired in the struggle, and the situation was not stabilized until he was able to stop the car and get assistance.

The boys told a much different story. Ozie said he paid thirty-five cents to an unidentified black kid to smuggle the knife to him in the Decatur jail. Ozie added he became convinced he and the others would not arrive in Birmingham alive when he heard the police officers talking about killing them all. The boys said Blalock was also cussing and ranting about the "Communist, Jew, Northern lawyers," when Ozie said, "I wouldn't give up the help I have for no damn Southern lawyer that I've seen." Ozie said he cut Blalock after Blalock slapped him for his sassy comment. Clarence and Roy denied there was any plan afoot to escape, citing the somewhat favorable recent verdict coupled with the poor odds of success in this heavily guarded caravan. The truth of this encounter was never completely known; however, it was a situation of the word of two white men versus the three black boys, and the outcome of that debate was never in doubt in Alabama. On January 28, Alabama Governor Graves issued a statement completely exonerating Sandlin and Blalock, and he praised their actions in handling "a most delicate and deplorable situation in an efficient manner."

The aftermath of the incident was predictable, as all hell did break loose: it fanned the flames of racial bias and hatred in the South; relit the torches of righteous indignation in the North; and fed the brimstone-like rhetoric rising from all directions.

Samuel Leibowitz heard about the incident in Chattanooga and immediately headed for Birmingham. In Birmingham, he had to force his way into the hospital to see Ozie, and the Birmingham jail to see the other boys. After talking to the boys, he was convinced they had not tried to escape and that the incident was precipitated by the constant haranguing the boys received in the Decatur jail and from Sandlin and Blalock in the car. Leibowitz released a not too subtle statement about the incident, saying, "Does the Sheriff of Morgan County claim that three Negroes shackled together in the rear seat of a rapidly moving automobile, with only two doors leading to the front compartment, with two men in that automobile armed to the teeth, this car preceded in front by an automobile carrying two other armed officers of the law and followed by still another car with armed guards and with State highway patrolmen as an escort, did attempt to escape using a pen-knife?"

On January 29, *The New York Times* responded to Governor Graves's assessment saying, while it was clear that Ozie Powell did slash the officer, "it strains belief that a handcuffed man could precipitate a struggle for the pistol of an officer in the seat in front and bring about a situation where he could be stopped only by a bullet in the brain."

Birmingham's *The Age-Herald* was typical of southern response when it mirrored the governor's views, saying the incident "should be an answer to unjust charges that Southern officers are always quick on the trigger when negroes accused of rape attempt to escape."

A most prophetic reaction came from Dr. Henry Edmonds, when he wrote, "The cutting and shooting affray near Cullman has seriously altered the whole aspect of the case." Edmonds added that Patterson's seventy-five year sentence "showed a new and hopeful attitude on the part of Southern juries in such cases," but concluded, "If Patterson were tried today he would get death. There is a new tenseness that bodes ill for the future trials."

17.

ALABAMA SCOTTSBORO COMMITTEE
1936

AFTER HAYWOOD PATTERSON'S FOURTH TRIAL and the Ozie Powell incident, Allan Chalmers was even more determined to forge a working relationship between the SDC and a group in Alabama. He was convinced such an alliance would provide a defense coalition that would lead to freedom for the Scottsboro Boys. Dr. Henry Edmonds, who was as liberal- and open-minded as almost any southerner you could find at the time, agreed, although skeptically, to meet with Chalmers in February of 1936 to discuss the feasibility of a North-South defense group.

The Magic Years Surely End

WAIGHTS WROTE OF HIS YOUTH IN BIRMINGHAM: "Could any other world ever have been filled with half the magic of those twelve years from 1918 to 1930?" Any magic leftover from 1930 for the family surely came to an end on March 11, 1936, when Angus died, finally succumbing to the effects of his earlier stroke and the business pressures caused by the Great Depression. In late 1935, Waights had returned to Birmingham from Mobile and his job with the *Mobile Register* newspaper. He found a position with the Birmingham Chamber of Commerce and was just getting settled into his new position when Angus died, the first of several events to unexpectedly redirect his life.

All the Taylor Boys returned home for what had to be the saddest day of their young lives. Angus, who had little formal education, had toiled all his life to see that his five sons were given the education that eluded him. The Board of Elders of Angus's church, the Independent Presbyterian

Church, wrote in a church resolution expressing appreciation for his life work in the church and the community, "These five stalwart sons were the glory and pride of his life."

After the funeral, the family gathered in the Sixteenth Avenue South home to deal with the financial realities of the situation. Angus had accumulated a large amount of bank debt over the last six years as he struggled to keep his business afloat. Margie, with the agreement of her five sons, decided to sell the Sixteenth Avenue South house, the adjacent "new lot," and Angus's business. The moneys from these sales were used to pay off the bank debt; however, since there wasn't enough money to cover the entire obligation, several banks agreed to forgive the remaining debt, as Angus had been a good customer over the years and was a respected member of the community. Family members then returned to their respective pursuits: Margie moved into an apartment, continued her work as a travel agent, and would soon open her own travel agency in Birmingham; Angus Jr. and Bill returned to their jobs with the FBI and Pan Am; Frank and Macey returned to the university to complete their college days; Waights continued working for the Birmingham Chamber of Commerce, but he was soon to be interrupted by two very different demands for his time and attention.

In April, Waights was on a date with a young lady friend at a party at a friend's house when he saw Rose for the first time. Waights asked his date who she was.

"Oh, that's Ethel Rose Dawson."

Rose was a beautiful, auburn-haired twenty-one-year-old. Waights took his date home early, returned home, and called the Dawson household. Rose knew who Waights was; the Taylor Boys were well-known young men on the Birmingham scene. After some brief chitchat, Waights asked Rose for a date the next evening. When she replied she was busy, he asked about the following night, and she said she was also busy that evening. Thinking he was being put off, he asked one more time for a date a few days later, and, to his surprise, Rose said yes.

On their eventual date, Waights and Rose had a delightful evening, and they soon saw each other on a regular basis, a regularity that would last a lifetime.

Rose lived with her mother, Madge, and her fourteen-year-old sister, Anne. Rose was born on July 13, 1914 in Perry, Florida, a town in northern Florida's Panhandle near the Georgia border. Her mother, Madge Buckels, was born in 1894 in Jasper, Florida. In 1912 at age eighteen, Madge married Samuel Dawson, born in 1892 in Georgetown, South Carolina, and the family moved to Birmingham soon after Rose was born. After the Great Depression started, Samuel's lumber business declined precipitously, and he moved to California to seek his fortune. Madge, as headstrong a woman as you'll ever meet, refused to go with him. Samuel left Birmingham in 1930 without his family, he and Madge were divorced in 1934, and Rose would see her father again on only two short visits to California before his death in 1971. Rose missed her father terribly, and the separation was a burden she carried the rest of her life; even in her nineties, Rose talked about the loss she felt when Samuel left in 1930. Madge had a difficult time financially after Samuel went to California, as he apparently left the family little financial support. Madge had to sell the family home and rent a house for her and the two girls. They received assistance from family and friends, and Madge found a job with the Welfare Service Department in Birmingham as a social worker. Now, knowing Madge's strong personality and feelings of racial superiority over blacks, imagining her as a social worker is like imagining Attila the Hun dispensing social services to the needy in one of his conquered cities. Yet, a social worker she was, and would continue to be until 1942.

Alabama Scottsboro Committee

WHILE WAIGHTS SETTLED INTO HIS NEW JOB and continued wooing Rose, Allan Chalmers waited until the initial furor over the Powell cutting and shooting incident subsided. He then traveled to Birmingham for a meeting on February 20, 1936, with a small group led by two Birmingham clergymen, Episcopal Bishop William G. McDowell and Dr. Henry Edmonds. The meeting, which was led by McDowell on the Alabama side, was brief and did not lead to a definitive agreement. Chalmers returned to New York, exchanged a few letters with both McDowell and Edmonds, and realized he should work more directly with Edmonds, as McDowell was proving to be more rigid in his views than Chalmers first realized. At first it appeared an agreement could not be reached with Edmonds either, as the two sides were in disagreement on several issues. Edmonds and his small group wanted Scottsboro Defense Committee's agreement on three major issues: one, replace Leibowitz as the chief defense counsel with a prominent Alabama lawyer; two, convince the ILD to refrain from issuing inflammatory press releases; and three, do not require the Alabamians to state publicly that the Scottsboro Boys were innocent. Edmonds's group felt all three issues needed to be addressed to minimize negative Alabama public opinion if the case was to be resolved in the Alabama courts to the boys' benefit.

After Chalmers and Edmonds exchanged several more letters, Edmonds finally agreed in April to form a committee, the Alabama Scottsboro Committee, with the single goal of securing the Scottsboro Boys an unprejudiced trial. Edmonds immediately proceeded to organize the core of the committee, which included James Chappell, president and general manager of the *Birmingham News* and *Age-Herald*; Forney Johnston, a prominent Alabama attorney and the son of a former governor; Donald Comer, another son of a former governor and the owner of Avondale Mills; and Guy Snaveley, president of Birmingham-Southern College. Edmonds also knew he needed an energetic young man to serve as executive secretary to the committee, as Edmonds and the other members of the committee were too busy to do the day-to-day work. So, Edmonds did what any smart manager or organizer would do; he turned to an individual he knew well with the personal and writing skills the position required, Waights Taylor.

Waights, now twenty-three years old, had just recently met Rose Dawson and was more interested in pursuing his relationship with her and his new job at the Birmingham Chamber of Commerce. At first, he resisted Edmonds's offer, but Edmonds, Waights's lifelong minister, persisted and Waights soon acquiesced. To understand why Waights yielded to Henry Edmonds's entreaties to work for the Alabama Scottsboro Committee, one only has to look at Edmonds's background and his relationship to the Taylor family.

Henry Morris Edmonds was born in 1879 in York, Alabama in Sumter County, the heart of the Black Belt. Unlike Thomas Knight Jr., Edmonds would grow out of his youthful years in the Black Belt with a more liberal view of the South's racial situation and the need for change. Edmonds graduated from the University of Tennessee in 1899 and the Louisville Presbyterian Seminary in 1907. In 1913, he accepted the pastorate at the South Highland Presbyterian Church in Birmingham. While at South Highland, Edmonds had to come to grips with his current theological views being much more liberal than many in his congregation and the orthodox Southern Presbyterian Church views, and his desire to expand his ministry into social programs in the community.

He did not believe the Bible was a consistent body of divine revelation, he rejected the Presbyterian belief that man is totally depraved, and he considered God a loving, forgiving father. However, his view on the Atonement, the Christian orthodox belief that Jesus died a vicarious death to satisfy God's demand for justice for man's sins, would create his biggest problem with orthodox Presbyterian principles. Edmonds believed, and argued, that Jesus did not come to die for our sins but came to teach us what a good life is and how to live one, and that God forgives us because he loves us. Edmonds also embraced the tenets of the Social Gospel movement, a late nineteenth-century and early twentieth-century Protestant Christian intellectual movement that applied Christian ethics to social problems. Edmonds had ideas for several social programs he wanted to develop within the framework of the church to assist those less fortunate in the Birmingham community. In his first two years at South Highland, Edmonds established an employment bureau and several missions in industrial areas around Birmingham. When asked what an employment bureau had to do with the church, he replied, "Get a man a job, get him bread—then ask him to pray for you and come to church with you. A successful and well-conducted employment bureau in a church, for instance, is of equal value, if not greater importance than prayer meetings! There's something odd!"

Throughout the summer of 1915, an aging, influential elder of the church had made it clear to all that he was unhappy with Edmonds and his liberal views. In September 1915, Edmonds's beliefs came to a head with the Session, the church's ruling body of elders. The Session met several times over the next few weeks to discuss the issue, and, although Session members were almost evenly split in their support or opposition to Edmonds, the matter was referred to the North Alabama Presbytery for resolution. The Presbytery, a group of elders and ministers who governed the churches in North Alabama, met with Edmonds and several of his supporters on October 19 to consider his theological views. After two days of interviews and discussion, the Presbytery issued a report finding Edmonds's views on the Atonement at odds with the orthodox Presbyterian belief. Edmonds was asked to reconsider his view on the Atonement "by further reflection, study and prayer," and instructed not to preach or write about the disputed point for six months until the Presbytery met again to issue a final finding.

Henry Edmonds was unwilling to accept either of the Presbytery's findings, and, on October 23, he resigned his position at South Highland Presbyterian Church. Edmonds and several of his South Highland supporters started work on the formation of a new church the day after the Presbytery's report was issued. On Sunday, October 24, 1915, the first service of the newly created Independent Presbyterian Church was held in Temple Emanu-El. Edmonds's good friend, Rabbi Morris Newfield, had offered the new church the use of the synagogue, which was just a few blocks from South Highland. Over the years, Independent Presbyterian Church would grow to become one of the more influential and successful Christian churches in Birmingham.

Soon after Independent Presbyterian started services, Angus and Margie Taylor joined the church. Angus was an early elder in the church and was a strong supporter of it until his death. All the Taylor Boys attended the church, and the entire family became close and valued friends of Henry Edmonds. Waights could not refuse his request to become the executive secretary of the Alabama Scottsboro Committee.

The first formal meeting of the Alabama Scottsboro Committee was on April 28, 1936, where Edmonds was formally elected committee chairman and Waights was confirmed as its executive secretary. Besides handling all of the committee's correspondence and meeting minutes, Waights was assigned the task of traveling the state to enlist the support of prominent Alabamians to the committee's position and objective. He was paid $37.50 per week plus his travel expenses for his full-time effort.

Waights immediately started work on one of his principal Alabama Scottsboro Committee assignments, traveling the state to elicit the support of prominent Alabamians. He regretted the travel, as it limited his opportunities to date Rose, but, over the next six weeks, he covered most of the state and was quite successful in lining up support for the committee's position. Waights was a charming young man, persuasive, and well spoken. He used these skills and the name of Dr. Henry Edmonds to enlist over fifty supporters. The list was impressive and included George H. Denny, president of the University of Alabama; A. J. Farrar, dean of the University of Alabama Law School; Thomas E. Kilby, a former governor of Alabama; James Mills, editor of *The Birmingham Post*; Dr. W. D. Partlow, superintendent of Alabama's state mental hospital; Algernon Blair, a Montgomery building contractor; Judge W. H. Tayloe, Uniontown; F. T. Raiford, Selma publisher; Harry M. Ayres, Anniston publisher; Dr. E. T. Belshaw, Mobile; Roderick Beddow, Birmingham attorney; Rabbi Morris Newfield, Birmingham; and William Mitch, president of the Alabama Federation of Labor.

Waights and Edmonds were also in contact with Files Crenshaw Sr., President of the Alabama Bar Association, requesting the services of prominent Alabama lawyers to handle the case. Crenshaw was noncommittal but agreed to pursue the request with several of his colleagues.* In the interim, the committee was able to get one prominent Alabama lawyer to commit to the case; Congressman Archibald Hill Carmichael, representing Alabama's Eighth Congressional District in the northwest corner of the state, agreed to join the defense team. Although Carmichael believed in segregation as a social necessity, he also believed the Scottsboro Boys were innocent, and said he would do all he could to secure their unconditional release.

The Alabama Scottsboro Committee tried to work in complete secrecy during this period of establishing the committee's framework and supporters. Edmonds wanted to wait until all the pieces were in place before announcing the committee's existence, its list of supporters, and any new

---

* It's little wonder that Crenshaw Sr. was noncommittal. In 1936, his son Files Crenshaw Jr. coauthored a book titled *Scottsboro: The Firebrand of Communism*. The book held that the Scottsboro Boys were guilty based on their own testimony in several of the trials. The book also charged the Communists for the continuation of the trials and for plotting revolution and discord in Alabama; the latter charge would be used for years by Alabama politicians and newspapers during any labor or civil rights disputes.

Alabama lawyers on the case. Thomas Knight would again try to thwart any activities aimed at improving the defense effort or securing the boys' release. From an unknown source, Knight obtained a copy of committee letters to Files Crenshaw Sr., and on June 9, Knight sent the contents of the letters to the press along with his own scathing comments about their contents.

On June 10, the *Montgomery Advertiser* printed a lengthy article based on the material Knight released. The article said, "Waights M. Taylor, of Birmingham, who signed [the correspondence] as secretary of the Alabama committee, said the group was 'confident that the request for designation of Alabama counsel to assist in the defense will come from the defendants themselves, after the withdrawal of Mr. Leibowitz from the case...this committee has nothing to do with the action of Mr. Leibowitz—nor does it intend in any way to influence his action—but the committee does have assurance from other sources that this action will be that which I have mentioned.'"

Knight wrote with his release of the Alabama Scottsboro Committee's correspondence, "I have nothing to say as to who shall be appointed to represent these defendants," but added, "Apparently Dr. Edmonds and Mr. Chalmers are working in unison on a committee to secure adequate representation for the defendants in the 'Scottsboro' case. The defendants, to the best of my recollection, have been represented by 21 lawyers, part of whom were native Alabamians, and the rest of the array of counsel were from the Empire State of New York...Whatever publicity Dr. Edmonds and Mr. Chalmers, of the New York committee, desire to give to the defense is a matter of no consequence to me..."

Samuel Leibowitz immediately responded to the contents of the released correspondence saying, "There is not the slightest bit of truth [in the Alabama committee assertions]...The American Scottsboro Committee with headquarters in New York is the one in charge of this case. The Alabama committee has nothing to do with it." Leibowitz went on to say that he had never heard of the Alabama committee chairman, Dr. Henry Edmonds. A few days later, Waights said Knight "sat back and gleefully waited for the feathers to fly" after releasing the letters, as Knight was sure his action would turn public opinion against the newly formed committee.

The "feathers" did fly for a few days, as Edmonds came to the stark realization of the lengths Knight would go to successfully prosecute and execute the nine boys. Chalmers had to use all his charm and powers of persuasion to calm Leibowitz down; after Chalmers told Leibowitz he would be involved in the approval process of any prospective Alabama lawyers, Leibowitz agreed to stay home for the next trials if a well-known, well-qualified southern lawyer was available to defend the boys.

To Knight's surprise, his strategy backfired, as he underestimated Edmonds's resolve, determination, and support. On June 11, Edmonds left Birmingham with Waights in tow to visit their supporters who were wavering after Knight's ploy. The trip was successful as the support coalition held, and the Alabama press was generally on Edmonds's side in the aftermath of Knight's latest move. Birmingham's *The Age-Herald* wrote on its editorial page, "The dual objective implicit in the formation of the Alabama Scottsboro Committee must command the unqualified support of all good citizens of Alabama...The objective obviously is at once specifically to obtain and expedite justice for the defendants...and in general to uphold the law and the good name of this state...It is difficult to see how Lieut. Gov. Knight, special prosecutor in the case, reasoned that he was at liberty to release the correspondence. It is easier to agree literally that, as he said, he 'took' the liberty."

Edmonds advised Chalmers that the situation was improving when he wrote, "We are making very definite and rapid strides in the direction of our goal." It was thought Callahan would not preside over the next trials because of poor health, and that Knight might be persuaded to step down as chief prosecutor. In July, Edmonds's hopes were short lived when all these expectations proved wrong; Callahan and Knight were showing no willingness to withdraw, and, to make matters worse, the Scottsboro Defense Committee considered Representative Carmichael's demand for ten thousand dollars for the first trial and five thousand for each additional trial completely unacceptable and beyond their budgetary resources. At this point, Leibowitz announced he would be present at the coming trials, as he could not, in good faith, leave the boys at such a critical time in their defense.

As usual, through all this back and forth between the two committees, Knight, and Leibowitz, the condition and plight of the Scottsboro Boys remained in the background. Unfortunately for the boys, the Birmingham jail sheriff had seen fit to place seven of the boys in solitary confinement because, as the sheriff stated, "when prisoners of their prominence are allowed to mix with other prisoners there is difficulty." Chalmers became so concerned about their mental health and welfare that he asked the Alabama committee to intervene on the boys' behalf and get them returned to more normal cells. In August, Waights wrote to Morris Shapiro, the executive secretary of the Scottsboro Defense Committee, on behalf of the Alabama committee, "Much as we deplore the fact that the boys are being kept in solitary confinement, it has been the general contention of our committee all along that our work will be more effective if it is confined primarily to the effort of securing a fair and impartial trial…pressure might ultimately do the defendants more harm than good." Chalmers and his committee were quite upset with this attitude and response, and Chalmers came to the conclusion that the solitary confinement was a deliberate attempt by the state to break the boys through isolation, minimal social contact, and no exercise.

Any rapport between the two committees started to rapidly unravel from August on, as they were unable to resolve the issues that separated them. The Alabama committee was strapped for funds, and the wide support it had garnered started to fade; there was, in fact, a Scottsboro case fatigue settling in with many in Alabama, who just wished the whole affair would come to an end. The Alabama Scottsboro Committee ceased its formal activities at year end, and Edmonds, in language uncharacteristically harsh for his nature, wrote Chalmers in January 1937 chastising him for the New York committee's failure to meet its obligations to the Alabama committee: "You were to keep the Communist group silent; you were going to get Leibowitz out; you were going to furnish the money necessary to pay the Alabama counsel." Edmonds soon apologized to Chalmers for his brusque language, and the two men remained close friends and continued to work together for years on a personal level as they sought a satisfactory resolution to the plight of the Scottsboro Boys.

The overall impact of the Alabama Scottsboro Committee on the ultimate resolution of the case was marginal, at best. The committee was unable to deliver on its primary objective of securing the Scottsboro Boys an unprejudiced trial led by a team of well-qualified Alabama lawyers. The committee's one achievement was to raise the awareness throughout the state of the prejudicial trials that occurred under Callahan and Knight. The committee also succeeded in uncloaking Knight's unseemly character and intentions with their prompt reaction to Knight's release of the committee's correspondence. It is interesting to read the later reactions of Chalmers and Leibowitz to the Alabama Scottsboro Committee. Chalmers worked for years with Edmonds and several other Alabama committee members on the case, and he wrote in his book about the Scottsboro case, *They Shall Be Free*, "In all, a group of some forty-nine prominent Alabama citizens formed the Alabama Scottsboro Committee and we have worked in complete harmony through these years."

Leibowitz had a more critical view of the committee's work. He felt the committee had accomplished little, although he did respect the character and reputation of the men on the committee. Their willingness to speak out provided a shock to the southern press, who had pushed as hard as Thomas Knight for the boys' conviction.

Both Chalmers and Leibowitz are correct from their different perspectives and involvement with the Alabama committee.

Waights's work for the Alabama Scottsboro Committee came to an end in November 1936, and, fortunately, he was able to return to his job with the Birmingham Chamber of Commerce. When Donald Rasmussen interviewed Waights in 1947, Waights said the following about the Scottsboro case:

> I went to work for the Alabama Scottsboro Committee—a group of liberal Southerners who tried to see that justice was done in that case. I didn't do that because I was burning up over the issue…We just heard a lot about it and I went to a meeting Dr. Edmonds organized to help the boys and to keep in touch with the northern organizations. I did some volunteer work for them. Then they needed a full time person so I did that for a few months…When I worked on the Scottsboro Committee, several Negroes were on it too—mainly ministers. We had several interracial meetings without segregation. This was not a problem to me.

When Rasmussen asked Waights if he ever used the n-word, Waights replied:

> Frankly, I still do sometimes although I correct myself when I can. I do use Nigra quite often and I am only gradually getting natural about using Negro. Since you speak of traces of prejudice, there is one thing that I have a hard time getting out of my system, and that is addressing Negroes without [using a] title—Doctor, Professor, Reverend, Boy, etc. Yes, but it almost hurts me physically to call them Mr. Yet, I am increasingly getting used to it.

The Alabama Scottsboro Committee and the Scottsboro Boys were obviously not a crusade for Waights, but something he did because he was asked to by Dr. Edmonds. It is also obvious that this southern "liberal" was a far cry from a true liberal in 1936 and was still struggling with his thoughts on race in 1947. Waights's "liberal" racial views were molded more by Clarence Cason than Joseph Gelders, a true liberal by any measure. Change in the South's racial attitudes and social customs would not come from the large number of southern white "liberals" who shared Waights Taylor's background and opinions.

18.

THE LAST TRIALS
1937

WAIGHTS PROPOSED TO ROSE in December 1936. Rose readily accepted, but they initially waited before deciding on a wedding date. However, in early 1937, they changed their minds and were married on February 27, 1937, by Dr. Edmonds. As the newlyweds were quietly settling into married life, events surrounding the Scottsboro Boys moved forward at an even more rapid pace.

Alabama Almost Yields

MOST OF THE PARTIES involved with the Scottsboro Boys were now looking for ways to bring an end to the continuous process of trial and appeal that characterized the case. In January 1937, Allan Chalmers become so concerned about the boys' year in solitary confinement that he asked a physician from Tuskegee Institute, Dr. George C. Branche, to visit the Birmingham jail and do a psychiatric examination of their condition. Not surprisingly, after more than six years in various jails and courtrooms, Dr. Branche reported that the mental and physical condition of the boys had deteriorated by varying degrees with several showing significant signs of prison neurosis, an advanced neurotic reaction to prison confinement. Dr. Branche also tested the boys' mental acuity, and found both Ozie Powell and Willie Roberson with IQs of sixty-four and mental ages of about nine. Interestingly, Dr. Branche did not comment on Clarence Norris's condition, presumably because he was coping reasonably well with prison life. While Clarence's autobiography certainly doesn't sing the virtues of prison life, he seldom writes of the experience in the harsh tones of Haywood Patterson's autobiography. This more centered aspect of Clarence's personality is seen throughout his life and certainly comes to the fore much later.

With the exception of Clarence Norris, Chalmers's concerns about their condition had been verified, and he now sought to find a compromise to bring an end to the case and get the boys released. Even State of Alabama officials were quietly seeking ways to conclude the proceedings. Alabamians and Alabama newspapers had grown weary of the inability of the courts to conclude the matter, and they were equally weary of the negative press the state received from many quarters, including some within the state and in other southern states. While the Scottsboro Defense Committee and the Alabama Scottsboro Committee were struggling to find a resolution to their differences in late 1936, there were signals the state was prepared to make some compromises in the Scottsboro case. In a brief meeting in October 1936, Governor Graves told Allan Chalmers the boys should plead guilty to a charge of miscegenation. Chalmers and the Scottsboro Defense Committee would not agree to such a condition. Clarence Watts, the Huntsville attorney, met with Attorney General Carmichael, also in October, to discuss having all charges dropped against Olen Montgomery, Willie Roberson, Eugene Williams, and Roy Wright. Watts told Carmichael the defense would be willing to have the other five boys plead guilty to a charge of simple assault if the state would agree to release the five boys shortly after sentencing. Carmichael balked at the proposal saying the state would accept nothing less than twenty years for the charge of rape.

Just as it was looking hopeless for any compromise, Lieutenant Governor Knight and Attorney General Carmichael were in New York City during the 1936 Christmas holidays and asked Samuel Leibowitz to meet with them in their hotel room. Knight knew the political capital he'd garnered from the Scottsboro case in his run for the Lieutenant Governor position was waning as he looked ahead to a run for the Governor's seat. Leibowitz joined the two men in their room, and Knight proposed to let an undefined number of the boys go free if Clarence Norris, Haywood Patterson, and some undefined other of the boys pleaded guilty to rape. Leibowitz was incensed by the proposal and flatly refused it. At a later meeting between Leibowitz and Carmichael in January 1937 in Washington, DC, the two agreed to proceed based on the following conditions: Haywood Patterson's appeal would be withdrawn; Ozie Powell would be tried only for the assault on Deputy Sheriff Blalock; Clarence Norris, Charlie Weems, and Andy Wright would plead guilty to some form of assault with the sentences to be less than five years each; Haywood Patterson would be released later, and his time served would not exceed the five years of Norris and the others; and, it was presumed, the other four boys would be released as soon as the overall agreement was implemented. The Scottsboro Defense Committee was initially opposed to the proposed agreement, but reluctantly agreed to it as options seemed few and far between.

Even though Attorney General Carmichael got cold feet about implementing the proposed agreement soon after he and Leibowitz crafted it, two later events would end all hopes of a compromise. In every deck of cards, there are usually two wild cards, and, at this moment in the Scottsboro case, two such cards would come into play. On May 17, 1937, thirty-eight-year-old Lieutenant Governor Thomas Knight Jr. died unexpectedly of complications from liver and kidney ailments. Knight had been the driving force behind the state's efforts to prosecute the boys after the initial four trials in the city of Scottsboro in 1931. Allan Chalmers and the Scottsboro Defense Committee thought the State's resolve to continue the case would end with Knight's death, but it was not to be. Judge William Callahan proved to be the other wild card in any potential agreement to end the proceedings. Judge Callahan still presided in the court where any subsequent cases would be tried. He steadfastly refused to agree with the proposed settlement and pleas, saying they were only a "fifty-dollar fine for rape." He also announced the new trials would commence in July 1937.

Influential members of the Alabama Scottsboro Committee tried to convince Carmichael to overrule Callahan and live up to the agreement with Leibowitz. Several Alabama newspapers joined the chorus, writing publicly that it was time for a compromise and conclusion to the case. Carmichael, realizing his political future would be shaped by the implications of Knight's death and Callahan's intransigence, ignored the advice and pressure. He abandoned the compromise and let the trials proceed.

On June 14, 1937, the Alabama Supreme Court upheld Haywood Patterson's guilty verdict and seventy-five year sentence from the January 1936 trial in Decatur stating, "When the record is examined, as has been done, we find no reversible errors." Although the defense was preparing an appeal to the U.S. Supreme Court, the appeal process would have no bearing on the soon to start trials of the other boys.

The Last Trials

ON JULY 12, 1937, Clarence Norris looked around at the now familiar surroundings of the Decatur segregated courtroom as he was brought into the room in handcuffs on a beastly hot summer day. After the handcuffs were removed from Clarence's wrist and he took his seat at the defense table, both he and Leibowitz had a feeling of optimism about the trial since talk of compromise was still in the air, and Patterson's last trial had at least ended without a death sentence. This was to be Clarence's third trial in this long-running case, which now totaled nine trials for all the boys. What he was about to experience was like attending three theatrical productions of the same play with mostly the same actors and a script unwavering in its content and delivery. It is difficult for a writer and his readers to stay focused on a set of events so repetitive in content and outcome, but it is important to realize the significance of the flow and subtle changes in the trials as they moved to their conclusion. With no interest in what the future might hold or the present and past injustices against blacks, southern politicians, courts, and many of its white citizens were attempting to maintain a way of life and belief in segregation and racism that was doomed to fail.

Judge Callahan continued his courtroom style of obvious prejudice against the defense and the defendant while aiding the prosecution with his restrictions on what issues and lines of questioning the defense could pursue. The selected jury was all white, as the prosecution struck the two qualified Negroes in the pool of potential jurors. With Lieutenant Governor Knight's death, the prosecution team leadership should have fallen to Attorney General Carmichael; however, Carmichael, who had made himself incommunicado at an out-of-state vacation retreat, assigned the case to Assistant Attorney General Thomas Lawson. It appears Carmichael did not want to face Leibowitz after reneging on the compromise agreement, and he likely wanted to avoid what was now a potential political albatross for an aspiring Alabama politician. Samuel Leibowitz and Clarence Watts were the defense attorneys, and Leibowitz continued to let Watts conduct most of the defense's case. Victoria Price was, as always, the principal prosecution witness, and she told her story with her usual vigor and embellishments. The defense did bring several new witnesses forward, including Ruby Bates's mother Emma Bates, to try to show the true character and background of Victoria Price. The prosecution also agreed to let the defense read to the court the medical testimony of the now dead Dr. Bridges from an earlier trial.

On Thursday morning, July 15, Judge Callahan charged the jury saying, "...where the complaining witness was a white woman, and the defendant a Negro, they could put out of their minds all questions of consent, that even though they did not believe some parts of Mrs. Price's story, they need not discard her whole testimony, and that under Alabama law her own unsupported word was sufficient to warrant conviction."

The jury took the case for deliberation at eleven o'clock that morning and, less than three hours later, returned with a verdict reading, "We the jury find the defendant guilty and fix his punishment at death."

Clarence sat stoically, showing no emotion, as the verdict was read. Leibowitz, his face showing the strain and disgust of the situation, was greatly disheartened by the verdict. Allan Chalmers, who was in England at the time, received a telegram advising him simply and bluntly, "NORRIS SENTENCED TO DEATH." Chalmers was attending a religious conference at Oxford, and as he left the meeting that evening he later wrote, he was "sick, bewildered, and alone," and "As we came out of the church...I suddenly broke down and leaned against the wall of the alley that ran beside the church and began to cry."

Just as the case seem to be turning in the defense's favor, just as a compromise in the case seemed to be at hand, just as Victoria Price's true character was more evident to most people, just as the Scottsboro Defense Committee and the Alabama Scottsboro Committee seemed to be making some progress locally, just as many influential Alabama newspapers were stressing a need to end the case with some even questioning the guilt of the boys, the Alabama politicians lost heart and courage for a compromise. The Alabama courts, personified by Judge William Callahan, were determined to see the boys prosecuted, convicted, and executed. The verdict in Norris's third trial returned the case to where it had started in Scottsboro on April 7, 1931.

In a broad sense, the third trial of Clarence Norris can be seen as the nadir, the low water mark, in the South's period of Jim Crow laws and segregation. About twenty years later, the civil rights movement fully emerged with the leadership, energy, and resolve needed to force the change so long overdue. While arrests, beatings, and deaths were constant threats to the civil rights participants, their push for change was engaged with no one looking back.

Judge Callahan and the prosecution rushed to complete the remaining trials from July 19 through July 24. Andy Wright was brought to trial on July 19, at which time the prosecution announced it would not call for the death penalty in any of the remaining trials. On July 21, Wright was found guilty and sentenced to ninety-nine years imprisonment. Judge Callahan immediately sentenced Wright and Norris, but Norris's execution, set for September 24, 1937, was automatically stayed when Leibowitz filed a notice of appeal. On July 22, Charlie Weems entered the courtroom for what would prove to be the eleventh and last trial in the Scottsboro case. On Saturday, July 24, the jury found Weems guilty and sentenced him to seventy years in prison. Ozie Powell was then brought into the courtroom, and Judge Callahan told him that while the state had dropped the charge of rape against him, he still faced a charge of assault with intent to commit murder when he slashed Deputy Sheriff Blalock's throat. Powell pleaded guilty to the assault charge, and Callahan sentenced him to twenty years in prison.

After Powell was sentenced, Assistant Attorney General Lawson approached the bench and quietly informed Callahan that the state had decided to *nolle prosequi* all of the indictments against the remaining four defendants: Olen Montgomery, Willie Roberson, Eugene Williams, and Roy Wright. It meant quite simply that, after six and a half years and eleven trials, the State of Alabama was dropping the rape charges against five of the boys. Four would be released immediately, and, while Powell wouldn't be tried for rape, he would have to serve the just-imposed sentence for assaulting the deputy. Even before Callahan called an end to the day's activities, Leibowitz dashed out of the courtroom with a copy of the court order to release the four boys. He went straight to the Decatur jail, showed the order to one of the jailers, and took the four boys to two waiting cars. Dr. Newman Sykes, an African American Decatur dentist, provided the two cars. Dr. Sykes had testified at the Decatur courtroom hearings in 1933 that led to the U.S. Supreme Court decision that Negroes had been systematically excluded from the Scottsboro and Decatur juries. As the cars were preparing to leave for Tennessee, under escort by state policemen to the Alabama state line, Decatur Sheriff Sandlin, thinking the boys were being taken back to the Birmingham jail, shouted at Leibowitz, "Why don't you get in there with your clients, you —— [bastard]?" Only after the cars had pulled away toward the east and not the south was Sandlin told the boys had been released, and it was then that Leibowitz also told the boys they were free. Victoria Price viewed the boys' departure from a courthouse window, and one can only imagine what her thoughts were at that moment.

The prosecution issued a statement explaining that they were convinced all of the defendants tried to date were guilty of raping Victoria Price. However, the statement continued with:

> But after careful consideration of all the testimony, every lawyer connected with the prosecution is convinced that the defendants Willie Roberson and Olen Montgomery are not guilty.

The prosecution's statement added that Willie Roberson and Olen Montgomery were a case of mistaken identity. The statement finally explained their reason for the release of Roy Wright and Eugene Williams. Since the two boys were juveniles when the crime was committed (Roy was twelve years old and Eugene was thirteen years old) and both had already served six and one-half years in jail, the State considered justice had been served. The two were released on the condition that they leave Alabama and never return.

The state's sophistic explanation is full of inconsistencies that leave the state's prosecutors looking like the emperor who wore no clothes. The state's admission that Victoria Price mistakenly identified Olen Montgomery as being in the gondola and a rapist opens up the entire line of reasoning that Judge James Horton used in dismissing the guilty verdict against Haywood Patterson after the April 1933 trial. Horton showed quite convincingly in his decision to dismiss the verdict that Victoria Price's testimony was full of uncorroborated statements, inconsistencies, and apparent lies. The state ignored most of Horton's findings in the explanation for their actions on July 24. Many newspapers, North and South alike, argued that if two defendants could be released based on an assumption of mistaken identity, certainly the same argument should hold for the other defendants.

Although it now appeared the state was implementing at least one part of the agreement Leibowitz and Carmichael had agreed to, there was never a clear understanding of the state's full intentions or motives. A letter that Forney Johnston, a prominent Birmingham lawyer and a member of the Alabama Scottsboro Committee, wrote to Allan Chalmers on October 5, 1937, probably best summarizes the situation:

> We have never known here the facts leading up to the dismissal of the remaining cases...My guess is that the very great pressure which had been brought on the attorney general and the Court, and the certainty that this pressure would blow up if the prosecutions were continued throughout the entire panel of defendants, resulting in convincing the prosecution that it must retreat in order not to create a revulsion in the state...

On October 26, 1937, the U.S. Supreme Court made the debate about the compromise moot, effectively closing any further legal appeals to the highest court, when it announced without any comments that it would not review Haywood Patterson's appeal. The appeal was based on two issues: denial of Patterson's request in the state court to be tried in a federal court, and the language in Judge Callahan's charge to the jury, which allowed conviction if Patterson was involved in a conspiracy to rape even if the rape had not been committed. The appeal argued that both of these issues denied Patterson his constitutional guarantee of due process of law.

———

ONE OTHER EVENT IN 1937, while of no great global significance, was greeted with fanfare and enthusiasm in the Taylor family: I was born on September 26, 1937, in Birmingham, the first Taylor in the next generation of the family. I was named Waights McCaa Taylor Jr. and was baptized by Dr. Henry Edmonds in the Independent Presbyterian Church on Easter Sunday, April 17, 1938, the same day Mother Rose became a member of the church.

And yes, if you are taking a moment to count the months on your fingers, I was a "premature" baby.

PART THREE

OUR SOUTHERN HOME

1938–1955

19.

THE GROWTH OF AN ACTIVIST
1938–1955

Maxwell Field

ROSA BOARDED THE BUS, took the first seat in the front row across
from her friend Rose, and sat back comfortably to enjoy the ride, if
for only a few minutes. It was 1941, and she was working as a secretary at Maxwell Field, an Army Air Force base in Montgomery, as she
started her short ride home on one of the few nonsegregated buses in
Alabama. This anomaly in public transportation in Montgomery came
about when Franklin Delano Roosevelt directed all U. S. military bases to
prohibit segregation in public places and on public transportation. Although
there were employees on the base with strident racial views, Rosa was never
challenged on the base because of her race. She had formed a friendship
with a white woman originally from Mississippi, who lived on the base.
Rosa and the woman, named Rose, would frequently ride the same base bus
toward town. Rose and her nine-year-old son would sit together, and Rosa
would sit just opposite Rose. The two women would chat away as friends
will do.

Rosa knew, only too well, that when the military bus reached the base's
main gate, she would have to change to a city bus and return to the segregated world of Montgomery and the South. Rose and her child would sit in
the front, and Rosa would have to sit in the back. Rose's little boy would
look back and forth from his mother to Rosa with a quizzical expression on
his face as if to ask, "Momma, why's your friend sitting back there?" All of
these experiences just added to the "humiliation" Rosa endured on the
Montgomery buses.

Her passage between these two worlds was like moving through a
veiled barrier: a somewhat open and understanding world looking through

an always-present barrier to a world of prejudice and hate. The experiences on Maxwell Field caused Rosa to first realize there was a way forward from the only life she had known in Alabama. Rosa later said, "You might just say Maxwell opened my eyes up. It was an alternative reality to the ugly racial policies of Jim Crow."

That fateful day in Montgomery in December of 1955 when Rosa Parks refused to move from the white section of the bus to the black section did not happen by accident. Rosa seemed destined for that day from the moment she met Raymond Parks in 1931, when he introduced her to the plight of the Scottsboro Boys. Just about everything she experienced and learned from 1931 forward, along with the strong character and self esteem her mother and grandparents taught her, had prepared her for the momentous day. Her experience on the Maxwell Field bus in 1941 was only one of the small steps she took to ready herself for what was to come.

Scottsboro Boys Support

RAYMOND AND ROSA HAD CONTINUED their quiet work raising money for the defense of the Scottsboro Boys, although Raymond always insisted she stay in the background for her safety. In June 1938, the Alabama Supreme Court upheld Clarence Norris's death sentence, and the following month Alabama Governor Graves commuted the sentence to life imprisonment. When Raymond was confident none of the boys would be executed, he curtailed his fundraising activities although there was still a need for money to support the continuing efforts to get the five boys still in prison released. Raymond and Rosa then turned their interests and efforts to voter registration. Few blacks could vote at the time in Montgomery, and the registration process was consciously designed to prevent blacks from voting.

Voter Registration and the NAACP

THE REGISTRATION PROCESS FOR BLACKS in Alabama was onerous both by law and by local practices. Alabama law required blacks to have a white person vouch for them at registration, and then they had to pass a written literacy test based on questions about the U.S. Constitution. In addition to the legal requirements, registration offices did not keep regular hours. Hours for registration would be scheduled, but not posted, at various times like ten o'clock to noon: a difficult time for most voting-age, working blacks to come to the office. When too many blacks came on a particular day, the registrar personnel would purposely drag their feet, forcing many in the line to come another day. If a black person was able to overcome all the legal and other obstacles, and actually receive a voter certificate, he or she still had to pay the annual poll tax of $1.50. Also, when people over twenty-one years of age were finally able to register, they had to pay the poll tax from their twenty-first year even though they hadn't been allowed to vote. Thus, a person thirty-five at the time of registration would have to pay $21 to become eligible to vote and continue to pay $1.50 every year thereafter.

As Raymond and Rosa became more involved with the voter registration issue, they learned a startling and sad fact: segregation and Jim Crow laws caused a social bias even among black people. The middle class and professional blacks in Montgomery lived in an area of town called Centennial Hill, four blocks south of the downtown business district and the Capitol. A few of the blacks living in Centennial Hill were registered because they were willing to work with the whites to get through the onerous process. The poorer, working-class blacks, the vast majority of the black population in Montgomery, lived on the west side of town, and the Centennial Hill blacks looked down on them. Raymond was even told by some well-to-do blacks to stop trying to register poor blacks and get on with his normal business. Raymond never tried to register in Alabama because he considered it degrading to submit to such a racist process, but he did finally register to vote years later in Detroit, Michigan.

Up until 1943, Raymond had been Rosa's primary mentor into the world of black activism, but the roles and positions going forward were about to change. In 1943, fed up with the NAACP because he thought the group represented the haughty outlook of some of Centennial Hill's blacks, he resigned from the association. It seems Raymond preferred to work quietly in the background, as he did in his fundraising activities for the Scottsboro Boys, and his pride prevented him from getting involved in activities that belittled his self-respect and self-esteem. Rosa was more sanguine than Raymond about the situation, and, despite the racism of Alabama laws and practices and the attitude of wealthier blacks, she was determined to work on voter registration. Their change in interest in activism did not alter their personal relationship; Raymond and Rosa were still very much in love and dedicated to one another. Raymond usually supported Rosa's activities, although he continually worried about her safety.

There were two other reasons Rosa was so determined to work for voter registration—she wanted to be able to vote for Roosevelt in the 1940 election, and her brother, Sylvester, was drafted into the Army in the early 1940s as U.S. participation in World War II ramped up. Rosa was unable to register to vote in the 1940 election, and it particularly rankled her that Sylvester could be called to fight for his country even though he wasn't allowed to vote.

Rosa was considering joining the Montgomery NAACP branch when she saw, in a local black periodical, a picture of a women identified as a member of the NAACP named Mrs. Johnnie Mae Carr. Rosa was sure it was one of her classmates from her days at Miss White's School when Carr's maiden name was Rebecca Daniels. Rosa went to her first NAACP meeting in December 1943 in hopes of seeing Carr to confirm it was her old school friend. Although Carr, the only woman in the Montgomery NAACP branch, was not at the meeting that night, at subsequent meetings she and Rosa would meet and renew their friendship. Rosa joined the NAACP that first evening, paid her dues, and was elected secretary of the branch. It happened it was election night for officers, and, as Rosa was the only woman present along with about fifteen men, she agreed to accept the position. None of the men wanted to be labeled secretary, and Rosa later said, "I was the only woman there, and they said they needed a secretary, and I was too timid to say no. I just started taking minutes, and that was the way I was elected secretary."

The president of the Montgomery NAACP branch was Mr. E. D. Nixon, and he would be Rosa's next mentor in her growth as an activist. Edgar Daniel Nixon was born in Montgomery in 1899, one of seventeen children. His father was a Baptist minister, but his aunt, a devout Seventh Day Adventist and strict disciplinarian, raised him in the rural Black Belt of Alabama. Nixon had little formal education, and by age fourteen, he was working to support himself. He finally became a Pullman car porter, and in 1928, he founded the Montgomery branch of the Brotherhood of Sleeping Car Porters, the union founded by A. Philip Randolph in 1925. Nixon was a tall, imposing man with a dignified presence. His lack of formal education and sophistication coupled with his Black Belt rural speech style made him popular with West Montgomery blacks, but Centennial Hill blacks thought Nixon an unsophisticated ward-style politician below them in the social pecking order. It is surprising Raymond could not find a way to work with a man like Nixon.

Although Rosa continued to handle the secretarial duties of the Montgomery NAACP branch, she soon found herself more the personal secretary to Nixon. Rosa had a very high regard for Nixon, and she would spend hours working in his home office at no pay handling his correspondence and organizing his busy schedule around his frequent long trips out of town as a Pullman porter. Nixon developed an equally high regard for Rosa and came to realize he now had a person who could help with his two principal concerns: voter registration and bus desegregation. While their working relationship was friendly, Nixon, who was a male chauvinist as most men of his generation were, would say to Rosa, "Women don't need to be nowhere but in the kitchen." Rosa would reply, feigning she was going to quit, "Well, what about me?" He would plaintively reply, "But I need a secretary and you are a good one." The repartee was half-jest and half-truth.

E. D. Nixon wanted to marshal a voter registration drive in Montgomery, and he set two actions into motion to facilitate his plan. Initially, he organized a Voter's League made up of local people who wanted to help with the drive. Rosa joined the Voter's League, and she and others worked tirelessly on the issue, mostly in Rosa's home. Rosa had a list of the black registered voters in Montgomery; the list numbered thirty-one, and several on the list were dead. It was then that Rosa realized how completely the Jim Crow laws had succeeded in preventing blacks from registering to vote.

Second, Nixon asked a black civil rights lawyer, Arthur A. Madison, practicing in Harlem, to come to Montgomery to help organize the drive and educate local drive participants. Madison, an Alabama native, was a fiery individual, and he leapt into the racially embroiled situation with full abandon. He told the drive participants they did not need to have a white person vouch for them when they registered, and, although he explained to them how to prepare for the test to prove they could read, write, and understand the U.S. Constitution, he told them the test was unconstitutional. Madison also filed a voting rights class action suit on behalf of Montgomery blacks. Several of the plaintiffs were schoolteachers, including Madison's cousin, Sarah Pearl Madison. The Montgomery authorities became so angry and concerned about Madison's lawsuit that he was arrested on the charge of barratry.* When Alabama authorities threatened to fire the schoolteachers, six of the teachers, including Sarah Pearl, testified that Madison had used their names in the lawsuit without their permission. Madison was found guilty, fined $500, and disbarred from practicing law in Alabama. Under court order, Madison had to abandon the voter registration drive in Montgomery and return to New York City.

Rosa was determined to register to vote, and she was not about to let any of the South's legal and cultural barriers prevent her from doing so. Rosa planned her first visit to the registrar's office in 1943 when Arthur Madison was still in Montgomery working on the voter registration lawsuit. Although the registrar's office was open the day she intended to go, she had to cancel her visit because she had to work. The next day was her day off, and fortunately the office was open. She took the test but never received a voter certificate in the mail. She observed that whites received their certificates immediately after completing the test, while African Americans had to wait to receive theirs in the mail. Rosa tried again late in 1943 but was told that she didn't pass the test even though she was sure she had. Finally, in April 1945, Rosa went to the registrar's office accompanied by E. D. Nixon. She took the test for the third time, and this time she copied her

---

* Barratry is a rarely used, obscure legal charge. It is the creation of legal business by stirring up disputes and quarrels, generally for the financial benefit of the lawyer.

answers to the twenty-one questions to a blank sheet of paper to use in a lawsuit against the registration board if necessary. It didn't come to a lawsuit, however, as she soon received her voter certificate in the mail. She then had to pay her poll tax, which amounted to $16.50—about $350 in today's dollars—to cover the annual fee of $1.50 plus the annual amounts due since she was twenty-one.

After Rosa's second attempt to register to vote in November 1943, she experienced a situation that might simply be called a coincidence, or possibly a harbinger of things to come. Rosa left the registrar's office in the afternoon and prepared to board a Montgomery public bus for her ride home. As Rosa boarded the bus at the front door and paid her fare, she noticed that all the seats and standing space in the black section in the back of the bus were full, even the steps in the well of the back door. She walked toward the back when the white bus driver stood and yelled at her, ordering her to exit the bus out the front door, walk to the back door, and reenter the bus in the black section at the rear. The driver was a tall, heavyset man named James F. Blake, known to be a virulent racist. He gave all the blacks a hard time, but he was particularly mean and disrespectful to black women, frequently calling them "bitch" and "coon." She refused, saying it was too crowded to board through the back door, and, why should she, when she was already on the bus. Blake walked up to her, grabbed her by the sleeve of her coat, and pulled her toward the front door. As he pulled her forward, Rosa dropped her purse and sat in an open seat while she picked it up. This only made Blake madder, and he yelled, "Get off my bus," looking like he might hit Rosa. As he threatened her, Rosa said to him, "I will get off. I know one thing. You better not hit me." Blake didn't hit her. She got off the bus, but didn't re-board through the back door. Rosa waited for the next bus and decided then and there to never board a bus driven by Blake saying, "I didn't want any more run-ins with that mean one." Yet, twelve years later Rosa would have another run-in "with that mean one."

Virginia Foster Durr

THERE WERE A NUMBER of other people Rosa admired and tried to emulate as she grew as an activist. She was particularly influenced by Walter White, executive secretary of the NAACP, and Ella Baker, national director of the NAACP's branch offices and founder of the Student Nonviolent Coordinating Committee (SNCC) in 1960. However, it would be a white woman, born and raised in Birmingham, who would provide her the friendship, encouragement, support, and guidance for Rosa's next encounter with James Blake. Virginia Foster Durr was a true liberal in every sense of the word, a far cry from most of the southern "liberals" of the time. Some even considered her a radical.

Virginia Foster was born in Birmingham in the parsonage of South Highland Presbyterian Church in August 1903. Her father, Dr. Stephen Foster, was the minister of the church and, in a few years, would suffer the same fate with the church's conservative membership as Dr. Henry Edmonds did in 1915. The church asked Foster to declare under oath that the biblical story of Jonah being swallowed by a whale and spewed up alive three days later was the literal truth and word of God. When Foster said he did not believe the story was literal truth, he was dismissed from the church, taken before the Presbytery on heresy charges, and was never offered another church. Unlike Edmonds, who founded a new church, Foster went on to manage his parent's plantation and cotton business to support his family.

Virginia's younger years gave no indication to the path her adult life would follow. A well-to-do, prominent family raised her to be a proper southern belle, and it was expected she would follow the South's segregation-ist social and racial traditions. Virginia followed the family expectations reasonably well until 1921, when she enrolled in Wellesley College, the famous woman's college in Boston. At Wellesley, Virginia had her first encounter with blacks in an open society and started her journey to liberalism. She had to drop out of Wellesley after her sophomore year and return to Birmingham because her father could no longer afford to send her to the college; his cotton business had suffered immensely in the boll weevil crisis in the 1920s. In 1925, she met Clifford Durr, a young Birmingham lawyer. Clifford was born in Montgomery to a wealthy Presbyterian family, earned a Phi Beta Kappa key at the University of Alabama, and was a Rhodes Scholar. He and Virginia were married in 1926, and all the parents felt the southern traditions of both families were now well in hand.

The Great Depression would impact the Foster and Durr families equally hard. Virginia's parents lost the plantation and their cotton business, and had to move into Virginia and Clifford's apartment in Birmingham. During these early years of the Great Depression, Virginia had her first real awakening to the huge economic, social, and racial inequities in the country and the South. She later said, "Up to this time I had been a conformist, a Southern snob. I actually thought the only people who amounted to anything were the small group I belonged to...What I learned during the Depression changed all that...I saw the world as it really was."

Soon after Virginia's parents had moved in, Clifford lost his job with a Birmingham corporate legal firm and was rescued by Hugo Black, the husband of Virginia's older sister, Josephine. Hugo Black was then a U.S. Senator representing Alabama and would be appointed to the U.S. Supreme

Court by Roosevelt in 1937. Black advised Clifford that there were jobs available for lawyers in Washington, DC, in the Reconstruction Finance Corporation. Clifford got the job, and he and Virginia moved to Washington in 1933. Virginia and Clifford would live in Washington for sixteen years during which time Virginia's metamorphosis from a sweet southern belle to a liberal activist would be complete.

Virginia met Eleanor Roosevelt at a garden party soon after arriving in Washington and was so inspired by Eleanor that she joined the Women's Division of the Democratic National Party, where she became involved in the national effort to repeal the poll tax. Virginia worked for two organizations that were later accused of being controlled by Communists only because the two groups fought against racism and segregation: the Southern Conference for Human Welfare and the National Committee to Abolish the Poll Tax. When Hitler started his invasions of European countries in 1939, most of the United States favored a hands-off policy of isolation; however, the Durrs were outspoken interventionists, convinced that the United States needed to enter the war to protect against attack and to defend Britain.

In 1948, the Democratic Party Convention was fractured by the issues of racism and segregation, causing two groups to bolt from the Democrat Party: the racist and states' rights Dixiecrat Party led by Strom Thurmond, and the Progressive Party led by Henry Wallace. Virginia, determined to press for social and racial equality for all, was the only member of her family to support the Progressive Party. To prove her support and convictions, she chaired the Progressive Party in Virginia and ran for the U.S. Senate from that state on the party's ticket.

In 1949, after Harry Truman narrowly won reelection as President, he asked Clifford to remain on the Federal Communications Commission, a commission Clifford was appointed to by Roosevelt in 1941. To accept the reappointment, Clifford would have to sign and enforce an anti-Communist loyalty oath instituted by the Truman administration in 1947. Clifford refused to sign the oath even though he knew his position of income, power, and influence in Washington would be over. Virginia supported Clifford completely in his decision, knowing it meant difficult times for their family that now included four children. Clifford opened a law office in Washington and offered services to people accused of "disloyalty" under the loyalty oath, foregoing any opportunity to attract corporate clients. Virginia went to work as an English teacher to augment the family's income.

Unable to make a reasonable income in his Washington legal practice, Clifford accepted a job offer from the Denver Farmers' Union in 1950, and the family moved to Denver. In less than a year, the Durrs' conscience and commitment to their principles again cost Clifford his job. As the Korean

War ratcheted up in intensity with the entry of China into the war, the United States was considering bombing China—General Douglas MacArthur even suggested the use of atomic bombs. Virginia made her opposition to this policy public. When, with Clifford's agreement, she refused an offer to save his job by retracting her position, he was again jobless with few, if any, opportunities open to him. To make matters worse, Clifford, who suffered from severe back problems, had to have a back operation that would require a long recovery period.

In 1951, faced with Clifford's situation, the Durrs had to return to Montgomery and move in with Clifford's mother. While Clifford recovered from his back operation, Virginia found a job in the state's insurance department at $125 per month.

After his recovery, Clifford opened a law office in Montgomery, and Virginia worked with him as his secretary. Clifford offered legal services to poor blacks, who found themselves in impossible financial situations with whites, either having been cheated outright or forced into tenuous legal agreements. E. D. Nixon, whom the Durrs became close friends with, also brought Clifford NAACP cases. Although Virginia decided not to enter into any other outside activities to avoid putting her mother-in-law in jeopardy, the family was ostracized by most of Montgomery's white population.

The next few years were very frustrating for Virginia, as she wanted to get involved with those in Montgomery combating racism and segregation. However, she honored her commitment to herself to keep a low profile for her mother-in-law's sake. Things were soon to change when, in March 1954, she was served a subpoena to appear before a hearing of the Senate Internal Security Subcommittee, the Senate counterpart to the House Un-American Activities Committee, chaired by the racist senator from Mississippi, James Eastland. This was the "Red Scare" period in American history, personified by Senators Joe McCarthy and James Eastland. The House and Senate committees held contentious hearings where people were accused of being a Communist or a Communist sympathizer with little or no proof. Although Virginia was never a Communist, she was presumably called to testify since she did not hesitate to accept the support and help of any individual, including Communists, if it would further her activities, such as the effort to repeal the poll tax. However, Virginia knew Eastland's ulterior motive for subpoenaing her; he was really after Hugo Black, Virginia's brother-in-law, and, through her, he wanted to imply that Black and the Supreme Court had Communist leanings.

Eastland's hearing was held in New Orleans, and Clifford went with Virginia to the hearing. She was disgusted by what she heard and saw the opening day of the hearing—Eastland berating witnesses and threatening them with contempt of court and jail. She spent most of the night drafting a statement she intended to read the next day. When she was called before the committee, she was not allowed to read her statement, which read in part, "I have the highest respect for the investigatory powers of the Congress. I think that is an important function. But from what I saw going on yesterday, this is not a proper exercise of Congressional powers—this is nothing but a Kangaroo Court...I stand in utter and complete contempt of this committee." When questioned, she did not claim protection under the First or Fifth Amendments, but chose to say simply, "I stand mute." The hearing lasted five days, investigating other Southerners including the Durrs' close friends, Myles Horton, co-founder of the Highlander Folk School, and Aubrey Williams, publisher of *Southern Farmer* magazine in Montgomery. At the end of the hearing, Eastland said he would have all the defendants cited for contempt and then jailed. Newspaper reports of the hearing were so negative about the unfairness of the procedures that Eastland's threat never came to pass, and his plan for a second hearing was abandoned.

Virginia returned to Montgomery feeling she had been released from a cage. With the publicity she received from Eastland's hearing in all the Montgomery newspapers, she now felt free to pursue her work to overcome racism and segregation. The Durrs did move into their own apartment to offer some protection to Clifford's mother, as they feared attacks or burnt crosses by the Ku Klux Klan or others. Nothing violent came to pass against the Durrs other than threatening and hateful phone calls. However, the family did suffer another trauma after the Supreme Court issued its historic unanimous ruling on May 17, 1954, that stated, "separate educational facilities are inherently unequal," effectively making segregated schools in the South unconstitutional. The Durr children were harassed by their teachers, classmates, and friends to the point the children had to be sent to school in Massachusetts.

Notwithstanding all of the harassment, Virginia jumped back into activities in Montgomery with enthusiasm. She attended meetings of the Council on Human Relations, the only interracial group in the city. She supported the Woman's Political Council of Montgomery, a group of educated black women working to improve the lives of blacks. However, the most significant meeting occurred quietly when E. D. Nixon came to her house and told her there was someone he wanted her to meet. Virginia accompanied Nixon back to his house and was introduced to Rosa Parks. Virginia and Rosa would become the best of friends, but, equally important, Virginia would prove to be Rosa's last mentor in her growth as an activist.

Their friendship started out simply enough when Virginia learned that Rosa was a skilled seamstress. Virginia was in constant need of someone to mend and make clothes for her family, as the Durrs were so poor they bought few new things and depended on hand-me-downs from her sister, Josephine Black. Virginia asked Rosa to do her mending work and Rosa agreed, although the two women were always at odds over price; Virginia knew Rosa's prices were ridiculously low and had to press her to take more money. Rosa attended integrated prayer meetings at Virginia's house, but, more importantly, the two women just spent time alone together discussing books, and the racial situation in Montgomery and the South. Rosa insisted on calling Virginia *Mrs. Durr*, adhering to the southern custom requiring blacks to use *Mrs.* or *Mr.* when addressing whites. Virginia responded in kind by calling Rosa *Mrs. Parks*, and telling her she would continue to do so until Rosa called her Virginia. It would be twenty years before the two women finally called each other by their first names.

On March 2, 1955, the NAACP nearly got the impetus it wanted and needed to start a legal case against Montgomery's segregated bus policies. Claudette Colvin, a fifteen-year-old high school junior, boarded a bus in front of Dexter Avenue Baptist Church, where twenty-six-year-old Martin Luther King Jr. was minister. She took a seat with several other older black women in the middle section of the bus. The bus was empty except for the few blacks, and the driver said nothing; however, after some whites boarded the bus, the driver ordered all the black women to move to the rear. All the women moved except Claudette. The bus driver called the police and pointed Claudette out to them; one of the cops said, "That's nothing new... I've had trouble with that 'thing' before." Claudette refused to get up, and the policemen dragged her from the bus as she kept screaming, "It's my constitutional right!" She was arrested and booked on charges of assault, disorderly conduct, and violating the segregation law.

E. D. Nixon and the other NAACP members, including Rosa, thought they now had the individual they could use in a lawsuit challenging the constitutionality of the Montgomery law. Rosa was delighted Claudette would be the individual to serve as the plaintiff in this case, as she was the great-granddaughter of Gus Vaughn, a Pine Level resident, and as a young girl Rosa played with Claudette's mother. The process started smoothly but came to an abrupt end when it was learned that Claudette was several months pregnant. Nixon knew the case couldn't go forward with a plaintiff who was an unwed pregnant minor. In addition, Claudette was very out-spoken, immature, and frequently cursed when excited. The white press and public reaction would have been brutal. Rosa was distraught for Claudette, but she agreed it would be a mistake to take the case forward at this time. The Montgomery NAACP meetings, with Rosa as the secretary, were now faced with finding another individual to serve as the plaintiff in a bus case.

Highlander Folk School

IN THE SUMMER OF 1955, amidst all the turmoil of Claudette's situation, Virginia got a phone call from her friend Myles Horton at the Highlander Folk School in Monteagle, Tennessee. He said that he had a two-week scholarship available for an upcoming seminar titled Radical Desegregation: Implementing the Supreme Court Decision, adding he would prefer a black community leader from Montgomery. Virginia immediately told Horton she knew just the person to attend the seminar: "Rosa Parks."

Highlander was located forty miles west of Chattanooga and forty-five miles north of Scottsboro, Alabama, in the Appalachian Mountains. Horton, born in Tennessee in 1905 to a poor white family, co-founded the school in 1932 with an initial focus on the labor issues in the South; and in the 1950s, the school expanded its role to work with the emerging civil rights movement. The school, a two-hundred-acre sanctuary in a broad landscape of intolerance, offered a venue for oppressed people of all races and political persuasions to gather, discuss, debate, and plan courses of action on vexing problems in a completely open and integrated environment. The Durrs had visited Highlander as attendees and teachers several times in the 1940s and knew well the powerful individual and group experience Highlander offered all its participants.

Virginia told Rosa about the opportunity, and she was eager to go; however, two obstacles stood in Rosa's way. One, Raymond was opposed to the idea; he considered Highlander "suspect," probably thinking they were too left wing even for the black community. Second, Rosa did not have fifteen dollars for the round-trip bus fare to Chattanooga. At this point in their lives, Raymond and Rosa had reversed roles from the early days in their marriage. Raymond had ceased being an activist; he now worked quietly as a barber and helped at home with Rosa's aging mother, who now lived with them. Rosa, of course, had continued to grow as an activist since the day she met Raymond, and she was not about to let him deny her this opportunity. Although Virginia couldn't afford to pay the bus fare either, she solved the problem. Virginia approached her good friend Aubrey Williams, a Montgomery white liberal who published the *Southern Farmer*, a magazine supporting civil rights and other liberal issues, and explained Rosa's financial plight to him. Williams readily agreed to pay Rosa's travel expenses, and she departed for Highlander in late July 1955.

As Rosa boarded the bus for the trip, she was apprehensive and unsure of what to expect. Apparently, Virginia hadn't made it clear to Rosa that the school was founded and operated by whites, and she came to realize this only after she arrived. Her first few days were spent quietly trying to get comfortable with the surroundings and the classroom situations. This was

Rosa's first experience in a completely open and integrated environment, where everyone, black and white alike, shared in everything—work, dining, play, and the classroom. Everyone in attendance was assigned a different work task each day: one day whites would cook and serve everyone, and the next day it might be an all-black or a black/white cooking staff. Rosa slowly overcame her apprehension and shyness, and became a full participant in all the activities. The high point of this wonderful experience for Rosa was meeting Septima Clark, a black activist from South Carolina. Clark was a working activist for equal education and civil rights well before the movement started in earnest in the late 1950s. She maintained an active role in the civil rights movement until 1970, when she retired as Director of Education and Teaching from the Southern Christian Leadership Conference. When Rosa met Clark, she was a workshop teacher at Highlander, and Rosa left Highlander in early August with Clark firmly in mind as a role model for what black women could achieve.

Rosa said of her experience at Highlander, "...it was one of the few times in my life up to that point when I did not feel any hostility from white people...It was hard to leave, knowing what I was going back to, but of course I knew I had to leave..." Rosa returned to Montgomery with one additional comment.

"And back to the city buses, with their segregation rules."

20.

BOYS ON THE STAGE

1937–1959

A S THE CURTAIN WENT UP ON THE STAGE, four black youths, their hair slicked to a bright polish, strutted forward dressed in flashy, new suits and sporting canes. Olen Montgomery, Willie Roberson, Eugene Williams, and Roy Wright faced yet another audience, but unlike the Alabama courtrooms they had come to know so well, the sea of faces now in front of them was mostly black. It was August 20, 1937, and they were performing in a vaudevillian-type production in the famous Apollo Theater in Harlem. The boys participated in a play that reenacted the Scottsboro case courtroom scene during the hour of their release; the play was sandwiched between the Harlem Playgirls Band and the All-Girl Revue billed as "Fifty Fascinating Females." The four boys felt they were now set for the big time; they had an agent, a black minister from Brooklyn, and, as they understood their contract, they would be making good money.

The years between the end of the trials in 1937 and the final release of all the Scottsboro Boys were a period of broken promises and disappointments for all involved in the process: the four boys released in July 1937; and the five boys still in prison, and all those working on their release—Samuel Leibowitz, Allan Chalmers, Henry Edmonds, and the others who helped in the effort. And, of course, the big elephant in the room was the issue of whether or not any of the boys would be able to return to some semblance of normal life, given their backgrounds and the Scottsboro case ordeal.

When Samuel Leibowitz and the four Scottsboro Boys arrived at Pennsylvania Station in New York City on July 26, 1937, a crowd of two thousand people met the train. Olen, Willie, Eugene, and Roy were treated as heroes; they were overwhelmed by the boisterous reception and especially flustered when the crowd pushed around them and tried to touch them in praise and adulation. Later in the day, Leibowitz made it clear to reporters that the four boys would not be exploited, as numerous offers were made to the boys within hours of their arrival for events from theatrical performances to barnstorming tours, all hoping to take financial advantage of the boys' instant celebrity status.

Ignoring the outside offers, Leibowitz asked the boys what they would like to become: Olen replied a lawyer, physician, or musician; Eugene wanted to be a jazz musician; Willie wanted to be an airplane mechanic; Roy said he would like to be a teacher or a lawyer. Realizing these were unrealistic short-term, and likely even long-term, job opportunities for the boys, Leibowitz told them he would arrange to get them into a vocational school. Over the next few days, the four boys started to chafe under his control and influence. After a week, they confronted Leibowitz, accusing him of profiting at their expense, and they turned to the Reverend Thomas Harten as their mentor. Harten, a black Brooklyn minister with a reputation for making shady deals and mishandling funds, arranged the contract with the Apollo Theater, and the boys went on the stage thinking they were in the clover. Soon they got their first paychecks and realized they were in a situation no better than the sharecropper system in the South. Although the contractual salaries were generous, by the time deductions were made for Harten's management fee and the theater's fee for costumes and accessories, the boys were left with meager amounts. They angrily left Harten and the Apollo Theater, and turned to Allan Chalmers and the Scottsboro Defense Committee, where discussions were held about their futures, resulting in some immediate arrangements for each of the boys. These arrangements were effective entry points for the four boys into a free, more normal life, if, in fact, they could ever achieve such an existence after their almost seven years in southern jails and courtrooms. Chalmers constantly worried about their activities and behavior, knowing that Alabama authorities would construe any missteps as evidence that the five boys still in jail were not ready for parole.

Eugene Williams chose to join relatives in St. Louis, where Chalmers hoped to get him to enroll in the Western Baptist Seminary. However, when he got to St. Louis, he ignored Chalmers's advice and did not enter the seminary. Since little is known or has been written about Eugene's life beyond his initial move to St. Louis, it is not unreasonable to assume he adjusted well and led a quiet life.

Willie Roberson remained in New York City and took one of the many jobs offered the boys. Willie was able to hold a steady job and became somewhat settled in the Big Apple; however, his bad luck associated with his arrest in the Scottsboro event and his chronic asthma were his constant companions. His bad luck again came into play in 1942 in a Harlem social club when a fight broke out. He was not involved in the fight, but he was among those arrested, charged with disorderly conduct, and jailed. While in jail, he wrote to an ILD friend, "I guess a whole lot of people think I've let them down, but just the opposite. I am again a victim of inconcievable maglinity and though I hartily dislike the role of myrter I have been cast in that role and it seems impossible to escape it." Escape came in either 1958 or 1959 when Willie was found dead in his Brooklyn apartment, apparently having suffocated during one of his severe asthma attacks.

Roy Wright and Olen Montgomery agreed to go on a two-and-one-half month national tour arranged and led by the Scottsboro Defense Committee on behalf of the five boys still in jail. Upon their return to New York City in early 1938, Roy enrolled at a vocational school. Roy's tuition and living expenses were paid by the singer/dancer Bill "Bojangles" Robinson. Mr. "Bojangles" had met Roy at an earlier rally for the boys, where he pledged to help Roy with his schooling. Olen wanted to study music and was offered a scholarship by a New York music school, but, unlike Roy, he did not have a benefactor to pay his living expenses, and he was unable to enter the school.

Of the four boys, Olen proved to be the major problem for Allan Chalmers and the Scottsboro Defense Committee. The committee agreed to provide him some financial support while he tried to find a part-time job and a sponsor, so he could pursue his musical training. Olen's physical limitations—blind in one eye and severely nearsighted in the other—coupled with his emotional problems, lack of motivation, and minimal education, made finding work, other than menial tasks frequently requiring hard labor, a difficult proposition. Over the ensuing years, Olen developed a serious drinking problem and found himself in and out of jail and drunk tanks wherever he was: New York City, Atlanta, Detroit, or Hartford. At some point in the 1950s, Olen returned for good to his hometown of Monroe, Georgia and disappeared into obscurity. His death was not even reported in any newspapers or in any of the many books written about the Scottsboro Boys.

Roy made what appeared to be the best adjustment from prison life to a normal life. After he completed vocational school, he went into the U.S. Army for a few years, got married, and found a good job as a merchant marine. Then tragedy struck.

On August 16, 1959, he returned home to New York City from an extended trip at sea to find his wife had been living with another man. In his rage, he shot her and shortly thereafter, full of remorse, he shot himself.

21.

THE WAR YEARS

1940–1945

WORLD WAR II WAS A TRANSFORMATIVE PERIOD for the United States. Besides the obvious outcome of defeating the Fascist and totalitarian regimes in Mussolini's Italy, Tojo's Japan, and Hitler's Germany, the war years led to profound economic, political, and social changes in the country. Economically, the vast productive effort created in the country to support the war effort brought a final end to the Great Depression and built the framework for the post-war boom that was to follow. Politically, the war established the country as the world's predominant political and economic power, setting the country up as the leading opponent of the Soviet Union in the soon to start Cold War.

The social changes that came about during and after the war were equal to, if not more profound than, the economic and political ones: a vast migration of blacks and poor whites to the industrial centers in the North and West changed the demographic outlines of the country; young men and women from all races and regions in the country experienced fighting and working abroad beyond anything their young lives had ever imagined, and many were afforded the first opportunity to work alongside someone of another race or ethnic background; Japanese-Americans, predominantly those located on the West Coast, were forced into interment camps soon after the war started, demonstrating that the country's racial bias and xenophobia was not limited to the South; the middle class in the country exploded in size and political clout after the war; the baby boom led to unprecedented population growth; and, although black soldiers returning home from the war found the South, and much of the country, as segregated and racially bigoted as before the war, the civil rights movement started to grow and slowly flex its muscles, leading to the momentous events of the 1950s and 1960s.

The Taylor Boys

THE TAYLOR BOYS WERE INDEED A "BAND OF BROTHERS," both at the University of Alabama and in World War II. All five brothers were reserve Army officers as a result of their ROTC (Reserve Officers' Training Corps) days at the university and were called to active duty as the war started and progressed. Waights, Frank, and Macey were called into active service in early 1941 as the country began mobilizing its forces even before formally entering the war after the Japanese surprise attack on Pearl Harbor on December 7, 1941; the three served in North Africa and Europe. Angus was in Honolulu when Pearl Harbor was attacked, was called to active duty shortly after the attack, and served in the Pacific. Bill first served as a civilian in the Pan Am operations supporting the war effort in North Africa and the Pacific. In January 1944, Bill asked to be commissioned, and he became a first lieutenant serving the remainder of the war in the Pacific, supporting the air operations against the Japanese in the island campaigns on Saipan, Tinian, the Philippines, Guam, Iwo Jima, and Okinawa.

Waights's first assignment was in Fort Bragg, North Carolina, where he was placed in charge of a group of new Negro recruits. When Don Rasmussen interviewed Waights, he had this to say about how the war changed his attitude about Negro soldiers and their capabilities:

> My real change took place in the Army. I heard that they supposedly broke down in combat, but if they did that it was because they were poorly trained and not because of their race…My first assignment was with Negro troops at Ft. Bragg. I was with them for two years when I was transferred to the command of white troops. After a year with them I was again put in command of Negro troops and I completed my Army career with them in an anti-aircraft unit in Germany. These transfers gave me a first hand experience with troops of both races and it convinced me that Negroes made as good soldiers as whites. I met quite a few Negroes overseas and I appreciated them as equals. I think many Southern boys changed in the Army. In fact, the best First Sergeant that I ever saw in the Army was a Negro.

Waights was sent to North Africa in March 1944 and served in Morocco and Algeria for six months. On August 15, 1944, the second D-Day in Europe occurred when the 7th Army invaded southern France, landing on the Riviera in an area between Toulon and Cannes. In October, Waights's unit was sent to Marseille and then to Dijon and Epinal, near Nancy, to support the 7th Army. He was sent to Germany in January 1945, and spent time in Kaiserslautern, Darmstadt, Manheim, and Heidelberg before the Germans surrendered. His unit, which included Negro soldiers under his command, was generally assigned to work with field hospitals in the various areas they were sent to. This was in keeping with the Army's segregated policies in World War II; although many Negro troops fought in combat situations, most were assigned to non-combat units, like Waights's, such as hospital service, maintenance, and guards in prisoner of war facilities.

Macey's unit, the 26th Anti-Aircraft Artillery Group, was sent to Normandy through Omaha Beach on July 5, 1944, about one month after the D-Day invasion. His unit supported the Battle of Normandy for several weeks and then moved through northern France, Belgium, Luxembourg, Holland, and into Germany. After the Germans surrendered on May 9, 1945, the unit was sent to Munich as part of the mop up operation and the start of occupation. The unit's historian wrote an interesting, but macabre, entry dated June 13, 1945, about their time in Munich, "We moved from our tents into Hitler's apartment house at #16 Prinzregenten Straus. The 179th Division had pretty well ransacked the place. Major Taylor slept in Hitler's bed. The Group offices here were where the Munich Pact of 1939 was signed by Hitler and Chamberlain." After months in tents, mud, and poor sleeping conditions, Macey was probably delighted to sleep in a bed, even if it was Hitler's, but imagine the nightmares he must have experienced.

Frank was first sent to Panama where he served as a logistics officer with the troops assigned to the country to protect the Panama Canal, a vital sea transportation link during the war. Frank's son, Frank Jr., tells a humorous story about his father's days in Panama. It seems good American beer was hard to come by, and Frank, in the best tradition of Sergeant Bilko, traded a jeep for a number of cases of beer with the officers on a ship passing through the canal. Apparently, the ship's officers used the jeep to scurry about the deck performing their duties, but there's no problem imagining what happened to the beer.

Much more serious, on December 28, 1944, Frank was bound for Le Havre, France, with part of the 15th Army on the HMS Empire Javelin, a British troop carrier, when a German U-Boat torpedoed the ship off the coast of France. Local vessels in the area saved all but thirteen of the over seven hundred men on the ship. Frank's unit continued on to France and then Germany, where, by one of those coincidences of war, three of the brothers were brought back together.

Macey, Waights, and Frank found themselves in Lenggries, Germany, on July 1, 1945. Lenggries is about thirty miles south of Munich and only eight miles from the Austrian border. On the back of a photograph taken of the three at Lenggries, a handwritten note reads, "A meeting of the 'Big Three,'" probably a tongue-in-cheek comparison to the meetings Roosevelt, Churchill, and Stalin held in Tehran and Yalta during the war, and the soon-to-be-held meeting between Truman, Churchill, and Stalin at Potsdam on July 18, 1945.

Fortunately, all five returned safely from the war, and their mother, Margie, did not have to suffer a *Saving Private Ryan* experience. The Taylor Boys arrived home to loving families with their old jobs or with new jobs readily available to them. Bill rejoined Pan Am, and Angus went to a new job at the Justice Department in Washington, DC. Waights, Frank, and Macey returned to Birmingham: Waights to a new job as editor of a fledging newspaper aimed at Birmingham's youth, Frank back to his advertising business, and Macey to his law practice.

Sylvester McCauley

IT WAS CHRISTMASTIME 1945, and Sylvester McCauley, Rosa Parks's brother, had just returned from his wartime service. As he walked down one of Montgomery's main streets in his uniform, a group of white rednecks approached him, taunted his being in uniform, and spat on him. When he complained to the police about the incident, they told him he was being "uppity," and ignored his complaint.

Sylvester had been drafted soon after the war started and was assigned to the 1318th Medical Detachment's Engineering Services Regiment. He was first sent to Europe, where he was a stretcher-bearer in the Battle of Normandy. He was then sent to the Pacific Theater, where he did similar work, ending his combat duty on Okinawa.

As the Taylor Boys did, Sylvester arrived home after the war to a loving family: his sister and mother, his wife, Daisy, and their two young children. However, any comparison to the Taylor Boys' experience ends there, as he was unable to find employment in Montgomery, and, overwhelmed by his return to a segregated society that seemed even worse than what he left, Sylvester moved with his family to Detroit. He found a janitorial job in a Chrysler factory, never to return to Alabama, not even for a short visit with his sister and mother. Rosa visited Sylvester in Detroit a few months after he moved, and, on her first trip out of Alabama, was initially amazed at the apparent openness of the city. She came to realize it was a façade; Detroit had suffered a terrible race riot in 1943 when a white mob attacked a black housing project leading to fighting between whites and blacks that resulted in numerous deaths. Wartime factory production came to a standstill in the city and was only restored after President Roosevelt sent military police into the city to restore order. Rosa left Detroit understanding that racial tensions and prejudices were nearly as rampant there as in Montgomery.

Sylvester's experiences were similar to most of the one million blacks that served in World War II. About half of these men served overseas, and the other half served in this country. Those men serving overseas, especially in Europe, experienced, for the first time, a world devoid of lawful segregation and much of the social racism so prevalent in America. Young black men fraternized freely with white women in Europe and married young white women in England, France, Italy, and Germany, prompting Alvin Owsley, the former national commander of the American Legion, to write Dwight Eisenhower in 1946, "My dear General, I do not know…where these Negroes come from, but it is certain that if they expect to be returned to the South, they very likely are on the way to be hanged or burned alive at public lynchings by the white men of the South." Owsley, a native of Denton, Texas, was reiterating the southern white man's views of his "manhood" that resulted in the consistent guilty verdicts in the Scottsboro cases: touch, flirt with, or insult a white woman, much less have sex with her, and you're a dead man. The black soldiers came home to a country yet unwilling to change any of the social customs and laws that so disenfranchised blacks. Many black men in uniform in the South were threatened and attacked, at least one in uniform was killed, and many were beaten senseless.

James Baldwin, the famous black author, best sums up the situation after the war and the black reaction to the war in his book *The Fire Next Time*: "The treatment accorded the Negro during the Second World War marks, for me, a turning point in the Negro's relation in America. To put it briefly, and somewhat too simply, a certain hope died, a certain respect for white Americans faded."

War Travels of the Taylor Family (or Dragged Around by the Army)

WORLD WAR II WAS MY AWAKENING to the world around me. Those vague memories, a series of cameo snippets, have been formed and reinforced by a photo album Dad and Mom kept of the family's travels throughout the country as Dad was transferred from location to location prior to being sent overseas. Father Waights and Mother Rose now had two young boys in tow: me and my brother Gibbs, who was born on November 13, 1939. Dad gave the album the title of this chapter subsection, and we were "dragged around by the Army," as so many in America were at the time. Our family odyssey started in Birmingham in January 1941 and ended back in Birmingham in March 1944.

In those three years, we spent varying amounts of time with Dad at Army facilities scattered about the country in this order: Fort Bragg, North

Carolina, where we lived in Southern Pines; Edgewood Arsenal, Maryland, where we lived in Bel Air; Fort Cronkhite, California, where we lived in Sausalito; Camp San Luis Obispo, California, where we lived in Morro Bay; back to Fort Cronkhite, where this time we lived in Larkspur; Westport, Washington, where we lived in Aberdeen; Camp Stewart, Georgia, where we lived in Glennville and Savannah; and back to Birmingham just before Dad shipped out for North Africa in March 1944.

Rosie, our loving nickname for Mom, had a favorite story she loved to tell about those vagabond years. At her ninetieth birthday party in 2004, as we were going around the room of about fifty family members and close friends telling Rosie stories, my brother Gibbs told her favorite story to the delight of all present, especially the grandchildren who love to hear about their grandparents' foibles.

The story goes something like this: In early 1943 when we lived in Aberdeen, Washington, I was five years old and Gibbs was three. Mom had just purchased a new set of cosmetics, probably rather expensive and hard to get during the war years, to highlight her natural beauty. She and Dad had gone out for the evening, leaving us with a baby-sitter. Apparently the baby sitter did not pay much attention to what we were doing. Gibbs and I went into Mom and Dad's bedroom, sat down at Mom's dressing table adorned with all these lovely bottles and vials of lotions, crèmes, perfumes, lipstick, and other magical cosmetics. We proceeded to prepare an exotic olio of all these ingredients, adding, as the *pièce de résistance*, the tobacco from a pack of cigarettes on the table. Suffice it to say, the olio was an awful mess, the dressing table was an awful mess, and we were an awful mess. While we were still engaged in our experiment in cosmetology, Mom and Dad returned home. Mom came into her bedroom, took one look at us and the mess, and, while there is no definitive record of what she said, her verbal reaction seemed to turn the air a distinct color of blue. She took us straight-away to the bathroom, cleaned us up as best she could, gave us both a well-deserved spanking, and put us to bed. After cleaning up her bedroom, she sat in the living room and tried to relax, but the more she thought about what had happened, the madder she got. Rosie best described what happened next when she delivered her punch line.

"I got so mad all over again, I went back into the boys' room, woke them up, and spanked them again."

22.

FINAL STRUGGLES FOR FREEDOM
1937–1952

FROM THE MOMENT THE FOUR BOYS were released in July 1937, Allan Chalmers continued to work unceasingly for the release of the five boys still in prison: Ozie Powell, Clarence Norris, Haywood Patterson, Andy Wright, and Charlie Weems. The U.S. Supreme Court's refusal in October 1937 to hear Haywood Patterson's appeal effectively served notice that any further appeals would be denied by the highest court in the land. Chalmers realized the only viable approach was now through the state, preferably straight to Governor Bibb Graves, since he had the authority to pardon the boys remaining in prison. Dr. Henry Edmonds, Forney Johnston, and others from the now defunct Alabama Scottsboro Committee assisted Chalmers in working with Governor Graves to craft an approach all parties would agree to implement.

Negotiations, Agreements, and Broken Promises

ALABAMA GOVERNOR BIBB GRAVES was not one you would expect to be sympathetic to the plight of the Scottsboro Boys. He had been an ardent supporter of the Ku Klux Klan, and the Klan reciprocated in kind in his first term as governor from 1927 to 1931. However, Graves was a devoted Roosevelt and New Deal supporter, and he had instituted government services and social welfare programs during his two administrations. In addition, a number of Alabama newspapers were encouraging the governor to bring closure to the case, which many considered not only an embarrassment to Alabama, but also a miscarriage of justice. Chalmers and his Alabama supporters hoped Graves would be amenable to using his pardon powers in the case as he approached the end of his second term.

After Graves received a letter from Chalmers and a petition signed by Edmonds, Johnston, and the editor of the *Birmingham Post* newspaper, both asking him to pardon the five boys, he agreed to meet with the group on December 21, 1937. The meeting went very well, and afterwards the group was sure they had the governor's commitment to pardon the boys after all pending appeals were exhausted. Nothing happened of any consequence through the first half of 1938 until June, when the Alabama Supreme Court ruled on the boys' appeals, upholding Norris's death sentence, and Weems and Wright's prison sentences. On July 5, Governor Graves lived up to his commitment in the Norris case, commuting Clarence's death sentence to life imprisonment. However, this action, while welcome, raised the first red flag in Chalmers's mind about Graves's true intentions: If he intended to release the boys, why did he bother to go through the unnecessary step of commuting Norris's sentence? Chalmers's concern was well founded.

After more discussions and reviews by the Alabama authorities, it was announced that Graves had decided to parole Norris, Patterson, Weems, and Wright on October 31 at 11 a.m. Ozie Powell was excluded from the announcement since the state decided he should remain in prison longer for his admitted stabbing of Deputy Sheriff Blalock. Chalmers proceeded to make detailed plans for meeting and handling the four boys upon their release; however, on October 29, 1938, Graves announced the boys would not be released as planned. Graves made it official on November 15, announcing he would not parole the boys based on a set of personal interviews he had with them, having told one of Chalmers's Alabama associates, "They are anti-social, they are bestial, and they are unbelievably stupid, and I do not believe they can be rehabilitated in freedom..."

Chalmers, never one to give up, tried another tactic to persuade Graves to change his mind; Chalmers had Walter White visit Eleanor Roosevelt in the White House and ask for her husband's help. Clarence Norris's ex-employer agreed to help, and he invited Governor Graves to visit him at the Warm Springs Little White House during the 1938 Thanksgiving holidays. Graves had visited Roosevelt at the Little White House in 1937, showing his adulation for the man and his programs by exclaiming, "Every enemy of Roosevelt's is an enemy of mine." Graves declined this later invitation, saying he had too much state work requiring his presence. Roosevelt did not let the matter rest; on December 7, he wrote a personal letter to Graves commending him on his public record and all he had done "for the cause of liberalism in the State of Alabama." However, Roosevelt went on to say, "...you said definitely and positively that you were going to commute the sentences of the remainder of the Scottsboro boys... warm friends of yours all over the United States relied on what they thought was a definite promise." For the second time, Graves ignored an entreaty from President

Roosevelt and refused to change his mind. On December 12, Chalmers met with the governor one last time but was also unable to sway him from his decision. Although Graves always said it was the personal interviews with the boys that changed his mind about the paroles, the more likely reasons are the mail he received from his constituents largely opposed to the paroles, and the pressure he got from a number of Alabama politicians advising him he was committing political suicide. The door to freedom, which seemed to be slowly opening for the boys a year ago, was now slammed shut in their faces.

On January 16, 1939, Frank Dixon was sworn in as the new Governor of Alabama, and any hopes for immediate paroles evaporated; Dixon had no interest in dealing with the case as he moved ahead with his new administration. In November 1939, Dixon appointed the first three members to the newly created Alabama Pardon and Parole Board. The board would now handle all pardon and parole requests, giving the governor some political cover from the process.

Chalmers and his Alabama associates would now have to establish relationships with three new individuals and a new board. They would find working with the new parole board as frustrating as it was with Governor Graves: full of broken commitments and Alabama politics. It would be almost four years before another Scottsboro Boy was paroled.

Shortly after his appointment, the chairman of the new parole board said he was interested in seeing the boys paroled soon. However, when the board considered parole requests at their February 1940 meeting, parole was denied to all five boys. The board again denied parole to all five boys in November 1941 and July 1942. During this time, the five boys continued to have different problems in Alabama prisons, known to be among the worse in the country. Haywood Patterson was having sex with other men in prison, not an uncommon occurrence for men who are incarcerated for lengthy periods of time. His sexual experiences aside, Patterson was always the most outspoken and defiant of the nine boys and was considered a problem by prison authorities and the parole board. Andy Wright showed continued symptoms of prison neurosis. Clarence Norris was in and out of trouble in prison and used what little money he could get to support his gambling habit. Ozie Powell and Charlie Weems, while not model prisoners, seemed to cope with prison life better than the others.

On November 17, 1943, after years of persistent negotiations with the parole board, a break in the case finally came about; Charlie Weems was paroled. As he was about to leave for his hometown of Atlanta, Charlie told reporters that he wanted to put "the part of his life just past [behind him], work hard, and make [himself] a man." He started work at a laundry, later married, and lived a quiet, uneventful life in Atlanta.

The parole board followed Weems's release with the releases of Clarence Norris and Andy Wright on January 8, 1944. Chalmers had arranged jobs for Clarence, now thirty-two years old, and Andy, now thirty, in Cleveland, Ohio, but the Alabama parole board would not let them leave the state. Instead, the two had to work at a lumber company near Montgomery in poor living conditions and under hard, irregular working hours for thirty-five cents an hour. A few months later both married young women—Clarence married Dora Lee from Montgomery, and Andy married Ruby Belle from Mobile—and tried to settle down to some semblance of home life. Clarence's parole officer, an ex-deputy warden at Kilby Prison, allowed him to move to another lumber company at forty cents an hour, but the working conditions proved to be harsh, like a "chain gang"; Clarence later said he started thinking about jumping his parole. Andy was having health problems, and in September 1944, Andy and Clarence both left Montgomery, violating the terms of their paroles.

Clarence left his wife in Montgomery and went to New York City, hoping Chalmers and the Scottsboro Defense Committee would protect him from the Alabama authorities. Although the Scottsboro Defense Committee had disbanded earlier in 1944, Allan Chalmers refused to stop his ceaseless efforts on behalf of the Scottsboro Boys, and he saw to it that Clarence had lodging and money while he worked on alternatives with the Alabama parole board. After the board agreed not to send Clarence back to prison if he returned to Alabama, Chalmers was able to convince a reluctant Clarence that his return was the best thing to do. He explained to Clarence that an action like this would hopefully lead to the releases of Patterson and Powell.

Andy went to Mobile to live with his wife's mother. He stayed there until E. D. Nixon, Rosa Parks's NAACP friend in Montgomery, convinced him to return to Montgomery as well, telling Andy he would appear before the parole board on his behalf. Nixon was able to convince the parole board not to put Andy back in prison and to let him change jobs because of his health.

Both Andy and Clarence returned to Montgomery in October 1944, and, true to the parole board's commitment, they were not sent back to prison. Andy went to work for a grocer, a job E. D. Nixon had found for him that was less physically taxing than the lumber company work. Clarence was not so fortunate; he was sent back to the same parole officer who insisted Clarence return to the lumber company where he was worked as if on a "chain gang." After a few weeks, Clarence complained to his parole officer about the conditions at the lumber company. The officer told Clarence he was tired of his constant complaints; he called the prison warden and told him Clarence wouldn't work. Clarence was immediately returned to prison, and the parole board told him he would not be eligible for parole consideration for two years. Clarence, angry and distraught, later said, "I was filled with rage and hatred. Going back to prison hurt me more than when I was sentenced to the chair...I could have killed every cracker in Alabama and been happy doing it. I was sick to my soul."

Ozie Powell, who was still serving his twenty-year sentence for knifing Deputy Sheriff Blalock, was paroled in June 1946. He immediately returned to his home state of Georgia, found work, and little was ever heard of him again.

Andy worked for the grocer for almost two years when he had an incident with a white man, forcing him to flee to Chicago, again in violation of his parole. When Andy returned to Montgomery in October 1946 to get his new wife—he and Ruby Belle had broken up—he was arrested and put back in prison. Andy inquired about Clarence, only to learn Clarence had been paroled for the second time the month before.

Clarence had been released from prison in September 1946, and his parole officer, the same man he was under earlier, found him a job with a gas company digging ditches. Clarence wasn't about to hang around to be harassed by his parole officer and another white employer, especially after he learned Dora Lee was with another man. On September 30, 1946, Clarence went to Atlanta, where he spent an evening with Charlie Weems and his wife, who put him on a train the next night to Cleveland. Thirty years would pass before Clarence Norris returned to Alabama under vastly different circumstances.

Andy was paroled for the second time in December 1946, and then had, in quick succession, three revolving door experiences in and out of prison: the first time his prospective employer discovered he was a Scottsboro Boy and would not hire him, and he was returned to prison; the second time he was fired because he refused to "steal from the Jews" for his employer, and he was returned to prison; and the third time he was involved in a truck accident and charged with reckless driving and driving without a license. After the truck accident, Andy went back to prison in the summer of 1947.

In many ways, the most tragic figure of the nine Scottsboro Boys was Haywood Patterson. In 1948, Haywood was still languishing in Alabama's Atmore Prison Farm, a notoriously bad prison, with no apparent hope for parole. In the summer of 1948, while on a work gang, Haywood quietly escaped and somehow eluded search dogs and airplanes for the next week. He made it to Atlanta and then to Detroit to join his sister. He tried to keep a low profile for the next two years, but the Federal Bureau of Investigation finally found and arrested him. The governor of Michigan, G. Mennen Williams, refused to cooperate with Alabama's request to extradite Haywood, and the Alabama authorities gave up on the extradition effort. In

1950, Haywood collaborated with a Detroit writer, Earl Conrad, on his autobiography, *Scottsboro Boy*, which brought Haywood some recognition at the time. In December 1950, Haywood visited a Detroit bar to sell his book, and later, a barroom brawl broke out and a twenty-seven-year-old black man was killed with a knife. Initially, Haywood denied to police he was even in the bar, but then he admitted he killed the man in self-defense. After two mistrials, Haywood was found guilty of manslaughter and sentenced to six to fifteen years in the Michigan State Prison, where he was soon diagnosed with cancer. On August 24, 1952, at age thirty-nine, Haywood Patterson died in the Michigan prison.

Andy Wright walked out of Kilby Prison in Montgomery on June 9, 1950, with $13.45 in his pocket, his "parole" pay. It was his third and final parole, and he was headed for New York where he had been promised a job. Outside the gates of the prison, a reporter asked him how he felt. Andy replied he was not angry with anyone. When pressed about Victoria Price, he said, "I'm not mad because the girl lied about me. If she's still living, I feel sorry for her because I don't guess she sleeps much at night." After over nineteen years since he'd first been jailed in Scottsboro, Andy was the last of the Scottsboro Boys to be released from an Alabama prison for the final time.

In June 1950, after his release from prison, Andy Wright first went to Albany, New York without his wife and daughter for a job in a candy company. Apparently Andy's prison neurosis continued to haunt him because he found it difficult to hold a job, and he wanted to be alone, both at work and from his parole officers. Over the next five years he bounced between jobs in Albany, New York City, and Cleveland, never able to hold a job for long or stay put. Andy wrote Allan Chalmers complaining, "Doc, when are you coming to see me. I feel like a rabbit in a strange wood." Much more seriously, in 1951, a woman Andy had known since he moved to Albany accused him of raping her thirteen-year-old daughter. When Andy denied the charge to the police, they beat him with their fists and hoses, and tried to get him to sign a confession. Thurgood Marshall, the NAACP's special counsel, who became a U.S. Supreme Court Justice in 1967, and the attorney Marshall hired to defend Andy were able to prove to the court that the woman, whom Andy had dated, had charged Andy out of vindictiveness, and an all-white jury found him not guilty. After the trial, Andy Wright wrote to Allan Chalmers, "Everywhere I go, it seems like Scottsboro is throwed up in my face…I don't believe I'll ever live it down."

Unfortunately, this could serve as an apt epitaph for all the Scottsboro Boys.

The Scottsboro Girls—Victoria Price and Ruby Bates

THE TWO GIRLS WHO MADE the rape charges that precipitated the Scottsboro Boys trials were also victims in this long saga—victims of a system that bred poverty among poor whites and blacks to maintain a ready pool of low wage labor, and a caste system that placed poor whites just above blacks in the social and legal order, leading to inevitable situations like the Scottsboro events. When found on the train with the nine black boys, Victoria and Ruby knew that the only recourse they had to reclaim some social redemption in the moment was to accuse the black boys of rape.

After the trials concluded in 1937, the state of Alabama and the media soon forgot both girls. Victoria Price moved to rural Tennessee in 1938 after the Huntsville mill she worked in closed. In 1940, Allan Chalmers, having heard that Victoria might recant her testimony, sent a Scottsboro Defense Committee member to meet with her. She agreed to do so if paid a large sum of money, which Chalmers was unwilling to pay. During World War II, she married a man named Frank Roland, but they lived together for less than three years. In the early 1950s, she married, for her fourth marriage, a Tennessee sharecropper named Walter Street, and Victoria became known as Katherine Queen Victory Street.

Ruby Bates toured with the ILD as a speaker for a few years while the later trials were still in progress, but as the story faded from the headlines, the interest of the ILD and others in Ruby faded as well. She worked briefly in a spinning mill in upstate New York but returned to Huntsville in the late 1930s and lived with her mother. In 1940, Ruby moved to Washington State's Yakima Valley and did migrant farm labor work for two years. In 1942, she married a Washington man, Elmer Schut, and became known as Lucille Schut. The couple briefly returned to Alabama in the 1960s when Elmer needed to visit a Veterans Administration hospital there. Ruby found her family members still ostracized her for the position she took in the Scottsboro case and for working with the Communists at the ILD. By this point, Ruby was an embittered woman, and years later she would change her story again, claiming the boys had raped them.

23.

LIVINGSTON, ALABAMA
1949–1952

OUR SOUTHERN HOME in the late 1940s and early 1950s was in Livingston, Alabama, the county seat of Sumter County. Livingston is in west central Alabama, some fifteen miles from the Alabama/Mississippi state line, in the heart of the Black Belt.

Even though the Black Belt was initially built from the seeds of king cotton and on the backs of slaves, the region did develop more than cotton. I have always been fascinated by the fact that Monroeville, in Monroe County on the southern edge of the region, produced the celebrated authors Harper Lee, Truman Capote, and Mark Childress and was designated the "Literary Capital of Alabama." Harper Lee's *To Kill a Mockingbird* is one of my favorite books of southern fiction. Atticus Finch, the principled protagonist in the book, remains a hero of mine and, of course, I see him as Gregory Peck, who won the Best Actor Oscar for his portrayal of Atticus in the 1962 movie. Although Harper Lee denies the assertion, many readers assume she tailored the character Dill after her childhood friend Capote in her famous and only novel, for when Scout, Atticus Finch's daughter and the narrator of the story, describes him in the book she says:

> Dill was a curiosity. He wore blue linen shorts that buttoned to his shirt, his hair was snow white and stuck to his head like duck-fluff; he was a year my senior but I towered over him. As he told us the old tale his blue eyes would lighten and darken; his laugh was sudden and happy; he habitually pulled at a cowlick in the center of his forehead.

Considering the small town they lived in, it's hard to imagine this description as anyone other than Truman Capote. He was a year Harper Lee's senior and short of stature as an adult, while she grew to be a tall and stately woman. The blue eyes and persona certainly matches what one would imagine the younger Truman to be.

A more recent and incredible example of the creative talent in the Black Belt region is the story of the African American quilt makers of Gee's Bend, a small town on a huge bend in the Alabama River about thirty miles south of Selma. For over one hundred years, generations of Gee's Bend women, many descended from slaves on the Pettway plantation in the area, quietly produced remarkable quilts that had gone unnoticed until an exhibit opened at New York City's Whitney Museum of American Art on November 22, 2002. Initial reaction to the exhibit was subdued until Michael Kimmelman, chief art critic of *The New York Times*, wrote a week after the opening that the quilts constitute "some of the most miraculous works of modern art America has produced. Imagine Matisse and Klee (if you think I'm wildly exaggerating, see the show) arising not from rarefied Europe, but from the caramel soil of the rural South in the form of women, descendants of slaves when Gee's Bend was a plantation." *The Times of London* offered an interesting insight: "For once black Americans are admired and lauded for what they have achieved for themselves, not because their artistic gifts have conformed to what is expected of them."

Dad must have been getting itchy to move along again because in late 1948 he became aware of a newspaper opportunity in Livingston, where, incidentally, his good friend from his trip to Scandinavia in 1928 and at the University of Alabama, Andy Allison, was now living. The owner of the newspaper, an elderly lady named Mrs. Lawrence, was looking for someone to serve as editor and manager of the small weekly newspaper. Dad leapt at the opportunity, and we soon found ourselves moving to Livingston.

Livingston had a population of about two thousand people, a majority of whom were black, although I don't think this included the student population at Livingston State Teachers College, the town's claim to academic and cultural enlightenment. The western and southern sides of the town are bounded by the Sucarnoochee Creek—at least an atlas labels it as a creek. But to me it was, and always will be, a river—the river of my youth—both a symbol and a reality of freedom of growth and expression.

In the center of town was the ubiquitous town square, holding the county seat offices and the courthouse, a red brick building with a big white cupola. The square was well treed with magnolias and other native shrubbery. There was, of course, a statue and monument to the soldiers of the Confederate States of America who came from this area. There was a bandstand on a corner of the square where one could escape the summer sun and the winter rains. To me, the town square represented the center of the universe—the natural gathering place for a peaceful, harmonious community. Unfortunately, the square was also the occasional meeting place of the local Ku Klux Klan. Our first home in Livingston was only one block from the square and whenever those hateful meetings took place, Mom and Dad would ensure that my two younger brothers and I were safely in the house and remained there.

All roads emanated from the town square—one to the north through Tuscaloosa to Birmingham, one to the east through Selma to Montgomery, one to the south to York, Alabama and then on to Meridian, Mississippi, and one to the west to our later home in Livingston.

The road to the west wasn't a Yellow Brick Road to a magical place like the Land of Oz, but it was certainly a special road to me. It was only about one-half mile long with houses on either side for the first three blocks. The houses varied from small, single story homes to larger, southern plantation-style mansions. The last block of the road was unpaved and dead-ended on a bluff above the Sucarnoochee River. There were only a few homes on this last part of the road, and all were on the north side of the road.

Our house was the last house on the road on the bluff above the river. We represented the sentinel outpost above my mighty river. No one could approach the river without passing my outpost.

It was a small wood frame house with two bedrooms, a small living room, kitchen, and a single bath. When we first moved into the house in 1949, I was eleven years old, and my two younger brothers and I shared one of the bedrooms. Later my parents had the back porch screened with a translucent plastic material and created my first private bedroom.

I still remember the joy and serenity of having my own private space. I learned that while I needed intellectual, emotional, and physical contact with others, I equally needed the quiet, alone time. To this day, I value and require time and space alone to both reflect on the activities around me and on my own thoughts.

Although we lived modestly, but comfortably, the years our family spent in Livingston at our southern home were, for me, a golden time of growth, discovery, and challenge as the South moved past the cusp from its segregated past to the civil rights movement.

The times they were a changin'!

24.

OUR SOUTHERN HOME
1949–1952

OUR SOUTHERN HOME was also the name of the Livingston and Sumter County weekly newspaper Dad and Mom managed and edited. So, as with the Black Belt, our southern home has a significant double meaning for me. I spent the formative years of ages eleven to fourteen in this small Black Belt town, and just as Jem in *To Kill a Mockingbird*, I experienced and observed life in a way that molded what I am and how I think.

The newspaper, one of the oldest in Alabama, started publishing circa 1835 in a single-room wooden building on Monroe Street. The small building was still the location of the newspaper when Dad and Mom took it over in late 1948. Dad handled the primary publishing responsibilities from 1948 to late 1950, at which time he was recalled into active military duty at the start of the Korean War. Mom then served as the publisher from 1950 to 1952 with long distance help from Dad.

To watch the weekly preparation and publication of *Our Southern Home* was to view a process that was more mid-nineteenth century than mid-twentieth. As you entered the front door of the building, you felt like you were stepping back into a scene from a Victorian novel. Although the room was by no means dirty, it was cluttered with work furniture and equipment. The lighting, while not dark, was dim enough to cast a somber tone over the room, and the wooden floor was thoroughly impregnated with ink stains. A single aisle running down the center of the room divided desks and worktables, which held all the equipment necessary to publish the paper. Equipment to prepare the paper for the printing press included typewriters, typesetting trays, and page plate trays. Once the printing was complete, the pages were cut, folded, and addressed. All of this work was done by hand from the typesetting to the folding and addressing.

Dad and Mom either wrote or edited all the articles that were printed in the paper. Articles were submitted by local reporters from each of the small towns and villages in the county. Rarely did the local news go beyond events of local interest—club meetings, school events, and of course, births, marriages, and deaths. Dad's one real writing joy was his weekly editorial and, as he soon learned, one had to either adhere to a conservative political viewpoint or become the center of controversy in this decidedly conservative and segregated county.

Dad wrote an editorial decrying the emergence of the States Rights Party (more popularly known as the Dixiecrat Party) in the 1948 presidential race. A group of Southerners led by then governor of South Carolina, Strom Thurmond, stormed out of the 1948 Democratic National Convention over the civil rights plank in the party's platform. Thurmond ran that year as the segregationist Dixiecrat Party presidential candidate. Part of the Dixiecrat Party platform read, "We stand for the segregation of the races and the racial integrity of each race…We oppose the elimination of segregation, the repeal of miscegenation statues, the control of private employment by Federal bureaucrats called for by the misnamed civil rights program." The Dixiecrats carried four southern states—Alabama, Louisiana, Mississippi, and South Carolina—and won thirty-nine electoral votes. Although the defection of the Southerners from the Democratic Party did not lead to the defeat of Democrat Harry Truman in the presidential election, Dad's editorial argued that the action by the Dixiecrats was politically irresponsible to both the Democratic Party and the ideals of the New Deal, and would favor the Republican Party candidate in the 1948 presidential election.

Dad received little support in the county for this point of view, and many labeled him a Communist. The local Ku Klux Klan threatened to burn a cross in our yard, and I was jeered at and kidded by elementary school classmates who must have overheard some heated comments about the editorial from their parents. I remember going home crying to Dad and Mom who comforted me and told me that our principles were correct, and that we had nothing to be ashamed of.

I think Dad's prescience in this matter is borne out by the transition that took place in southern politics over the succeeding years as conservative southern Democrats transformed into the Republican Party, changing the political face of the United States. His insight is further underscored by an event that occurred in 2002 involving two southern politicians who were part of the migration from the Democratic Party to the Republican Party: Strom Thurmond and Mississippi's Trent Lott. Senate Majority Leader Lott was invited to speak at Senator Thurmond's one-hundredth birthday party on December 5, 2002. Lott said, "I want to say this about my state: When Strom Thurmond ran for president, we voted for him. We're proud of it. And if the rest of the country had followed our lead, we wouldn't have had all these problems over all these years, either."

Many southern politicians were and are great chameleons (e.g., Trent Lott, Strom Thurmond, and George Wallace). They all changed their political appearance from white to black (as racist as this metaphor sounds, it is absolutely accurate in this case) as the times demanded in order to survive politically. Nothing forced this change more dramatically than the 1965 Voting Rights Act that outlawed literacy tests and poll taxes as a way of assessing whether one was fit or unfit to vote. With this landmark legislation, disenfranchised blacks registered to vote in large numbers and gained the vote majority in many areas. Yet, despite the southern politicians' public personas, these politicians' racist feelings are frequently just under the surface as Lott demonstrated, to his chagrin.

Of course, Dad's editorials had to find the printed page, and this task fell to the crown jewel of the newspaper—the printing press. In the center of the back of the room stood the press, which was about five-feet high, six-feet wide, and six-feet deep with an extended tray on the back rear to catch the printed pages as they exited. The old press was as well used as the building and the other equipment in it. Other than the fact that the press did indeed print the paper's pages, its operation was anything but automated; all of the operations of the press were performed by hand.

My brother Gibbs and I were part-time participants in this highly automated publishing process. We both learned how to set type and were allowed to set an occasional article. After each story was set, a copy impression was made for proofreading, and incorrect characters were replaced. This was laborious work, as you would have to remove the offending character with tweezers and slip the correct character in its place while maintaining the sanctity of the entire line of type and the article.

Gibbs and I also had another critical task to perform. The newspaper had to be printed one page at a time. Assuming the week's run was a four-page newspaper, the plate for pages 1 and 4 would be loaded into the press (by hand, of course). One person would work as the feeder and stand on a small platform about one- to two-feet high and reach over the top of the press onto a long, flat feed area large enough to accommodate a stack of paper. The feeder would hand-feed each sheet of paper into the press, and the challenge was to develop a coordinated rhythm matching the rotational rate of the press to maximize the print rate. The piece of paper rotated around a cylinder and was impressed onto the page plate in the bottom bed of the press that moved back and forth under the cylinder in rhythm with the rotation. The printed sheet was ejected out the rear of the press onto a catcher assembly shaped like a long, straight rake that was supposed to catch the printed sheet and gently set it on the finished stack of printed pages.

There was one minor problem: the catcher assembly never seemed to work as the designer intended, and the just-completed page would frequently be sent on its way like a leaf on a gentle autumn breeze. If left unattended, finished pages would soon be everywhere, and eventually pages would get jammed in the catcher mechanism. The press would have to be shut down to clear the jam.

Solution: Position a person behind the press to serve as a human catcher to ensure the finished pages settled down on the completed stack in an orderly fashion. When my brother or I was available, we were assigned this job. Otherwise, the feeder usually had to serve double duty: feed papers into the press, and at the same time, monitor the printed pages coming out, which required one to leap back and forth to maintain some kind of state of equilibrium.

Finally, there was the inevitable mad dash to the post office to meet the Thursday deadline, so the newspapers could be delivered on Friday. After a brief respite to savor a completed production, everything had to be cleaned up and knocked down before starting the process all over again for next week's publication.

Thus were about two thousand copies of *Our Southern Home* published each week. The newspaper was not a financial success. To make ends meet, Dad made a bartering deal with one of the two grocery stores in Livingston—a weekly ad for food. Yet, we did something few families experience: We worked together in a family-run enterprise conditioned by a high set of moral principles. These experiences help set the tone and tenor for the values my brothers and I took with us into our adult years.

Years later my father would wonder aloud: Who influenced my oldest son to become such a liberal? I should have said to him, "Papa, you did. You sowed the seeds in Livingston when you were publishing *Our Southern Home.*"

25.

BOYHOOD PASTIMES
1949–1952

THE SUCARNOOCHEE RIVER was the central thread holding together the surrounding forests, fields, streams, and ponds that served as the amphitheater upon which my brothers and I played out our childhood games and fantasies. The river was literally out our back door, as our house stood on a bluff overlooking the river at the edge of town.

Willie Jr. and Yank

WE WERE AIDED AND ABETTED in wilderness treks by two knowledgeable and capable companions and teachers: Willie Jr. and Yank, two black boys who lived with their families in the black section of Livingston in housing that only in a moment of extreme generosity could be called adequate. And yet, we played and visited constantly, as if we lived next door to one another. One of the unwritten rules of southern society at that time was that young black and white children under the age of puberty, especially boys, were allowed and expected to play together, as if the segregated barriers of the day didn't exist. At puberty, generally as one entered high school, the dark barrier slammed back into place, and both black and white children were then expected to observe the written rules of the segregated South.

Willie Jr. and Yank were not only our companions and friends; they were our guides and instructors. We had spent our years prior to Livingston in mostly larger urban areas like Birmingham and Mobile and knew little of small-town life and the rural setting at our doorstep, anchored by our wonderful river. Willie Jr. and Yank took it upon themselves to educate two skinny, red-haired white boys in all the wonderful adventures to be had exploring the river area. Since Dad was not an outdoorsman, we were very much in their hands for our extracurricular education, and they did not fail us.

The lessons were not sequential and certainly not scheduled, but over time they showed us all the trails leading in, out, around, and through the river, streams, and fields that were out our back door. Although I was usually with Yank, Willie Jr., my brother, or other friends, I would frequently go for long exploratory hikes alone as I came to know the area better. For me this was the start of a lifelong pleasure of hiking and exploring alone. I am not a solitary person, but I find the occasional hike alone both exhilarating and rewarding. Your thoughts and perceptions are yours and yours alone, unencumbered by interruptions or comments by others. It is an opportunity to clear your mind of all the extraneous flotsam and jetsam of our hurried world and return in a more tranquil state of mind.

As we explored the fields with Willie Jr. and Yank, they introduced us to the decadent pleasure of smoking corn silks. As we were much too young and timid to smoke real tobacco, we opted for this cheaper and more readily available product in the fields. Using any type of paper we happened to have, we would pick the corn silks off the corncob cluster, preferably silks that were more aged, as they burnt better than a greener silk, and wrapped the silks in our paper. Then we would sit down and light up and smoke, as if we were some grand potentates or important businessmen. I honestly don't remember how our corn silk cigarettes tasted, but it's safe to say they weren't habit forming, as I've never met a corn silk addicted smoker.

Willie Jr. and Yank also introduced us to the joys of fishing southern style—trot lines and pole fishing. Trot lines (or trout lines) are an effective, simple way to catch catfish, the ugly but tasty fish that inhabit the rivers and streams of much of the continental United States, especially the southeast. Today trot lines are pretty sophisticated, but our homemade trot lines consisted of one long main line about twenty to thirty feet in length. Every two to three feet along the main line, we tied off a series of small lines with a hook at the end. After all the hooks were baited, one end of the main line was tied to a secure object on the river bank, and the entire line was either thrown or towed out into the river and anchored to the bottom by a heavy weight at the end of the main line.

Once our trot line was set, we were free to pursue other activities and could return to check the line for fish or the need for more bait as often or as infrequently as we wished. Supposedly, the term trot line comes from the need to trot out frequently to check the status of your line. I don't remember taking home a substantial number of fish, but I do fondly remember the fun and camaraderie of working and playing with Willie Jr. and Yank, as we struggled to properly set and arrange our trot lines.

Pole fishing was just that, a six- to twelve-foot bamboo pole with a line, float, sinker, hook, and bait (apologies to Norman Maclean, as we did use old coffee cans filled with worms, not the elegant handmade flies of his youthful fly fishing days in Montana). Pole fishing was an idyllic pastime composed of quietly sitting on a pond or river bank tending your pole, monitoring the motion of the float for a strike, and generally doing nothing. Depending on your frame of mind and point of reference, it is either the most relaxing and meditative form of fishing or the most boring.

Great outdoorsmen we did not become, but we romped the fields, and swam and fished the ponds and streams with Willie Jr. and Yank, and our other white friends as though the whole expanse belonged to us with no other world beyond its narrow borders.

I've often wondered whatever became of Willie Jr. and Yank. I never saw them or heard from them again after I left Livingston in 1952 at age fourteen. They would have grown into young adulthood as the civil rights movement was gaining momentum in the late 1950s and early 1960s and then been prime candidates for the draft as the insatiable demand for manpower ensued with the Vietnam War. One of the many sad facts of that war is the disproportionate number of young black men who were drafted into that conflict and became casualties. This may well have been the fate of either Willie Jr. or Yank, but I fervently hope that concern is wrong and that one day they will read this and smile at the memory of those two red-headed white boys they helped guide through their boyhood years.

Other Boyhood Pastimes

A VERY DIFFERENT ACTIVITY I initially learned in Livingston was golf, and this did not include Willie Jr. and Yank, as even the unwritten rules for young children did not cross the segregated barrier into the lily-white world of golf. One of my good, white friend's father, a wealthy lumberman with a large cattle ranch just east of town, along with some of his golf-loving buddies, built a golf course in one of his large cow pastures.

The tees were an area of the pasture more neatly trimmed than the remainder of the pasture, which served as the fairways, and were kept trim by the constant grazing of the cattle. The greens were anything but green, as they were sand mixed with oil, and each "green" had to be fenced with barbwire to keep the cattle out. Once you had navigated your ball from tee to "green" around the cows, the cow piles, and the barbwire protecting the "green," you had to scrape a path from your ball over the cup with a heavy metal scraper to give yourself a relatively flat and smooth putting surface.

My young buddies and I took our first golf licks on this course and became experts at trying to avoid the cow piles, especially the fresh ones.

Of course, the local rules allowed a free drop from the cow piles, but one did have the odious task of retrieving and cleaning the ball. My buddies and I would occasionally cancel the cow pile lift and drop rule, forcing us to play the ball as it lay. To say the least, this led to some humorous and messy scenes, but such is the stuff young boys are made of.

In the summer of 1950, I attended the second national Boy Scout Jamboree in Valley Forge, Pennsylvania, along with most of my Livingston scout troop members and our scout leader. Although Willie Jr. and Yank were friends with most of the white boys on the trip, our two black buddies were excluded from participation by the ever-present harsh barrier of segregation. We could play together in the fields and streams but were precluded from any social or educational interactions that might lead to lasting change. Our troop departed Livingston on June 26 on the Southern Railway and arrived in Valley Forge on June 27, where we camped until July 7 along with over forty-six thousand other scouts from across the nation and nineteen foreign countries. President Truman and soon-to-be-president General Eisenhower came to the jamboree to give speeches. Both men talked about the need to protect our country and the world against the evils of communism and the necessity to respond to the North Korean attack on South Korea on June 25, 1950, just the day before we had left Livingston on our great journey.

I still have the boyhood album I put together after the jamboree and in one of his letters to me, Dad wrote, "Don't worry about the war news from Korea. I don't think it will amount to much. I think the Russians will back down and give up – because they are afraid to go to war with the United States." While I am sure Dad was mostly trying to assuage any youthful anxiety I might have over the war news, his prognostications proved quite inaccurate, as the war lasted three years until July 27, 1953, and it was Mao Tse-tung's People's Republic of China, not Joseph Stalin's Russia, that proved to be the intractable force assisting the North Koreans.

One delightful memory of the jamboree revolves around one of the highlights, where scouts were asked to bring artifacts and objects indigenous and representative of their area of the country or world to be used as trading material. Scouts were encouraged to barter and trade objects as a way to get to know one another better and to share experiences. Although I wish our troop could take credit for this nefarious scheme, it was actually another Alabama troop that came up with the most innovative trading object of all. These fellas came to Valley Forge with a load of cockleburs, a one-to-two-inch spiny seed covered with spikes that will both stick you and stick to anything. They had dried the cockleburs so they were a dark brown color. The Alabama boys traded these off to Yankees and other unsuspecting scouts as porcupine eggs. They reaped a bountiful harvest from their trade endeavors and proved conclusively that Yankees aren't so smart after all. The Yankees may have won the Civil War and have a superior industrial base, but they sure are gullible.

After the Jamboree concluded, our troop traveled to New York City for two days of sightseeing, where I got to see my beloved Boston Red Sox beat the New York Yankees 4–2 in Yankee Stadium. The Birmingham Barons baseball team was a part of the Red Sox farm system, and I was a rabid Red Sox fan from my youngest years until I settled in the San Francisco Bay Area in 1968 and changed my allegiance to the San Francisco Giants. Oh, how fickle we mortals are!

Our troop spent a day touring Washington, DC, on our way back to Livingston, and we arrived home on July 10, 1950, concluding a long and exciting trip that, for most of us, was our first big experience alone away from home.

Horseback riding was another new adventure for me in Livingston, one that unfortunately led to a life-threatening accident. On reflection, it's a miracle I ever survived childhood—I was an accident looking for a place to happen. I broke one of my arms on two separate occasions as a child, fell out of a swing and gashed the back of my scalp requiring a number of stitches to repair, and, most traumatically, suffered the horse accident.

The period of time immediately preceding the horse accident, and the accident itself, has always been a blank in my memory, as it is not unusual to suffer a short-term memory loss for the period surrounding a severe head injury. I had always thought I was with my good childhood friend, Dickie Allison, that day. In 2006, I visited Dick (he had long since dropped the ie in his first name) in Atlanta and showed him what I had written in this book to that point. After reading it, Dick told me I had one important fact wrong in the story. He said I was with his younger brother, Louis, that day, as Dick disliked horseback riding. I called Louis when I returned to California and asked him if he remembered that day. He replied, "Waights, it's etched in my memory. I'll never forget it."

Then, fifty-seven years after the accident and for the first time, I heard Louis's eyewitness account of that fateful day in my life. Louis's mother, Lillis Allison, drove us out to their farm east of Livingston in the spring of 1949. They called the farm Tornado Place because the antebellum home Louis's grandfather built on the farm had been destroyed by a tornado when Louis was five years old. Miss Lillis left us with Eugene Evans, a black man who worked for the family and was caretaker of the farm and its horses. He took us into the corral where there were two or three horses, and, as he herded the horses into a corner of the corral to harness them, he told us to stand about twenty feet back in the middle of the corral. As Evans approached the horses to start putting bits and reins on two of them, one of the horses bolted forward. I was on Louis's right, and the horse ran straight at me, taking only two or three strides to reach me. It all happened so fast, I just froze, leaned or knelt down, and the horse tried to jump over me, but either his knee or a hoof hit me in the right side of my head. Louis said it looked "just horrible." I immediately collapsed, was bleeding profusely, and did not move. There was no telephone on the property, but Evans found another black man who was working on the property that day. The man had an old bobtail pulp wood truck, and Evans picked me up, cradled me gently in his arms, and held me in his lap in the truck while the other man drove to town. Louis had to stay at the farm and didn't see me again until after I came home from the hospital a couple of weeks later.

After Eugene Evans and the bobtail truck driver got me into town, my parents and the Allisons had an ambulance take me to Rush Memorial Hospital in Meridian, Mississippi, about thirty-five miles west of Livingston. It turned out I needed surgery. A brain surgeon was flown from Birmingham to perform the surgery. I had suffered a skull fracture and severe brain concussion, and but for the horse's leap and the grace of a fraction of an inch, I would have either died or suffered serious brain damage. After the surgery, I laid in my hospital bed overnight and did not regain consciousness until the next morning.

I still remember my awakening with a special sense of awe. Mom had stayed at the hospital with me, sleeping on an extra bed in the room, but it so happened that when I awoke she had briefly stepped out of the room. I distinctly remember, as I opened my eyes and looked around at what for me was a surreal scene framed in a beautiful sunlit glow, I actually thought this must be heaven. I pinched myself to see if I had feeling in my body, which I did. After I lay there for a short period of time trying, with no success, to piece together what had happened and where I was, Mom came back into the room. Mom's initial reaction was one of tearful joy to see and hear me alert, as there was, of course, a concern about whether or not I had suffered any significant brain damage. Mom explained to me what had happened and where I was.

Although I had to visit the doctor in Birmingham several times over the next few years for follow-up examinations, I fully recovered. I still have a one-inch by two-inch area of my skull that is slightly indented, and it is one of several youthful scars I collected as badges of honor on my way to manhood.

In 2007, Mom, at age ninety-three, told me one other interesting facet of the story. At the time of the accident, Mom and Dad were struggling to make ends meet. The newspaper was not a profitable venture, and Dad's only medical insurance policy had a maximum benefit of $700, which would have covered only a fraction of the cost of my medical treatment for this accident. Andy Allison, Dad's childhood friend who accompanied him on the trip to Scandinavia in 1928 and the father of Dickie and Louis, paid all the remaining medical costs. It must have been substantial, and I feel a strong linkage and debt of gratitude to this family, who helped us, and me in particular, so generously.

This was not to be the end of Eugene Evans in our family's story. In about 1960, Andy Allison sold his business interest in Livingston and Sumter County, and Evans moved to Birmingham and was employed by Frank Taylor for years. My brother Gibbs remembers meeting Evans at Frank's house in the 1960s and discussing my accident. Frank even considered using Evans as a member of his football film crew for the *Bear Bryant Show* in the 1970s, but, apparently, that never came to pass. Too bad, I'll bet Eugene Evans would have made a great football film man.

AND, BY THE WAY, EUGENE, I'm sorry I never got a chance to thank you for saving my life.

Part Four

Unsettled Times

1955–1977

26.

MONTGOMERY
December 1, 1955

Two events in the 1950s served as precursors to the start of the modern civil rights movement.

On May 17, 1954, the U.S. Supreme Court issued its long-awaited decision invalidating the "separate, but equal" education laws practiced in southern states, calling segregated schools "inherently unequal." The "separate, but equal" laws were nothing more than a well-managed method to keep blacks in segregated schools offering educational programs that were anything but equal to those available in white-only schools. However, some states and politicians would once again prove that a court ruling did not automatically lead to willing and effective compliance.

On August 28, 1955, Emmett Till was brutally murdered in Money, Mississippi. Emmett, a fourteen-year-old black boy from Chicago, was visiting his uncle in Money. He was not schooled or raised in the ways of the segregated South and purportedly whistled at Roy Bryant's wife, a white woman, in their store. He was later abducted from his uncle's home, and his mutilated body was found three days later in the Tallahatchie River. An all-white jury acquitted Bryant and his half-brother, J. W. Milam, of the murder, but Milam later confessed that they had indeed committed the heinous crime. Emmett's mother's decision to hold a public, open-casket funeral service for her son so people could see his mutilated face and body drew national attention to the murder, and the subsequent publicity and magazine articles shocked the nation.

Montgomery, Alabama—Thursday, December 1, 1955

The first day of December 1955 was a cold day in Montgomery. The Christmas lights and displays shined brightly in the store windows, and a festive spirit enveloped the whole community. Just after five o'clock in the late afternoon, Rosa Parks finished her day's work as an assistant tailor at the Montgomery Fair Department Store and walked to the Court Square bus stop to catch the bus to her home. Still upset by Emmett Till's murder, she was anxious to get home and relax with Raymond and her mother. Raymond would be getting home about the same time from his job as a barber at Maxwell Air Force Base, and they would all sit down to a dinner prepared by Leona. Rosa let the first bus pass; it was too full, and she hoped to be able to sit after a long day. The next bus drove up, not quite as full, and she got on quickly, paid her ten-cent fare, not paying any attention to the driver, and rushed to the one open seat, an aisle seat, in the middle section of the bus. The middle section was like being in limbo for blacks; they could sit there if the bus was not full, but the driver, at his discretion, could move the "Colored" sign back a few rows if he wished. The bus picked up several whites at the next two stops, and one white man was finally left without a seat. The driver stood up, and as he walked to the middle section of the bus, Rosa recognized James Blake, the white driver who had put her off the bus in 1943. Blake said to Rosa and the other three blacks sitting in the middle section, "Let me have those front seats." When nobody moved, the bus was deadly silent as he barked, "Y'all better make it light on yourselves and let me have those seats." The man next to Rosa and the two women opposite her all moved to the back. Rosa quietly slipped over to the empty window seat. Blake asked her again, "Are you going to stand up?"

Rosa sat quietly for a few seconds, and, while she didn't think of it consciously, the culmination of years of preparation for this moment—her strong sense of self and dignity instilled in her by her parents and grand-parents, her meeting and marrying the activist Raymond Parks and hear-ing of the injustices suffered by the Scottsboro Boys, her work with E. D. Nixon and the NAACP, her struggle to register to vote, the compassion and sorrow she felt for what young Claudette Colvin had to endure, and her friendship with Virginia Durr leading to her two weeks at Highlander Folk School—came together, as she replied to Blake, "No."

Blake, frustrated and unsure what to do next, threatened her with, "Well, I'm going to have you arrested."

Rosa replied with four words that required Blake to quickly consider the moral and legal implications of his threat, and, most importantly, four words that would provide the spark for the beginning of the modern civil rights movement: "You may do that."

After uttering her now famous words, events would move at a dizzying speed for the next five days, creating both the leader and the first major confrontation of the civil rights movement. Soon after the impasse with Blake on the bus, Rosa was arrested and taken to the city jail where she was booked and fingerprinted, and her mug shot taken. Initially, the police wouldn't let Rosa make a phone call, but they finally relented, and she called her husband and mother and told them of her arrest. A black woman on the bus with Rosa called a friend and told her of Rosa's arrest, and this woman, a friend of E. D. Nixon, immediately called him. Nixon called the police, but they were rude to him and refused to answer any of his questions about Rosa's situation. Nixon called Clifford Durr to seek his assistance, and Durr called the police who told him her bail was one hundred dollars. Durr didn't have the money since his law business was doing so poorly, but Nixon said he had the money. Nixon, and Clifford and Virginia Durr went to the jail to post the bail for Rosa's release. Rosa was released unharmed physically and in a tranquil state, as she knew she was right and this action was long overdue. Her trial was scheduled for the following Monday, December 5, when she would be formally charged with violating the city's segregation ordinance.

After arriving at Rosa's home, Nixon approached her about becoming the plaintiff in a lawsuit challenging the legality of Montgomery's ordinance. After thinking about it for a while, concerned about the safety of her mother and Raymond, Rosa agreed to be the plaintiff, even though Raymond had pleaded with her not to do it, saying repeatedly, "Rosa, the white folks will kill you." E. D. Nixon is reported to have said, upon hearing of Rosa's decision, "My God, look what segregation has put in my hands," as he knew Rosa's impeccable character, background, and demeanor would make her the perfect plaintiff.

When Nixon got back to his home just before midnight, he knew he had to make some phone calls to start organizing the effort to defend Rosa; his job as a Pullman Car porter required him to leave town the next morning for a scheduled train trip from Montgomery to Atlanta to New York and back. He would return home in time for Rosa's trial on Monday, but much of what had to be done couldn't wait. Knowing he had to arrange for Rosa's defense in court on Monday, he first called Fred Gray, a twenty-four-year-old black Montgomery attorney in his first year of practice.

Gray, one of the two black attorneys in Montgomery, was born in Montgomery, received his law degree at Case Western Reserve University in Cleveland, Ohio, in 1954, and returned to Montgomery to practice law. Clifford Durr befriended the young lawyer, gave him advice and help as he got started, and explained to him how best to deal with the political and legal machinations in the Montgomery courts. Gray would become one of the major lawyers conducting the legal efforts of the civil rights movement. In 2002, he became the first African American elected to be president of the Alabama State Bar Association.

Nixon explained Rosa's situation, and Gray, who had handled Claudette Colvin's case earlier, readily agreed to handle Rosa's case. He and Nixon also discussed the need to contact the national offices of the NAACP to get their support, both financially and legally.

Gray called Jo Ann Robinson, an English professor at Montgomery's all-black Alabama State University, the same school at which Rosa attended tenth grade, and where her mother, Leona, took summer courses to maintain her teacher's license. Robinson was largely responsible for the success of the upcoming boycott. Initially, Robinson was not given the credit due her for her role in the boycott, but later books have told her story well and with proper recognition. As the head of the Woman's Political Council, the largest and most active integrationist group in the city, she had prepared a bus boycott plan just for this day and was ready to go into action. Robinson told Gray she had heard about Rosa's arrest and was already preparing to announce a one-day bus boycott for Monday, December 5.

Friday—December 2, 1955

Jo Ann Robinson, two of her students, and another professor went to the university offices after midnight, ostensibly to grade exam papers, and by 4:00 a.m., they had a handbill announcing the one-day boycott prepared and mimeographed. They distributed the handbills around the city early the next morning.

At 5:00 a.m., Nixon called several Montgomery black ministers, including twenty-nine-year-old Ralph Abernathy and twenty-six-year-old Martin Luther King Jr., before he was to board the train for his scheduled run. Abernathy immediately agreed to Nixon's request to support a boycott; however, King initially hesitated, telling Nixon he needed some time to think about it and would get back to him. Abernathy ultimately convinced King he should support the boycott. It was agreed the group of ministers would meet that evening at King's Dexter Avenue Baptist Church.

Nixon, ever the consummate politician and planner, didn't waste any opportunities to publicize Rosa's arrest and the boycott. Before he left for the train station, he called Joe Azbell, the progressive city editor of the *Montgomery Advertiser*, and told him to meet him at the station to get the "hottest story you've ever written." Azbell met him on a platform at the station, and Nixon told Azbell about Rosa's background and solid reputation in the community and then filled him in with all the details of the Monday bus boycott, knowing full well it would be in Saturday or Sunday's newspaper, thus, spreading the news all over town.

Rosa got up early as usual on Friday morning and prepared to go to work. She read on page nine in a *Montgomery Advertiser* article headlined "Negro Jailed for 'Overlooking' Bus Segregation" that she was news;

however, the article did not identify her by name, although it did give her place of employment. She was determined to go to work, so she called a black taxi company and took a taxi to work, as she had vowed to herself to never ride another segregated bus. When she got to work, her direct boss was surprised to see her, as most employees in the department store knew Rosa was the woman arrested. Soon after she arrived at the store, her supervisor came into the basement tailor shop, glared at her, and walked out. She knew then that her job was in jeopardy, and, as she suspected, the following month she would be fired. When she left work, she was able to avoid a reporter looking for her in the store. Rosa got home with no further encounters and spent the remainder of the day quietly thinking about the tumultuous events unfolding about her. She was also pleased to hear King would be involved in the protest, as she had a high regard for him.

Friday evening, Rosa joined about fifty black ministers and other black leaders in the community at their meeting at King's church. The first part of the meeting was a rather contentious debate about the wisdom of proceeding with the boycott. However, after Rosa spoke of her arrest and the need for urgent action to stop these hateful and degrading practices, most of those in attendance, even those initially opposed, supported this brave woman and the need for a boycott. After the meeting adjourned, Rosa remained to help King, Abernathy, and a few others draft a shorter version of Robinson's handbill, adding to it an invitation to all to attend a mass meeting at seven o'clock on Monday evening at the Holt Street Baptist Church to receive further instructions on the boycott.

Saturday—December 3, 1955

Saturday morning Rosa got a phone call from her new, young friend, twenty-seven-year-old Reverend Robert Graetz, the white minister of Montgomery's all-black Trinity Lutheran Church.

Graetz, who was born in West Virginia, had finished his seminary education and training in Ohio earlier in 1955 and was then assigned by the Lutheran Church to succeed the outgoing black minister in Montgomery, Nelson Trout. Years later, Trout would become the first African American Lutheran bishop in the United States. Graetz, his wife Jeannie, and their two young sons arrived in Montgomery in the summer of 1955 and moved into the new parsonage that Trout had built and occupied. Graetz and his family were immediately ostracized by Montgomery's white community and joined the handful of white liberals who supported the black community and the abolishment of segregation including Virginia and Clifford Durr, Aubrey Williams, and Myles Horton. Graetz also developed a close friendship with King and supported him and the black community throughout the bus boycott and beyond. His house, the parsonage, was bombed twice, but no one was hurt. A third bomb was planted at the house, but it did not explode. Had it exploded, the entire family would likely have been killed, as the bomb was made up of eleven sticks of dynamite and a container of TNT.

Graetz's conversation with Rosa is both humorous and illustrates her humility and self-deprecation. She was not interested in being a hero; she just wanted justice for black people. After the usual opening pleasantries in their phone conversation, Graetz commented to Rosa, "I just heard that someone was arrested on one of the buses Thursday."

Rosa replied, "That's right, Pastor Graetz."

"And that we're supposed to boycott the buses on Monday to protest," Graetz said.

Rosa answered again, "That's right, Pastor Graetz."

Graetz asked, "Do you know anything about it?"

Rosa acknowledged she did, "Yes, Pastor Graetz."

Graetz pressed on, "Do you know who was arrested?"

Rosa said, "Yes, Pastor Graetz."

Graetz, now somewhat exasperated at Rosa's apparent reticence, exclaimed, "Well, who was it?"

Rosa paused, and finally answered, "It was me, Pastor Graetz."

Graetz immediately drove over to Rosa's home to hear all the details about the arrest and boycott first hand. The next morning he told his all-black congregation about Rosa Parks's arrest and urged them to honor the boycott, as he and his family would. The congregation murmured its approval.

Sunday—December 4, 1955

On Sunday morning, Montgomery woke up and read the *Montgomery Advertiser* with their coffee and breakfast. As Nixon had hoped, there was an article on the front page about Rosa and Monday's boycott. In addition, Jo Ann Robinson's handbill and the amended handbill were liberally quoted in the article, ensuring most of Montgomery would now know about the boycott.

Many blacks flocked to their churches that morning, where the ministers emphasized the importance of honoring the bus boycott to show Montgomery's white citizens and power structure that the black community was not going to tolerate the status quo. However, Abernathy, King, Nixon, Robinson, Rosa, and everyone else involved in the effort were worried and unsure how successful it would be. The weather was forecast to be rainy; King felt a 60 percent participation rate would be a success assuming the black-owned taxi companies in the city cooperated as they had promised.

Monday—December 5, 1955

Monday morning was a rainy, cool day, not conducive to avoiding the buses as the black population of Montgomery awoke and prepared to go to work and start their day. Rosa was up early and watched buses go by her Cleveland Avenue house, and saw that most of them were empty. King and his wife, Coretta, were also up early, sitting in the kitchen in their house on Jackson Avenue, along the route that carried more black riders than any other in the city. When the six o'clock bus came by, Martin and Coretta looked out their window and saw an amazing sight—there was a not a black face to be seen on the bus. The results were the same citywide with nearly 100 percent participation. The one-day boycott was a rousing success.

Later that morning, Rosa, accompanied by her husband and E. D. Nixon, went to the city courthouse for her 9:30 a.m. trial to find a huge crowd of black people standing around the front of the building. As she worked her way through the crowd to the front door of the courthouse, a young member of Montgomery's NAACP Youth Council, Mary Frances, called out to the crowd, as the impeccably dressed forty-two-year-old woman passed, "Oh, she's so sweet. They've messed with the wrong one now." Those words would become the mantra of the movement throughout the remainder of the boycott: "They've messed with the wrong one now."

Rosa's trial was short—only five minutes. The prosecution brought three witnesses to the stand. First up was James Blake, whose testimony was reasonably accurate about the events on the bus, except when he claimed there was an empty seat in the rear black section of the bus, which Rosa could have used. Two white women were then called to testify, and they corroborated Blake's testimony about the empty seat. It was not true; there was not an empty seat. One of Rosa's NAACP associates, who was observing the trial, leaned over to Nixon and whispered, "You can always find some damn white woman to lie." Fred Gray chose to ignore their testimony and only argued for the defense that the city's segregation ordinance was unconstitutional. Of course, Gray, Nixon, Rosa, and all the other black leaders wanted a guilty verdict. Without it, they had no basis for an appeal. However, they needn't have worried; the judgment was never in doubt, as the judge ruled Rosa had violated the city's segregation ordinance, and he fined her ten dollars plus four dollars for court costs.

The ministers and other black leaders met that afternoon to discuss formation of the newly created Montgomery Improvement Association and the agenda and approach for the evening's mass meeting. Several of the ministers were still unsure about continuing with the boycott and wanted any voting done by secret ballot to protect their identities. Nixon stood and literally scolded the ministers for their timidity and lack of courage, and said it was time to record opinions openly, not in a secret ballot. He said he would expose the men as cowards and added, "Let me tell you gentlemen one thing. You ministers have lived off these wash-women for the last hundred years and ain't never done nothing for them…We've worn aprons all our lives. It's time to take the aprons off…If we're gonna be mens, now's the time to be mens." Just before he finished his stern lecture, King arrived at the meeting, heard the last part of Nixon's remarks, and immediately responded, "Brother Nixon, I'm not a coward. I don't want anybody to call me a coward." King added that he agreed with Nixon that voting should be done openly.

Before anyone else could respond, Rufus Lewis, a mortician and outspoken civil rights activist, stood up and moved that King be elected president of the new association. A close friend of Lewis's immediately seconded the motion. The group initially sat quietly, not sure what to make of the quick turn of events, but, after a brief discussion, no one else was nominated. Much to their chagrin, neither Abernathy nor Nixon was nominated, as they considered the young minister from Atlanta unqualified and untested to lead the group. Martin Luther King Jr. was elected president of the association, and the man who would become the charismatic leader of the civil rights movement with his elegant oratory and brave leadership was about to be thrust onto the nation and the world's stage for the first time.

The mass meeting was held at seven o'clock that evening in the Holt Street Baptist Church, located in an area of town that was predominately black. The attendance was overwhelming: about one thousand people crowded into one of the largest black churches in the city, and over four thousand overflowed in front of the church and on the surrounding streets. Loudspeakers were set up so the crowd outside could hear the speeches. Rosa joined King, Abernathy, Nixon, and others on the platform in the church. After an opening prayer and a statement by Nixon that the boycott should be extended, King walked to the pulpit to deliver his first speech as a civil rights leader.

King's speech started slowly, but he warmed to his subject, and the audience started to respond with "Yeses" and "Amens" when he talked about Rosa: "Just the other day—just last Thursday to be exact—one of the finest citizens in Montgomery—not one of the finest Negro citizens—but one of the finest citizens in Montgomery—was taken from a bus—and carried to jail and arrested—because she refused to give up—to give up her seat to a white person." And King later exclaimed, "And you know, my friends, there comes a time when people get tired of being trampled over by the iron feet of oppression," bringing the crowd to a fever pitch, shouting in agreement.

King made his position clear on the need for a nonviolent protest when he said, "Now let us say that we are not here advocating violence. We have overcome that...The only weapon that we have in our hands this evening is the weapon of protest." To make sure people understood this nonviolent protest was a far cry from the racist actions of the Ku Klux Klan and the White Citizens Council, he added, "There will be no crosses burned at any bus stops in Montgomery. There will be no white persons pulled out of their homes and taken out on some distant road and murdered. There will be nobody among us who will stand up and defy the Constitution of this nation."

And then King said what would become the most remembered line in the speech: "And we are determined here in Montgomery—to work and fight until justice runs down like water, and righteousness like a mighty stream!"

After King's speech, Abernathy discussed the bus boycott and proposed that it continue. The audiences inside and out roared their approval. The meeting concluded with a prayer. The black citizens of Montgomery held true to the boycott for thirteen months. There followed many violent moments caused by whites, including the bombings of the homes of Abernathy, Graetz, and King, and four black churches, but the community held together with a firm resolve. On November 13, 1956, the U.S. Supreme Court upheld without dissent a lower federal court's ruling that the segregation laws of Alabama were unconstitutional.

Several misconceptions have lingered surrounding Rosa Park's civil disobedience on December 1, 1955: the action was premeditated; she intended to become the test case in an appeal to the Supreme Court; and, she was too tired to give up her seat. None is true. She had not been planning any particular action that day; she just wanted to get home to her family. While she well knew a test case was needed to challenge the segregation laws, the action came about spontaneously in the circumstances of the moment. She later explained that she was not too tired or too old, adding "...the only tired I was, was tired of giving in." Rosa never had an easy answer as to why she acted when she did, only able to say, "When I declined to give up my seat, it was not that day, or bus, in particular. I just wanted to be free like everybody else. I did not want to be continually humiliated over something I had no control over: the color of my skin."

Great historical moments sometimes seem to get over glorified. This was not one of those moments. Twenty-four years earlier, the Scottsboro Boys were tried, found guilty, and sentenced to death in the short span of sixteen days. A young black woman, Rosa McCauley, grew as an activist out of that tragedy, and now, in five days, the black citizens of Montgomery had said in one voice, "We will not abide by your segregated laws any longer!"

and successfully conducted a bus boycott demonstrating the black community's resolve and ability to organize against years of racism and segregation. The civil rights movement—no—the revolution, had begun. Change would now be forthcoming because the oppressed had taken the initiative, tired of a timid federal government's reluctance to take action and an entrenched southern system determined to maintain the status quo.

University of Alabama—December 1, 1955

ON THAT SAME COLD, FIRST DAY OF DECEMBER, another eighteen-year-old Taylor boy was walking across the University of Alabama Quadrangle late in the afternoon, returning from one of his engineering lab classes. It was me, probably reciting to myself the litany of Deke nationwide chapters in as-established order, first to last, as required by my lowly status as a freshman fraternity pledge: "Psi–Yale; Theta–Bowdoin; Xi–Colby; Sigma–Amherst; Gamma–Vanderbilt; Psi–Alabama; Chi–Mississippi…" When I got to the fraternity house, we heard nothing about Rosa's situation for several days, and, even then, thought little about it. A black person having a run-in with a white bus driver was not exactly an unusual or newsworthy event in Alabama. Even as the situation developed into the bus boycott, our interest was minimal. Let's see, what were our interests? The list probably goes something like this in descending order: dreaming about sex, chasing coeds with mixed success, drinking beer with too much success, playing and watching sports, and, oh yeah, attending classes.

Southerners honor and follow their traditions with a single-minded dedication to the past—not very different from Tevye in *Fiddler on the Roof.* Tradition dictated my path to higher education, as it was my father's desire to see me follow in his footsteps and those of his four brothers at the University of Alabama, both as a student and as a member of their fraternity, Delta Kappa Epsilon, the Dekes. In the fall of 1955, I dutifully and quite willingly reestablished the Taylor legacy at Alabama when I enrolled as a freshman in the School of Aeronautical Engineering. We had left Livingston, Alabama, in June 1952 to join Dad after he had been recalled to active duty at the start of the Korean War. I graduated from high school in Killeen, Texas, the town adjacent to Fort Hood, the enormous Army base in central Texas. Mom drove me from Killeen to Birmingham, where Uncle Macey then drove me to the university in Tuscaloosa and helped me get settled in my dormitory.

The Dekes, when advised by Uncle Macey that another Taylor was at the university, immediately rushed me as if I was royalty. I felt quite regal from all their fawning attention and rush parties, but learned, soon after I agreed to join, that treatment of freshman pledges was anything but regal.

In addition to the Montgomery bus boycott, my freshman year was marked by an event that captured national attention in February 1956, when Autherine Lucy became, for a few days, the first black student to enroll at the university. I'm going to tell the story of those events from two perspectives. First, I'll tell the story as I remember it from my student days with the caveat that my memory is clouded by the passage of over fifty years. Second, I'll tell a much more factual story based primarily on the account in Diane McWhorter's excellent book, the Pulitzer Prize winning *Carry Me Home*.*

Autherine Lucy—An Account Based on My Cloudy Memory

Within the environs of our cloistered fraternity world and our narrowly focused interests, my fraternity brothers and I were mostly indifferent to the arrival of Autherine Lucy to the school. There were no strong desires to rush out and greet her or to chase her away. The first couple of days she was on campus, we went about our day-to-day activities in our normal fashion, and the campus was reasonably quiet. The weekend brought trouble, as most students now had no classes, and the off-campus world was generally free from work. The campus roiled with fierce mob activities, mostly at night, led by some students and faculty, Ku Klux Klan agitators, and local rednecks. The riots were an ugly scene and forced Miss Lucy to flee the campus for her own safety as neither local, state, nor federal authorities could or would provide her adequate protection. My fraternity brothers and I walked from our fraternity house to the periphery of the mob action and watched the mayhem as rioters tossed bottles and other objects, and bashed cars. I wish I could say we protested the actions or at least gave Miss Lucy our tacit support, but I'm afraid we stood silently by and did nothing. University officials expelled Miss Lucy after three days of riots, and, within a few days, campus life had returned to normal, as if nothing had happened.

Autherine Lucy—An Account Based on the Facts

Autherine Lucy was born in 1929 in Shiloh, Alabama, a small town in the Black Belt. After high school, she attended two all-black Alabama schools: Selma University in Selma and Miles College in Fairfield, a Birmingham suburb. She graduated from Miles in 1952 with a BA in English. Pollie Ann Myers, Autherine's classmate at Miles, convinced Autherine to join her in trying to enroll in graduate school at the University of Alabama. Knowing it would be difficult to get admitted, they approached the NAACP for help, and Thurgood Marshall, Constance Baker Motley,

---

* Although I now own a copy of Ms. McWhorter's book, when I first turned to it as a reference source, I checked a copy out of the Santa Rosa, California, library. On the title page, someone had written in ink: "More black baloney! Go home to Africa!"

and Arthur Shores, a Birmingham attorney prominent in the civil rights struggles in the city, were assigned to the case. Court action started in July 1953, and on June 29, 1955, a newly appointed federal court judge in Birmingham issued a court order instructing the university not to deny the two women admission based on their race. A few days later, the judge amended the order to apply to all African Americans seeking admission to the university. In October 1955, Supreme Court Justice Hugo Black, the ex-Ku Klux Klan member from Alabama, unilaterally upheld the lower federal court's decision, opening the door for the admission of the two women.

However, when they came to the university on Wednesday, February 1, 1956, to formally enroll, the university rejected Pollie's application, citing her premarital conduct. A detective the university hired to look into the women's backgrounds discovered Pollie was pregnant and unmarried when she submitted her application, although she was married before the baby was born. One can only wonder how many Alabama coeds would have been denied admission had they been subjected to similar background checks. Since Pollie was the more outspoken and outgoing of the two, the university hoped that the shy, soft-spoken Autherine would now withdraw. They badly misjudged the twenty-six-year-old young lady's resolve.

On Friday, February 3, Autherine went to her first class. Other students avoided the seats around her, but otherwise everything went smoothly. Fred Shuttlesworth, a black minister and activist in Birmingham and class-mate of Autherine's at Selma University, had accompanied her to Tuscaloosa for the enrollment process. He was so delighted with Autherine's first day in class, he telegraphed Emory O. Jackson, editor of the *Birmingham World*, a black newspaper, "Miss Autherine J. Lucy in class. Everything fine."

By Friday night, everything was not fine. A white student from Selma, sophomore Leonard Wilson, directed a group of male students, intent on a panty raid at a girl's dormitory, to the university president's campus house, and led the group chanting slogans like "Keep Bama white!" and "Hey, hey, ho, ho, Autherine's got to go!" Wilson pledged to the crowd bigger and better things, and Saturday night events grew to a full-scale riot. Rocks were thrown, cars with blacks that happened to drive past unknowingly were attacked and threatened, and a Greyhound bus was also attacked. The rioting resumed on Sunday night with the mob growing to include outsiders: town rednecks and Robert Chambliss, a Ku Klux Klan and White Citizens Council member.

Monday morning, February 6, Autherine started her second day of classes in an atmosphere that had turned tense and decidedly dangerous. She was escorted from her first class out a back door, but, even there, a riotous group found her, intent on chasing her from the campus. The mob pelted her car with eggs, and, when she ran into another building for her next class, she was hit in the back by an egg accompanied with cries of "Let's kill her, let's kill her." After being locked in the building for three hours, the Alabama Highway Patrol finally had to sneak her off the campus hidden on the floor of a car. Monday night, the university's board of trustees suspended Autherine "for her protection and for the protection of other students and staff members."

Autherine's attorneys filed a lawsuit asking the court to overturn her suspension. The federal court ordered the university to allow Autherine to continue her education, but Thurgood Marshall also pushed the court to rule that the university had not provided adequate protection for her. Unable to substantiate this charge to the court's satisfaction, Marshall withdrew the accusation and later admitted he had made a mistake. The university's board of trustees used this accusation as a justification for formally expelling Autherine, contending the lawsuit slandered the university. Thus, the University of Alabama and the State of Alabama had ignored a Supreme Court decision abolishing segregated education and three federal court decisions ordering the university to enroll Autherine as a student. The federal government, under the direction of the Eisenhower administration, was equally culpable in its inactions, as it had refused to enforce the decisions of its federal courts. It would be another seven years before the university would admit its first black students, and even that moment would be challenged by Governor George Wallace's infamous stand in the schoolhouse door.

In the month of February 1956, the emerging Montgomery bus boycott and the Autherine Lucy expulsion from the University of Alabama had set diametrically opposed directions for the two sides in the civil rights struggle. The bus boycott showed blacks could organize in a nonviolent manner to protest and try to right centuries' old injustices, while the capitulation of the university to the mob's actions gave white supremacy groups a renewed sense that mob action and violence could maintain the segregated status quo.

University Life Continues

After several months in the dormitory, I moved into the fraternity house and resided there for the remainder of my college days. Fraternity life in the Deke House was definitely a mixed blessing for me as a student in a strenuous academic program like aeronautical engineering with its heavy technical course load along with numerous lab sessions. I always envied the business and liberal arts majors who seemed to get by on fourteen-to-sixteen semester-hours of course work, while I was struggling under a load of eighteen-to-twenty and the additional labs.

Academically, there is no doubt I would have been better off living in a dormitory or off-campus rather that in the fraternity house where I was constantly challenged to a basketball game, a poker game, a bridge game, a bull session, or a party in the house or at the local bar. It's a testament to the resiliency of youth and my native intelligence that I did as well in school as I did. The distractions and temptations were constant and appealing, and unfortunately, I frequently succumbed to their siren call at the expense of my studies, my grades, and my wallet.

My sophomore year was highlighted by an event that changed the course of my professional life choices. At that time, male freshmen were encouraged to take two years of ROTC and to decide toward the end of their sophomore year whether to continue into Advanced ROTC in the junior and senior years, thus, having an opportunity to become a reserve officer in the military. I elected to take Air Force ROTC as a freshman and, in my sophomore year, was awarded the outstanding second year cadet award. I was proud, full of myself, and gung-ho about continuing into the advanced program with an opportunity to learn to fly. When I went to Maxwell Air Force Base in Montgomery, along with the other candidates for the advanced program tests and physical, I dutifully and honestly told the Air Force doctors about the accident I had with a horse at age eleven that resulted in a skull fracture and brain concussion.

This would prove to be my Achilles heel, as I was not accepted into the program for medical reasons. At the time I was extremely angry and hurt to realize I wouldn't be able to pursue this goal, and, at the time, I wished I had lied about the accident. Reflectively, I realize it was probably a godsend, as I would have been commissioned and trained in the early 1960s, and would have been a ripe candidate for the military's insatiable need for manpower as the Vietnam War ratcheted up.

I returned to campus for my junior year, having gotten over my pique at the Air Force for treating me so unkindly, free from the burden of any ROTC requirements, and maybe with a little more maturity. I had the best academic year of my college career. In one of my junior semesters I racked up a grade point average of 3.4 out of 4.0, although I never again duplicated it. At the end of my junior year, my fraternity brother, Charlie Beauchamp, who was graduating that year and was headed to Seattle to join The Boeing Company, suggested that I come along. Through Dad, I contacted Uncle Bill in Seattle who was then a vice president in Boeing's Commercial Airplane Division. Uncle Bill arranged summer employment for me at Boeing as an intern engineer; Charlie, Bay Lott (another fraternity brother), and I piled into Charlie's 1950 Chevrolet and started a memorable summer.

We first drove from Tuscaloosa to Carlsbad Caverns in New Mexico, and then on to El Paso, Texas, where Dad was stationed at Fort Bliss, and spent two days visiting my family and Juarez, the Mexican city across the Rio Grande from El Paso. We then drove through New Mexico into northern Arizona and through the many marvelous parks and vistas in the area—the Painted Desert, Grand Canyon, Lake Mead, and Boulder Dam. After a brief stop in Las Vegas, we drove through Nevada and past Mono Lake into California. We tried to cross the Sierra Nevada Mountains via Tioga Pass into Yosemite National Park, but the road was not yet open from the previous winter's snows, so we had to drive farther north to South Lake Tahoe to cross the Sierras and reach our San Francisco destination. We spent two days in the marvelous city by the Bay and then drove north through Northern California and the magnificent redwoods, through Oregon, and finally to Seattle.

Charlie and I found an apartment right on Lake Washington with incredible views and access to all that Seattle had to offer. Bay Lott found a job as a maintenance man working at the University of Washington and bunked with one of his workmates, who had a houseboat on Lake Union. Seattle may have a reputation for rainy and dreary weather, but this was one incredible summer. The weather was perfect except for a few days of rain right after we arrived and the last few days of our summer. I fell in love with everything about Seattle—the city, the lakes, Puget Sound, the mild climate, the mountains, and my work. I knew as soon as I left after that idyllic summer that I wanted to return to Seattle and work for Boeing when I started my professional career.

My senior year then became something of a blur, as I wished for it to end quickly and hoped I would receive a job offer from Boeing so I could return to Seattle. Well, sometimes your dreams do come true, and in the spring of 1959, Boeing offered me a job as an associate aeronautical engineer on the staff of the Commercial Airplane Division's Aerodynamics Department. In August 1959, I graduated from the university and prepared to move to Seattle.

―――――

SEPTEMBER 1959 would find two Southerners and one African making their way westward for very different reasons.

I arrived in Seattle in September 1959 to begin my professional career with Boeing. I have spent the ensuing years on the West Coast in Seattle and the San Francisco Bay area except for a year-and-a-half stint with the Lockheed-Georgia Company in Marietta, Georgia, near Atlanta, and frequent trips to visit my parents in Birmingham after they returned following Dad's retirement from the Army in 1965.

On September 17, 1959, Martin Luther King Jr. addressed the legislature of the State of Hawaii, newly created by an act of Congress on August 21, 1959. Hawaii is the most racially diverse state in the country, and King dwelt on this fact in his speech. He closed with a moving quotation from an old Negro slave preacher who said, "Lord, we ain't what we want to be; we ain't what we ought to be; we ain't what we gonna be, but, thank God, we ain't what we was."

In September 1959, a twenty-three-year-old African from Kenya enrolled at the University of Hawaii on a scholarship. In 1960, he met an eighteen-year-old white woman in a Russian language class; they started dating and were married in February 1961. On August 4, 1961, a baby boy was born in Honolulu to this Christian white woman from Kansas and a Muslim black man from Kenya. Named after his father, the baby boy was called Barack Hussein Obama II.

27.

MY BROTHER, MY UNCLE, AND BEAR BRYANT
1961—1962

N
OW Y'ALL PAY REAL GOOD ATTENTION. We're about to enter very sacred ground. In Alabama in the 1960s and 1970s (and even today), there was only one real deity, and he was called Bear—Paul William "Bear" Bryant—the head football coach at the University of Alabama from 1958 through 1982. He was "The Man." For you football trivia freaks, he played as the opposite end to the immortal Don Hutson on Alabama's great football teams of the 1930s culminating in their 1935 Rose Bowl victory over Stanford 29–13.

Y'all think I'm putting you on. Y'all gotta understand—football, Alabama, national championships, Bear Bryant—these were the things that answered some of life's more profound and perplexing questions. What is the meaning of life? Why are we here? Is there life after football?

Well, I gotta tell you, there was a time when any answers to those meaning of life questions were in serious doubt. I enrolled at the University of Alabama as a freshman in 1955, and in that year the football team's record was an ignominious 0–10. We didn't win a damn game!

The coach was J. B. "Ears" Whitworth. Now "Ears" has gone on to his reward, bless his soul, but oh my Lord, he was an awful football coach. Bart Starr was a senior quarterback at Alabama in 1955, but for reasons known only to "Ears" and whoever his football muse was, he used Starr very sparingly in that dreadful season. Yes, I mean to shout, the same Bart Starr who led the Green Bay Packers to their glory and wins in the first two Super Bowls in the 1960s. How can this be, you ask? I don't know. I told you, answers to these mysterious questions were in doubt in this terrible period.

Things didn't improve much in my sophomore and junior years of 1956 and 1957, as the team had 2 wins, 7 losses, and 1 tie in both seasons—an inglorious record of 4–24–2 in my first three years of college. So much for "Dixie's football pride, Crimson Tide," as Alabama's fight song proclaims.

The "tide" turned in 1958, when Bear Bryant returned to his alma mater as head football coach and led the team to a winning season record of 5–4–1. Four years later the team achieved a perfect record of 11–0 and won the first of Bear's six national championships over a period of twenty-five years, culminating in a total record of 232–46–9.

"Roll Tide," all was right with the world again!

After I graduated in 1959, my brother Gibbs enrolled as a freshman. One of the first things Bear did, after he got his coaching staff and first year team lined up, was to call his old friend from their college days, Frank Taylor. By this time Uncle Frank owned and managed an established and successful public relations and advertising company in Birmingham. Bear asked Uncle Frank if he would organize and manage a weekly television show featuring him during the football season. Now Uncle Frank was no dummy; he knew every advertising agency in Alabama would kill for an opportunity like this, so of course he said yes.

Uncle Frank had no problem lining up two preeminent southern companies, Coca-Cola and Golden Flake Potato Chip, to sponsor the *Bear Bryant Show*. The show was televised for one hour every Sunday afternoon at four o'clock during the football season and featured Bear live as he discussed the film from Saturday's game and the upcoming game. The show's ratings were phenomenal. Any program unfortunate enough to be scheduled against it inevitability finished a distant second to Bear, as did most of his football opponents over the years.

Now, Uncle Frank did have a prickly logistics problem. The show was telecast live from a studio in Birmingham, and Bear lived in Tuscaloosa, the main campus of the University of Alabama, about sixty miles from Birmingham. Now I don't want to talk out of school, but Bear was rumored to enjoy a drink, and I don't mean iced tea. Bear didn't like to drive, but he very much valued his privacy and didn't want to be chauffeured by just anybody. So, who could serve this important and somewhat secretive function of successfully chauffeuring Bear Bryant to and fro from Tuscaloosa to Birmingham, keep his mouth shut, and keep the Bear happy?

Uncle Frank wisely used an age-old method of control to solve the problem—nepotism. He hired his nephew, Gibbs, to serve this simple but critical task.

From 1960 through 1962, Gibbs became Bear's personal chauffeur and youthful confidant. The first time Gibbs performed the critical task he was, of course, quite nervous and apprehensive—y'all remember now, he held the life of the savior of Alabama football in his hands. After the show, Bear instructed Gibbs to stop at a local watering hole for some liquid libation. Bear ordered his "iced tea" and asked Gibbs what he wanted. Gibbs ordered a scotch and water. Bear initially said nothing. As the drinks were served, Bear said to Gibbs, "Son, enjoy your drink because it'll be your last one while you're with me. You do the driving and I'll do the drinking."

Years later, I asked Gibbs what Bear talked about, and Gibbs said, "Very little. He usually slept on the back seat because he was either tired from work, travel, or drink."

Bear had promised his freshmen players in 1958 that, if they believed in him and gave all they had, he would take them to a national championship in four years. In 1961, Bear took the Crimson Tide to the national championship as the team went 11–0, a remarkable turnaround in four years, as he promised, and a far cry from my four-year tenure at Alabama. The 1961 team had a good offense, but the defense was extraordinary. Over the course of eleven games, the defense allowed only two touchdowns and four field goals, as Alabama outscored all opponents, including its Sugar Bowl opponent Arkansas, 297 to 25. How did Bear achieve this kind of result, y'all ask? Hell, I don't know exactly, but I do know that he never blamed losses on his players or his young assistant coaches. He always said he didn't prepare the team properly on those rare occasions they lost, and the wins were always credited to the players and the assistant coaches. Bear had a real empathy for young people, and it showed in his coaching results.

In early 1962, Bear traveled to New York City to receive the MacArthur Bowl national championship award from President John Kennedy and General Douglas MacArthur, and returned to Tuscaloosa a conquering hero. There was an enormous crowd awaiting him as his car drove up to the Athletic Field House. On the steps of the field house stood the president of the university, other important state and university officials, the usual large contingent of the local press corps, and Uncle Frank. Gibbs stood off to the side, ever available to serve Bear and Uncle Frank. Bear walked toward the gathered dignitaries, all eagerly waiting to be the first to shake his hand and offer congratulations.

As Bear approached the group, he slowed, looked around, turned away from the dignitaries, and said in his Arkansas drawl as he walked toward him offering his hand, "Hiya Gibbs. Good to see ya."

28.

BOMBINGHAM
1963

AS I SETTLED INTO MY CAREER IN SEATTLE, far from the nonviolent civil rights protests and the violent reactions of white mobs and police in the South, my carefree young bachelor days were about to change. In February 1961, I met a beautiful black-haired young lady from Montana while on a ski vacation in Sun Valley, Idaho. Darlene Wold and I were married in September 1961, and our first son, Waights III, whom we've always called Judge, was born on September 29, 1963.

Judge certainly didn't know it, but he was born in the year my hometown earned the infamous sobriquet "Bombingham," as civil rights protests reached a crescendo in the city. The events in Birmingham in 1963 would push the civil rights movement from its nonviolent beginnings to a more violent form of reaction and protest in response to constant police brutality and frequent bombings. This culminated with the tragic and cowardly bombing of the Sixteenth Street Baptist Church on September 15, 1963, when four young black girls were killed. This wrenching period in our history led to the profound changes in our laws that started the second emancipation of African Americans and moved the South slowly away from its segregated past.

At that time, Martin Luther King Jr. called Birmingham "the most segregated city in America," a well-earned reputation that grew out of the iron-fisted actions city politicians and business leaders used to control the city. Bull Connor became the most infamous political face of the city, and the business leaders, a group of wealthy, powerful white men, were known as the Big Mules, an appalling name probably derived from what the black mine workers were called. The Big Mules, who were involved directly or indirectly with Birmingham's mining and steel industry, would ask after a mine accident took place, "How many mules did we lose?" The question implied more a concern with profit-and-loss than human life.

Birmingham's Unholy Triumvirate

BIRMINGHAM DID NOT EARN ITS REPUTATION as "the most segregated city in America" overnight or by accident. The first underpinnings were set soon after the city was founded in 1871, when emancipated blacks were used to work in the burgeoning mining industry. This was followed by the use of mostly black convict lease labor in the mines, a practice that continued until the Alabama legislature abolished it in 1928. The changes leading to the Birmingham Martin Luther King Jr. encountered in 1963 grew out of Roosevelt's New Deal era in the 1930s. The city's Big Mules, most quite conservative politically, were very concerned about the liberal policies coming out of FDR's administration; they considered the policies anti-business and pro-labor union with a strong socialist bias. In addition, the U.S. Communist Party was at its peak in the country and the South in the 1930s, and the Big Mules despised them and used them as scapegoats and targets in their actions to control the community. One of the Big Mules would become the kingpin in organizing their reaction to FDR and his policies, and he would proceed to put in place an informal triumvirate-type organization to combat these concerns and take control of the city. The organization, triangular in arrangement, had the Big Mules at the top of the triangle directed by the kingpin. On the two bottom sides of the triangle were two groups led by the kingpin's acolytes. On one side was the legal organization, the Birmingham Police Department, led by the Police Commissioner. The other side was the loosely organized illegal vigilante groups including the Ku Klux Klan and the security forces of the large mining and steel companies.

Birmingham's Machiavellian Prince

At his birth in 1890, one would not have predicted that James A. Simpson would become the Birmingham kingpin, a man who would truly operate like a Machiavellian Prince and become arguably the strongest politician in Alabama at the time. When James was nine years old, his father, a poor struggling farmer, led his family on a wild goose chase looking for utopia within the Ruskin Colony. The colony, an attempt to establish a socialist community in Dickson County, Tennessee, was short-lived, beset by issues of property ownership, distribution of the colony's meager income, and, even, free love between some members of the community. The Simpson family followed a group of the dwindling community to a new location in southern Georgia near the Okefenokee Swamp. The community settled on an old lumber mill site near the swamp where disease was rampant, the soil poor, and good water scarce. The Simpson family and the others lived in conditions of abject poverty. Although the family left the Georgia colony after only a year, the experience left such a lasting impression on young James—the squalid living conditions, the indignities his well-bred mother suffered, and the effects of centralized control on people and their attempts to accumulate some wealth—he developed an intense hate for government interference, socialism, and eventually communism.

James Simpson was able to earn a law degree, but, more importantly for his desire to climb from his poor, country boy background to a princely position in Birmingham society and politics, he married well; his wife was the heiress to one of Birmingham's pig-iron fortunes. In his early law practice in the 1910s and 1920s, he was frequently pitted against Hugo Black in the courtroom. Black would usually represent injured laborers, including convict lease laborers, and Simpson always represented the side of the corporations and big business. Black won many large settlements for his clients, but Simpson fought any awards tooth-and-nail, railing against the inherent threats of socialism and communism in the settlements.

In 1926, at age thirty-six, Simpson was elected to the state legislature to begin his climb in state politics. In 1932, he was elected to the legislature as a senator and soon thereafter would start his efforts to thwart the impact of New Deal legislation on the state, and particularly Birmingham. In 1934, he tried to push through the state body a piece of civil service legislation that would abolish Birmingham's patronage system for assigning city hall positions. Simpson proposed a system whereby appointees would be hired and fired using merit-based reviews of their performance. On its face, the bill sounded like a good idea; however, one of Simpson's major opponents in the legislature identified the real intent in the bill, which called for a non-elected personnel board to conduct the reviews. Simpson was trying to establish a group, controlled by him and other Big Mules, to appoint and direct the personnel board.

Simpson's opponent was an effective speaker with a rabble-rouser's intensity, who knew how to address the common man, a skill Simpson had long since lost in his climb up the social ladder. Simpson now realized he needed a person in the legislature whom he could control and who had the ability to speak the same language to the southern common man. His new Senate page, George C. Wallace, whom Simpson thought had a bright future in the rough and tumble world of Alabama politics, was only fifteen years old. Instead, he turned to a man recently elected to the legislature, who had the prerequisite bad grammar of a southern country boy and a good reputation with Birmingham's working class: Theophilus Eugene "Bull" Connor.

Plantersville Hog-Caller

"Ouuuuuuuuuut," shouted Connor, adding when the next batter stepped into the batter's box, "Th'ow that onion boy, th'ow it." The twenty-four-year-old was the baseball announcer for the Birmingham Barons, although he seldom saw the baseball game he announced. He was sitting in his radio studio booth frantically pulling the ticker tape off the telegraph machine as soon as it came across the wire, quickly translating the dots and dashes into his own colorful colloquy describing the action. He was already a celebrity, along with the entire baseball team, with the city's masses.

Connor was born in 1897 in Selma in the Black Belt, and was brought up in Plantersville, fifteen miles north of Selma. He was not a good student, constantly in and out of school; however, his father, a railroad dispatcher, took the time to teach Eugene and his three brothers how to read a ticker tape, which would prove to be Eugene's ticket to his future successes. In Plantersville, people called him "the Plantersville hog-caller" for his strong country accent. When he started baseball announcing, he became known as Bull because he also sounded like a bullfrog with his quick and hoarse discourse.

Bull's sports fans, mostly the working class of Birmingham, pleaded with him to run for the state legislature in 1934. At first, Bull balked at the entreaty; he was convinced he couldn't win, telling the *Birmingham News*, "I'm going to tell the truth…I had no more idea of being elected than beating Lou Gehrig out for first base with the Yankees." But he eventually did decide to run, and he won, after spending the handsome sum of $64 on his campaign. Simpson took Bull under his wing in the legislature, even to the point of treating him like a long-lost son. Bull, of course, responded gratefully to one of the more powerful politicians in Alabama, and he helped get Simpson's civil service bill passed. In 1935, the bill was signed into law, and Simpson had one of the cornerstones he needed in place to control Birmingham.

Simpson soon realized he could use Bull in a much more effective manner than as a state legislator. In early 1937, he got Bull to run for Public Safety Commissioner on Birmingham's city commission. Bull was elected, and he took office in the fall of 1937. He would hold this office for twenty-two of the next twenty-six years: 1937 to 1953, and 1957 to 1963. When Bull was first elected, he immediately went to work molding the department into his personal police force, aided by additional laws Simpson had passed assigning more power to the police. Bull would soon get a chance to demonstrate to Simpson both his allegiance and the unique skills he brought to his new job to keep Birmingham racially agitated and segregated.

A remarkable event was about to take place in Birmingham, the Southern Conference for Human Welfare. The conference was the brainchild of Joseph Gelders—one of two University of Alabama professors who had a significant influence on Waights Sr. while he was a student. Gelders, in spite of having been nearly beaten to death in 1936 by four vigilante thugs, its leader hiding behind his position as a security officer for the U.S. Steel Corporation, approached President Roosevelt with his idea to hold a conference in Birmingham bringing together the various groups associated with the New Deal. Roosevelt was enthusiastic about the idea and agreed to support it because he saw it as an opportunity to broaden his base of support in the South with midterm elections approaching. Eleanor Roosevelt agreed to attend the conference, and Supreme Court Justice Hugo Black agreed to speak at the conference. Gelders then got the Birmingham arm of the Congress of Industrial Organizations, the CIO, to provide needed financial and organizational help for the conference. When the Big Mules and big steel heard the CIO was integral to the success of the conference, they became determined to undermine the conference, since they considered the unions the biggest threats to their economic interest and survival.

The conference attracted liberal thinkers, educators, labor leaders, sharecroppers, and tenant farmers, black and white, from all the southern states and beyond. Over fifteen hundred delegates, 250 of them black, gathered for the opening of the conference on Sunday, November 20, 1938. More than three thousand attended the first night of the conference in Birmingham's Municipal Auditorium, and the opening night mood was so positive and ecumenical that the black attendees ignored the "Colored" entrance and walked through the front doors. Seating was not segregated, so the attendees commingled in one happy crowd. Alabama Governor Bibb Graves was also in attendance with his wife. Only a week earlier Graves had snubbed an invitation from Eleanor Roosevelt's husband to join them at the Little White House in Warm Springs over the upcoming Thanksgiving holidays to discuss pardons for the Scottsboro Boys, and then announced on November 15 that he would not grant any pardons. The first night attendees also included Virginia and Clifford Durr, Aubrey Williams, and Myles Horton, all big New Deal supporters just getting their feet wet in the civil rights arena. The Swedish social scientist, Gunnar Myrdal, was there as a guest to observe as he did research for his landmark book, *An American Dream*. Gelders and other conference organizers hoped to keep the conference's focus on New Deal issues, keeping the elephant in the room—segregation and racism—in the background much as President Roosevelt preferred. However, the opening session's keynote speaker, Frank Graham, the white president of the University of North Carolina, immediately spoke to the hidden issue of southern politics and racism when he said, "The black man is the primary test of American democracy and Christianity." The attendees erupted into a standing ovation, and Virginia Durr later wrote, "He set the tone for the meeting, and we all went away from there that night just full of love and gratitude. The whole South was coming together to make a new day."

Gunnar Myrdal commented that he was overcome by "this new and unique adventure."

The conference attendees came to the Municipal Auditorium the next day, still full of enthusiasm after a morning of integrated workshops on New Deal issues, only to find the building surrounded by police cars with a short, stout man running about shouting out orders to his police. Bull Connor, eager to show the Big Mules he could handle this situation to their satisfaction, let fly with what would become the first of his many convoluted statements, "White and Negro are not to segregate together." Bull then had his men run a cord from the front door down the center of the main aisle in the auditorium, instructing whites to sit on one side of the cord and blacks on the other to comply with the city ordinance prohibiting the races to commingle in public places. When Eleanor Roosevelt arrived, she sat in the black section of the auditorium. The police ordered her to move into the white section, and she defiantly dragged a folding chair to the center of the aisle, where she sat for the remainder of the conference. The conference continued, deflated and heavily policed, and on the last night the auditorium was half empty as Hugo Black made the closing speech. As confusing and silly as Bull's statement sounded, he had moved the conference's agenda from the New Deal back to race and segregation, right where Simpson and the Big Mules wanted it.

Simpson had his first acolyte in place and now controlled Birmingham's police department. With the loss of company-controlled vigilante groups, under the guise of their security and private police forces, because of the publicity fallout from Gelders's assault, Simpson wanted more control over the remaining vigilante groups in the city to deal with things in ways even too illegal for the corrupt police to undertake. To do this, he had Bull Connor enter into a Faustian bargain with a Ku Klux Klan member who had a penchant for handling dynamite and making bombs: Robert E. Chambliss.

Bombingham's Dynamite Bob

At 10:45 p.m. on August 18, 1947, a bomb consisting of six sticks of dynamite exploded under the frame house of a black mine worker and CIO member. The blast collapsed the uninsured house, which represented the entire life savings of the black owner. Dynamite Bob had struck for the first time to make a racist, political statement.

The month before, a federal judge had ruled on a lawsuit brought by the NAACP's Arthur Shores, a Birmingham lawyer. The judge ruled Birmingham's 1926 zoning law, which zoned the city along racial lines with the express purpose of keeping blacks from living in white neighborhoods, was unconstitutional. Even with the ruling, the plaintiff in the case, the black mine worker, was too scared to move into his new house in the white neighborhood; Dynamite Bob spoke to him in the only language he knew.

Bob Chambliss was born in Pratt City, a Birmingham suburb, in 1904. Chambliss, always proud of his Irish background, grew up to be a tough brawler and drinker, and, at age twenty, he joined the Ku Klux Klan. He was first introduced to dynamite while working at a local quarry and later continued his dynamite education in the mines of one of the city's iron producers. In the 1930s and 1940s, the Klan set out to disrupt the activities of the CIO and to penetrate the upper ranks of the local CIO union. The efforts were so successful that the local union essentially became an arm of management. The sad irony of this strategy was that the Klan members, mostly lowly laborers in the mines and steel plants, were marginalizing the effectiveness of the only organization in Birmingham that represented their financial and work safety interests.

In 1946, Bull Connor was ready to cement his association with the Klan to gain more control over the vigilantes. He decided he didn't want to work directly with one of the Klan leaders, but, rather, with a confidante within the Klan organization. At the time, Chambliss was working in a city garage as a mechanic, and Bull tapped him as his man. Chambliss became a favorite of Bull's, was able to continue his bootleg activities with impunity, and would soon launch his Dynamite Bob career. From 1947 through 1963, over fifty bombs exploded in the Birmingham area, and all but a few of the explosions went unsolved. Chambliss didn't personally set all the bombs, but his leadership and fingerprints were on many of them.

Simpson's unholy triumvirate was in place.

Project C

SINCE THE MONTGOMERY BUS BOYCOTT in 1955 and 1956, Martin Luther King Jr. had avoided confronting Birmingham because of its reputation for violence and racial hatred. This son of a middle class black family in Atlanta was well educated. He attended Morehouse College in Atlanta, Crozer Theological Seminary in Pennsylvania, and Boston College where he earned a PhD. He freely and easily studied and learned from whites, including his friend and mentor Allan Knight Chalmers, and was introduced to the writings and practices of Gandhi and other disciples of nonviolent protest. King was concerned he would fail in Birmingham, putting the work he had achieved to date seriously in jeopardy.

It took a fiery black Birmingham preacher to goad, almost shame, King into coming to Birmingham. If King was the nonviolent, consensus-building conscience of the civil rights movement, Fred Shuttlesworth was the movement's hard-driving, uncompromising, abrasive, bombastic alter ego. While King was content to work with whites to seek legal and moral solutions to the South's racial dilemma, Shuttlesworth had little interest in the whites and what they thought; he was ready to mount whatever actions, violent or nonviolent, were necessary to confront racial injustice. He was so unconcerned about his personal safety that he became known as "the Wild Man from Birmingham." Between 1952 and 1965, Shuttlesworth was arrested, beaten, and tortured a number of times; his house and his church were bombed, and he was targeted for assassination. On Christmas night 1956, Robert Chambliss, Bull's man in the Klan, struck again. He threw a bomb made of six dynamite sticks directly at the bedroom wall of the church parsonage where Shuttlesworth and his family were preparing for bed. The bomb blew the wall and floor of the bedroom out; the roof caved in, and appliances were torn from the kitchen wall. Chambliss's intent was to kill all or some of the family, but miraculously all survived with minimal injuries.

Fred Shuttlesworth was King's opposite in almost all respects. He grew up in a poor, undereducated black family in Birmingham's Oxmoor district, home to a U.S. Steel scrapyard and mines. He graduated from high school as class valedictorian in 1940, demonstrating his sharp intelligence and photographic memory; however, he didn't have the money to immediately attend college, and it would be another seven years before he entered an oratorical contest and won a scholarship to Selma University, the black Baptist college in the Black Belt. In 1952, he moved back to Birmingham and became the minister of the Bethel Baptist Church.

In late 1962 and early 1963, months of negotiations and planning took place with King and others in the Southern Christian Leadership Conference (SCLC) before Shuttlesworth finally got his wish, and Project C (for Confrontation) was initially scheduled to start in Birmingham on March 14, 1963. During this planning period, George C. Wallace, Simpson's protégé and Senate page from twenty-nine years earlier, was inaugurated for his first term as governor of Alabama on January 14, 1963. His first inauguration speech that day included the infamous line, "And I say, segregation today, segregation tomorrow, segregation forever."

Birmingham was also holding a mayoral election on March 5. This election was necessitated by a referendum passed in the November 1962 elections changing the Birmingham city government style from a commission to a mayor-city council. The commission style was one of the tools the Big Mules used to control the city's politics. A group of moderates and the few liberals in the city, all members of the Young Men's Business Club, put the referendum forth with the expressed intent to eliminate the Public Safety Commissioner position and get Bull Connor out of office. Bull Connor was not about to go without a fight; after the referendum passed, he decided he would run for mayor against the other two announced candidates. The Young Men's Business Club's candidate was Tom King, a good friend of several of the moderates, and one-time aide to U.S. Congressman George Huddleston Jr., who was elected to the same congressional seat his father had held from 1916 to 1936. Huddleston Jr. had been elected to Congress in 1954 when Macey Taylor, who was Huddleston's law partner, served as his campaign manager and Frank Taylor handled the campaign's publicity and public relations. The third candidate was Albert Boutwell, the choice of other "moderates" and some of the Big Mules in the city, as even this group had now abandoned Bull. Boutwell was as much a segregationist as Bull, but he didn't exhibit Bull's bombastic style and willingness to use violence as a tool. The "moderates" endorsed Boutwell in hopes his proven political background and experience would bridge the seeming inevitable flow of desegregation, while minimizing the impact on their business interests.

None of the three candidates received a plurality of the votes, necessitating a runoff election to be held on April 2 between Bull Connor and Albert Boutwell. The SCLC decided to postpone the start of Project C until after the runoff election; they didn't want to give Bull any additional material to use as campaign rhetoric. Boutwell won the runoff election by eight thousand votes, his margin of victory secured when he received almost the entire ten thousand votes cast by blacks; however, Bull and two other commissioners serving under the old city government structure made it clear they did not intend to vacate their offices in city hall on April 15, the day Boutwell was to be sworn in as mayor along with the new city council members. The three planned to serve their full four-year term ending October 1, 1965, contesting the legality of the election held under the terms of the recently passed referendum.

Notwithstanding Bull's intransigence, national newspapers hailed Boutwell's election as a new opportunity for the city, and the next morning's *Birmingham News* touted Boutwell's election with this headline, "New Day Dawns for Birmingham." The paper's editor, one of the city's moderate Boutwell supporters, had no idea how truly prophetic his headline was. The same day, Wednesday, April 3, 1963, Project C started; Birmingham, the South, and the nation would never be the same.

Project C started rather quietly with a series of sit-ins in several downtown lunch counters. Most of the businesses and Bull Connor ignored the actions hoping they would soon pass, but the manager of one store complained to the police, and a total of twenty demonstrators were arrested. Not an auspicious start for Project C.

Project C continued rather low key for the first week, unable to elicit a vigorous or violent response from the police, or to get much news coverage from the local or national press. King and the others in the SCLC became concerned the movement was losing its steam and the whole effort would go for naught. Bull Connor saved the day when he asked a local judge to issue an injunction against any additional sit-ins, kneels-ins, or mass marches in the city. The judge granted the injunction. At 1:15 a.m. on April 11, one of Connor's deputies delivered the injunction to King, Abernathy, and Shuttlesworth surrounded by a mass of reporters at the Gaston Motel, located one block from the Sixteenth Street Baptist Church. King and the movement now had the impetus they needed for concerted action. Any protest would lead to mass arrest, giving the movement the press coverage it needed to bring nationwide political and public attention to its cause.

Letter from Birmingham Jail

On the afternoon of Good Friday, April 12, King and Abernathy led a group of fifty people out of Zion Hill Baptist Church on a march toward downtown Birmingham. When the marchers got into the center of downtown, Bull ordered the marchers to halt. King and Abernathy knelt, followed by the other marchers, and then the entire group was arrested, shoved into paddy wagons, and taken to the Birmingham Jail, the home to the Scottsboro Boys off and on throughout their ordeal.

That same day, Good Friday, a copy of a statement signed by seven white Christian ministers and a rabbi was published in the *Birmingham News*. The statement, although well intended, was another example of southern "liberals" preaching to the tenets of gradualism and, in the extreme, the status quo. After two opening paragraphs, the one-page statement said, "However, we are now confronted by a series of demonstrations by some or our Negro citizens, directed and led in part by outsiders. We recognize the natural impatience of people who feel that their hopes are slow in being realized. But we are convinced that these demonstrations are unwise and untimely." The statement closed with the appeal, "We further strongly urge our own Negro community to withdraw support from these demonstrations, and to unite locally in working peacefully for a better Birmingham. When rights are consistently denied, a cause should be pressed in the courts and in negotiations among local leaders, and not in the streets."

The seven ministers and rabbi could not have imagined the response their statement would evoke—a response that was later compared to Lincoln's Gettysburg Address and Émile Zola's *J'accuse* (I accuse), an open letter Zola wrote in 1898 to the President of France, accusing the government of anti-Semitism and the unlawful jailing of Alfred Dreyfus. Five days after the clergymen and rabbi's statement was published in the newspaper, King wrote his response to them in his cell on whatever scraps of paper he could find. The scraps of paper were smuggled out of the jail by King's associates, typed up in their motel office, and then taken back to King to read and edit. The final letter was almost fourteen pages in length and covered so well the history of Christianity and nonviolent protest, and the distinction between a just, moral law and an unjust, immoral law that the eight religious leaders would later have to defend their reputations against the charge of bigotry despite their sincere and honest effort to find a way forward in a most difficult time.

King first responded to the statement by the eight religious men that the demonstrations are "directed and led in part by outsiders." King explained he was in Birmingham because he was invited by the Birmingham SCLC affiliate, and then he wrote, putting the eight men in a box labeled religious hypocrisy containing the roots of their Jewish and Christian pasts, "But more basically, I am in Birmingham because injustice is here. Just as the prophets of the eighth century B.C. left their villages and carried their 'thus saith the Lord' far beyond the boundaries of their home towns, and just as the Apostle Paul left his village of Tarsus and carried the gospel of Jesus Christ to the far corners of the Greco-Roman world, so am I compelled to carry the gospel of freedom beyond my own home town. Like Paul, I must constantly respond to the Macedonian call for aid."

King's letter illustrates a broad reach of knowledge of religion and philosophy when he either quoted from or wrote about an impressive group of people: Apostle Paul, Socrates, Reinhold Niebuhr, St. Augustine, St. Thomas Aquinas, Martin Buber, Paul Tillich, Jesus, Martin Luther, Amos, John Bunyan, Abraham Lincoln, Thomas Jefferson, and T. S. Eliot. Perhaps the more damning and revealing part of the letter is the section on white southern moderates or "liberals."

> First, I must confess that over the past few years I have been gravely disappointed with the white moderate. I have almost reached the regrettable conclusion that the Negro's great stumbling block in his stride toward freedom is not the White Citizens' Counciler or the Ku Klux Klanner, but the white moderate, who is more devoted to "order" than to justice; who prefers a negative peace which is the absence of tension to a positive peace which is the presence of justice; who constantly says: "I agree with you in the goal you seek, but I cannot agree with your methods of direct action"; who paternalistically believes he can set the timetable for another man's free-

dom; who lives by a mythical concept of time and who constantly advises the Negro to wait for a "more convenient season." Shallow understanding from people of good will is more frustrating than absolute misunderstanding from people of ill will. Lukewarm acceptance is much more bewildering than outright rejection.

King closed the letter with an eloquent statement about hope for the future, which was preceded by a brilliant passage about the indiscriminate use of "nonviolent" means to achieve an immoral objective: "It is true that the police have exercised a degree of discipline in handling the demonstrators. In this sense they have conducted themselves rather 'nonviolently' in public. But for what purpose? To preserve the evil system of segregation... But now I must affirm that it is just as wrong, or perhaps even more so, to use moral means to preserve immoral ends...As T. S. Eliot has said: 'The last temptation is the greatest treason: To do the right deed for the wrong reason.'"

In fact, King's eloquent and morally powerful letter had no immediate impact on his imprisonment or the current situation in Birmingham. His associates tried to find a news outlet interested in publishing the letter with no success. The reporters on the scene looked at the letter as another of King's sermons, a long-winded one at that. It would be a month later before the letter appeared in print when the *New York Post* newspaper featured the letter on pages one and two of its Sunday edition on May 19, 1963. *The New York Times*, which was planning to put an edited version in its magazine section on the same Sunday, pulled the article in a professional snit when the *Times* realized the *Post* would scoop them. In quick succession, several other publications featured the letter, and *The Atlantic Monthly* used the letter in a summer issue, elevating the letter to the status of another New Englander's work who influenced King: Henry David Thoreau's essay "On Civil Disobedience."

Dr. King's "Letter from Birmingham Jail" is now generally considered the most important written document to come out of the civil rights movement.

The Incredible Children's March

The day King was jailed, James Bevel, the charismatic twenty-six-year-old SCLC field secretary in Mississippi, came to Birmingham. Bevel would later be one of the principal architects of the Selma Voting Rights Movement, when Alabama state troopers and local lawmen viciously attacked the Selma marchers on what is now known as "Bloody Sunday." Soon after "Bloody Sunday," King, Bevel, and others led the historic march from Selma to Montgomery in March 1965.

Bevel's arrival in Birmingham had been prearranged with King to help fill the void that King's time in jail would create. Even as Bevel was preparing to come to Birmingham, the white establishment sensed the movement was faltering, and they canceled a scheduled meeting with the movement's major people. Bevel was an outstanding organizer, and he immediately saw the flaws in the current Birmingham situation. With King in jail, the movement again lost its impetus and the support of many of the adult blacks in Birmingham. If the adults wouldn't march, there would be no arrest, and the national interest in Birmingham would quickly fade from view. Bevel conceived and implemented a plan that would make him the Pied Piper of Birmingham, when he lured the black children out of their schools to become the effective protesters their parents and other black adults were either afraid or reluctant to become. Bevel's plan would succeed beyond his wildest dreams, and the children's march, predicated on the Gandhian principles of nonviolence, would show to the nation and the world the extremes southern whites in authority would go to maintain their power and the status quo.

Bevel immediately turned to those in the black community he knew could communicate and influence the young blacks of Birmingham: two black disc jockeys, Shelley Stewart and "Tall Paul" Dudley White, who had the young peoples' ears every day. With the help of the black DJs, Bevel first invited the city's black beauty queens and football stars they knew from school dances to the church to hear Bevel's talk about the plans for the children's march. As the word spread, vast numbers of kids started coming to Sixteenth Street Baptist Church to hear Bevel. Bevel didn't disappoint them as he reminded them how their grandparents, and even their parents, had stood quietly aside as they were subjected to racism and second-class citizenship. The kids went crazy over Bevel's comments, having never been asked to express their own views on the current situation, and they were raring to go. Bevel also instructed the kids on the importance of the nonviolent approach and stressed that no weapons were allowed, after a number of knives and other weapons were collected from the kids.

While Bevel was organizing the youths, King and Abernathy posted a $300 cash bond on April 20 and were released from jail. They both recognized that their value as jailbirds was coming to an end, and they would better serve the movement on the outside. Three days later, on April 23, a Birmingham judge ruled Connor and his commissioner colleagues were not the legitimate government of the city; however, James Simpson, now a falling star in Alabama and Birmingham politics, had his law firm appeal the judge's decision to the Alabama Supreme Court, thus giving Connor and his two commissioner cohorts a reprieve from being evicted from office. King's release from jail allowed him to pursue his movement, while the appeal also allowed Connor to pursue his movement with his sit-in at city hall.

After King was released from jail, Bevel told him about the plan for the youth march. King was not sure he wanted to see children used in this manner, so he and Bevel took the plan to the SCLC committee overseeing the Birmingham activities. Most of the committee members were adamantly opposed to using the children as marchers, and the meeting broke up with no clear resolution to the issue.

Bevel and his lieutenants were determined to proceed with the children's march in spite of the lack of support from King and the SCLC committee. Bevel set Thursday, May 2, for the start of the march. He called it "D-Day," borrowing the term from the day allied troops landed on the beaches in northern France to start the liberation of Europe from the grips of Fascism, to honor his young troopers storming the streets of Birmingham to liberate the city and the South from centuries of racial Fascism. Early Thursday morning, Birmingham's black children woke up to hear a call-to-arms from the black DJs: "Kids, there's gonna be a party at the park. Bring your toothbrushes because lunch will be served." The kids knew the code words "party at the park" meant gather at the Sixteenth Street Baptist Church across the street from Kelly Ingram Park, and "bring your toothbrushes" meant be prepared to go to jail. While about eight hundred kids missed roll call that morning, many others left school after they had arrived even though some principals and teachers tried to keep them in school. By 8 a.m., the church was filled with kids from ages six to twenty, and their ranks would grow to over one thousand before the march started.

At about one o'clock in the afternoon, Bevel directed the first wave of children out of the church and onto the street. A large crowd of spectators gathered on the street and in the park to cheer the children on. The children came out clapping and singing. While some of the younger children ran in fear when the police approached, most of the children did as they had been instructed: they knelt and prayed. Just as the police thought they had the first wave under control, Bevel sent the second wave onto the street to be followed by succeeding waves, allowing the kids to take four different routes toward downtown and city hall. When the paddy wagons and school buses arrived, the children eagerly ran toward them even before the police told them they were under arrest. Bevel's Gandhian strategy had worked beyond his wildest expectations; over six hundred black children were taken to Birmingham's jails.

During the march and arrests, a policeman, amused at the sight of such young children in the march, leaned over to a little girl of about eight and asked kindly but with a mock gruffness, "What do you want?" The little girl answered for generations of African Americans, "F'eedom."

King spent most of the day in his motel, still unsure of whether or not he would support the children's march. Early that evening, realizing the sagging movement had been reignited by the children's march, King came out in support of Bevel even as some of his SCLC committee members still held out; they insisted Bevel be disciplined for his insubordination. At a church meeting that night, King, Shuttlesworth, and Bevel made it clear to a crowd of two thousand cheering, feet-stomping adults that the movement was now fully reengaged.

Bevel had already planned to designate Friday, May 3, "Double D-Day." Over fifteen hundred children were absent from school, as Governor George Wallace threatened teachers and principals with investigations and punitive actions. Again, the children streamed out of the church at about one o'clock and marched toward city hall. After walking two blocks around Kelly Ingram Park, the marchers found the entire area around the park and the church blockaded by policemen, police cars, and fire trucks. Bull ordered the marchers to stop, telling them if they came any closer, the fire hoses would be turned on them. The children hesitated and then continued to march forward. Connor ordered the hoses turned on, and the firemen, reluctant participants in what they considered a police responsibility, turned on their hoses, first at a gentle, fine spray level that was almost playful. When some children refused to back away, the firemen turned their hose nozzles to full pressure.

The scenes that have forever been imprinted in our minds and in history by the photographs and television images that followed started to unfold. Children were knocked to the ground and rolled over and over by the strong blasts of water; some were pinned to buildings and doorways. When the crowd of over one thousand onlookers cheered the kids and booed the policemen and firemen, the hoses were turned on the crowd. Some of the crowd, on the roof of an adjacent building, started throwing bottles, bricks, and chunks of any loose material they could find at the police and firemen.

Connor then turned to one of his deputies and said, "Bring the dogs." The dogs bit a number of people, and three had to be taken away in ambulances. Although their handlers never released the six dogs from their leashes, they frightened the crowd and children, and did enough damage to force Bevel to assist the police in ending the demonstration. By three o'clock, the crowd had disbursed and headed home. Connor and the other authorities thought it was a relatively uneventful day; a few people got wet, and a few got dog scratches. James Simpson thought it was an excellent example of good crowd and riot control. The nation's news outlets would see it quite differently, and so would most of the nation.

Two young television news correspondents were in Birmingham that day: CBS's thirty-one-year-old Dan Rather, and NBC's twenty-eight-year-old R. W. "Johnny" Apple Jr. Rather would later become the lead correspondent on the *CBS Evening News*, and Apple would become a highly respected correspondent for *The New York Times*. On Friday evening, May 3, however, they were both in a Birmingham television station vying for time to file their stories with their New York networks. Bayard Rustin, an early proponent of Gandhian nonviolence protests and an advisor to Martin Luther King Jr., said their reports on the nation's two major networks were "television's greatest hour."

Connor had not only metaphorically unleashed the dogs, he had unleashed the moment in which an enduring, arguably the *most* enduring, photograph of the civil rights movement was created: a photograph of Walter Gadsden, a high school sophomore, challenging one of the dogs and his handler. The young man has his torso thrust forward as the German shepherd leaps up at him, snarling with teeth bared. When Associated Press's Bill Hudson's photograph was first developed by one of his associates in the *Birmingham News* darkroom, the associate later said his initial reaction to the picture was the rush of adrenaline he got after he developed his first Pulitzer Prize winning photograph: a woman jumping from an upper-story window in a terrible Atlanta hotel fire in 1946. He was right; one of the iconic images of the civil rights movement had been created. The photograph has been immortalized in news releases, books, and paintings over the last forty-seven years.*

On Saturday morning, May 4, the children were eager to continue the march, as it was not necessary to skip school to participate. Over three thousand children came to the church to find the approach much different than the two previous days. The children were sent out of the church in twos instead of a wave to avoid an instant confrontation with the police. After a number of children were on the streets, they gathered in groups and moved forward in raincoats provided by the DJs for the overcast, rainy day. The kids shouted at the police and firemen, and a pretty black teenager called out to the police and firemen a taunt harking over the centuries of black-white relationships in the South, "Y'all don't like us but you like our pussy."

When Connor arrived on the scene, he ordered the fire hoses into play again. The children were scattered by the blasts from the hoses. Some boys had their shirts ripped off, and some girls were stripped to their slips and underwear by the sheer force of the hoses. The surrounding crowd started

---

* One of the paintings, by the artist Jack Levine, is displayed in San Francisco's de Young Museum.

hurling the standard fare—bottles and other available objects. Bevel had to borrow a bullhorn from the police to quiet down the crowd and bring some semblance of order to the situation. Only 127 were arrested on Saturday, bringing the three-day total to upwards of one thousand. Connor and Birmingham's finest, at Connor's direction, had performed efficiently while providing the civil rights movement a set of actions and images that would endure and change the legal and political landscape of this country.

Gunnar Myrdal, who was at the meeting in Birmingham in 1938 when Bull Connor first flexed his segregationist muscles for the Big Mules, was also in Detroit during the children's marches. His book, *An American Dream*, was now a best seller in its twenty-sixth printing. Myrdal, when asked to comment on the current events in Birmingham, "predicted that all formal segregation, in the legal sense, would be eliminated in the next 10 years." Myrdal was correct in his prognostication with one exception: it would be only two years before the legal underpinnings were in place to outlaw segregation and voter disenfranchisement in the United States.

The *Pas de Deux* Ends

PRESIDENT JOHN KENNEDY AND THE JUSTICE DEPARTMENT, led by his brother, Attorney General Robert Kennedy, had taken a hands-off posture on the situation in Birmingham. In spite of pleas by King, Shuttlesworth, and others, the administration steadfastly refused to send any federal troops into the city, concerned there was no federal law or federal court order being violated to justify such an action. Kennedy did finally send Burke Marshall, the Justice Department's civil rights chief, to seek a solution to the situation. However, President Kennedy made his views clear on King's role in Birmingham when he personally phoned the black comedian Dick Gregory and pleaded, "Please, don't go down to Birmingham." Gregory's reply to Kennedy was direct and explicit, "Man, I will be there in the morning," as he proceeded to join the march on May 6.

Unfortunately, the administration's views were strongly influenced by J. Edgar Hoover's FBI and the reports they fed the President and the Justice Department about the situation in Birmingham. Hoover insisted on linking King and some of his associates to the Communist Party with hardly a scintilla of evidence to back the assertions. The FBI had agents in Birmingham and an informant in the Klan, Gary Rowe; however, the FBI insisted on chasing bombing leads based on false rumors and innuendos about black men having set the bombs, rather than the real culprits, the Klan. The FBI never seemed concerned, or chose to ignore, that Rowe's initial calls to them about a bombing came right after the bomb exploded and from a location near the scene. The first federal indictment brought in sixteen years concerning a bombing case in Birmingham was against a black laborer, Roosevelt Tatum, based on FBI information that Tatum was lying when he said the police were involved in the bombing of A. D. King's house.

After the May 4 march, when the hoses were used so indiscriminately against the children, the organized marches continued for three more days. The last children's march occurred on Tuesday, May 7, and was called "Operation Confusion" since, rather than staying grouped in the area around the church and Kelly Ingram Park, the children were sent in smaller groups to various stores in the downtown "white" retail area. Later in the day, Fred Shuttlesworth was busy herding a group of kids safely back to the Sixteenth Street Baptist Church. Firemen were standing ready with their hoses, and as Shuttlesworth started down the steps to the church's basement, he heard someone shout, "Let's put some water on the Reverend." Shuttlesworth turned just in time to be greeted by a full pressure blast of water that hurtled him down the stairwell, slamming him against the wall at the bottom. Shuttlesworth was rushed to the hospital, diagnosed with serious chest injuries, and told he would have to be hospitalized for at least four days and then recuperate slowly. Since the start of Project C on April 3, most injuries were minor: a few scratches, dog bites, numerous hose showers, and, now, Shuttlesworth, who was probably the most seriously injured in all the activities.

There were two principal reasons for the lack of serious injuries and extreme violence to this point in Bombingham's year of 1963. First, as unorganized as the marchers seemed at times, and as vicious as the police and firemen could be, the two parties were performing a carefully choreographed *pas de deux*. With a few exceptions, the marchers followed an agreed upon march route and adhered to a strict nonviolent protocol. The police and firemen, while generally following Bull's orders, did not try to indiscriminately hurt or harm the marchers. At the May 4 march, even Bull Connor showed restraint when he bellowed in response to white hecklers in the crowd, "Goddammit, that's what causes trouble, them white people. Run 'em off! I don't want anybody here to get hurt." Second, the Klan had been told by Bull on behalf of himself, the Big Mules, and others in the city government to stay away from the downtown area and the protests, and to cease all their other nefarious activities. To this date, the Klan had followed Bull's orders. Both situations were soon to change, violently so.

Good and Bad Comes in Threes

The number three (3) has religious/mystical meanings in addition to its numerical properties. Three has many unique mathematical properties: three is the first odd prime number (also called the first lucky prime number); and three is the third Fibonacci number that is unique in the series, where the ratio of consecutive Fibonacci number converges on the Golden Ratio, 1.618033, a ratio many think defines perfect form in art, architecture, and the natural world. Religious meanings of three are numerous including the Holy Trinity in Christianity, and the three Abrahamic religions, Judaism, Christianity, and Islam. Three is considered both a lucky and an unlucky number, as in "the third time's the charm," or "three strikes and you're out." To that list can be added the frequent occurrence of events and individuals in threes throughout this book, and especially the events related to Birmingham during the late spring and summer of 1963.

May 10, 11, and 12

The first of these triads occurred in Birmingham over three days, May 10, 11, and 12. After Burke Marshall arrived on the scene, a series of meetings were held over the next few days with both the SCLC and a group of white business leaders, including representatives of the Big Mules, to try to hammer out an agreement that would end the demonstrations. On May 9, just as it appeared a four-point agreement was acceptable to both parties, the SCLC made it clear it couldn't go forward until agreement was reached on releasing all the people, mostly children, who were still in jail. SCLC asked the city leaders to drop all charges against the demonstrators, or to release those still in jail without a prohibitive bail bond requirement. Over eight hundred were still in jail, and with the bail bond set at $300 each, it would require about a quarter of a million dollars to get everyone released, money the SCLC did not have. The city would not agree to either stipulation, and the bail crisis was at an impasse, when Robert Kennedy called United Auto Workers (UAW) president Walter Reuther, a staunch Democrat and an early supporter of civil rights, and asked him if he and his union could help with the bail money. The UAW and the United Steelworkers agreed to put up $80,000 between them. The bail bond needs were still $160,000 short when the Steelworker's national counsel called fifty-year-old Jerome "Buddy" Cooper, the longtime CIO lawyer in Birmingham.

Jerome Cooper and Waights Taylor had been close friends since grammar school. After their grammar and high school days, Cooper earned his law degree at Harvard, and then worked as Hugo Black's first law clerk at the Supreme Court from 1937 to 1940. When he returned to Birmingham, none of the city's law firms would hire him because of his Jewish faith and association with Black, so he turned to the CIO for employment. A poignant, yet humorous, Taylor family story involved both young boys. When the Taylor family church, the Independent Presbyterian Church, was first established, the church had no building for its service, so the Jewish Rabbi let the Presbyterians use the temple on Sundays. One Sunday morning, young Jerome happened to go to the temple, where he saw Waights. Jerome rushed home and exclaimed to his mother, "Momma, I just saw Waights at the temple. I didn't know he was Jewish." About twenty-five years later, when the closet Jew was interviewed for Donald Rasmussen's 1947 study on southern liberals, Waights suggested to Rasmussen that he also interview his old friend Jerome Cooper. Cooper's comments to Rasmussen give an interesting insight to the dichotomy, almost split personality, in views that many southern "liberals" felt on race issues at that time. Cooper opened by making it clear to Rasmussen that he was comfortable with segregation and was in no hurry to see it abolished.

> I am not for social equality. I don't want it. I am not for abolishing racial segregation right now. I agree with the fellow who said that the black man doesn't care where he sits when he is in the bus, but he wants the ten cents in his pocket in order that he can ride it instead of walking.

However, Cooper than went on, in the classic dichotomy of the southern "liberal," to express a number of social views that were decidedly liberal, if not occasionally paternalistic about blacks.

> I do a good deal of work for the trade unions and if you want to call me liberal because of that, you can...I believe that any man whether white or black or what not should get decent pay for the work he does. And when Negro workers work with white workers on the job together then they should get the same advantages and pay. What difference does it make that at union meetings Negroes sit on one side and whites on the other?

> I am against the poll tax and other voter restrictions because they withhold from citizens their civil rights...We don't have fair trials now. There are not many white lawyers who will take a civil rights case for Negroes. People...see our problem as one of race. Well, it isn't primarily. It is one of employment, and education and public health and housing and civil rights. All those problems happen to involve two races and can't be provided for one without getting them for the other.*

Cooper was reluctant to pursue the request of the Steelworker's national counsel; he easily saw the hypocrisy in it; unions were being asked to give

---

* These comments by Jerome Cooper in 1947, while accurate at the time, may not fairly represent his view on race in later years. Cooper was a co-counsel in a case before the U.S. Supreme Court, *Reynolds v. Sims*, that led to the court's historic "one man, one vote" ruling in 1964. Taken together with the passage of the Voting Rights Act of 1965, the voting patterns and political structures in the South and this country were changed dramatically.

union funds to activities that had nothing to do with their business, and, even more ironically, the funds would be used to help the Big Mules, the group that had fought against the unions tooth-and-nail for years. However, Cooper did contact the Birmingham unions, and they agreed to put up funds to support the bail requirements. With the additional moneys, the actor Harry Belafonte and Nelson Rockefeller were able to raise in New York, the bail requirements were met, and the SCLC agreed to the accord.

On May 10, the SCLC and the white business leaders announced in separate press conferences that an accord, which would end the protests and Project C, had been reached. The city leaders agreed to four stipulations. One, the fitting rooms in department stores would be desegregated within three days of the end of demonstrations. This was really a nonissue with several of the stores, as they had quietly done this over the last two years with no adverse reactions. Two, all signage on restrooms and water fountains—"White Only" and "Colored Only"—would be removed thirty days after the new city government was established. Three, lunch counters in the city would be desegregated sixty days after the new city government was in place. And four, stores would promote at least one black person, although the number of stores required to meet this provision was not specified. In addition, no timetable was attached to the fourth provision, and it would prove to be the most contentious issue to get implemented.

After all King and other SCLC officials and the children had been through, this accord appeared to many a Pyrrhic victory. Fred Shuttlesworth certainly thought so, but he reluctantly agreed to the terms and came to the SCLC announcement of the accord, although he was still recuperating from his chest injuries. However, in a larger context, the accord was quite significant. The solid center of segregation in the South had been cracked, and two of segregation's most adamant supporters, Simpson and Connor, were now marginalized.

On May 11, with the accord public knowledge, the Klan came out of hibernation. Birmingham Klan members were quite unhappy with the accord and the lack of support and direction from Bull and the Big Mules. A big Klan meeting was held that night in nearby Bessemer, and, after the meeting broke up, Robert Chambliss and his buddies decided it was time to get back in business. At about eleven o'clock that night, a car drove up to A. D. King's home, a man walked up to the house and placed a package next to the front porch, he returned to the car, and, as he drove away, he tossed an object out the window that exploded near the sidewalk. Several minutes later, the bomb by the porch exploded, which collapsed the ceiling of the house and blew the front door into the kitchen. Martin Luther King's brother was in bed, and his wife was sitting in the living room, but fortunately, neither one was hurt. This was the incident Roosevelt Tatum said he had witnessed, resulting in the FBI report that he was lying, which led to his federal indictment. Whether or not Tatum was lying never became absolutely clear, but what did become clear was that there was a Birmingham police-Klan conspiracy involved in a number of the city's bombings.

About an hour after the bomb exploded at King's house, another car drove toward the southwest corner of the Gaston Motel. As the car passed the motel, a bomb was thrown out the window just under Room 30, a large corner suite used by SCLC for its strategy meetings during Project C. The bomb exploded, ripped a huge hole in the side of the steel-reinforced building and also destroyed two nearby house trailers. The Klan thought Martin Luther King would be in the room that night, but he had departed for Atlanta earlier in the day. Several other SCLC members, who might normally have used the room, decided not to that night for various reasons. No one was killed, but it was obvious the bombing was an assassination attempt.

Soon after the bomb blast, about twenty-five hundred people gathered in the neighborhood around the motel in the early hours of May 12. The group included revelers and drunks who had been in the local bars and honky-tonks, and residents who lived in the area. The mob proceeded to burn an Italian grocery store and other stores and houses in the predominately black neighborhood. A policeman was stabbed, a taxicab was overturned and burned, and phone booths were destroyed. The rioters were finally subdued when heavily armed state troopers arrived, having just left the city earlier in the day when it seemed everything was under control.

Sunday morning, May 12, the movement, not wanting to yield on its nonviolent mantra, called the unfortunate event "freedom tensions." The national press all but ignored the event, maybe out of fear of inflaming more race riots. Few were ready to admit that the first black race riot since the start of the modern civil rights movement had occurred; the *pas de deux* had ended.

Later that evening, Ramsey Clark, a Justice Department lawyer who would later become Attorney General in Lyndon Johnson's administration, sat in the Memphis airport thinking about the events transpiring in Birmingham. At Robert Kennedy's direction, Clark had been in Oxford, Mississippi, reviewing the need to keep federal troops at the University of Mississippi. The troops had been sent to the university in September 1962 to enforce a federal court order requiring the school to admit its first black student, James Meredith. Clark was on his way back to Washington when Kennedy instructed him to go to Birmingham to provide an additional assessment of the situation. Clark decided to use his overnight time in the airport waiting for his early morning flight to write a memo to Kennedy outlining what would become the Civil Rights Act of 1964. The act, later called by many the "Second Emancipation Proclamation," outlawed segregation in public accommodations and employment.

May 21, 22, and 23

Three other important events occurred on May 21, 22, and 23. SCLC leaders were always concerned that the children arrested during the marches would be expelled from school. The concern became a reality on May 20, when the school board officially expelled all the children who had demonstrated. The outcome was almost a certainty, as the school board was under the thumbs of Bull Connor and James Simpson. Connor appointed the school board members as part of his Public Safety Commissioner responsibilities, and Simpson's law firm provided the board legal advice and counsel.

The next day, May 21, three black lawyers, Constance Motley, Arthur Shores, and Orzell Billingsley, went before Birmingham's federal district court Judge Clarence Allgood, to seek a reversal of the school board's action. Although Allgood had been a supporter of Alabama's New Deal politics and politicians for years, he was also a close friend of both Jim Simpson and Bull Connor, and his racist views were decidedly segregationist. Allgood would neither grant nor deny Motley's motion for dismissal of the school board's action. He insisted on continuing the hearing later before rendering a decision, although his intentions seemed clear when he said, "Would you have your children out in the streets demonstrating?" Allgood certainly ignored his delinquent roots in this situation. He had been expelled from high school, but he would suffer even more for his youthful indiscretions. At eighteen, Clarence Allgood—like another eighteen-year-old, Clarence Norris—hopped a freight train for his last free ride. As he pulled himself into the boxcar, a swinging door knocked him under the train, and the train's wheels cut off both his legs. He now walked on two cork legs with a permanent limp. Motley, realizing the likely outcome in Allgood's court, did an end run around the judge. She took a late afternoon flight to Atlanta and sought a judgment from Judge Elbert Tuttle with the Fifth Circuit Court of Appeals. At a hearing at seven o'clock that evening, Judge Tuttle granted the appeal over the objections of Simpson's lawyer, and ordered the children back to school.

On Wednesday night, May 22, fifteen hundred children joined a mass meeting to celebrate the court's decision. In the euphoria of the moment, few had heard President Kennedy's comments earlier in the day, when he made his first public announcement of what he called the "legal remedy," the civil rights legislation he would submit to Congress.

On May 23, Bull Connor was finally evicted from his city position and office by a unanimous decision of the Alabama Supreme Court. Bull was enjoying his lunch in Kelly Ingram Park when one of his aides came with the news. True to his character and his racist self, Bull said, "Well, I'm just going on up there and draw my pennies and get in line [for welfare] with the rest of the n------."

June 11

June 11, 1963, saw the occurrence of three events in three separate locations, all intertwined with the events in Birmingham. At about eleven o'clock that morning, George Wallace performed his infamous Stand in the Schoolhouse Door stunt at the University of Alabama in Tuscaloosa. The university was under a federal court order to enroll Vivian Malone and James Hood as its first black students since the riots over Autherine Lucy in 1956, and Wallace was under a separate federal court order not to obstruct the process. Wallace ignored both orders and read his prepared statement, which decried the actions of the federal government, on the steps of the school's Foster Auditorium. Deputy Attorney General Nicholas Kazenbach, who personally escorted Malone and Hood from Birmingham to the campus that morning, pointedly told Wallace he was there "to assure you that the orders of this court will be enforced." Wallace glowered at Kazenbach but retreated into the auditorium between his bodyguards. Malone and Hood were enrolled in school and assigned to their dormitories. Kennedy had nationalized the Alabama National Guard to be available if the situation at the university got out of hand. Later in the day, National Guard General Henry Graham was given the assignment of directly confronting Wallace on the steps of the auditorium. Standing erect, General Graham said, "Sir, it is my sad duty—." At that moment, overcome with embarrassment at having to speak to his state commander in such a manner, he continued in an almost inaudible voice, "to ask you to step aside under orders from the President of the United States." Wallace did as the general requested, but he would continue strutting like a bantam rooster on his segregation stage for years to come.

At eight o'clock that night, President Kennedy went on national television to make a fifteen-minute speech. John Kennedy knew the speech might mark the end of his and his administration's effectiveness, but he made it clear he was now ready to confront the nation's long-standing racial issue when he said, "We are confronted primarily with a moral issue. It is as old as the Scriptures and is as clear as the American Constitution." He then explained his forthcoming legislative proposal on civil rights: "Next week I shall ask the Congress of the United States to act, to make a commitment it has not fully made in this century to the proposition that race has no place in American life or law." Kennedy had set the agenda and timetable for the Civil Rights Act of 1964.

Later in the evening of June 11, Medgar Evers, the NAACP's representative in Jackson, Mississippi, was shot to death by a lone assassin. Evers had mounted a Birmingham-style protest in Jackson, demanding that the city fathers put into place a desegregation agreement similar to Birmingham's. The agreement discussions were at a stalemate when Evers got home late on June 11 after a strategy session with his team, only to be greeted with a bullet in his back fired by Byron de la Beckwith, an active member of the local White Citizen's Council and the Klan. Kennedy's encouraging speech now had a terrible punctuation mark.

The Bombing Triad

In addition to the bombings of A. D. King's house on May 11 and the Gaston Motel on May 12, the Klan struck for the third time on August 20. The day before, Judge Allgood had approved Birmingham's school desegregation plan as required by the decision of the Fifth Court of Appeals in July. The Klan, mistakenly thinking that Arthur Shores had supported Shuttlesworth's school desegregation efforts, placed a bomb at his house that collapsed his garage and damaged his cars. Shores was home alone watching television and was not injured. The Klan's string of bombings with no serious injuries or deaths was about to come to an abrupt and tragic end.

Summer 1963 came to a climax with the extraordinary March on Washington for Jobs and Freedom on August 28. Over a quarter of a million people converged on the nation's capitol including six busloads of people from Birmingham's Sixteenth Street Baptist Church. The people marched from the Washington Monument to the Lincoln Memorial, where they heard music and speeches exhorting the crowd to support Kennedy's proposed civil rights legislation and employment for blacks. The day was brought to a dramatic conclusion when Martin Luther King Jr. delivered his "I Have a Dream" speech—a speech many consider one of the greatest in American history.

10:22 a.m.—September 15, 1963

SEPTEMBER AT THE UNIVERSITY OF ALABAMA was all about returning to the football wars now that Bear Bryant had the team back on a winning track having won the national championship in 1961. Now, led by star quarterback Joe Namath, the team almost won the national championship in 1962 and was thought to have a good chance at the championship in 1963. The university was much better at fielding winning football teams than it was in welcoming its new black students. James Hood did not finish the summer semester, succumbing to pressures from both the black community and the constant harassment he felt from Wallace and his state troopers. The black community was upset by an editorial he wrote for the campus newspaper suggesting the civil rights struggle should move from the streets to the classrooms. Hood's room was bugged, and Wallace used his recorded words to constantly pressure the school's trustees to expel him. Vivian Malone continued in school and would become the first African American to graduate from the University of Alabama on May 30, 1965. Bear would not field a football team with a black athlete until 1971. Two years later, one-third of the team's starters were black; winning football games finally trumped racism.

Birmingham in early September was engaged in another war over the federal court mandate to integrate three white schools with the grand total of five black students. George Wallace was pressing Mayor Boutwell to postpone the opening of the schools, but Boutwell refused. When the schools opened on Wednesday, September 4, 1963, the Klan and a neo-Nazi group sent their members to the schools to harass the police and make it clear they would prevent the schools from being integrated. That afternoon Robert Chambliss bought a box of dynamite; the box contained about 140 sticks of dynamite and would become the most infamous box of dynamite in Alabama's history. Eager to use his new tools, Chambliss and a few of his Klan friends drove by Arthur Shores's house that evening. Chambliss laid a bomb near the front door; the blast blew the front door into the living room, where Shores was sitting. His wife was in the bedroom, but, for the second time in two weeks, neither was seriously injured. A riot immediately broke out in the neighborhood; the police killed one black man and another was seriously injured. The *pas de deux* had definitely ended.

Wallace ordered the schools closed the next day, September 5, in defiance of the federal court order. On Monday, September 9, the Kennedy administration got a federal court to issue a restraining order instructing Wallace not to interfere with the court's desegregation order. When Kennedy heard Wallace intended to use the National Guard for his own purposes, Kennedy nationalized the guard, putting them on alert to help enforce the court order if necessary. On Tuesday morning, September 10, the five black children were escorted into the three white schools. Chambliss and his Klan buddies drove around trying to look intimidating, while underneath they seethed with frustration and anger at the turn of events. The Klan not only felt deserted by Connor and Simpson, they now added George Wallace to their list, as they thought he capitulated to the federal government on integration at both the university and the Birmingham schools.

As Klan activity reached a fever pitch in Birmingham, Chambliss and his buddies set out over the next few days to prepare for and accomplish what they would consider their masterpiece. The Klan seemed to be in constant motion, cruising the city in their automobiles looking for trouble, and going from meeting to meeting to discuss and plan their next move. Some even found time during these last few nights preparing for the denouement to prove they were as promiscuous with the use of their personal "sticks" as they were with dynamite sticks. Most were married but many carried on affairs with girlfriends in parked cars and other convenient tryst locations.

To this point in Birmingham's bombing history, the technique was simply tie a bunch of dynamite sticks together, light the fuse, toss it at the target, and run like hell. Chambliss realized they needed to improve their technique if they were to make a more effective bomb: one that could be planted at night and timed to explode in the daylight. At an earlier Klan meeting there had been a demonstration on how to make a bomb with a timing device. Chambliss and his best friend, Troy Ingram, used that knowledge to start working on a timing device of their own design involving acid, and, on the night of September 13, they met to experiment with it. The final product would be a device that fit easily into a shoebox.

Saturday, September 14, Elizabeth Hood, Chambliss's niece, had stopped by the Chambliss house to visit her aunt. Hood, who had never gotten along with Chambliss, told him he should be careful in whatever he was doing or he might get arrested. Chambliss scoffed and said he had enough "stuff put away to flatten half of Birmingham."

Hood asked, "What good do you think any of that would do?"

"You just wait till after Sunday morning. They will beg us to let them segregate," Chambliss said.

"What do you mean by that?" she asked.

Chambliss replied, "Just wait. You will see." He would come to regret this response.

The details of all the comings and goings of the various Klan members on Saturday night, September 14, and early Sunday morning, September 15, have never been completely documented. A black woman, Kirthus Glenn, visiting from Detroit, was able to provide the only eyewitness account of what likely occurred at the Sixteenth Street Baptist Church that night. At 2:10 a.m. Sunday morning, Glenn returned to the house where she was staying after driving a friend to another part of Birmingham. As Glenn pulled up to the house, she noticed a parked car with the interior light on—she later described it as a 1955 or 1956 white over turquoise Chevrolet—with either three or four white men in it. The car immediately pulled out and sped away as Glenn parked her car, but she did get a good look at the man in the back seat on the passenger's side, and she wrote the license plate number down on a slip of paper. Unfortunately, the slip of paper was lost before the number was given to the police or the FBI.

Later investigation would piece together that the four occupants of the car were Robert Chambliss, Bobby Cherry, Tommy Blanton, and Herman Cash. Troy Ingram, the co-builder of the bomb and its timer, chose not to accompany them in the car to the church. Together they would perform the atrocity that would represent the culmination of the Faustian bargain James Simpson had Bull Connor make with Dynamite Bob in 1946. Although it was never determined as fact, it seems Bobby Cherry planted the bomb; he placed it under the stairs in the same stairwell where Fred Shuttlesworth had been blown by fire hoses down into the basement of the church and seriously injured.

At around ten o'clock Sunday morning, September 15, 1963, about 125 people were already gathered at the Sixteenth Street Baptist Church for Sunday services. In the basement, a number of children were attending Sunday school in preparation for a new program, Youth Day, when the youth choir would serve as ushers and sing at the eleven o'clock service.

Fourteen-year-old Cynthia Wesley, one of the choir members, was the adopted daughter of Claude Wesley, a grade school principal, and Gertrude Wesley, a nursery school principal. Cynthia played the saxophone in her high school band and was an honor student.

Her best friend, fourteen-year-old Carole Robertson, was also in the choir. Carole was the daughter of Alvin Robertson, a bandmaster at an elementary school, and Alpha Robertson, a librarian. Carole was an avid reader, a straight-A student, and active in many school clubs.

Denise McNair, the eleven-year-old daughter of Chris McNair, a Tuskegee University graduate and a freelance photographer, and Maxine McNair, a schoolteacher, was not in the choir, and was in a separate Sunday school classroom. Denise, who wanted to be a pediatrician, organized the kids in her neighborhood to help her with an annual fundraising event for muscular dystrophy. The kids would put on skits and dance routines, and read poetry in Denise's yard to an audience of local children and adults, collecting whatever each would donate to their cause.

The Collins sisters, fourteen-year-old Addie Mae, a choir member, and twelve-year-old Sarah, were also in the classroom with Cynthia and Carole. Addie and Sarah's father, Oscar Collins, was a janitor at a local restaurant, and their mother, Alice Collins, was a homemaker. Thus, the Collins family was not considered on the same social status as most of the church's congregation, although it's possible Oscar was the best known of all the children's fathers within Birmingham's white community. Oscar worked at Joy Young's, the city's best Chinese restaurant, where the black staff had turned the simple task of waiting tables into a ballet-like art form, making the production of food and service equally important and entertaining.

Shortly after ten o'clock, Cynthia, Carole, Addie, and Sarah were excused from their Sunday school class to go to the women's lounge to freshen up before their usher duties. Denise was excused from her classroom about the same time and joined the four girls in the lounge. The women's lounge was in the northeast corner of the church basement adjacent to the exterior stairwell, where the bomb was planted.

Cynthia, Carole, Addie, and Denise were standing by the stained glass window that looked out onto Sixteenth Street at ground level. Denise's hair looked perfect, but Cynthia said she needed to work with her hair a bit more. Sarah was on the opposite side of the room at a washbasin, when fifteen-year-old Bernadine Mathews entered the lounge and told the girls their teachers wanted them back in their classrooms. One can imagine the exchanges of chatter and laughter among these six young girls as they hurried to finish primping for their usher and choir duties.

At 10:22 a.m., the chatter and laughter ceased; the bomb exploded.

The bomb, later estimated at from fifteen to nineteen sticks of dynamite, blew a seven-by-seven foot hole in the wall of the women's lounge. The stairs and stairwell were demolished, along with the east side of the church and some of its foundation. Right after the blast, Sarah lay covered by the rubble crying out to her big sister, "Addie, Addie, Addie." When church adults and emergency personnel got into the basement area, Sarah and Bernadine were found alive and were rushed to a local hospital for treatment. After more rubble was dug away, the four bodies of Cynthia, Carole, Denise, and Addie were found laid side by side, as if to offer comfort to one another.

As the searchers looked more carefully, they discovered that Cynthia Wesley had been decapitated; her head was found nearby, severed from her body.

The Grand Jury Charge—R. Macey Taylor

THE KILLING FIELDS OF BIRMINGHAM were not yet closed on September 15. Rioters gathered around the church area after the explosion, but, given the enormity of the atrocity, the situation could have become much worse. However, a black sixteen-year-old, Johnnie Robinson, paid the ultimate price for his involvement in the riots. After Johnnie threw a rock at a car with racist messages written all over it, a policeman confronted Johnnie. He ran away in a downtown alley, and the policeman shot Johnnie in the back with a shotgun. Johnnie was dead by the time the ambulance arrived at the hospital.

Later that afternoon, two white sixteen-year-old boys, Michael Farley and Larry Sims, were riding around on Michael's motor scooter on the western edge of the city, when they saw two black boys on one bicycle. Thirteen-year-old Virgil Ware was riding on the handle bars, while his older brother pedaled the bike they had just picked up for their paper route. When the white boys got close to the two black boys, Larry, a straight-A high school student, pulled a small pistol out of his pocket and shot Virgil with no apparent provocation. Roderick Beddow, the best criminal lawyer in Birmingham, who almost became involved in the defense of the Scottsboro Boys, represented the two white boys in their trials. Larry got a sentence of six months in a juvenile detention facility, and Michael got probation. Virgil got death.

Prior to the September 15 tragedies, Judge Allgood had scheduled a special session of the Federal Grand Jury on September 16 to investigate and indict any individuals or groups that had interfered with the court's August order to desegregate Birmingham schools. When Allgood heard on Sunday about the events occurring in the city that day, he knew he was faced with a much more serious situation. Allgood immediately called Assistant U.S. Attorney Macey Taylor and asked him to write a new charge—a set of instructions—for him to read to the Grand Jury the next day. Macey had left his private practice in 1961, when Robert Kennedy appointed him to the federal position.

Macey worked the rest of the day and late into the night to write a bold legal statement. Macey gave the newly written charge to Allgood the next morning, Monday, September 16, and Allgood made only minor edits before he read it to the Grand Jury. Birmingham's Community Affairs Committee on Public Schools asked the *Birmingham News*, and the newspaper agreed, to publish Macey's charge to the Grand Jury in its entirety.

Macey's charge made clear the position of the court concerning the events on Sunday.

> In recent weeks we have witnessed what amounts to mockery of our laws, a mockery by those who would cut the very roots of our American system of justice; who in so doing would starve the growth of our way of life, and snuff out human life with insane fury and irrationality.

> Sunday's bombing of a Negro church—a place of worship—where the lives of four children were taken, is a hideous example. I can think of no greater heresy or a more blackening sin against humanity.

> Acts of terrorism and foolish intimidation of peaceful people for the misguided cause of "Southern tradition" is heresy.

There is nothing "traditional" in this country that says a person may murder, or intimidate, or mock the judgment of the law, or curse those who have chosen to respect a law no matter how distasteful or unpopular that law may be.

Those who resort to this type of violence in the pious name of freedom and tradition blaspheme their neighbor, their country and their God...This court is sickened by them as a court of law, and ashamed as a native Alabamian.

Macey added a lengthy section discussing the origins of the grand jury by briefly tracing the history of the development of our current legal system from the Babylonian king, Hammurabi, through the Roman Empire and Emperor Justinian, and through the English and the Magna Carta to the U.S. Constitution.

He then wrote the specific instructions to the grand jury on their investigation and responsibilities.

Litigation which has been pending in this court for several years has resulted in the issuance by this court of certain orders. These orders were in the process of being carried out by responsible and dedicated public officials of the City of Birmingham.

Completely in disregard of law, order, justice and plain common decency, certain individuals have undertaken to illegally and forcibly prevent the carrying out of the orders of this court... I ask you to investigate possible violations of this statute and violations of any other federal statutes, which may be applicable.

The key phrase in the instructions was "certain individuals have undertaken to illegally and forcibly prevent the carrying out of the orders of this court." It is an explicit statement that, if taken literally and absolutely, covers not only the Klan bombers but also George Wallace and anyone in his administration that defied the court's order. Macey then added a paragraph commending and congratulating the Birmingham Police Department. In part, he wrote:

These officers, in the performance of their difficult duties under great hardship and often personally distasteful, exemplify that which is fine and good in our system...respect for law and the administration of justice regardless of personal feelings.

While the statement does accurately reflect the performance and attitudes of many of the policemen, Macey either did not know about the possible involvement of a few officers in the bombings, or he chose to ignore it. It is unlikely he knew about the FBI's informant in the Klan, Gary Rowe, or other FBI findings, as the FBI kept most of that information secret for two more years.

The grand jury did not take Macey's charge literally and absolutely; instead they chose to focus on the crazies in the neo-Nazi party, which included some crossover Klan people. No charges or indictments were brought against Wallace, any of his aides, or the five men responsible for murdering the four young girls.

The same morning Macey's charge was read to the grand jury, another young Birmingham lawyer was writing a speech he was to give at the Young Men's Business Club's regular luncheon meeting that day. Charles "Chuck" Morgan Jr., a University of Alabama graduate, was thirty-three years old, and was so charismatic, politically ambitious, and capable that many assumed he would one day be elected governor of Alabama. Chuck's political ambitions in the state ended abruptly when his liberal racial views became apparent during Birmingham's racial turmoil in the early 1960s.* That morning, September 16, he agonized over his speech, as he wanted to make clear to his audience his views on the bombing and the death of the four young girls. A close friend advised him to give the speech and speak the truth. If Macey's grand jury charge was a bold legal statement, Chuck's speech was extraordinarily personal. Chuck made it clear that all of Birmingham was responsible for Sunday's horrible events: "We are a mass of intolerance and bigotry, and stand indicted before our young. We are cursed by the failure of each of us to accept responsibility, by our defense of an already dead institution…Every person in this community who has in any way contributed during the past several years to the popularity of hatred is at least as guilty as the demented fool who threw the bomb." He ended his speech with, "What's it like living in Birmingham? No one ever really has and no one will until this city becomes part of the United States. Birmingham is not a dying city. It is dead."

A few weeks later, in October, Chuck Morgan had to move himself, his family, and his legal practice to Atlanta for their safety. Since his speech, crosses had been burned on his front lawn, and he and his family had received numerous death threats.

1963 Staggers to an End

BIRMINGHAM 1963 HAD SEEMED for a time that it might be an *annus mirabilis* until the events of September 15 turned the year into an *annus horribilis*. Another tragic event finally closed out the year, adding a terrible coda to

---

* Morgan was involved with Jerome Cooper and other young Alabama lawyers in filing the lawsuit that led to the U.S. Supreme Court's historic "one man, one vote" ruling in 1964. Charles Morgan Jr. died on January 8, 2009, at age seventy-eight.

all that had occurred. On November 22, 1963, President John F. Kennedy was assassinated while riding in a motorcade through the city of Dallas, Texas. In the ensuing years, three of the major participants involved in Birmingham 1963 would suffer assassination or attempted assassination: Martin Luther King Jr. was assassinated on April 4, 1968, in Memphis; Robert F. Kennedy was assassinated on June 5, 1968, in Los Angeles; and George C. Wallace was crippled for life by four assassin's bullets on May 15, 1972, in Laurel, Maryland.

It would be fourteen years before justice found the first of the five men responsible for the September 15 bombing. In 1970, one of the first significant generational changes in Alabama politics growing out of the civil rights movement took place. Twenty-eight-year-old University of Alabama law school graduate William J. Baxley defeated Attorney General MacDonald Gallion, and became the youngest Attorney General in the state's history. Gallion, born in 1913, represented the old South and its segregated ways, while serving two terms as Attorney General: 1959 to 1963, and 1967 to 1971.

In 1961, Alabama native John Lewis, then a civil rights activist on the Freedom Rides through the South and now a congressman from Georgia, was beaten unconscious by a mob in Montgomery while the state authorities stood quietly to the side. After Alabama's state public safety director finally restored order to the scene, Gallion came forth and stood over Lewis. As a bloody Lewis struggled to get to his feet, Gallion read aloud a court injunction forbidding "entry into and travel within the state of Alabama and engaging in the so-called 'Freedom Ride' and other acts or conduct calculated to promote breaches of the peace." Welcome home John.

Baxley, who would serve as attorney general for eight years, reopened the investigation into the five men suspected of the murders soon after he took office in 1971. While the investigation continued, one of the suspects, Troy Ingram, died of a heart attack in 1973 behind the wheel of his volunteer fire truck. Baxley finally got an indictment against Chambliss in 1977, and he was brought to trial in Birmingham. The two principal prosecution witnesses against Chambliss were his niece, now Elizabeth Hood Cobb, and Kirthus Glenn. Cobb's testimony repeated the conversation she had with him the day before the bombing when he said, "Just wait. You will see." Glenn testified that Chambliss was the man she had seen in the back seat of the car she observed near the church the night the bomb was planted. On November 17, 1977, the jury returned a guilty verdict on the murder charges. Chambliss went to prison on multiple life sentences, where he died on October 19, 1985, at age eighty-one. Baxley did not have the witnesses to bring an indictment against the remaining three men, and the case lay dormant again. Herman Cash died in 1994, leaving only Tommy Blanton and Bobby Cherry as outstanding suspects.

In 1995, a Birmingham FBI official finally cooperated and assisted local authorities in reopening the investigation against Blanton and Cherry. After indictments were secured against both men, and just a week before the trial was to start on April 21, 2001, a judge ruled that Cherry was mentally incompetent to stand trial.

However, Cherry did not escape prosecution. In 2002, the state was able to convince a judge that Cherry was faking his mental incompetence. He was tried and found guilty on four counts of murder in May 2002. Bobby Cherry died in prison on November 18, 2004, at age seventy-four.

The April 21, 2001, trial against Tommy Blanton started on schedule. He was found guilty on May 1, assisted by the testimony of the last prosecution witness, Addie's sister, Sarah Collins Rudolph, who now wore a glass eye from the results of her injuries in the bombing. Sarah told the court about those terrible moments right after the bomb exploded, when she exclaimed in fear and horror, "Addie, Addie, Addie." Blanton is still in prison.

None of the five men responsible for one of the worst tragedies of the civil rights period ever admitted direct involvement in the Sixteenth Street Baptist Church bombing, nor did they express any regrets or remorse for any of their actions.

Hatred is a harsh companion.

———

FOR DARLENE, THREE-MONTH-OLD JUDGE, AND ME, 1963 ended in Killeen, Texas, where we had flown for the Christmas holidays. Dad had been reassigned to Fort Hood, where he would end his Army career. As I wrote this chapter, I continually thought back to that visit with Mom and Dad, trying to remember if we talked about the 1963 events in Birmingham. I could not dredge up one mention or conversation about the horrible year in Birmingham, so I asked Darlene if she remembered anything, but she drew the same blank. As in our brief encounter with Martin Luther King Jr. in 1967, we apparently said nothing to one another. I wish I could explain why. Were we too ashamed of Birmingham and the awful events? Were we so insensitive to the events that we had no interest in discussing them? Or, were we too concerned about where the conversation might go if we opened up to Mom and Dad?

On reflection today, I think it may have been the latter. Dad, fifty-one at the time, was starting to show signs of his political and social drift from his younger liberal years to the right and conservatism. Perhaps we didn't want to provoke his political ire, or were even afraid to do so.

29.

BOUND FOR SAFE HAVENS

Clarence Norris

ON OCTOBER 1, 1946, Clarence Norris waved goodbye to Charlie Weems and his wife as the train pulled out of the Atlanta station bound for Cleveland. Clarence would never see or hear from Charlie again. Clarence had just fled from Alabama, violating his parole for the second time in two years. When not imprisoned, his life had been one long odysscy, and the odyssey was about to resume.

Cleveland, Ohio: 1946–1953

Clarence was en route to Cleveland to join his mother, Ida, and two of his sisters. Ida was delighted to see Clarence; it had been over thirteen years since she last saw him in an Alabama prison. Clarence, knowing the authorities might look for him in Cleveland, changed his name to Willie Norris, his brother's name, and used Willie's birth certificate to get a new social security card and other identification papers. It proved to be a smart decision that saved him from being returned to Alabama. Soon after Clarence settled down in Ida's house, the FBI came to the house one evening looking for him. Ida told the FBI agents Clarence was not there and that she hadn't seen him in years. Clarence was resting on the sofa in the living room, and the FBI asked to see his identification. He said his name was Willie Norris and showed them his identification. The FBI left, only to return the next night demanding to know where Clarence was. Fortunately, Clarence was at the movies, and when he got home and learned what had happened, he immediately moved out of his mother's house to a boardinghouse, never again to hear from the FBI.

When he got his first paycheck from his job at a machinery company, he decided it was high time he found out why Southerners thought the only thing black men wanted to do was have sex with white women. He went to a whorehouse to explore "what all the mystery was concerning white pussy." After the madam set him up with a white woman, he said, "Of course all I found out was that women are alike in the sex department. Ain't no difference."

Ida introduced Clarence to a young woman named Gloria who worked with her at a downtown Cleveland hotel. Clarence and Gloria lived together for about a year, but he left her when he discovered she was having affairs with other men. He then moved to another boardinghouse and became close with his landlady, Mary Pierceson, a woman about twelve years his senior. Although Clarence told her he was not in love with her, when Mary pressed him to marry her, he agreed, and a justice of the peace married them. Clarence continued his gambling several nights a week, generally playing cards or the numbers. Mary, who tolerated his gambling before they were married, now started to nag him about it. Whenever he was out late, which was often, she would also accuse him of messing around with younger women. Clarence moved out several times but would return to Mary when she promised to stop fighting with him. Of course, they quickly reverted to their old habits, and Clarence finally left Mary for good.

After working several more jobs, Clarence hit the numbers with one of the gambling joints he frequented and won three thousand dollars. He went to see his mother to say goodbye because he had decided to move to New York City to test his luck in the Big Apple. He gave Ida some of his winnings, telling her it was money he earned doing carpentry work. Ida would not accept any of Clarence's gambling money.

New York City: 1953–1975

Clarence arrived in New York City in 1953 and went straight to the offices of the NAACP. Roy Wilkins got him a room in the 135th Street YMCA in Harlem, and then Clarence set out to find a job. With Clarence's lack of education and skills, it was a daunting task. He knew the first stumbling block would be his inability to fill out the job applications; the personnel people in the business would have to fill the applications out for him. He also quickly learned that his competitors for jobs were not whites but the large Spanish-speaking Puerto Rican population in the city. On the job front, New York City played blacks against Puerto Ricans to keep wages low, much the same as the South did with blacks against poor whites.

When sainthood and model citizen awards are passed out, Clarence Norris will not be high on the list of candidates. After leaving Alabama, most of his life was spent working menial jobs for minimal pay, gambling whenever he could find the time and money, and messing around with women, both married and unmarried. He also had more than his fair share of run-ins with the law, an occupational hazard one would think he would have tried to avoid given the risk of being identified and sent back to Alabama for parole violation.

For three years, he followed his usual pattern of going from one back-breaking job to the next. Clarence understood the social and economic position he was in when he said in his autobiography, "The shame of it is the hardest work pays the least. But without an education, I had to take what I could get. I have been told I needed a high school education to empty garbage cans." He then decided it was time to visit Samuel Leibowitz.

Leibowitz had been nominated in 1940 by the Democratic Party as its candidate for an open judge position in Brooklyn's Kings County Court. He won the election, and in January 1941, he started the first of two fourteen-year terms he would serve on the court. In 1962, the State of New York merged New York City's County Courts into the New York Supreme Court, and the immigrant from Romania became New York Supreme Court Justice Leibowitz. Ironically, after his experiences in Alabama courts with tough, prejudicial judges and death sentences, Leibowitz also became noted for handing out harsh sentences and for losing his temper with lawyers, defendants, and witnesses.

In 1956, Clarence went to Leibowitz's courtroom in Brooklyn and asked to see him. When court adjourned, two plainclothes policemen came to Clarence and asked why he wanted to see the judge. After Clarence explained to the two policemen who he was and why he wanted to see Leibowitz, one of the policemen took the answer to Leibowitz, and a few minutes later Leibowitz came out, stared at Clarence for a moment, and shouted, "I'll be damned, it's Clarence." He took Clarence into his chambers, and the two men talked for several hours, reminiscing about the Scottsboro trials. They talked about the death penalty, which Leibowitz was not bashful about using in his courtroom. Clarence told him he agreed with the use of the death penalty as long as the crime merited the judgment and the defendant was clearly guilty. When Clarence told Leibowitz he was unemployed, Leibowitz called a few places on Clarence's behalf but quickly found out he wasn't qualified for the open positions. One of the calls did find a position Clarence could have handled—a chauffeur—except that Clarence did not have a driver's license. Leibowitz finally arranged for Clarence to visit the union that handled city cafeterias, where he later got a job as a dishwasher. Clarence thanked Leibowitz for his help and left his chambers, never to see him again except on television.

The dishwasher job lasted about five months. This was somewhat typical for Clarence, as he worked many jobs in many locations: Harlem,

Brooklyn, Queens, Yonkers, upstate New York, and New Jersey. He finally landed a job with a plastics company in Manhattan that lasted three and a half years, only to be injured when he sprained a shoulder muscle loading a truck. He couldn't lift his arms, and he was out of work for two months when the company went out of business.

Desperate for help, he went to the offices of the International Labor Defense, where, to his great surprise, he saw Allan Taub, the first lawyer the ILD had sent to the South to work on the Scottsboro case. Taub was able to get Clarence an insurance settlement of about three thousand dollars for his accident at the plastics company, and he charged Clarence only one hundred dollars for his services. Taub took Clarence under his wing, showed him around town, and even tried to talk Clarence into letting him write his life story. Clarence told Taub it wasn't a good idea because of his outstanding parole violation. A friend Clarence met through Taub took him to a party, where he met a beautiful young lady named Melva. She had a two-year-old daughter, Bernadine. Clarence and Melva were married in 1960. It was Clarence's third and final marriage, and he and Melva would have two daughters and be together until Clarence's death.

However, Clarence's gambling habit continued to get him in trouble in New York City. On one of his frequent visits to a bar to gamble, he left with about four hundred dollars in his pocket. Three guys followed him out of the bar, beat him badly, and took his money. After that, Clarence decided to start carrying a gun for protection. Over the years, he was arrested several times for possessing a gun. The first time he was fined two hundred dollars and released. The second time he was running a gambling game when an undercover policeman arrested him. He pleaded guilty and was put on probation for two years. The last time was at the public housing apartment where he and Melva lived with their girls. Two boys banged on their door with a stick, demanding to get in to look for a friend of one of his daughter's. The boys threatened Melva, and Clarence chased after them with his gun. When he found them, the boys threatened Clarence with a knife, and he scared them off by firing a few shots over their heads. A neighbor called the police, and Clarence was arrested. In court, he pleaded self-defense and was fined two hundred dollars for not having a gun permit.

In addition to all these arrests, Clarence was arrested in numerous gambling raids over his years in Cleveland and New York City. He would be booked, fingerprinted, and then released after a short stint in jail. Why he was never traced back to his Alabama parole violation remains a mystery. Clarence later said, "But there are people the law just don't catch because the system fails a lot of the time. They [the police] make mistakes." That's probably the most likely explanation, but just maybe his "Willie" Norris persona worked better than he thought.

In 1970, Clarence decided it was time to try to clear his name, as he knew the situation in Alabama had changed dramatically since he'd left the state twenty-four years earlier. Clarence went to the NAACP to seek help getting a pardon, and the NAACP chief counsel wrote a letter to Fred Gray, Rosa Parks's lawyer in 1955–56 and now a prominent lawyer in Montgomery, asking Gray to approach the Alabama authorities on Clarence's behalf.

Clarence heard nothing from Gray for two and a half years. At one point, Clarence became so frustrated he called Governor George Wallace's office. He was told to call the Alabama Department of Corrections and Institutions, where he was told the state still wanted him back. When asked for his phone number and address, Clarence gave a phony number and address.

The NAACP then put one of their young lawyers on the case, James Myerson, who wrote to Gray again. Gray finally responded in July 1973 saying he had assigned an associate to look into the possibility of a pardon. Myerson continually wrote and called Gray's law firm, as nothing additional was forthcoming.

On one of Clarence's visits to the NAACP offices in 1973, he was told about the recent deaths of Dr. Allan Knight Chalmers and Judge James Horton Jr. Chalmers was the driving force behind the efforts to secure paroles for the Scottsboro Boys from 1935 to 1950. Without his determination and unceasing efforts, the paroles may never have come to pass. He was also a mentor, friend, and confidant to Martin Luther King Jr. from the moment they met at Boston University in 1951 until King's assassination in 1968. Dr. Chalmers died in 1972 at age seventy-four.

Judge Horton lost his reelection campaign for his seat on the bench in 1934 because of his courageous, but unpopular, decision in Haywood Patterson's trial in 1933. He then worked part-time for several years as a lawyer for the newly created Tennessee Valley Authority. One of the dams built in the TVA project in 1936 flooded most of Horton's farm near Athens. Horton used the moneys he received for his flooded property to buy a new farm near Decatur, and he spent the last years of his life farming and raising commercial cattle. Judge Horton died in March 1973 at age ninety-five.

During his campaign for reelection in 1934, Judge Horton scribbled a comment at the top of his campaign speech notes, "And Ye Shall Know the Truth, and the Truth Shall Make You Free." It was a prophetic comment, as the final impact of Horton's courageous decision in 1933 was yet to be felt in the Scottsboro drama.

In October 1974, another Gray associate, Donald Watkins, finally wrote to Myerson. He apologized for the lengthy delay, explaining the firm had been "completely inundated in trying to expose, ascertain the dimension and perimeters of and handle the Tuskegee Syphilis Study," the infamous experiment carried out by the U.S. Public Health Service at Tuskegee Institute from 1932 to 1972. Watkins further explained that it would be necessary to convince the Alabama Board of Pardons and Paroles that Clarence was innocent, the board would have to vote unanimously to grant a pardon, and the governor would have to agree and sign the pardon.

The following week Watkins met with Governor Wallace's legal advisor and the executive director of the pardons and paroles board. The upshot of the meeting was that a pardon was unlikely, but a transfer of Clarence's parole to New York was probable on two conditions. One, New York parole authorities would have to agree to accept the jurisdiction of Clarence's parole and perform a background check to verify he had been an upright citizen for the past twenty-eight years. Two, Alabama wanted Clarence to return to the state, turn himself over to the authorities, and admit he was a parole violator. He would also be jailed for one night, although Myerson thought they could get agreement to waive the jail requirement.

After what Clarence had experienced in the Alabama justice system, it's not surprising he said, "I told them to go to hell."

In 1976, it appeared the pardon possibility had reached a dead end until Myerson read in the newspaper about the new, young Alabama attorney general who was resurrecting old, unprosecuted civil rights cases and seeking indictments against the suspected perpetrators.

Myerson decided to approach Attorney General William Baxley.

Waights Taylor

THE SOUTHERN "LIBERAL," who was called back into the Army at the onset of the Korean War in 1950, left the state of Alabama, our southern home, and *Our Southern Home* newspaper in December 1951, bound for Okinawa. If there is a specific year marking the start of Waights's transition from a liberal to a conservative, it is likely 1951.

On Okinawa, where the Army was the occupying power, Waights's newspaper background led to his new assignment as editor and publisher of the island's Army newspaper, the *Ryukyu Times*. He had a staff of about ten enlisted men who helped write and publish the newspaper. He always enjoyed the company of enlisted men over officers in his career, a fact Rose was convinced hurt his career advancement in the Army. Waights and Rose would frequently entertain the men at their home, where food and drink were in abundance, and riotous laughter went on until late in the evening.

Waights and his family left Okinawa in November 1953, bound for Fort Hood near Killeen, Texas, in the central part of the Lone Star State. This was the continuation of Waights's Army odyssey for the next twelve years. Here he would be assigned to the public relations position for the post, and his responsibilities included writing speeches for the post commander, a general. There, as he discovered on Okinawa, one did not use an Army newspaper or a general's speech to broaden one's liberal views; one was restricted to a more conservative point of view, if not by direct command or orders, then certainly by the Army's culture and expectations and one's own sense of self preservation.

Waights was next transferred to Fort Bliss in El Paso, Texas, and in 1956, he was sent to South Korea for a sixteen-month tour of duty, while his family remained in El Paso. He returned to Fort Bliss in 1957 and was assigned to Fort Sam Houston in San Antonio, Texas, in 1959. His final transfer in the Army was back to Fort Hood in 1961, where he retired from his Army career in 1965.

After so many years in the state of Texas, it would not have been unreasonable or unexpected if Waights and Rose had decided to retire in Texas. Either San Antonio or El Paso, where Gibbs now lived, would have been attractive alternatives. Instead, unlike Clarence Norris and Rosa Parks, who had to flee Alabama for their own safety, in June 1965, Waights and Rose chose to return to Birmingham as their safe haven.

Waights and Rose arrived back in Birmingham less than two years after the Sixteenth Street Baptist Church tragedy. The Selma-to-Montgomery march had recently concluded, the Voting Rights Act of 1965 would be signed into law in two months, and the civil rights movement was about to move from its non-violent phase to a more confrontational, in-your-face, violent movement. Waights took a job with Birmingham's Carraway Hospital as Director of Public Relations, where he would have to interact, write, and give speeches in a politically and socially conservative environment. How all these things affected his drift to the right is not clear. It is clear that by this time he had become more conservative, and he would continue to move to the right until he was a full-fledged neoconservative.

Waights's political party shift started in the 1960s, as did the shift of a majority of white voters in the South; the solid Democratic South was about to abandon the party of Jefferson and Jackson and move to the Republicans. He voted for John F. Kennedy for President in 1960, he likely voted for Barry Goldwater in 1964, he definitely voted for Richard Nixon in 1968, and he voted strictly Republican thereafter. His youthful heroes of liberalism—Franklin Roosevelt, Clarence Cason, and Joseph Gelders—had all died along with Waights's more liberal beliefs and would be replaced by Barry Goldwater, Richard Nixon, George Herbert Walker Bush, and finally, his favorite neoconservatism mouthpiece, Rush Limbaugh, and his favorite conservative writer, Thomas Sowell, a Senior Fellow at Stanford University's Hoover Institute. Three of his four brothers, Angus, Bill, and Frank, followed him to the Republican side of the house, while Macey stayed true to the Democratic Party for his entire life.

Waights experienced another transition, or conversion, after he returned to Birmingham; he slowly immersed himself back into his church and, more significantly, his Christian faith. As he would come to learn, there is a huge distinction between attending church services and being a true believer. Waights and Rose had led a relaxed and somewhat indifferent religious life in their younger years and with the religious education of their sons. The boys did go to Sunday School for a few years, but, after the move to Okinawa, church attendance and religious training came to an end. When Waights and Rose moved back to Birmingham in 1965, they rejoined the Independent Presbyterian Church and attended Sunday services regularly. However, while Waights was working at Carraway Hospital, he showed minimal interest in becoming involved in church activities or exploring his religious beliefs.

Waights worked at Carraway Hospital until 1972, when he fully retired, initially devoting himself to writing his memoir, and writing book reviews and guest editorials for the *Birmingham News* and the *Birmingham Post-Herald* newspapers. The return to editorial writing, his old passion, was a joy for him, and his opinions clearly showed he was bound for conservatism. One measure of his move to the right can be seen in his editorial that was published in the *Post-Herald* on February 17, 1979. It was headlined "Subjectivism's poison is undermining values." In the editorial, Waights argued that the last twenty-five years had seen the nation traveling down a road that put at risk our values and very survival. He claimed the principal problem came from subjectivism, as he wrote:

> The primary source of our trouble is to be found in what the late C. S. Lewis called the poison of subjectivism, that is to say, the attempt by some to substitute their own value judgments for the wisdom, customs and objective moral principles of mankind. These values, slowly and painfully discovered over a period of thousands of years, have an objective existence of their own quite independent of man.

> Our traditional moralities of courage, honor, truth, fairness and prudence are eternal and were part of the universe long before we were. "The human mind," Lewis wrote, "has no more power of inventing a new value than of planting a new sun in the sky or a new primary color in the spectrum."

Waights then went on to excoriate all things liberal, calling it the "New Left." He spared no one, saying the milder forms of this subjectivism nonsense were represented by the "likes of John Kenneth Galbraith, Dr. Benjamin Spock, Anthony Lewis, Joseph Califano, Jane Fonda, Gloria Steinem, and Bella Abzug." Public education was next on his list, and he blamed "progressive education" on the American philosopher John Dewey and the Columbia Teachers College faculty. He finally took on Democratic Party politicians; he wrote that senators Edward Kennedy and George McGovern were in the vanguard of the group who seemed to invent their own values, and then that President Carter and his administration had so seriously reduced the nation's armed services capacity and national security that "This sort of thing is, well frightening."

However liberal or "liberal" Waights was thirty or forty years before, it is clear from this editorial that he had left his New Deal and youthful idealism behind and taken on the mantle of a complete, and at times harsh, conservative on political, social, and moral values.

But, equally significant to Waights's political and social changes was the transition to return, perhaps for the first time, completely to his religious roots and beliefs. Although he wasn't a Pentecostal or Evangelical Christian, what he was grappling with would certainly become a born-again experience. His journey of rediscovery was influenced and directed by the Bible and by the writings of one the most prominent Christian authors of the twentieth century, C. S. Lewis, whose impact on Waights is seen in the 1979 editorial.

It is certainly not true that all conservatives are deeply religious, or that those who take a deep interest in religion and the Bible are conservatives. However, in Waights's case, the latter was true; he melded what he came to think and believe about religion into his political and social beliefs. He used one to justify the other and vice versa.

This was the changing man I tried to understand over the last twenty years of his life.

Rosa Parks

ROSA PARKS AND HER FAMILY were constantly harassed by whites during the Montgomery bus boycott in 1955 and 1956. Even though the white harassment continued into 1957, Rosa was able to tolerate the insults and death threats. However, her husband Raymond and her mother Leona were very bothered and scared by them. Raymond got a pistol, which he kept by his bedside, and Leona would call friends in the evening and talk for a long time to tie up the phone to prevent hate calls. Although Rosa was concerned about Raymond and Leona's fears, she was equally, if not more, hurt by the reaction and comments she got from many in Montgomery's black community. The press outside the South had elevated Rosa to the status of sainthood because of her action on December 1, 1955. However, her widespread fame was perceived much differently in Montgomery. Male chauvinism reared its ugly head among the men involved in the movement. E. D. Nixon and Ralph Abernathy were jealous of Rosa and turned their backs on her. A black minister said to her one day as she entered his church, "Well! If it isn't the superstar!" Claudette Colvin, the young woman who refused to give up her seat before Rosa's action, was angry and hurt that she didn't get the attention she felt she deserved. The white business community had labeled Rosa and Raymond "troublemakers," making them unemployable.

Things finally came to a head when Rosa received a credible death threat, which drove Raymond to the point of suicidal despair. Rosa, realizing she had to do something to protect her family, yielded to the entreaties of her brother and cousin in Detroit and decided to move to the Motor City. When Montgomery's black community heard about Rosa's decision, the petty jealousies quickly turned to shame. Abernathy apologized to Rosa for his attitude and tried to talk her out of moving. Nixon probably expressed it best for the community when he later said, "I never realized how much I would miss Rosa. Her leaving was a low, low moment for us all."

In August 1957, less than two years since the bus boycott started, Rosa, Raymond, and Leona moved to Detroit. Her brother, Sylvester, lived in River Rouge in southwest Detroit with his wife and thirteen children. Sylvester, not surprisingly, had no spare rooms in his house, so the three stayed with Rosa's cousin, Thomas Williamson. After a month in Thomas's house, Leona found them a small apartment on Detroit's west side. The three of them were comfortable and now felt quite safe, but they had to live very frugally, as Rosa was not able to make much money sewing. Rosa contacted the local chapters of the NAACP and the Urban League shortly after she arrived in Detroit, and, soon thereafter, she was on the road again on a lecture tour. At the tour stop in Boston in October 1957, Rosa met Alonzo Moron, the president of the prestigious black college, Hampton Institute in Hampton, Virginia. Moron offered her a position at the school as the hostess of the guesthouse on campus for visiting guests and faculty. Rosa accepted the position, thinking she would be able to find a place for Raymond and Leona, which never came to pass. She missed Raymond and Leona, who both had health problems, and, after a year at Hampton, she decided to return to Detroit in December 1958.

Rosa then turned to her old standby, when she found a job as a seamstress with the Stockton Sewing Company in downtown Detroit. She was paid seventy-five cents for each apron and skirt she sewed. She worked ten hours a day and rode the city bus to work and back. This is the lady Montgomery blacks thought was getting too much attention for her civil rights activism.

While working at the Stockton Sewing Company in 1961, Rosa met a young part-time worker, a teenage girl named Elaine Eason Steele, who would later come to be her best friend and confidante. Elaine was sixteen years old and still in high school at the time. Her father, Frank Eason, was one of the black Tuskegee Airmen who performed so well and bravely in World War II. Elaine was born in Tuskegee, but her father moved the family to Detroit after the war ended. In her younger years, Elaine was a firebrand and joined several radical black groups, but as she got to know Rosa over the years, her radicalism mellowed, and she and Rosa became closer and closer.

Even with her demanding work schedule to make ends meet, Rosa continued to support the movement. She attended the SCLC convention in Birmingham in September 1962, took part in the March on Washington in August 1963, continued to attend other conventions and retreats, and made speeches whenever possible.

Rosa also participated in the mass march from Selma to Montgomery that concluded in Montgomery on March 25, 1965. The march, a protest over the unwillingness of Selma authorities to allow blacks to register to vote, is most remembered for the violence that occurred on March 7 during the first attempt to march to Montgomery. Late that Sunday afternoon, John Lewis, Hosea Williams, and Amelia Boynton Robinson led a group of about six hundred people from the church gathering place toward the Edmund Pettus Bridge, fully expecting to be arrested but not anticipating violence. When the marchers reached the crest of the bridge and looked down, they were faced by a phalanx of state troopers and local police, some on horseback. George Wallace, determined to thwart the marchers and their intentions, had sent state troopers to Selma. After a warning from the state troopers to disperse, John Lewis instructed the marchers to kneel and pray. The troopers and police put on gas masks and then charged forward on foot and horseback, flailing at the marchers with billy clubs—some the size of baseball bats—and bullwhips, as a highly toxic form of nausea-inducing tear gas was released. Hundreds of people were injured, and more than ninety were hospitalized including John Lewis, who suffered a fractured skull. Amelia Boynton Robinson, a Selma resident and one of the principal organizers of the voter registration drive, was nearly beaten and gassed to death. Lewis later wrote about the scene back at the church, "The parsonage next to the church looked like a MASH unit, with doctors and nurses tending to dozens of weeping, wounded people." The brutal attack was shown on television news programs around the world, and a photo of Robinson beaten and gassed, held in the arms of another marcher, was in newspapers and magazines worldwide. This tragic day in Alabama's history became known as "Bloody Sunday."

When the successful march arrived in Montgomery on March 24, the marchers camped at a Catholic complex for the night. The next day Rosa joined the marchers, now twenty-five thousand strong, as they proceeded to the state capital to press their grievances highlighted by Martin Luther King's "How Long, Not Long" speech.

Rosa learned that evening that another Detroit resident, Viola Liuzzo, had been killed that night while working for the Selma march organization. It was the third murder related to the Selma events. On February 18, Jimmie Lee Jackson, a twenty-six-year-old black man, was in a peaceful civil rights voting demonstration with his mother and grandfather in Marion, Alabama, twenty-five miles from Selma. State troopers and local police attacked the demonstrators, and Jackson led his mother and grandfather into a café for safety. The troopers followed them into the café, started beating the three, and, when Jackson tried to protect his mother, a trooper shot him twice in the abdomen. Jackson died in a Selma hospital on February 26. On March 9, a group of segregationist whites attacked three white ministers in Selma to support the protest. James Reeb, a thirty-eight-year-old Unitarian Universalist minister from Boston, was beaten so badly in the head he had to be taken to a hospital in Birmingham, after the Selma hospital for whites would not admit him, claiming to be full at the time. Reeb died in the Birmingham hospital on March 11.

With the national uproar over "Bloody Sunday" and Reeb's death, President Lyndon Johnson introduced the Voting Rights Act to Congress and the nation on March 15, when he uttered the famous civil rights slogan, "We shall overcome." Unfortunately, it had taken Reeb's death, not Jimmie Lee Jackson's, to capture the conscience of the nation and force Johnson to push this monumental legislation forward.

Viola Liuzzo, a thirty-nine-year-old white housewife and mother of five, was so horrified by the "Bloody Sunday" images she saw on television that she told her husband she had to go to Selma to assist the protesters. Liuzzo drove her 1963 Oldsmobile to Selma and was asked to use her car to ferry marchers back to Selma after the march. As she drove out of Selma on March 25 with the young black man who was assisting her, nineteen-year-old Leroy Moton, they noticed a car with four men following them. The four men, all members of the Ku Klux Klan, chased after Liuzzo for twenty miles before pulling up along the side of her car and firing two shots. She was hit in the spine and head, and the car careened out of control several hundred feet down the highway while Moton struggled to bring it to a stop. Liuzzo was dead, and Moton had to fake death when the four Klansmen stopped to inspect the car to see if the occupants were dead.

The Liuzzo murder would bring back into focus Gary Rowe, the FBI's Klan informant, and Macey Taylor, the Assistant U.S. Attorney who wrote the Grand Jury charge after the Sixteenth Street Baptist Church bombing. The FBI apprehended the four Klansmen within twelve hours of the murder. One of the men was Gary Rowe. The four men were taken before a United States Commissioner in Birmingham on March 26, where they were arraigned and jailed on charges of conspiring to violate the civil rights of Viola Liuzzo. When pressed by reporters about the rather oblique reference to murder in the charge, Macey Taylor, who represented the government in this arraignment, said, "…of course this is a murder case." At an April 7 hearing before the Birmingham commissioner, Macey Taylor had to explain to the court why suspect Gary Rowe was not present along with the other three men. *The New York Times* reported that "United States Attorney Macy [Macey] Taylor said as of now a preliminary hearing on the original warrants still was set for April 15. If the charges [against Rowe] are dismissed, he said, it will be done in Montgomery." At the April 15 hearing in Montgomery, another U.S. Commissioner dismissed the charges against Rowe at the request of the federal government; Rowe became the government's key witness in the case and testified against the other three at their trials. The three were first tried in state courts on murder charges and were either acquitted or experienced a mistrial. The federal government then tried the three men under an 1871 Reconstruction civil rights statute on charges of conspiracy; all three men were found guilty and sentenced to ten years in prison.

Gary Rowe, the FBI informant in the Klan, basically operated as a double agent. He fed the FBI information while participating in Klan activities, probably including several of the bombings. It was only later that the FBI came to realize that many of Rowe's reports on Birmingham bombings came from the bomb scene right after the explosion. Concerning the Liuzzo murder, Rowe was reported to have told a Birmingham policeman sympathetic to the Klan, "We had to burn a whore." Of course, Rowe was *persona non grata* with the Klan and other segregationists after his testimony in the Liuzzo trials. He was placed in the federal Witness Protection Program under the name Thomas Neal Moore and moved to Savannah, Georgia. In 1978, Alabama got a murder indictment against Rowe based on the testimony of two of the men he helped convict. Extradition attempts were blocked, and a federal judge rejected efforts by Alabama to prosecute him, saying it was based on highly prejudicial evidence. Rowe died in Savannah on May 25, 1998.

Viola Liuzzo's body was returned to Detroit on March 27, 1965, and the funeral service was held on March 30. Rosa had never met Liuzzo, but she was distraught over her murder and the family she left behind. Rosa attended the service, where she met Liuzzo's husband and children and extended them her condolences.

On August 6, 1965, Rosa was in Washington with Martin Luther King, John Lewis, and other civil rights notables to witness President Lyndon Johnson sign the Voting Rights Act of 1965 into law. Probably the most seminal piece of legislation to come out of the civil rights period, the act caused a dramatic change in the South; blacks would soon hold the voting majority in many counties and use that majority to elect many blacks to local political positions. On a federal level, the act contributed to the shift of southern states from their historic allegiance with the Democratic Party to the Republican Party. Lyndon Johnson reportedly said after signing the act that he was "signing away the South for fifty years," a prophecy that has proved remarkably accurate.

Less than a month before going to Montgomery for the march, Rosa had started a new career that would occupy her for twenty-three years. On March 1, 1965, she started work as a receptionist and office assistant in the Detroit office of the newly elected member of the U.S. House of Representatives, John Conyers. Thirty-five-year-old Conyers won the 1964 Democratic primary for the Congressional seat over six other Democrats by a razor thin margin of 128 votes, thanks in large part to an endorsement he got from Martin Luther King at the behest of Rosa. Conyers won the general election handily, and one of his first actions was to offer Rosa a position in his office. Conyers is the second longest serving member of the House of Representatives. He is only junior to John Dingell, another congressman from Michigan, and started his twenty-fourth term in office on January 11, 2011. Rosa retired from her position in Conyers's office in 1988 at age seventy-five. Conyers later described Rosa's gentle, non-arrogant, yet almost majestic, personality when he said, "I can't help but marvel at the fact that Rosa Parks essentially had a saint-like quality. And I use that term advisedly, because she never raised her voice. She was not an emotional person in terms of expressing anger or rage or vindictiveness. But she was resolute. And this was an unusual set of circumstances for a person who, as the Movement went on and the successes built up, she became more and more recognized as the person who had, without probably intending to initiate it, a resurrection of the Civil Rights Movement."

Conyers's comment that Rosa "was resolute" gave a hint to the complex interests and beliefs of this seamstress from Alabama. The popular conception of Rosa, a one-dimensional view grown mythic in its magnitude, is one of a woman who refused to move to the back of the bus, thus, sparking the modern nonviolent civil rights period led by Martin Luther King Jr. Rosa certainly admired Dr. King and followed his nonviolent leadership approach in Montgomery and beyond. However, she later revealed her overarching view on blacks' struggle for equality when she wrote, "To this day, I am not an absolute supporter of nonviolence in all situations. But I strongly believe that the civil-rights movement of the 1950s and 1960s could never have been so successful without Dr. King and his firm belief in nonviolence." Rosa's ambivalence on nonviolence was rooted in her family's history, as her grandfather had instilled into her a sense of independence and doing what was necessary to protect one's self. In addition to her grandfather's guidance, in 1931, Raymond Parks introduced her to activism and reinforced the need for self-protection.

Detroit was also the home of the Nation of Islam, the Black Muslim movement. While Rosa abhorred their policy of hatred toward whites, she did admire the work they did in the community in converting black men, especially those habitually in and out of jail, to lead a useful life, and in helping establish strong family relationships and independent business activities. She admired Malcolm X, the young Black Muslim firebrand who left the movement and then made a pilgrimage to Mecca, where he learned Muslims worldwide did not preach hatred of white people. After his return from Mecca, he founded an independent Muslim mosque and organization in New York City. Rosa met Malcolm X at a speaking engagement he had in Detroit on February 14, 1965. She had a brief discussion with him after his speech, and her beliefs and support in what this young man was doing were reinforced. Although he wasn't a supporter of nonviolence, Rosa liked the changes he had made in his views and speeches to be more inclusive of all races.

A week later Malcolm X was assassinated by members of the Black Muslim organization.

Rosa found the work in Conyers's office rewarding, and it gave her a level of financial security that she had seldom experienced. She continued making speeches and attending civil rights events for the next ten years, but in the 1970s, she experienced a difficult and sad period in her life. Rosa had to curtail most of her civil rights work when her stomach ulcers acted up, and she developed some heart problems as well. More seriously, her husband, brother, and mother became so ill, Rosa had to start working part-time in Conyers's office to help care for them in three different hospitals. Her husband, Raymond, died at age seventy-four in 1977, after a five-year bout with throat cancer. Brother Sylvester died three months later, also of cancer. Rosa's beloved mother, Leona, who was also ill with cancer, was in a nursing home for a year. After Rosa got an apartment in a building for senior citizens in 1978, she moved her mother into the apartment and cared for her until she died in 1979.

The three pillars of love and support in Rosa's life were gone.

PART FIVE

SEEKING FINAL CLOSURE

1976–2009

30.

REDEMPTION, CONVERSION, AND IMMORTALITY

Clarence Norris—Redemption

J UST WHEN IT APPEARED in early 1976 that it was not going to be possible to get the State of Alabama to grant Clarence Norris a pardon, his NAACP attorney, James Myerson, contacted Alabama Attorney General William Baxley's office. Although Baxley did not have the legal authority to directly grant a pardon—that authority lay with the Alabama State Board of Pardons and Paroles, followed by the approval of Governor George Wallace—it was hoped Baxley could influence the process. Myerson called Donald Watkins, his Montgomery contact in Fred Gray's legal practice, and asked Watkins how they should proceed on this matter. Watkins first approached his friend, Milton Davis, one of Baxley's African American assistant attorney general appointees. Davis asked Watkins to write a summary of the case they both could take to Baxley for his review. The two men met with Baxley in April 1976, and Baxley agreed that a full pardon was long overdue. Although Baxley knew he had to appear not to be pressuring the pardon board, he asked Davis to draft a letter to the board outlining their view that Norris was wrongly charged and not guilty.

The Truth Shall Make You Free

Baxley signed the letter Davis wrote, and it was sent to the board in August 1976, where his concerns proved to be well founded; Norman Ussery, the board chairman, was not fully satisfied. Ussery responded that Norris was a fugitive with an outstanding arrest warrant. Ussery wanted

Norris to return to Alabama, give himself up to authorities, and serve a three-year jail term before being able to apply for pardon consideration.

Myerson and the NAACP then organized a nationwide public relations campaign seeking support for Norris's pardon. The response was overwhelming; letters were sent to the pardon board and to Wallace from all over the country, including New York City Mayor Abraham Beame and New York Senator Jacob Javits. Press releases were sent to all the major news organizations. In October, Norris's situation was presented on the *CBS Evening News*, and *The New York Times*, *The Washington Post*, and the *Montgomery Advertiser* published editorials urging the State of Alabama to pardon Norris.

On October 13, Ussery announced he still wanted Norris to serve three years in jail before being considered for a pardon. The real turning point in the impasse came on Friday, October 22, when the other two board members, Sara Sellers* and William Robinson, abandoned Ussery's position and voted to withdraw Norris's warrant and reinstate his parole without supervision. Ussery met with Wallace to discuss the situation, and it was reported that Wallace urged Ussery to resolve the matter and issue the pardon. Ussery then asked Baxley to submit a second letter in support of the pardon application.

Milton Davis drafted the letter and reached back to Judge James Horton's decision, overturning the guilty verdict and death sentence in Haywood Patterson's second trial in 1933. Horton's well-written, well-reasoned decision, which was ignored by subsequent Alabama prosecutors and courts at the time, would finally be used to close the last chapter in this tragic case. Davis's main points in the letter were taken almost verbatim from Horton's decision, and on October 25, Baxley signed the letter and sent it to the pardon board. The letter concluded, "I again vigorously appeal to this board to review all the evidence in this case and swiftly grant to Clarence Norris a full and complete pardon. Mr. Norris will continue to live a nightmare until this board removes from him the unjust stigma of conviction for a crime which the overwhelming evidence clearly shows he did not commit." That afternoon, the board unanimously voted to grant a full pardon to Clarence Norris and sent the pardon to Wallace's office for his review.

The same day, Monday, October 25, 1976, Governor George Wallace —the boyhood Senate page of Big Mule James Simpson; the "segregation

---

* Macey Taylor's youngest daughter, Margie Ann Taylor Sellers, now lives in Montgomery with her husband, Philip Sellers. Sara Sellers, now eighty-five years old and also living in Montgomery, was married to Philip's cousin once removed—another unexpected connection.

today, segregation tomorrow, segregation forever" governor; the Stand in the Schoolhouse Door governor; the governor who helped create the acrimonious atmosphere in Birmingham leading to the bombing of the Sixteenth Street Baptist Church and the deaths of four young girls—finalized Norris's pardon with his signature. Forty-five years and seven months after Clarence Norris and the other eight boys were arrested and jailed in Scottsboro, the State of Alabama finally admitted what Judge Horton so correctly and courageously concluded in 1933: Clarence Norris, and, by logical and legal inference, all the Scottsboro Boys were not guilty. Clarence Norris was the only one of the nine Scottsboro Boys to ever be truly free.

Two days later, Clarence was told by reporters in New York City that one of his two accusers, Ruby Bates (now Lucille Schut), had died in Yakima, Washington, on October 25, 1976, the same day his pardon was approved. Ruby had recanted her testimony in the second trial in 1933, when she said the boys did not rape her or Victoria. She died a bitter woman, now claiming the boys had raped them.

On November 29, 1976, Clarence flew to Montgomery to formally receive his pardon from the Alabama Board of Pardons and Paroles in the state Capital building. After all he had endured in Alabama, Clarence would not get off the airplane until Myerson convinced him the hundreds of people waiting at the airport were well-wishers, not authorities ready to arrest him again. Clarence was rushed to the board's office, and Norman Ussery presented him his pardon along with a brief congratulatory speech. He was then taken to the Dexter Avenue Baptist Church, Dr. King's old church, for several speeches by persons involved in his successful pardon. Clarence also gave a press conference, where he said, "I have no hate, prejudice against them, creed or color. I like all people, and I think all people accused of things which they didn't commit should be free. I wish these other eight boys were around." He then stared at the cameras and the reporters, his face a stoic mask of sadness and sorrow, and seemingly fighting back tears, he silently expressed his lost years in Alabama prisons and the memories of his eight comrades. Late that night back at his hotel, Wallace called Clarence and said he'd like to see Clarence before he returned to New York. Clarence agreed to visit the governor in two days.

The next day, November 30, Clarence, Myerson, and others drove to Tuscaloosa, where Clarence made a speech to hundreds at the University of Alabama. When he saw black and white students walking to class, talking with each other, and sitting together, he realized how the South had changed.

On December 1, Clarence was ushered into Wallace's office along with a number of his supporters and the governor's staff. Wallace, who now relied on a wheelchair, asked Clarence to sit in the chair right next to him.

He held Clarence's hand and told him he was happy that he was the one to sign his pardon. He told Clarence race relations were now much improved in Alabama, although he qualified it saying, "We are not a utopia, we've got a long way to go as does every place else…"

Then a humorous, and some would say, revealing, exchange took place. Wallace told Clarence he looked good and prosperous and wanted to know his age. Clarence told him he was sixty-four, worked hard, and took care of himself. Wallace looked around the room, as he wondered aloud how black people stayed so young looking for so long. One of the meeting attendees, Alvin Holmes, a black member of Alabama's House of Representatives, answered, "That's because we eat a lot of soul food, fried chicken, collard greens and you whites eat a lot of steaks." Wallace replied, rather plaintively, as if not wanting to be excluded, "I like collards as well as you do. I used to eat cold coon and collards for breakfast." When the meeting concluded, Wallace invited Clarence to come see him anytime he was in Montgomery. The two never met again; this was Clarence's last visit to the state of Alabama.

The Last of the Scottsboro Boys

Clarence returned to New York City after completing a speaking tour around the country arranged by the NAACP. He continued in his job as a warehouseman for about six months, after which he retired in July 1977. He then started to work on a book with a New York writer, Sybil Washington. Sybil, who had accompanied Clarence on his trip to Alabama in 1976, taped hours of conversations with Clarence about his life and the Scottsboro case experiences. She then transcribed the tape into a book written in Clarence's voice. The book, *The Last of the Scottsboro Boys*, was published in 1979 and afforded Clarence some additional fame for a short period of time.

On January 11, 1978, Samuel Leibowitz, who retired from the New York Supreme Court in 1969, died in New York City at age eighty-four. Samuel—the Romanian immigrant, who became the successful Jewish lawyer from New York, only to be reviled by Alabamians and by Alabama courts—was, along with the ILD, largely responsible for keeping the boys out of the electric chair through appeals to the U.S. Supreme Court and constant pressure on the prosecution and the trial judges. He had been the one to safely escort the first four Scottsboro Boys released by the State of Alabama in 1937 out of the state and back to New York.

In 1982, Victoria Price (now Katherine Queen Victory Street) died. Victoria never apologized for her actions or testimony in the Scottsboro trials, insisting to her death that she and Ruby were raped.

About the time of Victoria's death, Clarence's health took a turn for the worse when he was diagnosed with Alzheimer's disease. Clarence died in

New York City on January 23, 1989. He was seventy-six years old. The NAACP arranged a memorial service for Clarence at New York City's Abyssinian Baptist Church on January 31. Only about a hundred people were in attendance to hear the church's pastor, Dr. Calvin Butts, say in his eulogy, "How can you judge the behavior of a man who has lived through living hell?" Butts added, leaning on his Christian faith, "We must believe that those who were responsible for the horrible indignities heaped upon the Scottsboro Boys will be, if not in our lifetimes, brought to justice."

Unless there is a judgment day in the heavens, Dr. Butts was incorrect; no one would be "brought to justice" for their transgressions against the Scottsboro Boys. History alone would judge the participants, since all the major figures in the tragic case that started on March 25, 1931, were now dead along with Clarence Norris, the last of the Scottsboro Boys.

Waights Taylor—Conversion

IN THE 1970S AND INTO THE 1980S, Waights found another's voice that gave him the guidance he needed to reestablish his Christian beliefs and values. C. S. Lewis's life experiences and incredible body of writing on the Christian faith provided Waights the touchstone and inspiration he needed to test and challenge his beliefs and ultimately complete his religious conversion. Waights's desire to pursue his Christian faith through Lewis's work may have also been influenced by two tragic events that occurred about this time: the deaths of his brothers Angus and Frank. On March 28, 1977, Angus died at age sixty-eight. He was the eldest of the Taylor Boys and had moved back to Guntersville, Alabama for his retirement years. Angus's second wife, Jennie, was a raging alcoholic, and Angus wasn't far behind her in the drinking department. At family events, it was not unusual early in the evening to watch Angus assist a tottering Jennie back to their bedroom after she had drunk herself into oblivion. Angus died shortly after Jennie's death, both succumbing to years of alcohol abuse. On February 19, 1979, Frank died at age sixty-five. When he died, Frank was doing one of the things he loved best, working on behalf of Bear Bryant. The local television station in Birmingham that had carried the hour-long *Bear Bryant Show* for twenty years was being forced by its national affiliate to reduce the show to thirty minutes to accommodate expanded evening news programming. Neither Bear nor Frank wanted to shorten the program, so Frank approached the other major television station in Birmingham about taking the program. On February 19, Frank was at a meeting in the other station's general manager's office discussing some of the details concerning the deal, when he collapsed and died shortly thereafter of a heart attack.

Waights's other voice, Clive Staples Lewis, was one of the great Christian intellects and authors of the twentieth century. He was born in Belfast,

Northern Ireland, on November 29, 1898. He and his three-year older brother, Warren, were the only two children of Albert and Florence Lewis. Lewis's intellect, first molded when he was homeschooled by his mother, became abundantly clear when he accomplished a not unheard of, but still remarkable, academic achievement. In the span of four years, he was awarded the highest grade available at Oxford, a "First" in three difficult and demanding curricula. In 1920, he received a First in Honour Moderations, a Classics course in Greek and Latin languages. In 1922, he received another First in Greats, a continuation of the study of the Classics including Classical Literature, Philosophy, Greek and Roman History, Archaeology, and Linguistics. And in 1923, he received a First in English. Lewis became a prolific author, writing and publishing over forty books including scholarly works, poetry, a science-fiction trilogy, a seven-volume children's fantasy, and a number of books on his Christian beliefs. It was Lewis's books on Christian apologetics and his children's fantasy, *The Chronicles of Narnia*, that would attract Waights's attention.

When Waights journeyed back to his Christian faith, there were three events in Lewis's life that likely resonated with him on a personal level. The first event occurred when Lewis was fifteen years old and abandoned his youthful Christian beliefs, declaring himself an atheist. He remained an atheist until his friendly arguments with authors J. R. R. Tolkien and Hugo Dyson, and the writings of G. K. Chesterton, led him to slowly rediscover Christianity. It was not an easy road back for Lewis; he supposedly said of the experience that he had to be led kicking and screaming into Christianity. The second event occurred when Lewis finally yielded to theism and a belief in one God in 1929 and wrote of the experience, "That which I had greatly feared had at last come upon me...I gave in, and admitted that God was God, and knelt and prayed: perhaps, that night, the most dejected and reluctant convert in all England." Lewis's belief in theism and one God did not make him a Christian; he still doubted Jesus was the Son of God, the Christian Incarnation. The third event and the final turning point in Lewis's conversion came in 1931, when he, Tolkien, and Dyson spent the early evening over dinner and most of the night discussing the question uppermost in his mind, "...and is it true, this most amazing tale of all?" Nine days later, Lewis took a day trip to the zoo in the city of Whipsnade. Lewis later wrote of the ride, "I was driven to Whipsnade one sunny morning. When we set out I did not believe that Jesus Christ is the Son of God, and when we reached the zoo I did." As offhand, almost flippant, as Lewis's comment sounds, much angst, thought, and soul-searching proceeded the moment he made a complete commitment to the Athanasius doctrine of Incarnation, the bedrock of Christian belief. Lewis then became a lifelong member of the Church of England.

C. S. Lewis died on November 22, 1963, one week before his sixty-fifth birthday. Two coincidences on the same day were the tragic assassination of John F. Kennedy and the death of author Aldous Huxley. Or was it a coincidence? Possibly it was a mystical concurrence, a connection through the ether of men's minds. Whatever choice one makes to this question, three men who had varying degrees of impact on Waights's life died the same day. Lewis was his mentor and guide back to his Christian faith; Kennedy was the last Democratic presidential candidate Waights admired and voted for; Huxley was the author Waights politely corrected on his Shakespearean error in *Brave New World*.

Although Waights was never known to be an atheist, he had certainly abandoned his interest and participation in his Christian faith during his younger years. After his immersion in Lewis's works, both his Christian faith and conservative political views became his primary interests. His conservative editorial opinions were frequently published in the Birmingham newspapers. He also devoted a significant amount of time and effort to the church the last twenty years of his life, serving as an Elder on the Session of the Independent Presbyterian Church from 1986 through 1989.

However, Waights's most enjoyable and remembered endeavor was the series of lectures he prepared and delivered at the church on Lewis's writings and other religious topics. I never knew the exact dates and content of his lectures until I recently found his lecture notes in a box of some of his and Mom's possessions. The notes, written in his usual precise and readable form, are detailed with the topic outline for each lecture along with quotations from other scholarly writers he used as reference material. Waights was a wonderful speaker; he used his deep knowledge of the lecture subjects, coupled with a generous dose of humor and anecdotes, to mesmerize the large audiences that clamored to hear his talks. In the fall of 1984, he gave his first lecture series: fifteen talks titled *The Theology of C. S. Lewis*. The lectures covered fourteen of Lewis's books with a strong emphasis on *Mere Christianity*. In the summer of 1985, he followed with nine lectures on the wildly popular children's series, *The Chronicles of Narnia*, which constituted seven fantasy novels. He seems to have honored Lewis's position on the Christian parallels found in the Narnia books. Lewis called the Christian aspects suppositional, not allegories as many people assumed them to be. Waights's notes do refer to some of the Christian parallels in the Narnia books, but the lecture notes are primarily focused on the characters and the stories.

Waights concluded his lectures in late 1985 with three talks on different topics and individuals. In September 1985, he lectured on the life, teachings, and influence of St. Francis of Assisi. Then came a lecture titled "The

Desert Fathers," a talk about the fourth-century Christian ascetics and monks who lived all or part of their lives in Egypt's Wâdi El Natrûn, a desert valley sixty miles west of Cairo. The most noted of these men were St. Anthony and St. Athanasius. Soon after Anthony's death, Athanasius wrote a biography about Anthony that is considered one of the great works from the early Christian period. The Desert Fathers' spiritual lives and humility served as a guiding light for the development of early Christian precepts highlighted by the adoption of the Nicene Creed at The First Council of Nicaea in 325. Waights's last lecture was about *The Testament of Devotion* by Thomas R. Kelly, a noted twentieth-century Quaker. Besides lecturing about Kelly's book, a series of five essays about God's presence in our lives and the need to seek a path to an inner spiritual journey, he gave his audience an overview of the founding of the Religious Society of Friends, more commonly called the Quakers or Friends, in the seventeenth century by Englishman George Fox.

Waights's political views had by the early 1980s become quite polarized. He had absolutely nothing good to say about the Democrats and Jimmy Carter, and, interestingly enough, Carter's southern background seemed to incense Waights as much as Carter's politics. He was ecstatic about the election of Ronald Reagan in 1980, and he remained in political bliss through Reagan's eight years in office and the four-year term of George H. W. Bush. When Bill Clinton was elected in 1992, Waights was back to Democrat bashing in earnest, as well as having another southerner in the White House to rail against.

On racial issues, Waights was reasonably sanguine about the progress blacks had made in the South and the nation. He supported the need for the change that led to the repeal of Jim Crow laws, educational advancements, and voter registration for blacks. Where he drew the line was with the group of black activist radicals and politicians that grew out of the civil rights movement. He grouped activists such as Stokely Carmichael, Angela Davis, Jesse Jackson, and Al Sharpton in his broad categorization of liberals in general. To look like, talk like, or be like a liberal was to invite and receive the wrath of Waights.

As Waights became even more politically conservative, he achieved the "far right" status of a neoconservative in the 1990s during the presidency of Bill Clinton. He espoused these politics until his death in 1997.

Good Night Sweet Prince

I'm often asked what I knew and understood about my father's political and religious conversions in the later years of his life. The honest answer is very little during the period of his change from 1965 to the mid 1970s. Once Mom and Dad moved back to Birmingham in 1965, I visited them once, maybe twice a year, for visits of a few days to no more than a week. From 1965 to about the mid 1970s, I perceived little change in Dad other than that he seemed to be more conservative politically and attended church more regularly than I remembered from my younger years.

The obvious changes in his political and religious views became much more apparent in the late 1970s, when his views, especially his political views, became more strident. During my visits in this period, Mom's first words to me when I entered their apartment would be, "Now, don't you and your father discuss politics or religion." Of course, I would no sooner get comfortable in Dad's study than we would start discussing politics and, occasionally, religion. The discussion would start rather civilized in a somewhat Socratic method of debate but would quickly become quite heated, as neither of us was willing to yield our positions. What surprised me most about Dad's conservative political views were his fanatical, angry outbursts when he felt I didn't get his point or had offered an opinion so ridiculous as to not be worthy of his consideration. Mom would invariably come into the room, her temperature boiling, not at either political or religious position, but at our angry voices, and say to us in a stern voice, "Stop it right now!" Like little boys, caught in a moment of mischievous behavior, we always dutifully obeyed.

What was more amazing than our raucous debates, if they even deserve that label, was our ability to immediately put them aside and move on to more mundane and safer subjects. I never lost any of my respect or love for my father as a result of our political differences. I know he felt the same way, although he frequently blamed my liberal views on my many years in California, a convenient scapegoat to explain his son's transgressions. I do wish I had made it clear to him that he was the source of the seeds of my liberalism.

Another of my regrets is that I never had the opportunity to hear one of Dad's lectures. Whenever I was in Birmingham, people would come up to me and say how much they enjoyed his talks, even to the point of saying he affected their lives and Christian faith.

A good friend of mine in Birmingham, Alan Head, was one of those people. Alan moved back to Birmingham in 1986 after living on the West Coast for years. He wanted to join a Birmingham church, but he was unsure which one to select. He attended one of Dad's lectures on a C. S. Lewis book, and Alan later told me that Dad's talk was one of the major factors in his choosing the Independent Presbyterian Church over other Birmingham churches.

Alan's father, James Head, is mentioned several times in Diane McWhorter's book *Carry Me Home*. McWhorter explains how James was one of the few truly liberal Birmingham businessmen who tried to broker a peace accord in the early 1960s between Birmingham's ruling segregationists and the black community. James's efforts were mostly unsuccessful, and he suffered financially and socially for it. I met and interviewed James in 2006. James Head died on December 21, 2010. He was 106 years old.

An amusing measure of Dad's commitment to his neoconservative views was his daily ritual of listening to the conservative talk show personality Rush Limbaugh. When I was visiting my parents, Mom would often ask me to drive her to the supermarket and other stores for her shopping rounds. Dad often accompanied us, since he did not like to be alone, but he always brought his transistor radio and listened attentively to his revered Rush as we walked the aisles in the stores. If we were in a building with a weak signal, Dad would walk outside to listen and wait for us, as a dedicated neoconservative will not be thwarted from getting the word according to Rush. Of course, after the broadcast, I patiently listened to his summary of Rush's "pearls of wisdom" and harsh tirades against all things liberal and said nothing to avoid another uncomfortable verbal encounter.

Dad's other daily ritual was watching the evening news shows. Sitting with him to watch the news was entertainment unto itself; one got to listen to Dad's constant repartee with the newscasters concerning the story being presented. If the views expressed matched his, he would nod his head knowingly and comment quietly in agreement. Dad seldom swore, but if the views expressed were liberal and provocative, he would shout, "Goddamn that liberal son-of-a-bitch. He can go to hell," and words that were even more profane. Fortunately for Mom, he kept his verbal assaults on the evening news in his study and would usually behave himself if guests were in the apartment.

These daily rituals continued until April 1997, when Mom and Dad moved to Reno, Nevada. This was not a move they had contemplated or wished to make, but both of them were now having serious health problems requiring our frequent attention. However, attention was a problem in itself. At the time, I lived in Guerneville, California; brother Gibbs lived in El Paso, Texas; and brother Richard lived in Reno, Nevada. From about 1995 forward, one of the three of us frequently had to be in Birmingham to help Mom and Dad with their health issues. Richard and his wife, Cheryl, finally suggested that they move to Reno into a nice assisted-living facility close to their home. Surprising us all, Mom and Dad agreed to move, and in April the move was accomplished. I went back to Birmingham to help them prepare for the move, Gibbs accompanied them on the flight from Birmingham to Reno, and Richard got them settled in their new apartment in Reno. Initially, it looked like it was going to be a rough transition. Dad said to Mom soon after they arrived in Reno, "My God Rose, what have we done?"

Their first six months in Reno went well, as they both enjoyed a period of reasonably good health. Mom settled in quite easily, probably a carryover from her days as a military wife dealing with frequent moves. Fortunately, Dad acclimated surprisingly well also. He came to enjoy the meals in the dining room, where he could dress in a coat and tie, a habit and custom he practiced his entire life. He also came to enjoy the extra activities in the facility, such as the songfest and lectures. In fact, by September of 1997 they were doing so well, they decided to fly to California and join us at my house in Guerneville for a big September family birthday party. September is a special month for the Taylor family: brother Richard was born on September 1, Dad on September 3, my grandson Dylan on September 20, me on September 26, and my son Judge on September 29. On a beautiful fall day on September 21, 1997, all the birthday boys except Richard were at the party. It was almost my sixtieth birthday, Dad was eighty-five, Dylan had just turned six, and Judge would be thirty-four in eight days. It was a joyous and magical day!

The joy and magic were short-lived, when, twenty days later, we lost Waights McCaa Taylor, our "Dukie." He died on October 11, 1997, of an extreme case of pneumonia. The youthful "liberal" and the aged neoconservative had left us, hopefully to experience the elation of the Christian afterlife he so fervently believed in.

On April 20, 1998, a memorial service was held for Dad at the Independent Presbyterian Church. The chapel was filled with about two hundred loving friends and family members. I was asked by Mom and my brothers to deliver the eulogy. It was difficult, but I was able to get through without choking up or tearing up until I got to the end, when I closed with the following two paragraphs.

> Dad loved music and had a lovely singing voice. His favorite composer was Mozart, and his favorite single piece of music was the second movement, the Andante, of Mozart's Piano Concerto No. 21 in C major. When I visited with Dad and Mom, he would frequently play it, and, as the passage opened with those beautifully melodic violins, Dad would say to me, "Judge-Waights-Man, listen. This is the most beautiful piece of music ever written by man." So I invite you to listen to "the most beautiful piece of music ever written by man" and reflect on your memories of your association with our father.

> And now to close, and, when thinking about our father, there is absolutely no other way to close but to offer a quotation from his beloved Shakespeare and could anything other than Horatio's words upon Hamlet's death be more appropriate.

> *Now cracks a noble heart.*
> *Good night sweet prince,*
> *And flights of angels sing thee to thy rest.*

Just before Dad's memorial service started, a woman quietly entered the chapel and sat in the rear pew. When I saw Mattie Ruth Rucker, whose story I will tell you briefly, I immediately went to her and escorted her by the hand up the aisle to sit with my family.

The Unwritten Rules

In the years of my youth, the dark veil of segregation hung heavy over Birmingham and the South. There was no escaping the shroud's suffocating effects. It mattered not whether you were black or white, rich or poor; the insidious veil clung to all aspects of daily life like a shirt to a sticky back on a hot, humid day. Of course, the black population was the target and direct recipient of this overt form of social manipulation and control.

How did people function in this stifling atmosphere on a day-to-day basis? There is, or there was, a set of unwritten rules governing the daily relationships between blacks and whites. The written rules were everywhere: White Only signs, Colored Only signs, separate schools, separate churches, separate restaurants, separate toilets, separate drinking fountains, separate ticket booths, separate waiting rooms, separate theater seating, separate seating on public transportation, poll taxes to inhibit blacks from voting, and on and on. In spite of all this, the unwritten rules allowed life to proceed in a more reasonable fashion, although certainly not a fair one.

The unwritten rules were generally convoluted and certainly unspoken to avoid a head-on collision with the written rules. I didn't then, and I don't now, know all the unwritten rules. I'm sure many were so obtuse that I never even recognized them. So the only way I can give you a sense of the unwritten rules is to tell you a story about the relationship between two southern ladies, Madge Buckels Cook and Mattie Ruth Rucker.

In Birmingham, there were two worlds: the blacks and the whites, the north and south side of town, those who used public transit and those who didn't, and families who didn't have help and families who did. White wealthy and upper middle class families invariably had "help," the southern euphemism for the blacks who worked in their homes. While the help included maids, gardeners, chauffeurs, and cooks, it was the maids who made up the large core of this workforce. Mattie Ruth Rucker was one of those maids.

Madge Buckels Cook, my maternal grandmother, whom I always called Nanny, was a fascinating woman, but very much an unreconstructed southerner. Nanny and her first husband and my grandfather, Samuel Dawson, separated in 1930. Nanny then had to forego the use of help as she struggled to support herself and her two daughters.

Nanny's marriage to Oscar Cook in 1942 substantially altered and improved her life. Mr. Cook, or Doc as we children were allowed to call him, was a fastidious gentleman who brought Nanny back to the established upper echelons of Birmingham society. Nanny moved into Doc's large, red brick home on the north side, and soon after opened an antique and Oriental rug business, which proved to be quite a successful venture.

The marriage to Doc also allowed Nanny to again practice the time-honored southern white woman's tradition, and some would say privilege, of having help. From age five to age twenty-two, I visited Nanny frequently in her red brick Birmingham home. There was always a buzz of activity about the house concerning her antique and Oriental rug business. She frequently had either a maid or a young black man to assist in the constant arrival, rearrangement, and departure of furniture pieces and rugs. It was during these years that I first observed Nanny's attitude and demeanor with African Americans. I don't want to be misunderstood, Nanny was not a mean person, nor did I ever see her directly insult any of her help; however, she was very clear in establishing her position of authority. Her instructions and commands invited no rebuttal, her body language always invoked an air of superiority, and the black help always entered and exited through the back door.

It was shortly after I had moved to Seattle that Mattie Ruth Rucker entered our lives. She started working for both my mother and Nanny in the 1960s and continued to do so until Nanny died in 1988 and my parents moved to Reno in 1997.

Mattie Ruth divorced her first husband when her three children, a son and two daughters, were still young. Unlike Nanny, she never remarried, but she raised her children to be successful and thoughtful adults. Her son worked for the Birmingham Transit Company as a bus driver, and her two daughters attended college and later moved to Atlanta, where they own and operate several successful businesses.

I came to know and appreciate Mattie Ruth over the years during my many visits to Birmingham, when she would frequently be at either Mother or Nanny's home. As I observed Mattie Ruth's calm demeanor and relationships with my mother and Nanny, it became apparent to me that this "maid" was becoming a close and valued friend. However, I was very bothered by Nanny's continued superior attitude and racial overtones with Mattie Ruth.

At Dad's memorial service in 1998, Mattie Ruth sat next to my mother and held her hand during the service. After the service, my wife and I drove Mattie Ruth to her house in a sparsely populated northwest suburb of

Birmingham. She and her family lived in a well-kept white wooden frame home on several acres of land. Mattie Ruth invited us in, and we met her sister and an elderly aunt, who was bedridden and was being cared for by Mattie Ruth. She showed us around her house, and in the dining room, there was an upright piano. On the wall above the piano, there was a large bulletin board covered with photographs. I walked over to look closer at the photographs, which included pictures of Mattie Ruth's family and friends, and there, near the center of the board, were several pictures of our family: Nanny, my mother and father, and me and my brothers. I looked at Mattie Ruth and, before I even spoke, clearly sensing my surprise, she said, "This is all my friends and family, including you." I stood quietly fighting back tears, now fully realizing what a dear friend this woman had become to my family and me.

A few days later I returned to my home in California still confused and perplexed by the relationship between Nanny and Mattie Ruth. I called my mother and explained my dilemma to her, but she had no ready answers. I finally asked Mom if she thought Mattie Ruth would be upset if I called her and asked her about their relationship. Mom said she was sure Mattie Ruth would be comfortable talking about Nanny.

So, with some trepidation, I finally called Mattie Ruth. After the usual greetings, I said, "Mattie Ruth, this is hard for me, but I've always been bothered by the way Nanny treated you. You were always so polite and helpful to Nanny—I never heard you utter a harsh or unkind word. But it seemed she was frequently nasty to you with her constant demands, 'Mattie Ruth do this,' 'Mattie Ruth do that,' 'Mattie Ruth come here right now.' Am I wrong?"

Mattie Ruth was silent for a few moments before saying, "Judge," using my childhood nickname, which put me on notice that what was to come was of utmost importance. "You have to understand. Your grandmother loved me, and I loved your grandmother." She offered no other explanation, and I asked for none.

I felt like the young child she had carefully chosen to address, having just received a kind, but firm, reprimand for tiptoeing into the area of the unwritten rules that governed day-to-day life and relationships in the segregated South.

Rosa Parks—Immortality

AFTER HER MOTHER'S DEATH IN 1979, Rosa was quite despondent and said, "I found myself all alone." In addition, Rosa's health had worsened; besides her chronic stomach ulcers, Rosa was now plagued with heart problems, eyesight issues, and a general feeling of fatigue. Fortunately, her friendship with Elaine Eason Steele had blossomed since they first met in 1961. Steele filled the void in Rosa's heart, and Rosa now considered Steele the daughter she never had. Steele became not only her best friend, but also her personal manager and confidante. Steele was now Rosa's gatekeeper, managing the constant requests from journalists and others to meet with Rosa and the incessant demands made to her for speaking engagements. In spite of her health problems, Rosa found time, with the help of Steele, to lead a productive and varied life. She accomplished many personal and professional achievements and had to deal with the multitude of honors and awards that were now coming to her.

On a professional level, Rosa was able to complete a lifelong ambition in 1987, when she established an institute to help young blacks improve and succeed in life. She and Elaine Eason Steele co-founded the Rosa and Raymond Parks Institute for Self-Development in Detroit. The institute's philosophy is based on one of Rosa's greatest attributes, "Quiet Strength." The institute's primary objective is to get young people involved in community development activities, to improve their life skills, and to broaden their understanding of their cultural heritage. The institute, which is still in operation, has five-week programs each summer where young people learn about the Underground Railroad and the civil rights movement through a travel experience called Pathways to Freedom. The Pathways program is augmented by an extended curriculum on the history of the black experience offered in many communities throughout the country. The institute also has workshops on life skills, and classes in academic subjects to aid those having problems at school.

In 1988, after working for John Conyers for twenty-three years, Rosa retired from her position in his office. In the same year, she had to have a pacemaker implanted in her chest to help deal with her worsening heart problems. Even so, she continued to attend as many NAACP meetings and speaking engagements as possible.

On a personal level, her interests broadened into new areas. She had become a vegetarian, she was now more active in women's rights issues, she started studying Buddhism, and she began work on a series of books. Elaine Steele introduced Rosa to her Los Angeles friends, Leo Blanton, a civil rights lawyer, and his wife Geraldine. The Blantons invited Rosa to spend her winters with them in Los Angeles, and she spent twelve enjoyable years in Los Angeles during Detroit's mostly nasty winters. While in the City of Angels in 1992, she met Dr. Daisaku Ikeda, a noted Japanese Buddhist philosopher, poet, and educator. Dr. Ikeda had an American campus in the Santa Monica Mountains near Los Angeles, and Rosa spent time on the campus, where her interest in Buddhism flourished. In 1994, she traveled to Tokyo at Dr. Ikeda's invitation to visit Soka University, where he was president. Rosa and Ikeda and his students explored ways to improve human rights issues through nonviolent means. The Japanese were so taken with this humble, matriarchal "Mother of the Modern Civil Rights Movement" that she was described in the Japanese media as a "great spirit" and a "natural Buddhist." Rosa left Japan convinced that the harmony of Buddhist meditation was a natural and logical addition to her lifelong habit of using Christian prayers in her daily life.

In the 1990s, Rosa wrote four books: *Rosa Parks: My Story* with Jim Haskins in 1992; *Quiet Strength* with Gregory J. Reed in 1994; *Dear Mrs. Parks: A Dialogue with Today's Youth* with Gregory J. Reed in 1996, which received the NAACP's Image Award for Outstanding Literary work for children; and *I Am Rosa Parks* with Jim Haskins in 1997.

In the later years of her life, awards and honors were bestowed on Rosa, as Dr. King said, "like an ever flowing stream." The list of awards and honors would read like a lengthy bibliography if listed in total. It included more than forty-three honorary doctorate degrees from universities worldwide; hundreds of plaques, citations, awards, and keys to many cities; the NAACP's highest award, the Spingarn Medal; the UAW's Social Justice Medal; the Martin Luther King Jr. Nonviolent Peace Prize; and the Rosa Parks Peace Prize in 1994 in Stockholm, Sweden. In September 1996, President William J. Clinton presented Rosa the Presidential Medal of Freedom. On May 3, 1999, Rosa was awarded the Congressional Gold Medal of Honor. George Washington was the first person to receive the Gold Medal of Honor, and only about 280 individual medals have been awarded in addition to a few organization and group medals. In 1998, Nelson Mandela became one of the few foreign world leaders to receive the medal. In 2000, the State of Alabama made Rosa a member of the Alabama Academy of Honor and dedicated the Rosa Parks Library and Museum, located on the corner in Montgomery, where Rosa was arrested forty-five years earlier.

Rosa was particularly proud of two other occasions when she was honored in Montgomery. The first concerned the bus line she rode on that momentous day, December 1, 1955; part of the line was called the Cleveland Avenue Line, and today Cleveland Avenue is named Rosa Parks Boulevard. The second was the dedication in 1989 of a civil rights memorial erected by the Southern Poverty Law Center, the world famous center founded by Morris Dees and Joseph Levin Jr. in 1971 that has successfully pursued civil lawsuits against civil rights crimes and hate group crimes for years. Architect Maya Lin, who designed the Vietnam War Memorial in Washington, DC, created the new memorial. The memorial, a circular black marble surface covered by Dr. King's "mighty stream," displays the names of forty individuals killed in the civil rights struggle between 1954 and 1968. Rosa was invited to participate in the dedication ceremonies of this moving memorial.

In the late 1990s, Rosa was forced to stay in her apartment more often because of her declining health. In 1998, Elaine Steele found her unconscious on the floor of the apartment. Rosa was hospitalized and recovered, and, although she now required a walker or a wheelchair, she continued to pursue her interests. For exercise, she took a water aerobics class. For her mind, she compiled recipes for a vegetarian cookbook. And, for her body and soul, she worked with Deepak Chopra, the famous doctor who is an outspoken advocate of holistic medicine and spirituality, on suggestions for the use of holistic medicines in lieu of traditional drugs. Her life slowed significantly when she was diagnosed with progressive dementia in 2004.

Rosa Louise McCauley Parks died on October 24, 2005, in Detroit. She was ninety-two years old.

Immortality Awaits

On rare occasions, the earth seems to slow on its axis or even come to a complete standstill. The death of the humble, self-effacing seamstress from Alabama brought forth one of those occasions. Rosa's coffin was flown to Montgomery on October 29 and taken in a horse-drawn carriage to her old church, St. Paul African Methodist Episcopal, where she lay in repose at the altar dressed in the uniform of a church deaconess. A memorial service was held the next morning in the church, and one of the speakers, Secretary of State Condoleezza Rice, an Alabama native, said, "I can honestly say that without Mrs. Parks, I probably would not be standing here today as secretary of state." Her coffin was then flown to Washington, DC, where it lay in honor in the U.S. Capitol Rotunda on October 31; Rosa was the thirty-first person, the first woman, and the second African American to be so honored in our nation's history. Her funeral service was held in Detroit on November 2, and thousands of people turned out to watch the horse-drawn hearse carry her to the cemetery. Rosa was buried between her husband and mother under a headstone she had earlier selected and prepared. It reads simply, "Wife, Rosa L. Parks, 1913—."

All the accolades and tributes paid to Rosa in the last years of her life and at her memorial services prior to being buried in Detroit pale when compared to one event in 1990 that illustrates the true measure of the woman and the impact she had on the world stage. In February 1990, Nelson Mandela was released from a South African prison after being imprisoned twenty-seven years by the South African apartheid government. Mandela would oversee the peaceful transition of South Africa from its apartheid past to the open and democratic Republic of South Africa. After the first multi-ethnic elections in the country's history, he would serve as president of the Republic of South Africa from 1994 to 1999. It was truly a remarkable achievement after so many years of oppressive governance, with the threat of racial violence a constant concern. The strength of character, leadership, and forgiveness Mandela demonstrated in this crucial transition has made him a beloved and revered figure worldwide.

After Mandela was released from prison, one of the first things he did was to visit the United States to bolster his ties with our government and people as he prepared to face the daunting tasks ahead in South Africa. One of the cities on his itinerary was Detroit. The city, wanting to roll out the red carpet for Mandela, invited a number of local business, religious, and political leaders to join the welcoming group at the airport the day Mandela was to arrive. A good friend of Rosa's noted her name was not on the list, and she told Rosa she would see that she was invited. Although Rosa admired Mandela and had followed his entire career as an activist and prisoner, she told her friend not to bother: "I just shouldn't be there. It's okay. They just forgot me." The woman persisted, and, after some additional arm-twisting with the committee, Rosa was invited to join the group. Even as she was being escorted to the airport to greet Mandela, she kept telling her friends, "He won't know me."

When Mandela's plane landed in Detroit in June 1990, the welcoming group was arranged in a receiving line on the tarmac near the stairway to the plane's door. Rosa was located near the front of the receiving line. Mandela came slowly down the stairway and started to walk toward the receiving line, when he froze in his steps, his gaze transfixed on one person.

He stood quietly for a moment and then walked toward Rosa, tears welling up in his eyes, as he chanted in a low voice that rose in a music-like crescendo, "Ro-sa Parks. Ro-sa Parks. Ro-sa Parks."

Seventy-one-year-old Mandela and seventy-seven-year-old Rosa fell into each other's arms, embracing and weeping, not tears of sadness, but tears of understanding that only these two icons of the civil and human rights struggle on two continents could comprehend.

———

THREE YOUNG PEOPLE, all eighteen years of age, each calling the South home—a young black man, a young white man, and a young black woman—with three very different life stories and outcomes. One would seek and receive redemption and offer forgiveness to his tormentors; one would start his political life as a Franklin Delano Roosevelt liberal and end his life a staunch neoconservative; and one would become an iconic figure of the twentieth century. But, on this day, March 25, 1931, all three were bound *by* Scottsboro.

EPILOGUE

*And because we have tasted the bitter swill of civil war and
segregation, and emerged from that dark chapter stronger and
more united, we cannot help but believe that the old hatreds
shall someday pass; that the lines of tribe shall soon dissolve;
that as the world grows smaller, our common humanity shall
reveal itself; and that America must play its role in ushering in
a new era of peace.*

> President Barack Hussein Obama
> Inaugural Address, January 20, 2009

Seeking Answers

How do I find closure to the people, events, and changes in the
period of the South's history and our nation's history over the last
one hundred years? Of course, there is no closure, only a
continuation of change, hopefully for the betterment of our nation and our
humanity. I have made two journeys through the South in the last fourteen
years seeking more definitive answers to my questions.

A Journey to My Youthful Past

In April 1997, after I saw my parents off with my brother Gibbs for their
flight to Reno, I rented a car and drove to Tuscaloosa and Livingston to
revisit the other two important places of my youth. While I had visited
Birmingham many times since I moved from Alabama in 1959, I had driven
through Tuscaloosa and Livingston only once, early in the morning in
1968.

I left Birmingham before dawn on Saturday morning, April 5, 1997, and, although there is now a modern interstate freeway to Tuscaloosa and Livingston, I purposely drove on old U.S. 11 to retrace the route I so frequently traveled forty to fifty years ago. As I drove slowly toward Tuscaloosa, I was amazed at how much of the road I remembered, with all its twists and turns that finally led to the main campus. I made a brief detour to visit the new Mercedes-Benz automobile manufacturing facility about fifteen miles east of Tuscaloosa, just one of the many symbols of the changes I was about to see and experience.

I arrived on the main campus of the University of Alabama at about nine o'clock in the morning, and, even though it was a Saturday, it must have been spring or semester break because the campus was essentially deserted. I parked my car and wandered around the Quadrangle where I'd earned my second year ROTC cadet award drilling and training my fellow corps members. As I quietly walked the Quadrangle grounds, I observed a black man and a white woman, walking hand-in-hand across the Quad some distance from me. It then hit me full force that I was in a different place in a different time from my earlier days on this campus. A scene like that was, quite frankly, unimaginable in my student days and would have resulted in a terrible incident, if not a lynching.

As I drove south out of Tuscaloosa on U.S. 11 toward Livingston in Sumter County, I finally realized that I was stepping back into the yesteryears of my life into an area with fond memories, but fraught with thoughts of racial inequities and unfair treatment.

In my youth, from ages twelve to thirteen in Livingston, I had traveled this highway many times, as I had to go to Birmingham at least once a month for two years on a Greyhound bus for orthodontic appointments. I would ride the bus alone from Livingston through Tuscaloosa to the Greyhound station in downtown Birmingham, a trip of about 120 miles. There I would take a Birmingham municipal bus to Nanny's house on the north side of Birmingham, usually have my appointment on a Saturday morning, and travel back to Livingston by the same mode on either Saturday afternoon or Sunday. I came to know every town, turn, and bridge on the route.

As I drove through the towns of Ralph, Eutaw, and Boligee, all brief stops on my Greyhound bus rides years ago, I could feel the clock rolling back to match the moment. I approached Sumter County over the flat plain leading to the bridge over the Tombigbee River, the county line. The road is on a levee on the north side of the river to allow passage whenever the Tombigbee flooded. I remember several occasions, while riding on the bus over the levee, when the surrounding area appeared as a lake from the river's high waters. The bridge actually climbs up into Sumter County, as the opposite side is a high limestone cliff, and I remember I always felt a sense of relief when the bus was successfully lifted from the flat plain into the higher reaches of my home county.

As I approached the outskirts of Livingston, past what were just farms and cow pastures years ago, I now saw a number of nice, red brick homes lining the road. I slowed and noticed that there were African Americans in the yards and driveways of some of the homes doing the same things all families do—washing their cars, mowing the lawn, or preparing for a trip. This was my first indication that things were different, as years ago most black families lived in housing best described as shacks in areas generally away from the public eye.

I drove past the campus of the University of West Alabama, Livingston State Teachers College in my youth, and, while some of the old buildings were still there, it was mostly new and much expanded beyond anything I remembered. The campus was relatively quiet as it was probably break time here also, but I did observe a mix of black and white students walking around the campus.

I parked the car on the town square and walked around the downtown area I had frequented so often in my youth. The square still had the old courthouse building in the center with the Confederate memorial statue next to it. Most of the stores and buildings around the square were new or significantly remodeled. The old movie house was gone, and a library had replaced the corner Piggly-Wiggly grocery store.

Our first house in Livingston, just one block off the square, was gone, replaced by a bank. There was little activity in the square on the Saturday of my visit, a stark departure from Saturdays fifty years ago when the square bustled with hundreds of people from the surrounding rural areas in town for market day in their cars, trucks, and horse drawn wagons. I was beginning to wonder if the entire state of Alabama had taken the day off.

I walked around the corner to the street where Dad and Mom's newspaper, *Our Southern Home*, was located. At first blush it looked completely different, as many of the old homes on the block had been torn down. I initially thought this had been the fate of the newspaper building, but as I slowly walked down the street, I realized that a small building still standing next to a recently demolished home was the old newspaper location. The building had been remodeled and freshly painted and was now a small business. All remnants of its use as a newspaper publishing facility had long ago vanished. I felt a mixed sense of sadness to see the past gone but was relieved to see the building continuing to serve the community.

I then drove from the square to the end of Main Street where our house had been on the bluff overlooking the river. The road was now paved and, lo and behold, the house was still there, my sentinel outpost by the river. The house had been remodeled and looked quite good. There was no one home, so I walked around the yard and over to the trails leading down to the river where my brother and I, Willie Jr., and Yank roamed so many years ago. Of course, now it looked decidedly smaller and less intimidating than when I was ten to twelve years old, but it still stirred my memories and my soul as I stood there over fifty years later.

I said my goodbye to Livingston and started my drive back to Birmingham late in the day. As I reflected about my day, I initially thought that what I had experienced seemed almost revolutionary, but quickly realized that, in fact, it had taken the civil rights movement decades to achieve what I had observed this day.

The University of Alabama had an all-white student population of about eight thousand in the late 1950s and has grown to a campus of over twenty thousand today, made up of numerous ethnic and racial groups with African Americans comprising about 14 percent of the total. At the 1992 university commencement, Autherine Lucy Foster, the lady who was, for a few days, the first black student at Alabama in my freshman year of 1956, earned a Master's degree in Elementary Education in the same ceremony that her daughter received a Bachelor's degree in Corporate Finance.

Livingston State Teachers College had an all-white enrollment when I lived in Livingston, and now the University of West Alabama has over twenty-five hundred students, about 41 percent of whom are black.

The Birmingham Civil Rights Institute combines a museum, an education and outreach program, and an archives division into a rich and sobering history of the civil rights period in Birmingham's past. The institute is located across the street from the Sixteenth Street Baptist Church and the Kelly Ingram Park, two landmarks in the city's civil rights struggle. The institute does not excuse or apologize for Birmingham's terrible reputation as "Bombingham" in the 1960s, as it states in its motto, "Inspired by the Past; A Vision of the Future."

Montgomery is the home of the Southern Poverty Law Center. What started as a small civil rights law firm in 1971 has grown to international renown for its programs fighting all forms of racial hatred. Morris Dees, the co-founder of the center, attended the University of Alabama the same years I did, but we never met. He was married and in a liberal arts program leading to law school while I was single in a fraternity house and an engineering curriculum, so our social and educational paths were quite divergent.

In 2000, Alabama had the second highest percent of black elected officials in the nation's fifty states. In 2009, the Birmingham mayor, police chief, and superintendent of public education were all black. The City Council membership included four black women, one white woman, and four black men—a far cry from the days of Eugene "Bull" Connor, Birmingham Commissioner of Public Safety in 1963, who epitomized the strident segregationist of the time.

Following the Trail of the Scottsboro Boys

As I worked on this book, and particularly the parts on the Scottsboro Boys, I made my second journey to Alabama. I wanted to do some research in local libraries and archives, and retrace the steps of the boys in several of the locations critical to their ordeal. I arrived in Birmingham late in the evening on Sunday, October 22, 2006. I had a very busy, but productive week as I drove over seven hundred miles and visited ten locations associated with some aspect of the Scottsboro trials. As I traveled around, I was also able to visit with several of my cousins and two old friends. Over the next five days, I spent numerous hours in libraries and archives in Birmingham, Montgomery, Atlanta, Chattanooga, Scottsboro, and Decatur. Of course, I found quite a bit of material on the Scottsboro Boys, but, to my delight, I also found newspaper articles and letters pertaining to my father's position as Executive Secretary of the Alabama Scottsboro Committee in 1936.

On Monday morning I met with Laura Anderson, the Assistant Archivist at the Birmingham Civil Rights Institute. Laura is responsible for the structure of this book, as she made me aware of my father's involvement in the Scottsboro Boys' tragedy. I spent about an hour reading through sections of Don Rasmussen's thesis, and Laura later sent me an entire copy of the document. The highlight of my trip was being able to see and experience the sense of the places where many of the events described in this book occurred.

In Montgomery, I first went to the Alabama Department of Archives and History to explore their files on the Scottsboro Boys. I then visited the Dexter Avenue Baptist Church, almost in the shadow of the state Capitol, where Martin Luther King Jr. was pastor when the Montgomery bus boycott started in December 1955 and continued until December 1956. I drove past the point Rosa Parks boarded the bus when she refused to move, providing the spark for the modern civil rights movement, and along the street renamed Rosa Parks Boulevard in her honor. Late that afternoon, I visited the Southern Poverty Law Center, hoping to meet Morris Dees. He was out of town, but Penny Weaver, the Public Affairs Deputy Director, gave me an excellent tour of the center. I spent the night in Montgomery with my cousin, Margie Taylor Sellers, the youngest of Macey's six children.

In Warm Springs, Georgia, I went to the golf course Franklin Delano Roosevelt built in the 1920s, and stood on the tees where fifteen-year-old Clarence Norris was a caddie in 1928. I explained to the pro in the golf shop why I was here and asked if this was the golf course I was seeking. He said it absolutely had to be, as no other golf courses were built in this part of Georgia until years later.

In Atlanta, the home of Charlie Weems, I searched the archives at the Robert W. Woodruff Library of the Atlanta University Center. And, I reconnected with my boyhood friend, Dick Allison, whom I hadn't seen in over fifty years when we were both fourteen years old in Livingston. It always amazes me how quickly you reconnect with someone from your past; the interval of the years gone-by collapse as quickly as an accordion. We compared stories, memories, and photos in a fascinating evening.

In Chattanooga, I walked part of the railroad yard where Clarence, Victoria Price, Ruby Bates, and others boarded the train on March 25, 1931. I saw an area near the yard, which may well have been the hobo jungle where Victoria, Ruby, Lester Carter, and Orville Gilley spent the night of March 24. I even found a section of an old, unused track near 23rd Street where Haywood, Eugene, Andy, and Roy, Chattanooga natives, boarded the train.

However, the most memorable part of my trip was the drive from Chattanooga to Stevenson to Scottsboro to Paint Rock to Huntsville, and finally to Decatur. It was soon after I left Chattanooga that I noticed the first of many signs commemorating the "Trail of Tears," the forced exodus of the Cherokees from the Southeast in 1838. It was then, and only then, that I realized I was on a route associated with two tragedies that befell the two groups most persecuted in our nation's history: the Native Americans and the African Americans. I later called the route the Scottsboro Boys' "Trail of Trials and Tears."

I stopped at each of the critical points along the Chattanooga-to-Decatur route. In Stevenson, I found the station where the train stopped briefly to add a boxcar. After the train left Stevenson, the fight broke out between the black and white boys, thereby leading to the train being stopped at Paint Rock by the posse. In Scottsboro, I visited the courthouse on the town square where the first four trials took place. It immediately reminded me of my childhood home in Livingston. As I walked around the outside of the courthouse, I could sense the huge crowd gathered for the first trial on "First Monday," the town's monthly marketing and socializing day.

I next stopped in Paint Rock, still not much more than a water-stop on the railroad, and walked the tracks where the boys were arrested, and the two girls tried to flee, but, when recognized, accused the boys of rape.

In Huntsville, the home of Victoria Price and Ruby Bates, I had lunch with my cousin, Debbie Joyner—the stepdaughter of Mother's sister, Anne.

In Decatur, where the last seven trials were held, the old courthouse building no longer exists. However, the Morgan County Archives had some interesting material and photographs pertaining to the case.

I returned to Birmingham late Friday, and I spent the night with my good friends, Dale and Alan Head. Saturday morning, October 28, 2006, Alan and I drove to the University of Alabama in Tuscaloosa. Alan and I were both Dekes at the university, and on a beautiful fall day, the trip was a homecoming of sorts for us.

It also happened that this was the official Homecoming Day for the football season, so the campus was mobbed with students, alumni, and Alabama football fans. Alan and I had a blast; we were like two young freshmen wandering the campus for the first time. We watched the Homecoming Day parade, we paid our respects at the Paul "Bear" Bryant Museum, and we wandered the Quadrangle looking at all the displays by the different colleges at the school, the many social and professional organizations, and the many companies wanting to associate themselves with one of the most famous football programs in the nation. We found the display for the Golden Flake Potato Chip Company, one of the major sponsors of the *Bear Bryant Show* produced by Frank Taylor. I introduced myself to Golden Flake's Director of Public Relations; she remembered Frank and my father, and she offered to provide me with any material they had that would be useful for my book.

On my entire trip, everyone I talked to—black and white alike—was helpful. I never encountered an individual who was unwilling to talk about and help me with my inquiries into the Scottsboro Boys' ordeal. Even in the city of Scottsboro, the courthouse and library staffs were quite open and helpful. I know there are individuals in Scottsboro and Alabama who still wish people would stop asking about the event, but I didn't meet one such person. In fact, in two of the archives I visited, the black person I talked to knew little or nothing about the Scottsboro Boys, but after I explained the tragic events, they expressed surprise that anything like that could have happened.

What I most remember about my day on the campus was the crowd. The campus was awash in crimson and white, the colors of the school, but it was the black and white mix of the crowd that is the most enduring memory. It was mixed in all aspects! The school band was black and white, the student body was black and white, the visiting crowd was black and white, and they all commingled in one happy-go-lucky throng, oblivious to my looks of amazement and joy, as I continually thought back to the dark days of the riots on the Quadrangle in 1956 when Autherine Lucy briefly enrolled in the school.

As I complete this book, I think back to January 20, 2009, when Barack Obama was inaugurated the forty-fourth President of the United States, the first African American and the first American with a mixed racial heritage, to be elected President. It is a historic moment, and it brings some closure to our racial past and to Martin Luther King's famous "I Have a Dream" speech on the steps of the Lincoln Memorial in 1963. However, Obama's election is but another step to an end to all racial injustice in this country.

I don't want to sound too Pollyannaish or naïve; there are still many racial and economic inequities in the South and in our nation. The city of Birmingham, the most populous city in the state, represents one sad fact of our continued racial divide. In the 1950 Census, the population of Birmingham was about 326,000: split 60 percent white and 40 percent black. In the 2000 Census, the population of Birmingham had fallen to about 243,000, and the split was reversed: 75 percent black to 25 percent white. White flight had affected Birmingham significantly as it has in so many urban areas. Over the years, much of Birmingham's white population moved south of Red Mountain to cities like Homewood, Mountain Brook, Vestavia Hills, and Hoover. Birmingham is left with the problems so common in large cities: urban blight and decay, and high levels of unemployment, crime, and drug use. In addition, the Black Belt counties in Alabama continue to be among the poorest in the nation on a per capita basis.

So, change has come to my home state and city, some for the better and some for the worse. Much of it lifts your spirits, yet the flames of racial prejudice and injustice still burn as bright as the torch in the raised hand of Vulcan, the symbol of Birmingham's days as the "Pittsburg of the South." The large statue of the Roman god of fire and forge overlooks the city from atop Red Mountain. Vulcan also gives the "moon" to the white suburbs to the south, as his apron does not cover his derriere, a symbol of looking backwards.

Whites and blacks in Alabama and the South need to finally accept that we are all figuratively and literally connected at the hip. Figuratively, we were dependent on one another throughout our troubled history; the development of the South's agriculture, our social values, and our successes and failures would not have proceeded without each group's tacit, but often unequal, support. Literally, we are connected at the hip through several centuries of interracial sexual activity, most of it imposed by white men upon black women, although there were some consensual relationships and even marriages. The descendants of these interracial relationships are now so common in our culture that one needs to seriously consider asking of a person, be they black or white in appearance: Am I possibly related to this person? The short-term answer may be yes or no; however, the long look at mankind's evolution "out of Africa" would always answer yes.

Seeking Final Closure

THE LAST TWO TAYLOR BOYS joined their three brothers in 2005. George William "Bill" Taylor died on June 5, 2005 at age ninety-four in Seattle. A week later, the youngest and the last of the Taylor Boys, Robert Macey Taylor, died on June 12 at age eighty-eight in Birmingham. Three years later, on September 19, 2008, Rose Dawson Taylor—our beloved "Rosie"—died at age ninety-four.

The Taylor Boys and Rose Taylor, the Scottsboro Boys, Rosa Parks, and the others of their generation so prominent in this history of change in the twentieth century are now gone, leaving to us the task of sifting through our memories of them to understand their accomplishments and shortcomings.

I see their images and hear their whispers in my dreams. Three young people, all eighteen years of age, and so many others call back to me, trying to explain the past, but are never able to break through the fog of sleep and memory. I try to decipher the meaning of their words and expressions as they float slowly through my night. The emotions vary from joy to sadness to tragic despair. Are they speaking from the Elysian Fields, a vast nothingness, or my muddled subconscious? They provide no answers, and I have no answers. I was only an observer and am now their chronicler.

I am haunted by my past.

ACKNOWLEDGMENTS

THIS BOOK OWES ITS EXISTENCE to one individual, Laura Caldwell Anderson, the Assistant Archivist at the Birmingham Civil Rights Institute. Ms. Anderson's determined pursuit on the Internet to find my father, Waights Taylor, who was interviewed in 1947 in a study on Southerners thought to be "liberal on the race question," led her to me. What I learned from Ms. Anderson started my five-year odyssey to write this book, and I thank Ms. Anderson profusely. She has since provided me additional materials from the institute's archives, read and commented on parts of my manuscript, and, more importantly, become my good friend.

My descriptions of the Scottsboro Boys and their trials would be much less comprehensive if it were not for the outstanding histories written about the events by noted historians Dan T. Carter and James E. Goodman. Carter's book, *Scottsboro: A Tragedy of the American South*, was initially published in 1969 and revised in 1979 and is the definitive history of the case. Goodman's book, *Stories of Scottsboro*, was published in 1994 and added to Carter's efforts, as well as providing a broader perspective of the South and the period. These two books were my primary sources on the Scottsboro Boys and their trials, and both authors provided me generous guidance in my search for reference material. I am deeply indebted to these two fine historians, and I hope they will find my book an acceptable addition to the Scottsboro story and stories of the South.

The more personal material on the Scottsboro Boys came from two autobiographies: *The Last of the Scottsboro Boys* by Clarence Norris and Sybil Washington, and *Scottsboro Boy* by Haywood Patterson and Earl Conrad. Sybil Washington was particularly helpful in answering some specific questions I had about Clarence Norris.

The material on Rosa Parks comes primarily from two sources: Parks's autobiography written with Jim Haskins, *Rosa Parks: My Story*; and a biography written by Douglas Brinkley, *Rosa Parks: A Life*. Parks's book is a very personal account of her life up to about 1991, and Brinkley expands her life story from a historian's perspective up to about 2000.

The chapter on Bombingham, 1963, would not be as complete and comprehensive as it is if not for Diane McWhorter's book, *Carry Me Home: Birmingham, Alabama, The Climactic Battle of the Civil Rights Revolution*. McWhorter's book, nineteen years in development, is incredibly well researched, documented, and written, as recognized by the Pulitzer Prize for General Nonfiction she was awarded in 2002. McWhorter's book covers the entire story of Birmingham in 1963 in extraordinary detail from both factual and personal perspectives, while my chapter only represents the tip of the iceberg. I owe Diane McWhorter a deep sense of gratitude and thanks for her personal help and friendship.

My information on Judge James E. Horton Jr. was enhanced immensely when Birmingham's Gillian Goodrich provided me a copy of her Master's Thesis titled *James Edwin Horton Jr.: Scottsboro Judge*.

I want to extend my thanks to several individuals in libraries and archives that were particularly helpful in my research: Director Ed Bridges and Archivist Nancy Dupree in the Alabama Department of Archives and History; Alma Surles in the Alabama Supreme Court and State Law Library; Director James Baggett and Archivist Don Veasey in the Birmingham Public Library's Archives Department; Catherine Milne, a Cornell University law student, in the Cornell University Law Library; Thomas Hutchins in the Huntsville Madison County Public Library; Archivist John Allison in the Morgan County Archives, Decatur, Alabama; Jennifer Cole in the Seeley G. Mudd Manuscript Library, Princeton University; and Matthew Turi at the University of North Carolina, Wilson Special Collection Library.

I also received generous help from the Chattanooga Public Library, the Library of Congress, the Robert W. Woodruff Library in Atlanta, and the Scottsboro Public Library. Unfortunately, I failed to keep a list of the individuals in these libraries who helped me, so I extend a broad thanks to all of them.

My brothers and cousins provided both moral support, and details and information to enhance my faulty memory. A loving thanks to my brothers Gibbs Taylor and Richard Taylor, and my cousins Margaret "Mimi" Taylor Akers, Patricia "Patty" Taylor Campbell, Cheré Dastugue Coen, Veronica Taylor Coker, Debbie Joyner, Margaret "Margie" Taylor Sellers, Frank Taylor Jr., and Thomas Macey Taylor.

A number of friends and acquaintances have given me assistance along the way. My men's writing group—Peter Chiarella, Kal Edwards, Tom Kennelly, and James Keolker—all of whom are published authors, gave me guidance by example, constructive input and criticism, and friendship. David Beckman—a poet, author, playwright, and my tolerant golfing companion—has given me constant encouragement and friendship. A number of others who read various versions of the manuscript and gave me encouraging feedback, or provided me useful information were Carylon Alexander, Louis Allison, Richard Allison, Mary Lynn Archibald, Foster and Mike Beigler, Andi Brady, Frank Burney, David Doll, Alex Frantz, Jack and Shirley Hirschberg, Marge Gelders Frantz, Karl Friedman, Annette Gooch, Jean Harris and Arturo Maimoni, Dale and Alan Head, James Head, Martha and Jeffrey Kahane, Danielle Marshall, Karen Hart, Linda Nelson, Mae Ziglin Meidav, Nancy Huddleston Packer, Donald and Lore Rasmussen, Bruce Roche, Jordan Rosenfeld, Jane Stuppin, Marvin Whiting, and Tom York.

My friend and graphic designer extraordinaire, Suzan Reed, did the cover design and the state map. Arlene Miller used her editing skills to save me from my propensity to make punctuation, spelling, and grammar errors. Thérèse Shere did the Index for the book, making a difficult and daunting task seem easy.

Finally, but certainly not least, is the loving and critical support I received from my wife, Liz Martin. Liz was an English major and English teacher. Her language skills far exceed those of an Aeronautical Engineer, but she critiqued my work in a positive manner, while respecting the professional boundaries between a man and a wife. Even more supportive was her tolerance of our shared office. Liz is, to put it mildly, a person who values neatness, and yet, she tolerated my mess in my half of our shared office. I had stacks of books and papers piled on the floor, on chairs, under my desk, and in any spare space we had in our already crammed bookcases. I promised her I would clean up my half of the office once the book was finished, but alas, I may have to break my promise when I start on my next literary project.

Abbreviations Used in Notes

ACLU   American Civil Liberties Union

ADAH   Alabama Department of Archives and History, Montgomery, Alabama

ASKF   Aggie Scribner Kapelman Files. These are the files David Scribner kept on his involvement in the Scottsboro Boys trials. Scribner left the files with his daughter, Aggie, before his death.

ASLL   Alabama State Law Library

AVP   Transcript of Testimony, *State of Alabama vs. Haywood Patterson*, Morgan County Court, March 31–April 10, 1933; Alabama Department of Archives and History

BCRI   Birmingham Civil Rights Institute

CMH   Diane McWhorter, *Carry Me Home: Birmingham, Alabama, The Climactic Battle of the Civil Rights Revolution*

CULL   Cornell University Law Library

CR   Quentin Reynolds, *Courtroom*

EU   Emory University Manuscript, Archives, and Rare Book Library, Atlanta, Georgia

HRR   Hollace Ransdell Report to ACLU, Report on the Scottsboro, Ala. Case, May 27, 1931: ACLU Records, Box 1887, Folder 1, Twentieth Century Public Policy Papers, Seeley G. Mudd Manuscript Library, Department of Rare Books and Special Collections, Princeton University Library

LSB   Clarence Norris and Sybil D. Washington, *The Last of the Scottsboro Boys*

NAACP   Scottsboro Legal Files (SLF) of the National Association for the Advancement of Colored People, Library of Congress

NYT   *The New York Times*

RPAL   Douglas Brinkley, *Rosa Parks: A Life*

RPMS   Rosa Parks with Jim Haskins, *Rosa Parks: My Story*

SB   Haywood Patterson and Earl Conrad, *Scottsboro Boy*

SOS   James Goodman, *Stories of Scottsboro*

STAS   Dan T. Carter, *Scottsboro: A Tragedy of the American South*

TSBF   Allan Knight Chalmers, *They Shall Be Free*

Besides the sources listed above, trial transcripts, court decisions, and other related materials were sourced from the Morgan County [Alabama] Archives, the Robert W. Woodruff Library, Atlanta University Center, and the University of North Carolina at Chapel Hill, Louis Round Wilson Special Collections Library. Material was also sourced from public libraries in Birmingham, Chattanooga, Huntsville, and Scottsboro.

Unless noted otherwise, quotations are taken directly from the source documents with no grammar, spelling, or punctuation corrections. The consistent exception to this rule is my refusal to spell out the N-word.

NOTES

INTRODUCTION—UNEXPECTED CONNECTIONS

xiv **"liberal on the race question"**: Rasmussen, unpublished PhD thesis, p. 71, BCRI.

xiv **"Communist"** and **"un-American"**: Author's meeting and interview with Rasmussen, December 22, 2004.

xv **Two months after the Rasmussens settled in Talladega**: The story about the Rasmussens' ordeal in the Birmingham jail is taken from their unpublished memoir, *Failing to Conform*, pp. 16–21, and the author's meeting and interview with the Rasmussens on December 22, 2004.

xvi **In 1956, Nancy Huddleston attended a dinner party**: Based on Packer, *Blood of the Liberals*, pp. 182–83.

CHAPTER 1. A SHAMEFUL DAY—1967

1 *Let us all hope that the dark clouds*: King, *Why We Can't Wait*, p. 112.

PART ONE. BOUND FOR SCOTTSBORO, 1897–MARCH 25, 1931

CHAPTER 2. MARCH 25, 1931

5 I took some literary license in Chapter 2 with Clarence, Waights, and Rosa, three of the principals in this book. It is factual that all three were eighteen years old on March 25, 1931, were at the locations described, and would become involved in the Scottsboro events in the different ways described throughout the book. However, their detailed activities and thoughts on March 25 are the author's creation to best introduce the three and propel the story forward. The remainder of the book is based on fact from the referenced sources, and from memory concerning some Taylor family stories.

CHAPTER 3. WARM SPRINGS, GEORGIA

9 **Indians of the Creek Confederacy**: Burke and Burke, *Warm Springs*, pp. 13, 25.

9 **It was Franklin Delano Roosevelt**: This account of Franklin Delano Roosevelt's life in Warm Springs is based on Burke and Burke, *Warm Springs*, pp. 39–69, 111.

10 **Clarence Norris**: This account of Clarence Norris's life is based on *LSB*, pp. 27–38.

10 **"Daddy stripped us buck naked"**: *LSB*, p. 34.

10 **"Those were good times"**: ibid., p. 29.

11 **"Your children didn't kill the horse"**: ibid., p. 32.

11 **"He had momma on the floor"** and **"screaming and hollering"**: ibid., p. 33.

11 **"Bubba, momma wants you to call me"**: ibid., p. 36.

CHAPTER 4. BIRMINGHAM, ALABAMA

14 **The first recorded instance**: Johnson and Smith, *Africans in America*, pp. 36–37, 41.

14 **"All servants imported and brought into this Country"**: ibid., p. 48.

14 **New York and New Jersey were the last northern states**: Wikipedia, "Slave State," http://en.wikipedia.org/wiki/Slave_state.

14 **Reconstruction, as envisioned by President Lincoln**: Kunhardt, *Lincoln*, p. 224; Olsen, *The American Civil War*, pp. 224–25.

14 **Birmingham was still a young city**: Birmingham's early history is based on McMillan, *Yesterday's Birmingham*, pp. 9, 38, 76, 78, 113; Packer, *Blood of the Liberals*, p. 34–35.

15 **The convict lease program was used...last state to abolish the convict lease program**. Based on Packer, *Blood of the Liberals*, pp. 36–38; Blackmon, *Slavery by Another Name*, pp. 5–7.

15 **"What is it that we want to do?"**: Packer, *Blood of the Liberals*, p. 49.

16 **The State Constitution was a byzantine document**: Based on Packer, *Blood of the Liberals*, pp. 48–52.

16 **in 1899, Angus's twenty-seven-year-old brother...In 1909, James moved to New Orleans**: Coen, *The Taylor Family*, pp. 30, 33.

16 **"unfortunate love affair and duel"**: ibid., p. 22.

18 **"Ef you right" and "Tell a hawg sump'n"**: Taylor, *Life on the Side of Red Mountain*, p. 16.

19 **"Yeh—an' I di'n't git it"**: Cohen, *Highly Colored*, p. 9.

20 **"Then there were Waights Taylor, the neighbourhood intellectual"**: Copeland, *The Game Player*, p. 4.

20 **"They told me boys from the South would fight."**: Barra, *The Last Coach*, p. 45.

Chapter 5. Tuskegee, Alabama

22 **The geological Black Belt**: Tullos, Allen, "The Black Belt," Southern Spaces, April, 19, 2004, http://www.southernspaces.org/contents/2004/tullos/4a.htm.

22 **However, the name Black Belt**: Wimberley and Morris, *The Southern Black Belt*, pp. 1–6.

23 **The first inhabitants in the Alabama Black Belt**: ADAH, "Alabama Counties—Macon County," http://www.archives.state.al.us/counties/macon.html.

23 **"Alabama fever"**: Wikipedia, "Black Belt," http://en.wikipedia.org/wiki/Black_Belt_(U.S._region).

23 **One likely beneficiary...Sanford Taylor...forty acres in adjacent Wilcox county in 1838.**: Coen, *The Taylor Family*, p. 8.

23 **In 1880, the State of Alabama**: Washington, *Up from Slavery*, pp. 89, 95; Tuskegee University, "History of Tuskegee University," http://www.tuskegee.edu/Global/story.asp?S=1070392; Wikipedia, "Tuskegee University," http://en.wikipedia.org/wiki/Tuskegee_University.

24 **I have often been asked**: Washington, *Up from Slavery*, p. 90.

24 **In 1896, Dr. Washington recruited George Washington Carver**: This account of George Washington Carver's life is based on McMurry, *George Washington Carver*, pp. 41–43, 72–73, 80–83, 124–27, 219–27, 256–63, 307.

24 **One of the more famous programs**: Wikipedia, "Tuskegee Airmen," http://en.wikipedia.org/wiki/Tuskegee_Airmen.

24 **The Public Health Service conducted**: Jones, *Bad Blood*, pp. 1–2, 100–03, 213.

25 **"voluntary participants"**: ibid., p. 208.

25 **"I thought they"**: ibid., p. 160.

25 **In the early 1990s, the town of Tuskegee**: Wikipedia, "Tuskegee University," http://en.wikipedia.org/wiki/Tuskegee_University.

25 **Rosa McCauley**: This account of Rosa McCauley's life is based on *RPMS*, pp. 4–21, 32–34; *RPAL*, p. 17.

Chapter 6. Three Odysseys—1928

27 **Waights Taylor—An Intellectual Wandering**: Waights's trip to Scandinavia and all the quotations are taken from on his unpublished diary, *Journal of a Voyage to Scandinavia*.

29   **"Could any other world"**: Taylor, *Life on the Side of Red Mountain*, p. 5.

29   **Clarence Norris—A Wandering Filled with Challenges**: Clarence Norris's odyssey is based on *LSB*, pp. 39–46.

30   **"Do you want some ice cream?"**: *LSB*, p. 40.

30   **"Yeah, but where you gonna get it?"**: ibid.

30   **"Follow me."**: ibid.

30   **"Eat, take all you want, they never miss nothing."**: ibid.

30   **"Boy where did you get those cigars?"**: ibid.

30   **"I bought them."**: ibid.

30   **"Let's go to Birmingham."**: ibid., p. 41.

31   **"Are you going to kill me, Bubba?"**: ibid., p. 44.

31   **"Get outta there, n-----."** : ibid., p. 45.

32   **"We are going to give you a chance to run for your life."**: ibid.

32   **Rosa McCauley—A Journey for an Education**: Rosa McCauley's odyssey is based on *RPMS*, pp. 19, 24–26, 38–56; *RPAL*, pp. 28–29, 34–37.

33   **"very quiet" and "staying out of trouble"** *RPAL*, p. 34.

34   **"She was a straight"**: ibid.

34   **"I did not complain"**: ibid., p. 37.

Chapter 7. Chattanooga, Tennessee

36   **Haywood Patterson**: The account of Haywood Patterson's early years is based on *SB*, pp. 6, 26–28; *STAS*, p. 39; *SOS*, pp. 92–93.

36   **"You had to fox your way out of such a spot."**: *SB*, p. 27.

36   **"The day after my dad slipped off"**: ibid.

37   **Eugene Williams**: The account of Eugene Williams's early years is based on the website, Famous American Trials—The Scottsboro Trials, http://www.law.umkc.edu/faculty/projects/FTrials/scottsboro/SB_bSBs.html.

38   **"Which Italian American player"**: PBS, The Power of Illusion: http://www.pbs.org/race/000_About/002_04-background-01-09.htm.

38   **"How can we get rid" and "Stop talking about it."**: CBS News, *60 Minutes*, http://www.cbsnews.com/stories/2005/12/14/60minutes/main1127684_page3.shtml.

38   **Andy Wright**: The account of Andy Wright's early years is based on *SOS*, p. 92.

38   **Roy Wright**: The account of Roy Wright's early years is based on *SOS*, p. 92.

39   **Charlie Weems**: The account of Charlie Weems's early years is based on *STAS*, p. 31; *SOS*, p. 235.

39   **Olen Montgomery**: The account of Olen Montgomery's early years is based on *STAS*, p. 46; *SOS*, pp. 236–37.

39   **Ozie Powell**: The account of Ozie Powell's early years is based on *SOS*, p. 260.

39   **Willie Roberson**: The account of Willie Roberson's early years is based on *STAS*, p. 45; *SOS*, p. 276.

40   **"I just got lazy"**: *SOS*, p. 276.

41   **Victoria Price**: The account of Victoria Price's early years is based on *STAS*, pp. 13–14; *SOS*, pp. 19–21, 184; *HRR*, p. 16.

41   **Ruby Bates**: The account of Ruby Bates's early years is based on *SOS*, pp. 19–21, 184; *HRR*, p. 15.

41   **"took men for money"**: *HRR*, p. 15.

41   **"notorious prostitutes"**: Walter White to Bob (Bagnell) and Herbert (Seligman), May 3, 1931, NAACP, SLF 1,

41   **"negro night" and "ask colored men"** *STAS*, pp. 78–79.

42   **"take on five negroes"**: ibid., p. 78.

Part Two. The Trial Period, March 25, 1931–July 24, 1937

Chapter 8. Sixteen Days in Scottsboro—March 25–April 9, 1931

45   The "Trail of Tears": The "Trail of Tears" account is based on Perdue and Green, *The Cherokee Nation and the Trail of Tears*, pp. 50–51, 91–95, 112–113, 123–127, 161; Long, *The Cherokee*, pp. 9, 34.

46   The Train Continues to Paint Rock: This account is based on *STAS*, pp. 3–6; *SOS*, pp. 3–4; *LSB*, pp. 18–20; *SB*, pp. 3–6.

47   "The next time you want," and "N-----, I don't ask you when I want by." and "You white sonsofbitches": *SB*, pp. 3–4.

48   Day 1—Wednesday, March 25, 1931: This account is based on *STAS*, pp. 7–10; *SOS*, pp. 4–5; *LSB*, pp. 20–21; *SB*, pp. 5–9.

49   "N-----, you know damn well": *SOS*, p. 5.

49   "Let those n------ out. If you don't": *SB*, p. 7.

49   Day 2—Thursday, March 26, 1931: This account is based on *STAS*, pp. 13–19; *SOS*, pp. 11–12.

50   "A whole bunch of Negroes suddenly jumped": *STAS*, p. 14.

50   "that the ends of justice could best" and "the evidence against": ibid., p. 17.

50   "doddering, extremely unreliable": Hollace Ransdell to Walter White, April 10, 1931, NAACP, SLF 1.

51   Dr. P. A. Stevens, became aware: Dr. Stevens to Walter White, April 2, 1931, NAACP, SLF 1.

51   Day 6—Monday, March 30, 1931: This account is based on *STAS*, pp. 20–21; *SB*, p. 10.

51   "It is my intention": *STAS*, p. 20.

52   Day 7—Tuesday, March 31, 1931: This account is based on *STAS*, p. 21.

52   Days 8 through 12—Wednesday through Sunday, April 1–5, 1931: This account is based on *STAS*, pp. 12, 21; *SB*, p. 11.

52   "First Monday": *SB*, p. 11.

52   "Fair Day": *STAS*, p. 21.

52   "horse-swapping day": *SB*, p. 11.

52   Day 13—"First Monday," April 6, 1931: This account is based on *STAS*, pp. 21–28; *SOS*, pp. 13–14, 26; *LSB*, pp. 22–23; *SB*, pp. 10–12.

53   "stewed": *STAS*, p. 22.

53   "If you appear" and "I think the boys" CULL, U.S. Supreme Court, *Powell v. Alabama*, 287 U.S. 45, November 7, 1932.

54   "I am willing" and "All right.": ibid.

55   "wasn't in no loving conversation": EU, Collection No. 777, Box 3, Folder 7, Transcript of Record, *Weems v. Alabama*, U. S. Supreme Court (No. 100, October Term, 1932), p. 2.

55   "Are you going to put out?" and "No, sir, I am not.": ibid.

55   "It took two of them": ibid., p. 29.

55   "beaten up" and "bruised up": ibid., p. 30.

56   "a great amount" and "short scratches" and "She was not lacerated" and "non-motile" and "possible": ibid., pp. 33–34.

56   "there was, I guess" and "We only got enough semen" ibid., p. 38.

57   "vagina was in good": ibid.

57   Day 14—Tuesday, April 7, 1931: This account is based on *STAS*, pp. 29–41; *SOS*, pp. 14–15; *SB*, pp. 12–14.

58   "put off five white men and take" and "I think I saw a plenty": EU, Collection No. 777, Box 3, Folder 7, Transcript of Record, *Weems v. Alabama*, U. S. Supreme Court (No. 100, October Term, 1932), pp. 49–50.

58   "I never saw these girls at all": ibid., pp. 53–54.

59   "everyone of them": ibid., p. 56.

59   "I saw that negro just on the stand, Weems": ibid.

59   "Mr. Roddy then sighed": *Chattanooga Daily Times*, April 8, 1931, p. 1.

60   "private parts penetrated": EU, Collection No. 777, Box 3, Folder 4, Transcript of Record, *Patterson v. Alabama*, U. S. Supreme Court (No. 99, October Term, 1932), p. 22

60   "I don't know what you are talking": ibid., p. 26.

60   "We find the defendants guilty of rape": *STAS*, p. 37.

61   "I saw two girls": EU, Collection No. 777, Box 3, Folder 4, Transcript of Record, *Patterson v. Alabama*, U. S. Supreme Court (No. 99, October Term, 1932), p. 34.

61   "I saw all but three": ibid., p. 37.

61   "nine negroes down there": ibid., p. 39.

62   Day 15—Wednesday, April 8, 1931: This account is based on *STAS*, pp. 41–48; *SOS*, p. 15; *LSB*, p. 24; *SB*, pp. 13–14.

62   "I was by my lonesome": EU, Collection No. 777, Box 3, Folder 4, Transcript of Record, *Patterson v. Alabama*, U. S. Supreme Court (No. 99, October Term, 1932), p. 46.

62   "the one sitting there with the sleepy eyes" EU, Collection No. 777, Box 3, Folder 8, Transcript of Record, *Powell v. Alabama*, U. S. Supreme Court (No. 98, October Term, 1932), pp. 22–23.

63   "pour it to her": ibid, p. 25.

64   "that ape n-----": *STAS*, p. 45.

65   Day 16—Thursday, April 9, 1931: This account is based on *STAS*, p. 48; *LSB*, p. 24; *SB*, pp. 13–14.

65   "Yes, I have something": *SB*, p. 14.

65   Sixteen Days in Scottsboro: This account is based on *STAS*, p. 50; *SOS*, p. 25.

CHAPTER 9. DIFFERING STRUGGLES—THE REMAINDER OF 1931

67   The Scottsboro Boys: This account is based on *STAS*, pp. 51–69, 71–78, 85–103; *SOS*, pp. 18, 24–25, 32–38, 82–84; *LSB*, pp. 57–61.

69   The NAACP, initially called the National Negro Committee: Harris, *History and Achievement of the NAACP*, pp. 20–26, 40–43, 90, 96.

69   "I have no objection": Walter White to Clarence Darrow, April 10, 1931, NAACP, SLF 1.

70   "over six feet tall": *LSB*, p. 59.

73   "My dear friend Just a few lines": Clarence Norris letter to Walter White, August 14, 1931, NAACP, SLF 3.

74   "Mr. White, if you can't trust your mother": *STAS*, p. 93.

75   "By formal resolution": NAACP Announcement, January 5, 1932, Seeley G. Mudd Manuscript Library, Princeton University Library.

75   "The NAACP put out in the papers": *LSB*, p. 59.

76   Hollace Ransdell: This account is based on *STAS*, pp. 70, 80–85; *SOS*, pp. 39–46, 53–59.

76   The ACLU was founded in 1920: Walker, *In Defense of American Liberties*, pp. 30, 44–45, 47, 52, 72.

76   Ironically, one on the other founders: Wikipedia, "Helen Keller," http://en.wikipedia.org/wiki/Helen_Keller.

77   "any theory that denies": Walker, *In Defense of American Liberties*, pp. 30, 44–45, 47, 52, 72.

77   "There is something you can do.": Forrest Bailey to Hollace Ransdell, April 29, 1931, NAACP, SLF 1.

77 **"stubbornly independent and often radical"**: Packer, *Blood of the Liberals*, p. 56.

77 **"We are venturing to suggest"**: Forrest Bailey to George Huddleston, May 6, 1931, NAACP, SLF 1.

78 **"He met me coldly"**: Hollace Ransdell notes from interview with George Huddleston, May 7, 1931, NAACP, SLF 1.

78 **"I interviewed the judge"**: Interview with Hollace Ransdall by Mary Frederickson, 6 November 1974 (G-0050), in the Southern Oral History Program Collection (#4007), Southern Historical Collection, Louis Round Wilson Special Collections Library, University of North Carolina at Chapel Hill. Hollace's last name is seen spelled Ransdell or Ransdall in various sources. I have consistently used Ransdell except where a quoted source uses Ransdall.

79 **"the lowest of the low" and "These mill workers are as bad"**: HRR, pp. 14, 15.

80 **"a large, fresh, good-looking girl" and "intense feelings" and "quiet and well behaved" and "respectable"**: ibid.

80 **"a lively, talkative young woman" and "that in spite of her low wages" and "quiet prostitute"**: ibid., pp. 16, 17.

80 **"a charming southern village" and "The people on the street have easy" and "They all wanted the Negroes" and "We white people just couldn't afford" and "The N---- must be kept in his place."**: ibid., pp. 18, 19.

80 **"With the contrasting picture in mind"**: ibid., p. 22.

81 **The CIC was an interracial group**: Ann Ellis Pullen. Commission on Interracial Cooperation. The New Georgia Encyclopedia, History & Archaeology, http://www.georgiaencyclopedia.org/nge/Article.jsp?id=h-2919.

81 **"kind-faced, elderly woman" and "if they re-tried"**: HRR, p. 5.

82 **"we are told that we must"**: Papers of the Commission on Interracial Cooperation, Robert W. Woodruff Library, Atlanta University Center (Microfilm, 1983).

82 **Rosa McCauley**: This account is based on *RPMS*, pp. 55–64; *RPAL*, pp. 38–40.

CHAPTER 10. THE SUPREME COURTS—1932

86 **The Supreme Courts**: This account is based on *STAS*, pp. 156–73; *SOS*, pp. 47–50, 85–89; Alabama and U.S. Supreme Court decisions.

86 **"My delay in writing"**: Clarence Norris to Walter White, November 10, 1931, NAACP, SLF 4.

88 **"The right of the accused"**: CULL, U.S. Supreme Court, *Powell v. Alabama*, 287 U.S. 45, November 7, 1932.

88 **"In the light of the facts"**: ibid.

89 **"But the court"**: *NYT*, November 13, 1932, p. E1.

89 **During the period of time**: Alabama Execution List; http://www.geocities.com/alajustus/execution_list.html.

89 **"There was nothing to do"**: *LSB*, pp. 48, 53–55.

90 **Rosa McCauley Parks**: This account is based on *RPMS*, pp. 59–66; *RPAL*, pp. 38–41.

91 **"Twelve hundred and fifty kilometres an hour"**: Huxley, *Brave New World*, p. 158.

CHAPTER 11. THE PERFECT LAWYER AND THE PRINCIPLED JUDGE—1933

94 **The Perfect Criminal Lawyer—Samuel S. Leibowitz**: This account is based on *STAS*, pp. 181–83; *SOS*, pp. 101–05; *CR*, pp. 19–24, 249–54.

96 **"We are anxious to engage"**: William L. Patterson to Samuel S. Leibowitz, January 28, 1933, ILD Papers. This letter is printed in *CR*, p. 250.

96 **"While, as you are quite aware"**: Samuel S. Leibowitz to William L. Patterson, January 31, 1933, ILD Papers. This letter is printed in *CR*, pp. 251–52.

96 **"The views you have expressed"**: William L. Patterson to Samuel S. Leibowitz, February 6, 1933, ILD Papers. This letter is printed in *CR*, pp. 252–53.

96   The Principled Judge—James E. Horton Jr.: This account is based on *STAS*, pp. 183–84, 193; *SOS*, pp. 173–74; Goodrich, *James Edwin Horton Jr.: Scottsboro Judge*, pp. 13–17, 22–38.

96   On March 6, 1933, Judge Alfred Hawkins: *NYT*, March 8, 1933, p. 14.

98   "The Decatur Jail was a hellhole.": *LSB*, p. 64.

99   Pretrial Hearing—Monday, March 27, 1933: This account is based on *STAS*, pp. 192–97; *SOS*, pp. 120–22.

99   Judge Horton was fifty-five: *STAS*, pp. 193–94; Goodrich, *James Edwin Horton Jr.: Scottsboro Judge*, p. 21.

100   "has got education enough" and "they will nearly all steal.": *STAS*, p. 195.

100   Pretrial Hearing—Tuesday, March 28, 1933: This account is based on *STAS*, pp. 197–99; *SOS*, pp. 122–23.

101   "Call him Mr. Sanford please." and "not in the habit of doing that.": *STAS*, p. 198.

101   "moral turpitude": ibid., p. 199.

101   Pretrial Hearing—Thursday, March 30, 1933: This account is based on *STAS*, pp. 200–01; *SOS*, pp. 123–24.

102   Leibowitz called Arthur Tidwell: *STAS*, p. 200.

102   "I don't know.": *NYT*, March 31, 1933.

102   "Do you mean to say that I would swear falsely": ibid.

102   "I know it is supposed to have one.": *STAS*, p. 201.

103   Pretrial Hearing—Friday, March 31, 1933: This account is based on *STAS*, pp. 201–03; *SOS*, pp. 123–24.

103   "He ought to be hung": *SB*, p. 38.

103   "Now gentlemen under our law": *AVP*, pp. 3–5.

104   First Decatur Trial—Monday, April 3, 1933: This account is based on *STAS*, pp. 204–14; *SOS*, pp. 125–28, 136–39, 194–95.

104   "I want to make a statement" and "This is one time that I might tell a lie": *SB*, pp. 258–59.

104   "evidence against the negroes at Scottsboro": Crenshaw and Miller, *Scottsboro— The Firebrand of Communism*, p. 91.

105   "Mrs. Price, shall I call you" and "Mrs. Price.": *AVP*, p. 17.

105   "Little pieces of rock gray in color?": ibid., p. 37.

105   "Of course when the negroes got off of you": ibid., p. 46.

105   "You said six negroes raped you?": ibid., p. 60.

106   "Some of these negroes were pretty heavy": ibid., p. 63–64.

106   "To the best of your recollection": ibid., p. 64.

106   "The last negro had just finished raping you": ibid., p. 57.

107   "Do you know a man by the name of Lester Carter?": ibid., p. 67.

107   "As you looked through the microscope": ibid., pp. 176–77.

108   First Decatur Trial—Tuesday, April 4, 1933: This account is based on *STAS*, pp. 214–20; *SOS*, pp. 126–29, 139–40, 175–76.

109   "My God, Doctor": *STAS*, p. 215.

109   "off the white girl Victoria Price": *AVP*, p. 292.

109   "To a place called in Chattanooga, Hoboes Jungle?": ibid., p. 110.

110   "my old man has gone uptown" and "white man": ibid., pp. 313, 314.

110   "Did you ever meet a man by the name of Florian Slappy?": ibid., pp. 99–100.

111   First Decatur Trial—Wednesday, April 5, 1933: This account is based on *STAS*, pp. 221–27; *SOS*, pp. 129–31, 140.

112   "Ozie tell us about how much schooling": *AVP*, p. 397.

112   "I ain't had over about three months.": ibid.

112   "The court wishes to make an announcement.": ibid., p. 398.

112 **"He then delivered his warning" and "There was talk there"**: *NYT*, April 6, 1933, p. 13.

113 **"Now gentlemen, this is for the audience"**: *AVP*, pp. 399–401.

113 **"I will ask you if you haven't"**: ibid., pp. 453–54.

114 **"I will ask you if when you were"**: ibid., p. 454.

115 **"I told you I don't know"**: ibid., p. 480.

115 **"lyncher in sheep's clothing"**: *STAS*, p. 225.

115 **First Decatur Trial—Thursday, April 6, 1933**: This account is based on *STAS*, pp. 227–35; *SOS*, pp. 131–32, 140–43.

116 **"They ran toward the engine"**: *AVP*, pp. 487–88.

117 **"I had intercourse with Ruby Bates"**: ibid., p. 540.

118 **"keep your temper"**: *NYT*, April 7, 1933, p. 3.

118 **Fosdick was a liberal theologian**: Wikipedia, "Harry Emerson Fosdick," http://en.wikipedia.org/wiki/Harry_Emerson_Fosdick.

119 **"Did any of those negroes rape you?"**: *AVP*, p. 676.

119 **"No sir."**: ibid.

119 **"Victoria Price told it that way"**: ibid., p. 717.

119 **"No, I didn't tell the truth then."**: ibid., p. 727.

120 **"Yes sir."**: ibid., p. 741.

120 **"Did I not tell you"**: ibid., p. 742.

120 **"Yes."**: ibid.

120 **"what you swore to at Scottsboro" and "what happened on that train"**: ibid.

120 **"She said she got it"**: ibid., p. 753.

120 **"The defection of Ruby Bates"**: *NYT*, April 7, 1933, p. 3.

120 **"It'll be a wonder"**: *STAS*, p. 223.

120 **"Attorney General Knight, he tried"**: *SB*, p. 41.

120 **"He accused Ruby Bates"**: *LSB*, p. 65.

120 **"Knight wasn't able to do much"**: *CR*, p. 273.

121 **"Samuel Leibowitz is showing himself"**: ibid.

121 **First Decatur Trial—Friday, April 7, 1933**: This account is based on *STAS*, pp. 235–36; *SOS*, pp. 132–34, 143–44, *CR*, pp. 274.

121 **"Ahhh-men."**: *CR*, p. 274.

121 **"couldn't tell you all the things that happened in New York"**: *NYT*, April 8, 1933.

121 **"That man Carter is a new kind of man"**: Pasley, *NOT GUILTY!*, p. 265.

121 **"Show them that Alabama justice"**: ibid.

122 **"What is the argument of the learned solicitor?"**: ibid., p. 266.

122 **"to see that the law"**: *NYT*, April 8, 1933.

122 **First Decatur Trial—Saturday, April 8, 1933**: This account is based on *STAS*, pp. 236–38; *SOS*, pp. 134–35, 144.

122 **"that thing" and "If you acquit this Negro"**: *NYT*, April 9, 1933, p. 1.

122 **"Take the evidence, sift it out"**: Famous American Trials—"The Scottsboro Boys," 1931–1937, "Without Fear or Favor: Judge James Edwin Horton and the Trial of the 'Scottsboro Boys,'" by Douglas O. Linder, http://www.law.umkc.edu/faculty/projects/FTrials/trialheroes/essayhorton.html.

123 **"Things may vex you."**: ibid.

123 **"We are a white race and a Negro race here together"**: ibid.

123 **"Let's Go Down to Jordan" and "I'm on the Battlefield for My Lord"**: *SB*, p. 43.

124 **First Decatur Trial—Sunday, April 9, 1933**: This account is based on *STAS*, pp. 238–40; *SOS*, pp. 145, *CR*, 275.

124 **"one of the finest jurists" and "I believe wholeheartedly"**: *NYT*, April 10, 1933. p. 1.

125 **Monday through Sunday, April 10-16, 1933**: This account is based on *STAS*, pp. 244-45; *SOS*, pp. 152-53.

125 **"If you ever saw those creatures"**: *STAS*, p. 244.

125 **Monday, April 17, 1933**: This account is based on *STAS*, pp. 246-47; *SOS*, p. 153.

125 **"I ain't had a fair trial,"**: *NYT*, August 18, 1933, p. 3.

126 **"wail of a contemptible loser"**: ibid.

CHAPTER 12. A REMARKABLE DAY—1933

127 **Birmingham Jail**: This account is based on *SOS*, pp. 155-57; *LSB*, pp. 20, 64, 149-53; *SB*, pp 45-48.

127 **"hellhole" and "cracker" and "convict's paradise" and "You could buy women"**: *LSB*, pp. 20, 64, 149.

128 **"Life is funny"**: ibid., p. 151.

128 **Pawns in Ideological and Political Disputes**: This account is based on *STAS*, pp. 247-64; *SOS*, pp. 153-54, 161-62.

128 **"The sentiment expressed"**: *NYT*, April 19, 1933.

129 **"was solely the tremendous"**: ibid.

129 **"remove from the already"**: *NYT*, April 11, 1933

129 **"effort to do what"**: *STAS*, p. 247.

129 **"We love justice"**: ibid., p. 253.

129 **"square deal"**: ibid., p. 254.

130 **"too far"**: ibid., p. 255.

131 **A Remarkable Day in an Alabama Courtroom**: This account is based on *STAS*, pp. 265-69; *SOS*, pp. 176-82; *LSB*, pp. 66-77; *SB*, pp. 48-49.

131 **"The case is now submitted"**: All of the quotations from Judge Horton's eighteen-page statement were sourced from CULL, *State of Alabama vs. Haywood Patterson*, Morgan Circuit Court, June 22, 1933.

131 **smiles broke out on the faces**: *NYT*, June 23, 1933, p. 1.

135 **The courtroom sat silent and stunned**: ibid.

135 **"What does that have to do with the case?"**: Goodrich, *James Edwin Horton Jr.: Scottsboro Judge*, p. 95.

CHAPTER 13. BACK TO BUSINESS AS USUAL—1933

136 **The Fallout from Judge Horton's Decision**: This account is based on *STAS*, pp. 269-72; *SOS*, pp. 208-09.

136 **"chief lyncher"**: *SOS*, p. 208.

136 **"political considerations mean nothing to him whatever"**: *STAS*, p. 270.

137 **The Prejudicial Judge—William W. Callahan**: The material about Judge Callahan's life is based on *STAS*, pp. 274-75; *SOS*, pp. 209-10, 215.

137 **"common sense"**: *STAS*, p. 274.

137 **The Second and Third Decatur Trials**: This account is based on *STAS*, pp. 276-77; *SOS*, pp. 203-04, 210-11.

138 **Recent lynchings also occurred**: The Lynching Calendar—African Americans who died in racial violence in the United States during 1865-1965, http://www.autopsis.org/foot/lynch.html.

139 **"a Negro named Royal was lynched"**: *NYT*, November 20, 1933, p.1.

139 **Patterson and Norris Pretrial Hearing—November 20-25, 1933**: This account is based on *STAS*, pp. 279-84; *SOS*, pp. 211-12, 216; *LSB*, pp. 79-80; *SB*, p. 49.

139 **"I mean everywhere, too."**: *NYT*, November 21, 1933, p. 1.

139 **"There ain't going to be"**: *STAS*, p. 279.

139 **"Be careful, be careful David."**: ASKF, David Scribner audiotape tape transcript, p. 4.

140 **"I must admit, I was pretty good at it." and "the Jew lawyer from New York"**: ibid., p. 5.

140 **"If them lawyers, especially that Jew lawyer"**: *NYT*, November 11, 1933.

140 **"It was very apparent, to me"**: ASKF, David Scribner audiotape transcript, p. 7.

141 **"Hugh Sanford. He's a Negro."**: *NYT*, November 24, 1933, p. 9.

141 **Patterson's Second Decatur Trial—November 27–30, 1933**: This account is based on *STAS*, pp. 284–99; *SOS*, pp. 212–13, 217–18, 224–29; *LSB*, pp. 79–80; *SB*, pp. 49–51.

141 **"hurry it along" and "that's enough on that"**: *STAS*, p. 284.

141 **"All you white sons-of-bitches unload."**: ibid., 285.

142 **"treat the lady with more respect" and "The more I shut you off"**: *NYT*, November 28, 1933, p. 11.

142 **"Let's don't take up time on that" and "go on to something else"**: *STAS*, pp. 286, 288.

142 **"an entertainer"**: ibid., p. 288.

142 **"a vicious attempt to get something before the jury"**: ibid., p. 293.

142 **"'bums,' 'loafers,' 'scum,' upon whose word neither side could rely." and "a white girl tramp"**: *NYT*, November 30, 1933, p. 40.

143 **"It is an appeal to passion."**: *NYT*, December 1, 1933, p. 1.

143 **"It is the glory of the law"**: ibid.

143 **"would authorize a conviction"**: *STAS*, pp. 297–98.

144 **Norris's First Decatur Trial—November 30–December 6, 1933**: This account is based on *STAS*, pp. 299–302; *SOS*, pp. 213–14, 224–29; *LSB*, pp. 79–81.

144 **"I make it a rule"**: *NYT*, December 2, 1933, p. 1.

144 **"This judge was a redneck"**: *LSB*, p. 79.

CHAPTER 14. SOUTHERN "LIBERALS"—1933–1935

148 **You Gotta Be a Football Hero**: The material on Paul "Bear" Bryant and Donald Hutson was primarily sourced from Barra, *The Last Coach*, pp. 3–33, 46–48.

151 **"I cannot trace the origin of my liberalism."**: Rasmussen, unpublished PhD thesis, p. 94 and Rasmussen interview notes, BCRI.

151 **A Southern Liberal—Joseph Gelders**: The material on Joseph Gelders is based on Brown, *Refusing Racism*, pp. 151–52; *CMH*, pp. 40–53.

153 **A Southern "Liberal"—Clarence Cason**: The material on Clarence Cason is based on *90° in the Shade* by Cason with Introduction by Bailey Thomson, pp. v–xx, 128, 185–86.

153 **He was born in 1896 in Ragland**: Encyclopedia of Alabama, "Clarence Cason," http://www.encyclopediaofalabama.org/face/Article.jsp?id=h-2456.

154 **"go fishing and forget the whole thing"**: Cason, *90° in the Shade*, p. xii.

155 **"Quite aside from such abstract concepts"**: ibid., p. 128.

155 **"On the whole, the South"**: ibid., p. 185–86.

155 **A Neophyte Activist Starts to Grow**: This account is based on *RPMS*, 63–69; *RPAL*, 39–42.

156 **"He didn't want me to go"**: *RPMS*, p. 66.

156 **"shot-gun house"**: ibid.

156 **"I was so frightened, I was shaking."**: ibid., p. 69.

CHAPTER 15. THE SUPREME COURT REDUX—1934–1935

157 **Chicanery—Southern Style**: This account is based on *STAS*, pp. 273, 302–06, 325; *SOS*, pp. 233, 238; Goodrich, *James Edwin Horton Jr.: Scottsboro Judge*, pp. 95, 115–17.

157 **"null and void"**: *STAS*, p. 305.

159 "**What does that have to do with the case?**": Goodrich, *James Edwin Horton Jr.: Scottsboro Judge*, p. 95.

159 **Alabama Supreme Court**: This account is based on *STAS*, pp. 306–08; *SOS*, pp. 238; *CR*, p. 286; *LSB*, p. 144.

159 "**solely because of their race and color**" and "**brazen, rank and amateurish forgery**": *NYT*, May 26, 1934, p. 10.

159 "**the judgment was entered on December 1**": *STAS*, p. 307.

160 **Fraenkel replied that Knight's** "**previous declaration about the date of the judgment should in common decency preclude him from claiming otherwise.**": ibid., p. 307n.

160 "**If this court, with no evidence**": ibid.

160 "**the jury commission did not**": ASLL, Alabama Supreme Court, 156 So. 550, *Norris v. State*, 8. Div. 582, June 28, 1934.

160 **The court set the date**: *NYT*, June 29, 1934, p. 9.

160 **Hoping the U.S. Supreme Court**: *NYT*, July 10, 1934, p. 23.

160 **On October 4, after the Alabama Supreme Court**: *NYT*, October 5, 1934.

160 **On November 16, the Alabama Supreme Court**: *NYT*, November 17, 1934.

160 **On January 7, 1935, the U.S. Supreme Court**: *NYT*, January 8, 1935.

161 **Chicanery—Northern Style**: This account is based on *STAS*, pp. 308–19; *SOS*, pp. 241–42; *CR*, pp. 285–87, 290–91; *LSB*, pp. 144–45.

161 "**good propaganda for the cause**" and "**assassinated the Scottsboro boys**": *STAS*, p. 311.

162 "**You're leaving your money.**" and "**It's not my money.**": *NYT*, October 2, 1934.

163 "**Until all secret manoeuvrings, ballyhoo**" and "**I have given of my best**": *NYT*, October 4, 1934.

163 "**Alabama lynch rulers**" and "**lying stories of attempts**": *STAS*, p. 312.

163 **Also on October 4, the governor of Tennessee**: *NYT*, October 5, 1934.

163 **Their cases were called to trial**: *NYT*, May 30, 1935.

163 **Leibowitz made the first bid**: *NYT*, October 11, 1934.

164 "**Alabama lynchers**": *STAS*, p. 313.

164 "**So there we were, stuck in the middle again.**": *LSB*, p. 145.

165 **Coda to Chicanery—Northern Style**: This account is based on the ASKF papers.

165 **David Schriftman had his name legally changed to David Scribner**: ASKF, City of New York, Borough of Manhattan, court order In the Matter of the Application of DAVID SCHRIFTMAN for Lease to assume the name of DAVID SCRIBNER, dated July 30, 1937.

166 **The transcript of the hearing shows**: ASKF, Transcript of the hearing Before Hon. Hill McAlister, Governor of Tennessee In the matter of extradition of S. KONE and DANIEL SWIFT, upon requisition of Governor of Alabama at Nashville, Tennessee, Thursday, October 3, 1934 at 2 o'clock p.m.

166 **a hearing seeking a writ of *habeas corpus* for Daniel Swift**: ASKF, Writ of *Habeas Corpus* To The Honorable Chester K. Hart, Judge of Division One of the Criminal Court of Davidson County Tennessee at Nashville, October 4, 1934.

166 "**have the body of Daniel Swift**": ASKF, Judge Hart's order to the Honorable L. A. Bauman, Sheriff of Davidson County, Tennessee, and B. F. Giles, Sheriff of Madison County, Alabama, to deliver Daniel Swift to Judge Hart's court on October 5, 1934 at 9 a.m., dated October 4, 1934.

167 **On October 10, 1934, Charles Norman Jr. swore to**: ASKF, Affidavit of Charles H. Norman Jr., dated October 10, 1934.

167 **The warrant was preferred by Victoria Price**: ASKF, Warrant of Arrest in the Inferior Court of Huntsville for the arrest of Daniel Swift, preferred by Victoria Price, October 9, 1934.

168 **"I told him I didn't want to read it." and "I didn't swear to no affidavit"**: ASKF, Transcript of Preliminary Hearing in the Inferior Court of Huntsville, November 2, 1934.

168 **Daniel Swift entered a statement to the charges**: ASKF, Affidavit of David Schriftman, arrested under the name of Daniel Swift, entered in the Inferior Court of Huntsville, November 2, 1934.

168 **"at the next term of the Circuit Court"**: ASKF, Circuit and Grand Jury Bond from Inferior Court of Huntsville, Ala., November 5, 1934.

168 **On November 27, 1934, the Madison County Grand Jury issued an indictment**: ASKF, Indictment, State of Alabama, Madison County. *NYT*, November 28, 1934.

168 **On December 4, 1934, after Daniel Swift got back to New York City**: ASKF, Notarized copy of document David Schriftman (aka Daniel Swift) filed with New York City court on December 4, 1934.

168 **"May 28, 1935 – Nolle Prossed on motion of Solicitor."**: ASKF, *State of Alabama vs. Daniel Swift* in the Circuit Court, Madison County, Alabama, May 28, 1935.

170 **"come along"**: ASKF, David Scribner audiotape transcript, p. 12.

170 **"The significance of that is quite obvious."**: ibid., p. 15.

170 **"Don't worry, we'll get you to the Huntsville" and "Notwithstanding these assurances"**: ASKF, David Scribner notes, p. 4.

171 **"She didn't just lie" and "I concluded my research"**: ibid., pp. 7, 10-11.

171 **So, how does one measure David's credibility**: ASKF, National Lawyers Guild, New York Chapter, 46th Anniversary Dinner, March 4, 1983; Supreme Court of the United States decisions.

173 **U.S. Supreme Court**: This account is based on *STAS*, pp. 319-25; *SOS*, pp. 243-44; *CR*, pp. 291-95; *LSB*, pp. 145-47.

173 **"Can you prove this forgery?"**: *CR*, p. 292.

173 **"I can, your honor"**: ibid., p. 293.

173 **"Let's see them." and "It's as plain as daylight."**: ibid.

173 **"special counsel"**: ibid.

173 **"selection"**: *STAS*, p. 320.

174 **"I cannot tell you"**: *CR*, p. 294.

174 **"sweeping characterization of the lack" and "That testimony in itself"**: CULL, U.S. Supreme Court, *Norris v. State of Alabama*, 294 U.S. 587, April 1, 1935.

174 **"And, upon the proof contained in the record now before us"**: ibid.

174 **"we cannot ignore" and "At least the state court"**: CULL, U.S. Supreme Court, *Patterson v. State of Alabama*, 294 U.S. 600, April 1, 1935.

175 **"This judgment shows"**: *NYT*, April 2, 1935.

175 **"Mr. Hughes's pontifical"**: ADAH, *Montgomery Advertiser*, April 2, 1935, p. 4.

175 **"a smashing confirmation" and "proof of the might"**: *STAS*, p. 324.

175 **"triumph for American justice"**: ibid., pp. 324-25.

175 **"You must think I'm drunk" and "A new trial"**: *NYT*, April 2, 1935.

175 **"we think the failure"**: CULL, U.S. Supreme Court, *Powell v. Alabama*, 287 U.S. 45, November 7, 1932.

176 **"constitutional interpretation" and "separate but equal"**: Klarman, *From Jim Crow to Civil Rights*, pp. 5, 21.

176 **"We conclude that"**: CULL, U.S. Supreme Court, *Brown v. Board of Education*, 347 U.S. 483, December 17, 1954.

CHAPTER 16. PATTERSON'S FOURTH TRIAL—1935–1936

177 **Alabama Implements U.S. Supreme Court Decision:** This account is based on *STAS*, pp. 325–29, 338; *SOS*, pp. 244, 250, 253; *CR*, p. 296; *LSB*, pp. 147–48.

177 **"This decision means that we must put the names of Negroes":** *NYT*, April 6, 1935, p. 1.

177 **"Prompt action by Governor Bibb Graves":** *NYT*, April 7, 1935, p. E6.

177 **"deadening silence":** *STAS*, p. 328.

178 **Thomas Knight, in an uncharacteristically:** *NYT*, September 22, 1935.

178 **The lone black member:** *NYT*, November 14, 1935, p. 1.

178 **"The letter of the court's injunction":** *NYT*, November 17, 1935, p. E7.

178 **Scottsboro Defense Committee:** This account is based on *STAS*, pp. 330–36, 340; *SOS*, pp. 244–45, 278–80; *CR*, p. 296; *TSBF*, pp. 43–53; *LSB*, pp. 167–68; *SB*, p. 61.

180 **During those years, he attended:** Clarence Watts obituary in *The Huntsville Times*, August 26, 1963; Fifield, *The American Bar*.

180 **Haywood Patterson's Fourth Trial, January 20–24, 1936:** This account is based on *STAS*, pp. 339–48; *SOS*, pp. 254–59; *CR*, pp. 297–300; *LSB*, pp. 161–62; *SB*, pp. 61–62.

181 **"Here, boy, sit over there.":** *NYT*, January 21, 1936, p. 2.

181 **"I didn't want no scared":** *SB*, p. 62.

182 **"I won't have insinuations"** and **"did not want to hear":** *NYT*, January 23, 1936, p. 1.

182 **"He couldn't get us to the chair fast enough.":** *SB*, p. 62.

182 **"fixed opinion":** *STAS*, p. 346.

182 **"We, the jury, find the defendant":** *NYT*, January 24, 1936, p. 1.

183 **"fix his punishment":** ibid.

183 **"Twant fair":** ibid.

183 **"justice done no matter":** *SOS*, p. 258.

184 **Leibowitz wouldn't agree, saying the doctor's testimony:** *NYT*, January 25, 1936, p. 1.

184 **"Yes sir, Your Honor, I am not guilty":** ibid.

184 **"It was no victory for me":** *SB*, p. 62.

184 **All Hell Breaks Loose:** This account is based on *STAS*, pp. 348–52; *SOS*, pp. 259–63, 281–82; *CR*, pp. 300–01; *LSB*, pp. 162–66; *SB*, pp. 62–64.

184 **The state organized a caravan of five cars to take the nine boys:** *NYT*, January 25, 1936, p. 1.

185 **"He was never the same as he was":** *LSB*, p. 166.

185 **"hasn't real good sense no way":** *STAS*, p. 351.

185 **"Communist, Jew, Northern lawyers"** and **"I wouldn't give up the help":** *LSB*, pp. 162–63. This dialogue was taken from Clarence Norris's autobiography, which was written over forty years after the event.

185 **"a most delicate and deplorable situation":** *NYT*, January 29, 1936.

186 **"Does the Sheriff of Morgan County":** *NYT*, January 26, 1936, p. 32.

186 **"it strains belief":** *NYT*, January 29, 1936.

186 **"should be an answer":** *STAS*, pp. 350–51.

186 **"The cutting and shooting affray"** and **"showed a new"** and **"If Patterson were tried today":** ibid., pp. 351–52.

CHAPTER 17. ALABAMA SCOTTSBORO COMMITTEE—1936

189 **Alabama Scottsboro Committee:** This account is based on *STAS*, pp. 352–61; *SOS*, pp. 280–89; *CR*, pp. 301–03; *TSBF*, pp. 56–70, 169.

190 **Henry Morris Edmonds was born:** The primary sources for the life of Dr. Henry Edmonds were two books by Marvin Yeomans Whiting: *An Enduring Ministry: A*

Biography of Henry Morris Edmonds, 1978-1969; and *The Bearing Day Is Not Gone: The Seventh-fifth Anniversary History of Independent Presbyterian Church of Birmingham, Alabama, 1915-1990.*

191 **"Get a man a job":** Whiting, *An Enduring Ministry*, p. 59.

191 **"by further reflection, study and prayer":** ibid., p. 69.

192 **He was paid $37.50 per week:** *STAS*, p. 356.

192 **The list was impressive, and included:** *Montgomery Advertiser*, June 10, 1936, Birmingham Public Library, Department of Archives and Manuscripts.

192 **In the interim, the committee:** *NYT*, June 18, 1936.

193 **From an unknown source, Knight obtained:** *STAS*, p. 357.

193 **"Waights M. Taylor, of Birmingham":** *Montgomery Advertiser*, June 10, 1936, Birmingham Public Library, Department of Archives and Manuscripts.

193 **"I have nothing to say":** ibid.

193 **"There is not the slightest bit":** ibid.

193 **"sat back and gleefully waited":** *STAS*, p. 357.

194 **"The dual objective":** Birmingham *The Age-Herald*, June 12, 1936, Birmingham Public Library, Department of Archives and Manuscripts.

194 **"We are making very definite":** *STAS*, p. 358.

194 **"when prisoners of their prominence":** ibid., p. 360.

194 **"Much as we deplore the fact":** ibid., p. 361.

195 **"You were going to keep the Communist group silent":** ibid., p. 359.

195 **"In all, a group of some forty-nine":** *TSBF*, p. 169.

196 **"I went to work for the Alabama Scottsboro Committee":** Rasmussen, unpublished PhD thesis, p. 94 and Rasmussen interview notes, BCRI.

196 **"Frankly, I still do sometimes":** ibid.

CHAPTER 18. THE LAST TRIALS—1937

197 **Alabama Almost Yields:** This account is based on *STAS*, pp. 362-68; *SOS*, pp. 274-76, 286-87, 289-93; *CR*, pp. 303-06; *TSBF*, pp. 88-104; *LSB*, pp. 168-69.

199 **On May 17, 1937, thirty-eight-year-old:** *NYT*, May 18, 1937.

199 **"fifty-dollar fine for rape":** *STAS*, p. 365.

199 **"When the record is examined":** *NYT*, June 15, 1937, p. 3.

199 **The Last Trials:** This account is based on *STAS*, pp. 369-79; *SOS*, pp. 302-09; *CR*, pp. 306-08; *TSBF*, pp. 102-04; *LSB*, pp. 169-71; *NYT*, July 25, 1937, p. 1.

200 **"where the complaining witness":** *NYT*, July 16, 1937, p. 1.

200 **"We the jury":** ibid.

200 **"NORRIS SENTENCED TO DEATH":** *TSBF*, p. 103.

201 **"sick, bewildered, and alone"** and **"As we came out of the church":** ibid., p. 104.

204 **"Why don't you get in there":** *NYT*, July 25, 1937, p. 1.

202 **"But after careful consideration":** ibid.

202 **"We have never known":** *TSBF*, p. 103.

PART THREE. OUR SOUTHERN HOME, 1938-1955

CHAPTER 19. THE GROWTH OF AN ACTIVIST—1938-1955

207 **Maxwell Field:** This account is based on *RPMS*, pp. 65-66; *RPAL*, pp. 42-44.

207 **"humiliation":** *RPAL*, p. 43.

208 **"You might just say":** ibid.

208 **Scottsboro Boys Support:** This account is based on *RPMS*, p. 71; *RPAL*, p. 41.

208 **Voter Registration and the NAACP:** This account is based on *RPMS*, pp. 71-83; *RPAL*, pp. 44-60.

210 **"I was the only woman there":** *RPMS*, p. 81.

210   **"Women don't need to be nowhere"** and **"Well, what about me?"** and **"But I need a secretary"**: ibid., pp. 82–83.

212   **about $350 in today's dollars**: Measuring Worth, http://www.measuringworth.com/uscompare/.

212   **"bitch"** and **"coon"**: RPAL, p. 58.

212   **"Get off my bus."** and **"I will get off."** and **"I didn't want any more run-ins"**: RPMS, p. 79.

212   **Virginia Foster Durr**: This account is based on RPMS, pp. 95–97, 111–12; RPAL, pp. 79–90.

213   **Virginia Foster was born**: The primary sources for information on Virginia Foster Durr's life were Cynthia Stokes Brown's Refusing Racism: White Allies and the Struggle for Civil Rights, pp. 23–50; Durr's Outside the Magic Circle: The Autobiography of Virginia Durr.

213   **"Up to this time"**: Brown, Refusing Racism, p. 32.

216   **"I have the highest respect"** and **"I stand mute."**: ibid., p. 41.

217   **"That's nothing new"** and **"It's my constitutional right!"**: Hoose, Claudette Colvin, pp. 31–31.

218   **Highlander Folk School**: This account is based on RPMS, pp. 101–07; RPAL, pp. 90–97.

218   **"suspect"**: RPAL, p. 94.

219   **"it was one of the few times in my life"**: RPMS, p. 106–07.

219   **"And back to the city buses"**: ibid., p. 107.

CHAPTER 20. BOYS ON THE STAGE—1937–1959

220   **Boys on the Stage**: This account is based on STAS, pp. 384–86, 399–402, 414; SOS, pp. 309, 313, 337–39, 356–61, 384; CR, pp. 308–09; TSBF, pp. 107–08; LSB, p. 225; NYT, July 27, 1937.

220   **As the curtain went up**: NYT, August 16, 1937.

222   **"I guess a whole lot of people"**: SOS, p. 361.

222   **On August 16, 1959, he returned home**: NYT, August 18, 1959.

CHAPTER 21. THE WAR YEARS—1940–1945

224   **"My real change took place"**: Rasmussen, unpublished PhD thesis, p. 94 and Rasmussen interview notes, BCRI.

225   **"We moved from our tents"**: Riggs, 26th AAA Group Activities and History.

226   **Sylvester McCauley**: This account is based on RPMS, pp. 90–93; RPAL, pp. 47, 62–67.

226   **"uppity"**: RPAL, p. 65.

227   **"My dear General"**: Fehrenbach, Heide, Race After Hitler. Princeton University Press, 2005. http://press.princeton.edu/chapters/s8048.pdf.

227   **"The treatment accorded the Negro"**: Baldwin, The Fire Next Time, p. 68.

CHAPTER 22. FINAL STRUGGLE FOR FREEDOM—1937–1952

229   **Negotiations, Agreements, and Broken Promises**: This account is based on STAS, pp. 379–84, 386–98, 402–14; SOS, pp. 312–33, 352–53, 368–75, 378–81; TSBF, pp. 108–50, 168–95, 197, 216, 217–23, 232–33, 237; LSB, 191–205; SB, 101, 156–68, 229–46.

230   **"They are anti-social"**: STAS, p. 390.

230   **"Every enemy of Roosevelt's"**: Leuchtenburg, The White House Looks South, p. 53.

230   **"for the cause of liberalism"** and **"you said definitely"**: STAS, p. 394

231   **"the part of his life"**: SOS, p. 370.

232   **"chain gang"**: LSB, p. 197.

233   **"I was filled with rage"**: ibid., p. 201.

233   **"steal from the Jews"**: SOS, p. 373.

234 **On August 24, 1952 at age thirty-nine**: *NYT*, August 26, 1952.

234 **$13.45 in his pocket, his parole "pay" and "I'm not mad"**: *TSBF*, pp. 232–33.

234 **"Doc, when are you coming"**: ibid., p. 237.

234 **"Everywhere I go"**: *SOS*, p. 374.

235 **The Scottsboro Girls—Victoria Price and Ruby Bates**: This account is based on *STAS*, pp. 415, 417–18; *SOS*, p. 388.

CHAPTER 23. LIVINGSTON, ALABAMA—1949–1952

236 **"Dill was a curiosity."**: Lee, *To Kill a Mockingbird*, p. 8.

237 **"some of the most miraculous works of modern art"**: *NYT*, November 29, 2002, p. E33.

237 **"For once black Americans"**: *The Times*, February 5, 2003.

CHAPTER 24. OUR SOUTHERN HOME—1949–1952

240 **"We stand for the segregation of the races"**: Platform of the States Rights Democratic Party, http://webcache.googleusercontent.com/search?q=cache:iZMZzgE1xpgJ:me mbers.cox.net/polincorr1/platform.htm+dixiecrat+party+platform&cd=1&hl=en& ct=clnk&gl=us&client=safari&source=www.google.com.

241 **"I want to say this about my state"**:"Lott apologizes for Thumond comment," by John Mercurio, CNN Washington Bureau, December 9, 2002, http://articles.cnn.com/2002-12-09/politics/lott. comment_1_dixiecrat-party-lott-strom-thurmond?_s=PM:ALLPOLITICS.

PART FOUR. UNSETTLED TIMES, 1955–1977

CHAPTER 26. MONTGOMERY—DECEMBER 1, 1955

253 **On May 17, 1954, the U.S. Supreme Court**: Klarman, *From Jim Crow to Civil Rights*, p. 292.

253 **On August 28, 1955, Emmett Till**: This account is based on *RPAL*, pp. 100–02; PBS Online, American Experience: The Murder of Emmett Till, http://www.pbs.org/ wgbh/amex/till/timeline/timeline2.html.

253 **Montgomery, Alabama—Thursday, December 1, 1955**: This account is based on *RPMS*, pp. 108–25; *RPAL*, pp. 104–18, 121.

254 **"Let me have those front seats." and "Y'll better make it light"**: *RPMS*, p. 115.

254 **"Are you going to stand up?"**: *RPAL*, p. 107.

254 **"No."**: *RPMS*, p. 116

254 **"Well I'm going to have you arrested."**: ibid.

254 **"You may do that."**: ibid.

255 **"Rosa, the white folks will kill you."**: *RPAL*, p. 114.

255 **"My God, look what segregation"**: *RPMS*, p. 125.

255 **Gray, one of two black attorneys in Montgomery**: Fred Gray website, http://www. fredgray.net/background.html.

256 **Friday—December 2, 1955**: This account is based on *RPMS*, pp. 126–30; *RPAL*, pp. 119–25, 127.

256 **"hottest story you've ever written"**: *RPAL*, p. 125.

257 **Saturday—December 3, 1955**: This account is based on Branch, *Parting the Waters*, pp. 125–27; Graetz, *Montgomery: A White Preacher's Memoir*, pp. 41–45.

258 **"I just heard that someone was arrested"**: The conversation between Graetz and Parks is sourced from Graetz, *Montgomery: A White Preacher's Memoir*, pp. 42–43.

258 **Sunday—December 4, 1955**: This account is based on *RPMS*, p. 130; *RPAL*, p. 129.

259 **Monday—December 5, 1955**: This account is based on *RPMS*, pp. 116, 130–40; *RPAL*, pp. 118, 129–40; Branch, *Parting the Waters*, pp. 136–37, 139–42.

259 **"Oh, she's so sweet. They've messed with the wrong one now."**: *RPAL*, p. 132.

259 "You can always find": ibid., p. 133.

260 He said he would expose the men as cowards and "Let me tell you gentlemen" and "Brother Nixon, I'm not a coward.": Branch, *Parting the Waters*, pp. 136–37.

260 "Yeses" and "Amens" and "Just the other day" and "And you know": Branch, *Parting the Waters*, p. 139.

261 "Now let us say" and "There will ne no crosses burned": ibid., p. 140.

261 "And we are determined": ibid., p. 141.

261 "the only tired I was, was tried of giving in": *RPMS*, p. 116.

261 "When I declined to give up my seat": *RPAL*, p. 118.

263 Autherine Lucy—An Account Based on the Facts: This account is based on *CMH*, pp. 95–99.

264 "Miss Autherine J. Lucy in class. Everything fine.": ibid., p. 97.

264 "Keep Bama white!" and "Hey, hey, ho, ho": ibid., p. 97.

265 "Let's kill her": ibid., p. 98.

265 "for her protection": *NYT*, February 17, 1957, p. 1.

268 "Lord, we ain't what we want to be": King and Cason, *The Papers of Martin Luther King Jr., Vol. V*, p. 281.

268 In September 1959: Obama, *Dreams from My Father*, pp. 9–10; Amanda Ripley, "The Story of Barack Obama's Mother," *Time*, April 9, 2008.

CHAPTER 28. BOMBINGHAM—1963

272 "the most segregated city in America": *Newsweek*, September 18, 2000.

273 "How many mules": *CMH*, p. 20.

273 Birmingham's Machiavellian Prince: This account is based on *CMH*, pp. 33–34, 36–37.

275 Plantersville Hog-Caller: This account is based on *CMH*, pp. 37–39, 46–47, 49–51.

275 "Ouuuuuuuuuut" and "Th'ow that onion boy": *CMH*, p. 38.

275 "the Plantersville hog-caller": ibid., p. 37.

275 "I'm going to tell the truth": ibid., p. 38.

276 "The black man is the": ibid., p. 50.

277 "He set the tone": Durr, *Outside the Magic Circle*, p. 120.

277 "this new and unique adventure": *CMH*, p. 50.

277 "White and Negro are not": *NYT*, April 12, 1960, p. 1.

277 Bombingham's Dynamite Bob: This account is based on *CMH*, pp. 72–73.

278 Project C: This account is based on *CMH*, pp. 22, 48–49, 60–61, 88, 307, 311–13, 315–17, 320, 323–24, 330–31, 341–42.

278 This son of a middle class: Wikipedia, "Martin Luther King Jr.," http://en.wikipedia.org/wiki/Martin_Luther_King,_Jr.#Early_life.

279 "the Wild Man from Birmingham": *CMH*, p. 22.

279 "And I say, segregation today,": ADAH, "The 1963 Inaugural Address of Governor George C. Wallace," January 14, 1963.

280 "New Dawn Dawns for Birmingham": *CMH*, p. 320.

281 Letter from Birmingham Jail: This account is based on *CMH*, pp. 345–46, 348, 353–55, 452.

281 "However, we are now confronted" and "We further strongly urge": TeachingAmericanHistory.org, http://www.teachingamericanhistory.org/library/index.asp?document=533.

282 "But more basically": King, *Why We Can't Wait*, p. 86.

282 First, I must confess: ibid., pp. 96–97.

283 "It is true that the police": ibid., pp. 109–10.

283 The Incredible Children's March: This account is based on *CMH*, pp. 355–63, 366–74, 376–78.

285 **"Kids, there's gonna be a party"**: *CMH*, p. 366.

285 **"What do you want?" and "F'eedom."**: King, *Why We Can't Wait*, p. 115.

286 **"Bring the dogs."**: *CMH*, p. 371.

287 **"television's greatest hour"**: ibid., p. 374.

287 **"Y'all don't like us"**: ibid., p. 377.

288 **"predicted that all formal segregation"**: *NYT*, May 5, 1963, p. 82.

288 The *Pas de Deux* Ends: This account is based on *CMH*, pp. 161, 166, 177, 236–37, 310, 347, 362, 377, 381, 392, 397–98, 404–05, 427–28, 483, 485.

288 **"Please, don't go down to Birmingham." and "Man, I will be there"**: *CMH*, p. 392.

289 **"Let's put some water on the Reverend."**: ibid., p. 405.

289 **"Goddammit, that's what causes trouble"**: ibid., p. 377.

290 **May 10, 11, and 12**: This account is based on *CMH*, pp. 413–22, 424–37, 440.

291 **"I am not for social equality."**: Rasmussen, unpublished PhD thesis, pp. 100–01 and Rasmussen interview notes, BCRI.

291 **"I do a good deal of work" and "I am against the"**: ibid.

293 **"freedom tensions"**: CMH, p. 437.

294 **May 21, 22, and 23**: This account is based on *CMH*, pp. 448–52.

294 **"Would you have your children"**: *CMH*, p. 451.

295 **"Well, I'm just going"**: ibid., p. 452.

295 **June 11**: This account is based on *CMH*, pp. 455, 459–65.

295 **"to assure you that the orders"**: *NYT*, June 12, 1963.

295 **"Sir, it is my sad duty—"**: ibid.

295 **"to ask you to step aside"**: *CMH*, p. 462.

295 **"We are confronted primarily" and "Next week"**: John F. Kennedy Presidential Library & Museum website, http://www.jfklibrary.org/Historical+Resources/ Archives/Reference+Desk/Speeches/JFK/003POF03CivilRights06111963.htm.

296 **The Bombing Triad**: This account is based on *CMH*, pp. 481–82, 486.

296 **10:22 a.m.—September 15, 1963**: This account is based on *CMH*, pp. 485–86, 494–502, 505–13, 515–17, 520–27.

297 **Bear would not field a football team with a black athlete until 1971**: ESPN Classic website, http://espn.go.com/classic/biography/s/Bryant_Bear.html.

298 **"stuff put away"**: The conversation between Chambliss and Hood is sourced from *CMH*, p. 510

300 **"Addie, Addie, Addie."**: ibid., p. 523.

300 **The Grand Jury Charge—R. Macey Taylor**: This account is based on *CMH*, pp. 531, 534–35, 563.

301 **"In recent weeks"**: R. Macey Taylor's Grand Jury charge is taken from his original draft and copies he saved that are now in his children's possession.

303 **"We are a mass of intolerance"**: *The Washington Post*, January 9, 2009.

303 **"What's it like living in Birmingham?"**: *CMH*, p. 535.

303 **1963 Staggers to an End**: This account is based on *CMH*, pp. 573–75, 586–87, 589–98.

304 **"entry into and travel within"**: Lewis with D'Orso, *Walking with the Wind*, p. 160.

305 **However, Cherry did not escape prosecution.**: *The Washington Post*, November 19, 2004; *NYT*, November 19, 2004.

Chapter 29. Bound for Safe Havens

306 **On October 1, 1946**: *STAS*, p. 418; *SOS*, p. 382; *LSB*, p. 205.

306 **Cleveland, Ohio: 1946—1953**: This account is based on *STAS*, p. 425; *SOS*, pp. 382–83; *LSB*, pp. 207–14.

307 **"what all the mystery was" and "Of course all I found out was"**: *LSB*, p. 208.

307 **New York City: 1953—1975**: This account is based on *STAS*, pp. 425–26; *SOS*, pp. 383–86; *LSB*, pp. 215–33.

308 **"The shame of it is"**: *LSB*, p. 216.

308 **"I'll be damn, it's Clarence."**: ibid., p. 217.

309 **"But there are people"**: ibid., p. 224.

310 **Judge Horton lost**: Goodrich, *James Edwin Horton Jr.: Scottsboro Judge*, pp. 116–21.

310 **"And Ye Shall Know the Truth"**: Goodman and Anker, PBS DVD. American Experience: Scottsboro, An American Tragedy.

310 **"completely inundated in trying to expose"**: *LSB*, p. 232.

311 **"I told them to go to hell."**: ibid., p. 233.

313 **"The human mind has no more power"**: Lewis, *The Abolition of Man*, pp. 56–57. The quote should read, "The human mind has no more power of inventing a new value than of imagining a new primary colour, or, indeed, of creating a new sun and a new sky for it to move in."

314 **Rosa Parks**: This account is based on *RPMS*, pp. 15, 161–81; *RPAL*, pp., 174–202, 209–10.

315 **"Well! If it isn't the superstar!"** and **"troublemakers"**: *RPAL*, p. 175.

315 **"I never realized"**: ibid., p. 177.

316 **Late that Sunday afternoon, John Lewis**: The description of "Bloody Sunday" in Selma, Alabama on March 7, 1965 is mostly from Lewis with D'Orso, *Walking with the Wind*, pp. 323–31.

316 **"The parsonage next to the church"**: Lewis with D'Orso, *Walking with the Wind*, p. 330.

317 **On February 18, Jimmie Lee Jackson**: Wikipedia, "Jimmie Lee Jackson," http://en.wikipedia.org/wiki/Jimmie_Lee_Jackson.

317 **On March 9, a group**: Encyclopedia of Alabama, "James Reeb," http://encyclopediaofalabama.org/face/Article.jsp?id=h-2054.

317 **With the national uproar**: ibid.

317 **Viola Liuzzo, a thirty-nine-year-old white housewife**: Encyclopedia of Alabama, "Viola Gregg Liuzzo," http://www.encyclopediaofalabama.org/face/Article.jsp?id=h-1377.

318 **"of course this is a murder case"**: *NYT*, March 27, 1965, p. 10.

318 **"United States Attorney Macy [Macey] Taylor"**: *NYT*, April 8, 1965.

318 **Gary Rowe, the FBI informant** and **"We had to burn a whore."**: *CMH*, pp. 572–73.

318 **He was placed in the Federal witness and Rowe died in Savannah on May 25, 1998**: *NYT*, October 4, 1998.

319 **On August 6, 1965, Rosa**: Lewis with D'Orso, *Walking with the Wind*, p. 346.

319 **"I can't help but marvel at the fact"**: Democracy Now: The War and Peace Report, October 25, 2005, http://www.democracynow.org/2005/10/25/john_conyers_on_rosa_parks_she.

319 **"To this day"**: *RPMS*, p. 175.

PART FIVE. SEEKING FINAL CLOSURE, 1976–2009

CHAPTER 30. REDEMPTION, CONVERSION, AND IMMORTALITY

323 **Clarence Norris—Redemption**: This account is based on *SOS*, pp. 385–86; *LSB* pp. 233–34.

323 **The Truth Shall Make You Free**: This account is based on *SOS*, pp. 386–88; *LSB*, pp. 234–46, 280–81.

324 **"I again vigorously appeal"**: *LSB*, pp. 280–81.

325 **"I have no hate"**: Galloway, Kirby, Ober, and Sorenson, *The Greatest Trials of All Time*, Cinetel Productions and Courtroom Television Network. Sara Sellers sent me

her copy of *The Greatest Trials of All Time* from which Norris's press conference remarks are taken. Sara was one of the three members of the Alabama State Board of Pardons and Paroles in 1976. In opposition to the board chairman, she and another board member voted to withdraw the outstanding arrest warrant against Clarence Norris, which finally led to Norris's full pardon on October 25, 1976.

326   **"We are not a utopia":** *LSB*, p. 246.

326   **"That's because we eat" and "I like collards":** ibid.

326   **The Last of the Scottsboro Boys:** This account is based on *SOS*, pp. 389–92; *LSB*, p. 226.

327   **"How can you judge" and "We must believe":** *SOS*, pp. 390–91.

327   **Waights's other voice, Clive Staples Lewis:** The primary sources for material on C. S. Lewis's life were C. S. Lewis's *Surprised by Joy*; Michael White's *C. S. Lewis: A Life*; A. N. Wilson's *C. S. Lewis: A Biography*.

328   **"That which I had greatly feared":** Lewis, *Surprised by Joy*, pp. 228–29.

328   **"and is it true, this most amazing tale of all?":** Wilson, *C. S. Lewis, A Biography*, p. 125.

328   **"I was driven to Whipsnade":** Lewis, *Surprised by Joy*, p. 237.

330   **Egypt's Wâdi El Natrûn:** Wikipedia, "Wadi El Natrun," http://en.wikipedia.org/wiki/Wadi_El_Natrun.

336   **Rosa Parks—Immortality:** This account is based on *RPMS*, pp. 181–88; *RPAL*, pp. 210–25.

336   **"I found myself all alone":** *RPAL*, p. 210.

337   **On a professional level:** Rosa and Raymond Parks Institute for Self-Development, http://www.rosaparks.org/.

338   **"great spirit" and "natural Buddhist":** *RPAL*, p. 221.

338   **In the 1990s, Rosa wrote four books:** Rosa & Raymond Parks Institute for Self-Development, "Rosa Louise Parks Biography," http://www.rosaparks.org/index.php?option=com_content&view=article&id=2&Itemid=2.

338   **In the later years of her life, awards and honors were bestowed on Rosa:** ibid.

339   **"I can honestly say":** *NYT*, October 31, 2005, p. A16.

339   **"Wife, Rosa L. Parks, 1913—":** msnbc, "Premium charged for plot near Parks" with photo of headstone, http://www.msnbc.msn.com/id/11675695/.

340   **After Mandela was released from prison:** The account of Mandela's visit to Detroit is based on *RPAL*, pp. 228–31.

340   **"I just shouldn't be there" and "He won't know me.":** *RPAL*, p. 230.

340   **"Ro-sa Parks":** ibid., p. 231.

EPILOGUE

341   **And because we have tasted:** President Barack Hussein Obama's Inaugural Address, January 20, 2009, *NYT*, January 20, 2009.

344   **In 2000, Alabama had the second highest:** Bositis, *Black Elected Officials*, p. 20.

344   **In 2009, the Birmingham mayor:** The Official Website for Birmingham Alabama, http://www.informationbirmingham.com/ (December 2009).

BIBLIOGRAPHY

Baldwin, James. *The Fire Next Time*. Dial Press, 1963.

Barra, Allen. *The Last Coach: The Life of Paul "Bear" Bryant*. New York: W. W. Norton & Company, 2005.

Blackmon, Douglas A. *Slavery by Another Name: The Re-Enslavement of Black Americans from the Civil War to World War II*. New York: Anchor Books, a Division of Random House, Inc., 2008.

Bositis, David A. *2000 Black Elected Officials: A Statistical Summary*. Joint Center for Political and Economic Studies: 2000.

Branch, Taylor. *Parting the Waters: America in the King Years 1954–63*. New York: Simon and Schuster, 1988.

———. *Pillar of Fire: America in the King Years 1963–65*. New York: Simon and Schuster, 1998.

Brinkley, Douglas. *Rosa Parks: A Life*. New York: Penguin Books, 2000.

Brown, Cynthia Stokes. *Refusing Racism: White Allies and the Struggle for Civil Rights*. New York: Teacher's College Press, 2002.

Burke Jr., David M., and Odie A. Burke. *Warm Springs*. Charleston, SC: Arcadia Publishing, 2005.

Carter, Dan T. *Scottsboro: A Tragedy of the American South*. Rev. ed. Baton Rouge: Louisiana State University Press, 1979.

Cason, Clarence, with Introduction by Bailey Thomson. *90° in the Shade*. Tuscaloosa: The University of Alabama Press, 2001.

Chalmers, Allan K. *They Shall Be Free*. Garden City, New York: Doubleday & Company, Inc., 1951.

Clarke, Gerald. *Too Brief a Treat: The Letters of Truman Capote*. New York: Random House, 2004.

Coen, Cheré Dastugue. *The Taylor Family*. Unpublished, 2009.

Cohen, Octavus Roy. *Highly Colored*. New York: Dodd, Mead and Company, 1920.

Copeland, Miles. *The Game Player: Confessions of the CIA's original political operative*. London: Aurum Press, 1989.

Crenshaw Jr., Files, and Kenneth A. Miller. *Scottsboro: The Firebrand of Communism*. Montgomery, Alabama: The Brown Printing Company, 1936.

Durr, Virginia Foster. Edited by Hollinger F. Barnard. *Outside the Magic Circle: The Autobiography of Virginia Durr*. University, Alabama: The University of Alabama Press, 1985.

Editorial in Jackson County Sentinel, April 23, 1931. Papers on the Commission on Interracial Cooperation, Robert W. Woodruff Library, Atlanta University Center (Microfilm, 1983).

Fifield, James Clark. *The American Bar, Contemporary Lawyers of the United States and Canada*. Minneapolis: Byron Printing Company, 1918.

Frederickson, Mary. Interview with Hollace Ransdall by Mary Frederickson, 6 November 1974 (G-0050), in the Southern Oral History Program Collection (#4007), Southern Historical Collection, Louis Round Wilson Special Collections Library, University of North Carolina at Chapel Hill.

Galloway, Scott, Lynne Kirby, Eric Ober, and Erik Sorenson. *The Greatest Trials of All Time.* Produced by Cinetel Productions, Knoxville, TN, in association with Courtroom Television Network, 1998.

Goodman, Barak, and Daniel Anker. *American Experience: Scottsboro, An American Tragedy.* PBS Home Video DVD. Boston: WGBH Educational Foundation, 2001.

Goodman, James. *Stories of Scottsboro.* New York: Vintage Books, 1994.

Goodrich, Gillian White. *James Edwin Horton Jr.: Scottsboro Judge.* Master's Thesis, University of Alabama at Birmingham, 1974.

Graetz, Robert S. *Montgomery: A White Preacher's Memoir.* Minneapolis: Fortress Press, 1991.

Hardesty, Von. *Black Wings: Courageous Stories of African Americans in Aviation and Space History.* New York: HarperCollins Publishers, 2008.

Harris, Jacqueline L. *History and Achievement of the NAACP.* New York: Franklin Watts, The African-American Experience, 1992.

Hoose, Phillip. *Claudette Colvin: Twice Toward Justice.* New York: Melanie Kroupa Books, Farrar Strauss Giroux, 2009.

Huxley, Aldous. *Brave New World.* New York: HarperPerennial, 1932, 1946.

Johnson, Charles, Patricia Smith, and the WGBH Research Team. *Africans in America: America's Journey Through Slavery.* New York: Harcourt Brace & Company, 1998.

Jones, James H. *Bad Blood: The Tuskegee Syphilis Experiment.* New York: The Free Press, A Division of Macmillan Publishing Co., Inc., 1981.

King, Jr., Martin Luther. *Why We Can't Wait.* New York: Signet Classics, New American Library, 2000.

King, Jr., Martin Luther, and Clayborne Carson, Senior Editor. *The Papers of Martin Luther King, Jr., Volume V: Threshold of a New Decade, January 1959–December 1960.* Berkeley: University of California Press, 2005.

Kinshasa, Kwando Mbiassi. *The Man from Scottsboro.* Jefferson, NC: McFarland & Company, Inc., 1997.

Klarman, Michael J. *From Jim Crow to Civil Rights: The Supreme Court and the Struggle for Racial Equality.* New York: Oxford University Press, 2004.

Kunhardt Jr., Philip B., Philip B. Kunhardt III, and Peter W. Kunhardt. *Lincoln: An Illustrated Biography.* New York: Alfred A. Knopf, 1992.

Lee, Harper. *To Kill a Mockingbird.* New York: HarperCollins Publishers, 40th Anniversary Edition published 1999.

Leuchtenburg, William E. *The White House Looks South: Franklin D. Roosevelt, Harry S. Truman, Lyndon B. Johnson.* Baton Rouge: Louisiana State University Press, 2005.

Lewis, C. S. *Surprised by Joy: The Shape of My Early Life.* New York and London: Harcourt Brace Jovanovich, 1955.

Lewis, C. S. *The Abolition of Man.* New York: Macmillan Publishing Company, 1947.

Lewis, John, with Michael D'Orso. *Walking with the Wind: A Memoir of the Movement.* New York: Simon & Schuster, 1998.

Long, Cathryn J. *The Cherokee.* San Diego: Lucent Books, Inc., 2000.

McMillan, Malcolm. *Yesterday's Birmingham.* Miami: E. A. Seemann Publishing, Inc., 1975.

McMurry, Linda O. *George Washington Carver: Scientist & Symbol.* New York: Oxford University Press, 1981.

McWhorter, Diane. *Carry Me Home: Birmingham, Alabama, The Climactic Battle of the Civil Rights Revolution.* New York: Simon & Schuster, 2001.

Norris, Clarence, and Sybil D. Washington. *The Last of the Scottsboro Boys.* New York: G. P. Putnam's Sons, 1979. Current book produced by the American Council of Learned Societies in the ACLS History E-Book Project.

Obama, Barack. *Dreams of My Father: A Story of Race and Inheritance.* New York: Three Rivers Press, 1995, 2004.

Olsen, Christopher J. *The American Civil War: A Hands-on History.* New York: Hill and Wang, a division of Farrar, Straus and Giroux, 2006.

Packer, George. *Blood of the Liberals.* New York: Farrar, Straus and Giroux, 2000.

Parks, Rosa, with Jim Haskins. *Rosa Parks: My Story.* New York: Scholastic Inc., 1992.

Pasley, Fred D. *NOT GUILTY! The Story of Samuel S. Leibowitz.* New York: G. P. Putnam's Sons, 1933.

Patterson, Haywood, and Earl Conrad. *Scottsboro Boy.* Garden City: Doubleday & Company, Inc., 1950. Current book produced by the American Council of Learned Societies in the ACLS History E-Book Project.

Ransdell, Hollace. Report to ACLU, Report on the Scottsboro, Ala. Case, May 27, 1931: ACLU Records, Box 1887, Folder 1, Twentieth Century Public Policy Papers, Seeley G. Mudd Manuscript Library, Department of Rare Books and Special Collections, Princeton University Library.

Rasmussen, Donald. PhD Thesis. Rasmussen Papers Archives, Birmingham Civil Rights Institute, Birmingham, Alabama. Unpublished, 1947.

Rasmussen, Donald, and Lore Rasmussen. *Failing to Conform—Memories of Life in Alabama, 1942-1955.* Unpublished, 2003.

Reynolds, Quentin. *Courtroom.* New York: Farrar, Straus and Giroux, 1950.

Riggs, E. Gary. *26th AAA Group Activities and History.* February 16, 1963.

Rodgers, Richard, and Oscar Hammerstein, 2nd. *South Pacific: A Musical Play.* New York: Random House, 1949.

Salmond, John A. *The Conscience of a Lawyer: Clifford J. Durr and American Civil Liberties 1899–1976.* Tuscaloosa: The University of Alabama Press, 1990.

Shields, Charles J. *Mockingbird: A Portrait of Harper Lee.* Owl ed. New York: Henry Holt and Company, 2007.

Taylor, George William. *Remembrances of George William Taylor.* Unpublished, 1975.

Taylor, Waights M. *Diary of Trip to Scandinavia.* Unpublished, 1928.

———. *Life on the Side of Red Mountain.* Unpublished, 1978.

Walker, Samuel. *In Defense of American Liberties: A History of the ACLU.* New York: Oxford University Press, 1990.

Washington, Booker T., edited by and an Introduction by W. Fitzhugh Brundage. *Up from Slavery.* Boston: Bedford/St Martin's, 2003.

Washington-Williams, Essie Mae, and William Stadiem. *Dear Senator: A Memoir by the Daughter of Strom Thurmond.* New York: HarperCollins, 2005.

Weatherford, Carole Boston. *Birmingham, 1963.* Honesdale, Pennsylvania: Wordsong, 2007.

White, Michael. *C. S. Lewis: A Life.* New York: Carroll & Graf Publishers, 2004.

Whiting, Marvin Yeomans, with Linda J. Nelson. *An Enduring Ministry: A Biography of Henry Morris Edmonds.* Birmingham, 2007.

Whiting, Marvin Yeomans. *The Bearing Day Is Not Gone: The Seventy-Fifth Anniversary History of Independent Presbyterian Church of Birmingham, Alabama, 1915–1990.* Birmingham: EBSCO Media, 1990.

Wilson, A. N. *C. S. Lewis: A Biography.* New York and London: W. W. Norton & Company, 1990.

Wimberley, Ronald C., and Libby V. Morris. *The Southern Black Belt: A National Perspective.* Lexington, KY: TVA Rural Studies, The University of Kentucky, 1997.

INDEX

PERMISSIONS ACKNOWLEDGMENTS

Courtroom: The Story of Samuel S. Leibowitz by Quentin Reynolds. Copyright © 1950 by Quentin Reynolds. Reprinted by permission of Farrar, Straus and Giroux, LLC.

Brave New World by Aldous Huxley. Copyright © 1932, 1946 by Aldous Huxley. Used by permission of HarperCollins Publishers, Inc.

To Kill a Mockingbird by Harper Lee. Copyright © 1960 by Harper Lee, copyright renewed 1988. Used by permission of HarperCollins Publishers, Inc.

90° in the Shade by Clarence Cason. Copyright © 1935 by The University of North Carolina Press. First Paperbound Edition published 1983 by The University of Alabama Press. Used by permission of The University of Alabama Press.

Cover Photograph Acknowledgments

Top left: Clarence Norris on March 26, 1931. © Bettmann/Corbis.

Top center: Rosa Parks with Martin Luther King Jr. in the background (ca. 1956). Public domain photograph. United States Information Agency.

Top right: Waights McCaa Taylor at the University of Alabama on April 9, 1933. Taylor family photograph.

Bottom: The nine Scottsboro Boys surrounded by the Alabama National Guard on March 26, 1931. From left to right, Clarence Norris, Olen Montgomery, Andy Wright, Willie Roberson, Ozie Powell, Eugene Williams, Charlie Weems, Roy Wright, and Haywood Patterson. © Bettmann/Corbis.

ABOUT THE AUTHOR

Waights Taylor Jr., born and raised in Birmingham, Alabama, lives in Santa Rosa, California. His professional career included twenty-four years in the aviation industry and then twenty-two years in management consulting. When his professional career was coming to an end, he turned to writing. He is an author, a poet, and a playwright. His first book, *Alfons Mucha's Slav Epic: An Artist's History of the Slavic People*, was published in 2008. He has written a number of short stories and plays. His first chapbook of poetry, titled *Literary Ramblings*, was published in 2011.